FRAMING CHINA

For my parents Gisela and Otto Knüsel

Framing China
Media Images and Political Debates in Britain, the USA and Switzerland, 1900–1950

ARIANE KNÜSEL
University of Zurich, Switzerland

Routledge
Taylor & Francis Group

LONDON AND NEW YORK

First published 2012 by Ashgate Publishing

2 Park Square, Milton Park, Abingdon, Oxon OX14 4RN
711 Third Avenue, New York, NY 10017, USA

Routledge is an imprint of the Taylor & Francis Group, an informa business

First issued in paperback 2017

British Library Cataloguing in Publication Data
Knüsel, Ariane.
  Framing China : media images and political debates in Britain, the USA and Switzerland, 1900-1950.
  1. China--Press coverage--Great Britain--History--20th century. 2. China--Press coverage--United States--History--20th century. 3. China--Press coverage--Switzerland--History--20th century. 4. Press and politics--History--20th century. 5. China--Foreign relations--Great Britain. 6. Great Britain--Foreign relations--China. 7. China--Foreign relations--United States. 8. United States--Foreign relations--China. 9. China--Foreign relations--Switzerland. 10. Switzerland--Foreign relations--China.
  I. Title
  327.5'1'00904-dc23

Library of Congress Cataloging-in-Publication Data
Knüsel, Ariane.
  Framing China : media images and political debates in Britain, the USA and Switzerland, 1900-1950 / Ariane Knüsel.
    p. cm.
  Includes bibliographical references and index.
  ISBN 978-1-4094-2559-5 (hardcover) 1. China--Press coverage--Great Britain--History--20th century. 2. China--Press coverage--United States--History--20th century. 3. China--Press coverage--Switzerland--History--20th century. 4. China--Foreign public opinion, British--History--20th century. 5. China--Foreign public opinion, American--History--20th century. 6. China--Foreign public opinion, Swiss--History--20th century. 7. Press--Great Britain--History--20th century. 8. Press--United States--History--20th century. 9. Press--Switzerland--History--20th century. I. Title.
  PN4888.C54K68 2012
  070.4'4995104--dc23

                                                                            2012005198

ISBN 978-1-4094-2559-5 (hbk)
ISBN 978-1-138-10929-2 (pbk)

Contents

List of Illustrations		*vii*
List of Tables		*ix*
Acknowledgements		*xi*
List of Abbreviations		*xiii*

Introduction   1

1   The Dragon Throne in the Dustbin:
Press Reactions to the Xinhai Revolution   25

2   The 1920s, the Red Menace and
Anti-foreign Agitation in China   73

3   'A terror which has been truly Asiatic':
The Evolution of Yellow Peril Imagery until 1945   127

4   The Rise of the Bamboo Curtain:
Perceptions of the Communist Victory in 1949   203

Conclusion   251

Bibliography   *259*
Index   *309*

List of Illustrations

I.1   Charles Henry Sykes, 'Yes, China is Awakening',
        Los Angeles Times (14.2.1927)   1

1.1   Paul Frenzeny, 'The Crisis in China',
        Illustrated London News (21.7.1900)   32
1.2   G.F. Morrell, 'The Great Rebellion', *The Graphic* (28.10.1911)   37
1.3   G.F. Morrell, 'Republics on the Rampage',
        The Graphic (3.12.1910)   41
1.4   Joseph Keppler, Jr., 'The Chinese Boycott', *Puck* (28.6.1905)   50
1.5   'The Concert of the Powers Will Soon Begin in China',
        Los Angeles Times (19.8.1900)   56
1.6   C.R. Macauley, 'Letting in the Light', *The World* (24.10.1911)   60
1.7   C.R. Macauley, 'Into the Light', *The World* (15.1.1912)   60
1.8   J.F. Boscovits, 'Closing Time in China', *Nebelspalter* (17.2.1912)   70

2.1   David Low, 'Much Ado About Next to Nothing',
        The Star (14.10.1924)   74
2.2   Bernard Partridge, 'On the Loan Trail', *Punch* (29.10.1924)   82
2.3   W.K. Haselden, 'Under which Flag? To-day's Choice',
        Daily Mirror (29.10.1924)   83
2.4   Bernard Partridge, untitled, *Punch* (8.7.1925)   89
2.5   Bernard Partridge, 'Communisty Singing', *Punch* (2.3.1927)   96
2.6   William Charles Morris, 'What China Really Needs',
        Los Angeles Times (18.7.1925)   108
2.7   William Charles Morris, 'Uncle Sam: "I Can't Hear You Boys!"',
        Los Angeles Times (15.12.1926)   110
2.8   René Gilsi, 'China', *Nebelspalter* (13.5.1927)   118
2.9   Otto Baumberger, 'China for the Chinese',
        Nebelspalter (17.6.1927)   121

3.1   G. Welby Wilkinson, 'Tientsin', *Fun* (18.7.1900)   128
3.2   E.H. Shepard, 'Crowded Out', *Punch* (4.2.1942)   129
3.3   Sir John Tenniel, 'The Avenger', *Punch* (25.7.1900)   135
3.4   David Low, 'Will the League Stand up to Japan?',
        Evening Standard (17.11.1931)   142
3.5   Bernard Partridge, 'Dawn over Asia', *Punch* (29.9.1937)   145
3.6   E.H. Shepard, 'Honourable Persuasion', *Punch* (12.1.1938)   149

3.7   E.H. Shepard, 'The Monkey Folk', *Punch* (14.1.1942)   153
3.8   Joseph Lee, 'Evolution', *Evening Standard* (27.3.1944)   154
3.9   David Low, 'The Admiral Comes on Board',
       Evening Standard (20.10.1941)   156
3.10   David Low, 'The Next Course Doesn't Come So Easily',
       Evening Standard (11.12.1941)   157
3.11   George Frederick Keller, 'A Statue for Our Harbor',
       The Wasp (11.11.1881)   159
3.12   John T. McCutcheon, 'While the Police Are Busy Elsewhere',
       Chicago Tribune (6.5.1915)   163
3.13   Harold M. Talburt, 'The Light of Asia',
       Washington Daily News (27.1.1932)   165
3.14   Carey Orr, 'When the Cops Are Away',
       Chicago Tribune (23.9.1931)   167
3.15   Keith Temple, 'Another Scrap of Paper?',
       Times-Picayune (13.10.1931)   168
3.16   Gene Elderman, 'Bushido', *Washington Post* (20.8.1937)   172
3.17   H.S. Wong, 'Baby amidst Bomb Rubble', *Life* (4.10.1937)   174
3.18   Bruce Russell, 'Japanese Print', *Los Angeles Times* (9.2.1942) 187
3.19   Arthur Szyk, 'December 7, 1941', *Collier's* (12.12.1942)   189
3.20   Gregor Rabinovitch, 'The Japanese War Council',
       Nebelspalter (11.2.1938)   195
3.21   *Schweizer Illustrierte* (28.7.1943)   200

4.1   Leslie Illingworth, 'The Red Flood', *Daily Mail* (24.1.1949)   204
4.2   David Low, 'Asked for Trouble – and Got It',
       Evening Standard (13.9.1949)   211
4.3   David Low, 'It's Different with the Americans in China, of course',
       Evening Standard (13.9.1946)   216
4.4   E.H. Shepard, 'The New Hunting Ground', *Punch* (30.6.1948)   218
4.5   E.H. Shepard, 'The Strengthening of the Keep',
       Punch (20.4.1949)   219
4.6   Tom Little, 'According to Tradition', *New York Times* (5.6.1949) 235
4.7   Bil Spira, 'Land of the Smile', *Nebelspalter* (6.1.1949)   243
4.8   Peter Bachmann, 'The White Man in China',
       Nebelspalter (7.7.1949)   247

List of Tables

I.1   British Newspapers   16
I.2   British Magazines   17
I.3   American Newspapers   19
1.4   American Magazines   20
I.5   Swiss Newspapers   22
I.6   Swiss Magazines   22

1.1   Share of the British Empire in China's External Trade   35

Acknowledgements

This book analyses British, American and Swiss press reports and political debates about China between 1900 and 1950 in order to demonstrate that perceptions of China were different in each country due to national interests, self-perceptions and cultural stereotypes. It combines approaches from history, international relations, media studies, cultural studies and political science. Needless to say, I am indebted to a vast number of scholars in those fields and their publications. In particular, I would like to thank John Dower, Jürgen Osterhammel, Arne Westad, Jan Rüger, Gary Rawnsley and Christof Dejung, who were under no obligation to answer my questions and read my chapters but were kind enough to do so. I deeply appreciate every minute they took to read my drafts and write their comments, which were incredibly helpful. At various conferences I was able to present parts of my research and received valuable feedback. The supervisors of my dissertation at the University of Zurich, Jakob Tanner and Andrea Riemenschnitter, have been very supportive. Katherine Meier took time off her own research to read my chapters and has been a great help over the years, ever since I discussed this project with her over tea breaks at the British Library. At the Forschungsstelle für Sozial- und Wirtschaftsgeschichte of the University of Zurich, I distracted Eva von Wyl, Niklaus Ingold and Res Zangger with my suitcases filled with books, cartoons and maps, and yet they still agreed to read my chapters. Thank you so much! Corinne Laube also took time to read and comment on earlier drafts, for which I am grateful. At Ashgate, Emily Yates has been patient and supportive, while the comments of the two anonymous reviewers have been immensely helpful for revising the manuscript. Discussions with various people have also helped bring this book to its current form, though to name them all, I would fill another book. Of course, any shortcomings that remain in the book are due to my own stubbornness and ignorance.

I would also like to thank all the staff in the various libraries and archives I have frequented during the past five years, in particular the people at Doe Library at UC Berkeley, who started sighing at the sight of me because they knew they would have to haul out more carts of heavy magazine volumes. I am also still amazed at the speed with which the staff at the National Archives in Kew makes documents available for its visitors. I would not have been able to do the research for this book without grants from the Schweizerische Nationalfonds, the Janggen-Pöhn-Stiftung and the Forschungskredit of the University of Zurich.

The Snell family, Silvia, Ladina, Bigi and the kiddos made sure I had a life outside of my thesis (Raclette, anyone?), and thanks to Julie I did not get rusty from sitting in front of my laptop or crawling around libraries and archives all day.

Throughout the years, Daryl has stoically read draft after draft and has supported me in every way imaginable so that I could finish the book. I hope that one day I can return the favour. This book is dedicated to my parents, Gisela and Otto Knüsel. They have always supported me, even when I chose to do research abroad yet again.

List of Abbreviations

AEPM	Allgemeiner Evangelisch-Protestantischer Missionsverein
BAR	Schweizerisches Bundesarchiv
CCP	Chinese Communist Party
CPGB	Communist Party of Great Britain
CPUSA	Communist Party of the USA
DDS	Documents Diplomatiques Suisses
FDR	Franklin D. Roosevelt
FO	Foreign Office
FRUS	Papers relating to the Foreign Relations of the United States
GMD	Guomindang (Chinese Nationalist Party)
HCP	House of Commons Papers
IWW	Industrial Workers of the World
KPS	Kommunistische Partei der Schweiz
MP	Member of Parliament
NA	National Archives (USA)
NATO	North Atlantic Treaty Organization
NZZ	Neue Zürcher Zeitung
PPP	Public Papers of the Presidents
PRC	People's Republic of China
SPS	Sozialdemokratische Partei der Schweiz
T	Treasury
TNA	The National Archives (UK)
TUC	Trades Union Congress
UCR	United China Relief
UEK	Unabhängige Expertenkommission Schweiz-Zweiter Weltkrieg
WO	War Office

List of Abbreviations

Introduction

Illustration I.1　Charles Henry Sykes, 'Yes, China is Awakening',
Los Angeles Times (14.2.1927)

In early 1927, anti-foreign sentiment erupted in China. Chinese activists occupied the British concession at Hankou and across the country demands for the abolition of the unequal treaties intensified. The American cartoonist Charles Henry 'Bill' Sykes drew an editorial cartoon in which he visualized the changing Chinese attitude towards the foreign powers (Illustration I.1). Sykes worked for various publications and his cartoons were also syndicated, so they reached a fairly large audience across the USA. Among the publications that printed his cartoons was the *Los Angeles Times*, one of the most important newspapers on the West Coast at that time. Sykes's cartoon portrays in a literal way the metaphor of China awakening on the international stage. China is yawning and stretching, thereby elbowing Uncle Sam (i.e. the United States) with its left arm and punching John Bull (i.e. Great Britain) with its right.

References to China as an awakening power were very popular in Western media between the Opium Wars and the Communist Victory in 1949, not least because China went through so many transformations – from dynasty to republic to a period of warlordism, civil war and finally to a communist system. As a result, China's awakening was portrayed both positively and negatively by the Western media, depending on how the changes were perceived in each nation. By placing media portrayals of China in the wider political, economic, social and cultural context of Britain, the USA and Switzerland, I analyse in this book how media images and political debates about China were shaped by national interests and perceptions, and how they contributed to the discursive construction of nationhood in each country.

At first glance, Sykes's cartoon 'Yes, China is Awakening' seems to depict China's awakening as dangerous to nations like the USA and Britain. However, a closer look at the historical context leads to a different interpretation of the cartoon. Great Britain, Japan, France and the USA all relied on (informal) imperialism to establish their presence in China and protect their interests there. Yet, their efforts were met in the mid-1920s with increasing anti-foreign agitation. This is portrayed in the cartoon by John Bull getting a full-on fist in the face and being quite outraged at this (Britain was indeed affected more than any other power). As will be shown in Chapter 2, in the 1920s, American newspapers and magazines heavily criticized Britain's behaviour in China and pointed out that the USA was different from the other imperial powers in that it wanted to help China become a modern and democratic nation. Since American media images of China were centred around the idea that China benefited from the USA's global mission to spread democracy and Christianity, American journalists and cartoonists could not portray China too negatively because this would have called into question the belief in American cultural and political superiority. Hence, Bill Sykes did not depict China as a menacing power. Although Uncle Sam is knocked in the cheek by China's elbow and is not enjoying his treatment, he appears to endure it stoically like a father figure who knows that eventually China will get it right and will be able to wake up and get out of bed without hitting anybody else. Sykes's cartoon, therefore, served as a reminder to his American audience that even though the USA was in bed with the other imperial powers, it reacted differently to events in China because it was on a global mission to spread democracy and bring progress to other nations.

While several books have been written on perceptions of China in foreign countries, most of them treat the West as a single entity.[1] Yet, the dichotomy between 'China' and 'the West' is highly problematic because it ignores the effect of national interests, beliefs and anxieties on these images, resulting in exaggerations and generalizations.[2] In this book, I focus on China images in three particular countries, namely Britain, the USA and Switzerland, to show that in order to fully understand media images of China, political debates in the respective countries have to be considered. Britain, the USA and Switzerland were chosen for this study because they had different interests in China. Until the early twentieth century, Britain dominated foreign relations with China and continued to be associated with the aggression of imperial powers in China. Because Britain was an imperial power, the British press tended to focus on the Empire to frame events in China. The USA was selected because – unlike Germany or France – it did not occupy Chinese territory and had no sphere of interest in China but it did have huge geopolitical aspirations in East Asia. Moreover, in the first half of the twentieth century, foreign missionary presence in China was predominantly American. Switzerland was included in the analysis because it had very limited interest in China, having no relations with it until 1918 and a negligible commercial and missionary presence there. As a result, domestic issues were often used in the Swiss press to interpret events in China.

Newspapers and magazines were the most important sources of news and the main forms of mass media in the first half of the twentieth century. Since newspapers and magazines were produced and consumed in a similar way and had a similar format, they can be analysed with the same method, which is crucial

---

[1]   John S. Gregory, *The West and China since 1500* (Basingstoke and New York, 2003); Henry A. Myers (ed.), *Western Views of China and the Far East, volume 2: The Early Modern Times to the Present (since 1800)* (Hong Kong, 1984); Colin Mackerras, *Western Images of China* (Hong Kong, 1991); Jonathan D. Spence, *The Chan's Great Continent: China in Western Minds* (New York and London, 1998); D.E. Mungello, *The Great Encounter of China and the West, 1500–1800*, 2nd ed. (Lanham and Oxford, 2005). Publications on American Images include: T. Christopher Jespersen, *American Images of China, 1931–1949* (Stanford, 1996); Jonathan Goldstein, Jerry Israel and Hilary Conroy (eds), *America Views China: American Images of China Then and Now* (London, 1991); Thomas Laszlo Dorogi, *Tainted Perceptions: Liberal-Democracy and American Popular Images of China* (Lanham, 2001); Wang Jianwei, *Limited Adversaries: Post-Cold War Sino-American Mutual Images* (Oxford and New York, 2000); Harold R. Isaacs, *Images of Asia: American Views of China and India* (New York, 1962).

[2]   James L. Hevia, *English Lessons: The Pedagogy of Imperialism in Nineteenth-Century China* (Durham and London, 2003), pp. 17–18; Haun Saussy, *Great Walls of Discourse and Other Adventures in Cultural China* (Cambridge and London, 2001), pp. 76, 117 and 185.

for the synchronic and diachronic analysis of China images. I will treat the radio and newsreel coverage of China only briefly because they were not accessible for a large part of society until the end of the period covered in this study and also because the amount of sources had to be limited for research purposes.[3]

There are various approaches that analyse the effects of the media on public opinion or policy making.[4] Stephen Koss regards the press in the early twentieth century as both the best possible indicator of public opinion, as well as the most important instrument in influencing it.[5] Slavko Splichal in turn focuses on the agenda-setting function of the press, claiming that media influence or even form public opinion because 'they help to determine and demonstrate the limits of legitimate public discussion in society'.[6] This book, therefore, not only compares media portrayals of China in Britain, the USA and Switzerland, but also analyses the way newspapers and magazines were influenced by public debates, cultural preconceptions, government policies, pressure groups and economic interests, as well as how they contributed to the discursive construction of nationhood. After all, newspapers do not mirror reality but represent it and as such contribute to the construction of social, cultural or national identities.[7]

British, American and Swiss perceptions of China are also diachronically analysed in order to examine the transnational circulation of visual and verbal images. In the first half of the twentieth century, newspapers and magazines sometimes printed articles or political cartoons from other countries. They also frequently used press agencies for information. Journalists, too, often relied on foreign articles or sources, which in turn influenced their perceptions of China.

---

[3]   William R. Lindley, *20th Century American Newspapers: In Content and Production* (Manhattan, 1993), pp. 43–4.

[4]   J. David Kennamer, 'Public Opinion, the Press, and Public Policy: An Introduction', in J. David Kennamer (ed.), *Public Opinion, the Press, and Public Policy* (Westport, 1992), pp. 1–17; Tamir Sheafer, 'How to Evaluate It: The Role of Story-Evaluative Tone in Agenda Setting and Priming', *Journal of Communication*, 57/1 (2007): pp. 21–39; Nicholas O. Berry, *Foreign Policy and the Press: An Analysis of The New York Times' Coverage of U.S. Foreign Policy* (New York, Westport and London, 1990); Ottfried Jarren and Patrick Donges, *Politische Kommunikation in der Mediengesellschaft: Eine Einführung, Band 2: Akteure, Prozesse und Inhalte* (Wiesbaden, 2002); Anders Hansen (ed.), *Mass Communication Research Methods, volumes 1–3* (London, Thousand Oaks, New Delhi and Singapore, 2009).

[5]   Stephen Koss, *The Rise and Fall of the Political Press in Britain, volume 2: The Twentieth Century* (Chapel Hill and London, 1984), p. 9.

[6]   Slavko Splichal, *Public Opinion: Developments and Controversies in the Twentieth Century* (Lanham and Oxford, 1999), p. 274.

[7]   Norman Fairclough, *Media Discourse* (London, 2002), pp. 55 and 103–4; Roger Fowler, *Language in the News: Discourse and Ideology in the Press* (London and New York, 1991), pp. 3–4 and 11–17; Pamela J. Shoemaker and Stephen D. Reese, *Mediating the Message: Theories of Influences on Mass Media Content* (New York and London, 1991), pp. 90–98.

Moreover, images of China and the Chinese were influenced by literature and film, which contributed to the transnational circulation of cultural stereotypes because many novels and short stories about China or Chinese immigrants were translated and published in various countries. Films were often shown in several countries, causing their portrayals of the Chinese and particular images associated with China to reach an international audience.

Images have recently received much attention in disciplines such as history and cultural studies, which treat them as cultural products.[8] For this study, images are defined as visual and verbal cultural constructs that not only represent but also influence mental images about cultural concepts like the perception of social groups or national identity.[9] Media images of China, therefore, include visualizations such as cartoons, photographs, newsreels etc. as well as verbal constructs like newspaper articles because they all generated mental pictures of China. Editorials are of particular interest because they serve as commentaries on the events and often take on a much more explicit stance than articles or summaries of telegrams.[10] Likewise, editorial cartoons are a significant source of media images of China because they were openly biased and blatantly relied on stereotypes and caricature to satirize, distort or ridicule facts.[11] In the first half of the twentieth century, most newspapers had an editorial page on which they printed one or more editorial cartoons. These cartoons were not printed as an illustration of an article but were commentaries that stood on their own. They are important for a study of media images and political debates because they frequently provided readers with a different perspective than regular newspaper and magazine articles. While the content of newspaper articles was restricted by editorial policy or word limit, editorial cartoonists usually had more leeway and some were even exempt

---

[8] Birgit Mersmann, 'Bildkulturwissenschaft als Kulturbildwissenschaft?: Von der Notwendigkeit eines inter- und transkulturellen Iconic Turn', *Zeitschrift für Ästhetik und Allgemeine Kunstwissenschaft*, 49/1 (2004): p. 91; Gustav Frank and Klaus Sachs-Hombach, 'Bildwissenschaft und Visual Culture Studies', in Klaus Sachs-Hombach (ed.), *Bild und Medium: Kunstgeschichtliche und philosophische Grundlagen der interdisziplinären Bildwissenschaft* (Köln, 2006), p. 185; William A. Gamson, David Croteau, William Hoynes and Theodore Sasson, 'Media Images and the Social Construction of Reality', *Annual Review of Sociology*, 18 (1992): p. 374.

[9] See also Gerhard Paul, 'Von der Historischen Bildkunde zur Visual History: Eine Einführung', in Gerhard Paul (ed.), *Visual History: Ein Studienbuch* (Göttingen, 2006), pp. 7–36.

[10] Robert Hodge and Gunther Kress, *Language as Ideology*, 2nd ed. (London and New York, 1993), p. 17.

[11] Chris Lamb, *Drawn to Extremes: The Use and Abuse of Editorial Cartoons* (New York, 2004); Keith Kenney and Michael Colgan, 'Drawing Blood: Images, Stereotypes, and the Political Cartoon', in Paul Martin Lester and Susan Dente Ross (eds), *Images that Injure: Pictorial Stereotypes in the Media*, 2nd ed. (Westport and London, 2003), pp. 226 and 232; Thomas Knieper, *Die politische Karikatur: Eine journalistische Darstellungsform und deren Produzenten* (Köln, 2002), pp. 72–97.

from having to obey editorial policy. Thus, I will show that editorial cartoons not only reflected existing discourses on China but also contributed to them.

When media images of China in Britain, the USA and Switzerland are placed within the broader political, economic, social and cultural context, it becomes evident that they were cultural constructs that contained more information about the country in which they were produced than about China. Since culture is not a homogenous entity but is constituted of several subcultures, of which each has its own values and discourses,[12] one has to keep in mind that various images of China existed simultaneously in a specific country.[13] Similarly, the decoding of the media images of China by contemporary readers did not happen in a uniform way.

The main argument of this study is that images of China contributed to the discursive construction of nationhood in each country and were therefore different in each nation. This presupposes that identity is constantly (re-)produced within representation and only works through exclusion. Stuart Hall points out: 'it is only through the relation to the Other, the relation to what it is not, to precisely what it lacks, to what has been called its *constitutive outside* that the "positive" meaning of any term – and thus its "identity" – can be constructed.'[14] In this book, I demonstrate how China figured as such an Other that was used to construct specific concepts of national identity. Any study that deals with such a topic has to mention the late Edward Said's groundbreaking book *Orientalism*, in which Said used Louis Althusser's notion that subjects are always interpellated by ideology in order to argue that every European who writes about the Orient is aware of the history between Europe and the Middle East or East Asia.[15] Said defined 'Orientalism' as:

> a certain will or intention to understand, in some cases to control, manipulate, even to incorporate, what is a manifestly different (or alternative and novel)

---

[12]   Nicholas B. Dirks, Geoff Eley and Sherry B. Ortner, 'Introduction', in Nicholas B. Dirks, Geoff Eley and Sherry B. Ortner (eds), *Culture/Power/History: A Reader in Contemporary Social Theory* (Princeton, 1994), pp. 3–4; William H. Sewell, Jr., 'The Concept(s) of Culture', in Victoria E. Bonnell and Lynn Hunt (eds), *Beyond the Cultural Turn: New Directions in the Study of Society and Culture* (Berkeley and Los Angeles, 1999), pp. 43–6; Joyce Appleby, Lynn Hunt and Margaret Jacob, *Telling the Truth about History* (London and New York, 1994), pp. 220–23.

[13]   See also Gregory B. Lee, *Chinas Unlimited: Making the Imaginaries of China and Chineseness* (Honolulu, 2003), p. vii.

[14]   Stuart Hall, 'Introduction: Who Needs "Identity"?', in Stuart Hall and Paul du Gay (eds), *Questions of Cultural Identity* (London, 1996), pp. 4–5 (quote). See also: Michel Foucault, *Power/Knowledge: Selected Interviews and Other Writings 1972–1977*, ed. Colin Gordon (New York, 1980), pp. 92–108; Michel Foucault, *The History of Sexuality, volume 1: An Introduction* (New York, 1978), pp. 92–102; Hall, 'Introduction', pp. 2–14.

[15]   Edward Said, *Orientalism* (New York, 1979), pp. 11–12; Louis Althusser, 'Ideology and Ideological State Apparatuses: On Ideology', in Hazard Adams and Leroy Searle (eds), *Critical Theory Since 1965* (Tallahassee, 1986), pp. 239–50.

world; it is, above all, a discourse that is by no means in direct, corresponding relationship with political power in the raw, but rather is produced and exists in an uneven exchange with various kinds of power ... Orientalism is – and does not simply represent – a considerable dimension of modern political-intellectual culture, and as such has less to do with the Orient than it does with "our" world.[16]

Accordingly, the Orient is produced and excluded to establish the West; it is absent, substituted, displaced, different, strange and inferior – in short: the non-West.[17] Although Said's influence on various disciplines dealing with relations and perceptions of the West and the Middle East, Africa or Asia cannot be overestimated, *Orientalism* has also received its fair share of criticism.[18] While Said focuses on the Middle East, the arguments in *Orientalism* can be applied to studies of China images. In fact, China tended to be perceived as part of the Orient, and the Chinese were often described as 'Orientals' although direct relations with China and particularly alliances with China had the effect that the term 'Orient' was deconstructed and the relationship between China and the Orient viewed as more complex. Nevertheless, it is problematic to portray China and the Chinese only as a discursive antithesis to the West. Haun Saussy points out: 'China most often enters discourse as the countercase to an essentialized West ... Naturally, China is not the only non-West; the West has a variety of antitheses; nor is the "West" the only "we" that needs a "they" in order to think through its own self-definition.'[19] Thus, while this study seeks to show that images of China were always influenced by political, economic, social and cultural factors that differed from country to country, it is important to remember that they were by no means unidirectional. Relations with China and the various ways in which people came in contact with Chinese people, the government, culture and products also affected how China was viewed. Even more importantly, however, there also existed Chinese images of Western countries and the West or Western imperialism.[20]

---

16   Said, *Orientalism*, p. 12.

17   Said, *Orientalism*, pp. 21–55, 93–5 and 208–9.

18   Daniel Martin Varisco, *Reading Orientalism: Said and the Unsaid* (Seattle and London, 2007); Catherine Hall, 'Remembering Edward Said (1935–2003)', *History Workshop Journal*, 57 (2004): pp. 235–43; Graham Huggan, '(Not) Reading Orientalism', *Research in African Literatures*, 36/3 (2005): pp. 124–36; Ibn Warraq, *Defending the West: A Critique of Edward Said's Orientalism* (Amherst, 2007); Mustapha Morrouchi, 'Counternarratives, Recoveries, Refusals', in Paul A. Bové (ed.), *Edward Said and the Work of the Critic: Speaking Truth to Power* (London, 2000), pp. 187–228; Lawrence Grossberg, 'Identity and Cultural Studies: Is That All There Is?', in Stuart Hall and Paul du Gay (eds), *Questions of Cultural Identity* (London, 1996), p. 95.

19   Saussy, *Great Walls*, p. 185.

20   Hua Meng and Sukehiro Hirakawa (eds), *Images of Westerners in Chinese and Japanese Literature* (Amsterdam, 2000); R. David Arkush and Leo O. Lee (eds), *Land without Ghosts: Chinese Impressions of America from the Mid-Nineteenth Century to the*

Various academic disciplines have developed theories and research related to discourse, for example linguistics, anthropology, history, sociology and political science. Most of them use Michel Foucault as a reference point, according to whom discourses organize and regulate reality, and define what can or must be said and what cannot or must not be said. Knowledge and discursive practices constitute each other and cannot exist without each other. Unfortunately, as Foucault's definition of discourse changed and he never wrote a detailed methodology for empirical research, the problem of defining discourse has lasted until today because no universal definition has been accepted.[21] As a consequence, historians who undertake discourse analysis have developed different methods and theories. *Begriffsgeschichte*, for example, analyses social knowledge through concepts in specific historical contexts among political and social groups and their diachronic change, while *Historische Semantik* treats semantic change as part of a change in social reality and analyses semantic fields of syntagmatically and paradigmatically structured words as well as the context in which they appear in order to find out the ways specific linguistic communities thought and spoke.[22] A more linguistic approach is that of Critical Discourse Analysis, which is concerned with the constitution of knowledge and its effect on subjects and society. Critical Discourse Analysis also analyses the social process and structures influencing the

---

Present (Berkeley, 1989); Carola McGiffert (ed.), *Chinese Images of the United States* (Washington, DC, 2005); Hong Zhang, *America Perceived: The Making of Chinese Images of the United States, 1945–1953* (London and Westport, 2002).

[21]   Michel Foucault, *The Archaeology of Knowledge* (New York, 1972), pp. 182–7; Foucault, *History*, pp. 92–102; Foucault, *Power/Knowledge*, pp. 141–2 and 52. See also: Reiner Keller, Andreas Hirseland, Werner Schneider and Willy Viehöver (eds), *Handbuch Sozialwissenschaftliche Diskursanalyse, Band I: Theorien und Methoden* (Opladen, 2001); Achim Landwehr, *Geschichte des Sagbaren: Einführung in die Historische Diskursanalyse*, 2nd ed. (Tübingen, 2004), pp. 68–89 and 106; Philipp Sarasin, 'Geschichtswissenschaft und Diskursanalyse', in Philipp Sarasin, *Geschichtswissenschaft und Diskursanalyse* (Frankfurt am Main, 2003), pp. 50 and 58.

[22]   For Begriffsgeschichte see: Reinhart Koselleck, 'Begriffsgeschichte und Sozialgeschichte', in Reinhart Koselleck, *Vergangene Zukunft: Zur Semantik geschichtlicher Zeiten* (Frankfurt am Main, 1989), pp. 107–29; Otto Brunner, Werner Conze and Reinhart Koselleck (eds), *Geschichtliche Grundbegriffe: Historisches Lexikon zur politisch-sozialen Sprache in Deutschland* (7 vols, Stuttgart, 1972–97); Hans Erich Bödeker, 'Reflexionen über Begriffsgeschichte als Methode', in Hans Erich Bödeker (ed.), *Begriffsgeschichte, Diskursgeschichte, Metapherngeschichte* (Göttingen, 2002), pp. 75–6 and 92. For Historische Semantik see: Rolf Reichardt (ed.), *Aufklärung und Historische Semantik: Interdisziplinäre Beiträge zur westeuropäischen Kulturgeschichte* (Berlin, 1998); Hans-Jürgen Lüsebrink and Rolf Reichardt, *Die Bastille: Zur Symbolgeschichte von Herrschaft und Freiheit* (Frankfurt am Main, 1990), pp. 259–64; Hans Erich Bödeker, 'Ausprägung der Historischen Semantik', in Hans Erich Bödeker (ed.), *Begriffsgeschichte, Diskursgeschichte, Metapherngeschichte* (Göttingen, 2002), pp. 12–15.

production, consumption and interpretation of texts.[23] Recent years have witnessed the emergence of *Historische Diskursanalyse* (Historical Discourse Analysis), which looks at how realities and identities are represented and is interested in the diachronic change of categorizations, social hierarchies and thought patterns of a society or a period.[24] This study is part of Historical Discourse Analysis because it analyses media images of China as cultural products and examines how they related to stereotypes, national interests and cultural values. As a method it relies on frame analysis and Ruth Wodak's method of recontextualization.

Framing theory is among the most popular research approaches in media studies but it is also used in various other disciplines. One of the consequences of its interdisciplinary popularity is that definitions of 'frame' increasingly vary.[25] In this study, frames are treated as culturally shared organizing ideas or principles that are used to structure facts and give them coherence and meaning. They, therefore, highlight certain aspects of issues and ignore others.[26] Journalists use framing devices on a syntactical, rhetorical and thematic level to organize facts and structure an article and its message.[27] As Robert M. Entman states: 'To report

---

[23] Ruth Wodak and Gilbert Weiss (eds), *Critical Discourse Analysis: Theory and Interdisciplinarity* (Basingstoke, 2007); Ruth Wodak and Michael Meyer (eds), *Methods of Critical Discourse Analysis* (London, Thousand Oaks and New Delhi, 2007); Siegfried Jäger, 'Diskurs und Wissen: Theoretische und methodische Aspekte einer Kritischen Diskurs- und Dispositivanalyse', in Reiner Keller, Andreas Hirseland, Werner Schneider and Willy Viehöver (eds), *Handbuch Sozialwissenschaftliche Diskursanalyse, Band I: Theorien und Methoden* (Opladen, 2001), pp. 81–111.

[24] Landwehr, *Geschichte*; Franz X. Eder (ed.), *Historische Diskursanalysen: Genealogie, Theorie, Anwendungen* (Wiesbaden, 2006).

[25] Jörg Matthes and Matthias Kohring, 'The Content Analysis of Media Frames: Toward Improving Reliability and Validity', *Journal of Communication*, 58/2 (2008): pp. 259–63; Baldwin Van Gorp, 'The Constructionist Approach to Framing: Bringing Culture Back In', *Journal of Communication*, 57/1 (2007): pp. 60–61; David Weaver, 'Thoughts on Agenda Setting, Framing, and Priming', *Journal of Communication*, 57/1 (2007): pp. 142–7; Stephen D. Reese, 'The Framing Project: A Bridging Model for Media Research Revisited', *Journal of Communication*, 57/1 (2007): pp. 148–54.

[26] Robert M. Entman, *Projections of Power: Framing News, Public Opinion, and U.S. Foreign Policy* (Chicago and London, 2004), p. 5; Stephen D. Reese, 'Prologue – Framing Public Life: A Bridging Model for Media Research', in Stephen D. Reese, Oscar H. Gandy, Jr. and August E. Grant (eds), *Framing Public Life: Perspectives on Media and Our Understanding of the Social World* (Mahwah and London, 2001), pp. 12 and 14–15; Van Gorp, 'Constructionist Approach', pp. 62–3; William A. Gamson, 'News as Framing', *American Behavioral Scientist*, 33/2 (1989): p. 157; Karen S. Johnson-Cartee, *News Narratives and News Framing: Constructing Political Reality* (Lanham and Oxford, 2005), pp. 158–60.

[27] Zhongdang Pan and Gerald M. Kosicki, 'Framing Analysis: An Approach to News Discourse', *Political Communication*, 10/1 (1993): pp. 58–62; Johnson-Cartee, *News Narratives*, pp. 161–2 and 174.

the news is to frame.'[28] However, frames not only affect the structure and content of news, they also contribute to the social construction of reality by defining and reaffirming values and beliefs.[29]

Frames can be applied to various topics but a topic can also be framed in different ways. Thus, frame analysiˢ can compare frames from other political and/ or historical contexts and deal with diachronic change or the context surrounding the decision to adopt a certain frame.[30] This study undertakes synchronic as well as diachronic frame analyses; not only does it examine how events in China were framed in a specific country but it also compares the frames used by the media in Britain, the USA and Switzerland, and then analyses how they developed or changed over time. Zhongdang Pan and Gerald M. Kosicki point out: 'Choices of words and their organization into news stories are not trivial matters. They hold great power in setting the context for debate, defining issues under consideration, summoning a variety of mental representations, and providing the basic tools to discuss the issues at hand.'[31] As a result, frames are analysed via keywords, figures of speech, catchphrases, pictures, metaphors and stereotyped images in newspaper and magazine articles and political cartoons.[32]

When analysing media images of China, it is important to remember that not all newspapers could afford to have correspondents in China. Often, events in China were also not deemed newsworthy. Even when events in China made it through the gatekeeping process, in which news is selected for publication in

---

[28]   Robert M. Entman, 'Foreword', in Karen Callaghan and Frauke Schell (eds), *Framing American Politics* (Pittsburgh, 2005), p. viii.

[29]   Loup Langton, *Photojournalism and Today's News: Creating Visual Reality* (Chichester and Oxford, 2009), pp. 72–3.

[30]   Van Gorp, 'Constructionist Approach', pp. 62–3 and 66–7; Reese, 'Prologue', pp. 15–18; Charlotte Ryan, 'Getting Framed: The Media Shape Reality', in Anders Hansen (ed.), *Mass Communication Research Methods*, volume 3 (London, Thousand Oaks, New Delhi and Singapore, 2008), pp. 56–9.

[31]   Pan and Kosicki, 'Framing Analysis', p. 70.

[32]   Philemon Bantimaroudis and Hyun Ban, 'Covering the Crisis in Somalia: Framing Choices by The New York Times and The Manchester Guardian', in Stephen D. Reese, Oscar H. Gandy, Jr. and August E. Grant (eds), *Framing Public Life: Perspectives on Media and Our Understanding of the Social World* (Mahwah and London, 2001), pp. 177–82; Susan Dente Ross, 'Unconscious, Ubiquitous Frames', in Paul Martin Lester and Susan Dente Ross (eds), *Images that Injure: Pictorial Stereotypes in the Media*, 2nd ed. (Westport and London, 2003), p. 31; Mark Miller and Bonnie Parnell Riechert, 'The Spiral of Opportunity and Frame Resonance: Mapping the Issue Cycle in News and Public Discourse', in Stephen D. Reese, Oscar H. Gandy, Jr. and August E. Grant (eds), *Framing Public Life: Perspectives on Media and Our Understanding of the Social World* (Mahwah and London, 2001), p. 114; Gamson, 'News', p. 158; Robert M. Entman, 'Framing: Toward Clarification of a Fractured Paradigm', in Anders Hansen (ed.), *Mass Communication Research Methods*, volume 3 (London, Thousand Oaks, New Delhi and Singapore, 2008), p. 29.

newspapers,[33] various factors influenced how an article was written and published. The technology used by a publication for example affected the number of issues it could print, its type and amount of illustrations, and determined the speed of communication between journalist and editor. Some newspapers could not afford telegrams so their correspondents in China had to communicate via mail which could take several weeks to reach the editor's desk. The newspaper's political orientation, style and policy often depended on the preferences of the newspaper's owner, publisher or editor, and influenced how a subject was framed. Economic objectives also played an important role in the selection and framing of stories, for example newspapers risked losing advertisers if they printed certain things. This was very serious, as newspapers generated their revenue through sales and advertising. Editors also had to make sure that articles and cartoons fit the interests or political leanings of their target audiences and framed events to cater to them. Journalists, of course, influenced press coverage through the frame that they selected for their article and the sources that they used; the same holds true for cartoonists. Foreign correspondents in China tended to rely on missionaries, political leaders, staff from embassies and consulates, official press statements, news agencies and representatives of business organizations. Usually, sources tried to persuade the journalist towards their own interests and perspectives, thereby influencing the frame that was selected for the story.[34] Since frames were always part of a specific culture, journalists did not always select frames consciously but also relied on a cultural stock of frames.[35] Charles Stangor and Mark Schaller point out: 'cultural norms are more than simply contributors to individual beliefs about groups; they are a social system through which stereotypes are represented

---

[33]   See Pamela J. Shoemaker, 'Media Gatekeeping', in Anders Hansen (ed.), *Mass Communication Research Methods*, volume 1 (London, Thousand Oaks, New Delhi and Singapore, 2009), pp. 333–46.

[34]   Shoemaker and Reese, *Mediating the Message*, pp. 123–4 and 136–82; Lucig Danielian, 'Interest Groups in the News', in J. David Kennamer (ed.), *Public Opinion, the Press, and Public Policy* (Westport, 1992), p. 67; Allan Bell, 'The Discourse Structure of News Stories', in Allan Bell and Peter Garrett (eds), *Approaches to Media Discourse* (Oxford and Malden, 1998), pp. 64–104; Fowler, *Language*, pp. 121–2; Jarren and Donges, *Politische Kommunikation*, p. 23; Berry, *Foreign Policy*, pp. 140–41; O.W. Riegel, 'Channels of Communication', *The Public Opinion Quarterly*, October (1938): pp. 655–6; Michael Schanne and Ruedi Matter, 'Auswahl und Inszenierung von Themen zur öffentlichen Kommunikation', in Michael Schanne and Peter Schulz (eds), *Journalismus in der Schweiz: Fakten, Überlegungen, Möglichkeiten* (Aarau, 1993), pp. 76–9; Chandrika Kaul, *Reporting the Raj: The British Press and India c. 1880–1922* (Manchester and New York, 2003), p. 9; Ross, 'Frames', p. 31.

[35]   Van Gorp, 'Constructionist Approach', p. 64 and 67; Ross, 'Frames', p. 31; Erving Goffman, 'A Reply to Denzin and Keller', *Contemporary Sociology*, 10/1 (1981): p. 63.

and perpetuated across individuals, across generations, and across time.'[36] Frames, thus, often reinforced stereotypical images of China.[37]

This study uses Ruth Wodak's approach of recontextualization to analyse the frames within the historical setting. As the production and interpretation of discourses are situated in time and space, discursive events have to be recontextualized on various levels, namely on the immediate (i.e. text-internal) level, on the level of intertextuality and interdiscursivity, on an institutional level and in the broader sociopolitical and historical context.[38] In the media analysis, the following levels of recontextualization were used: individual newspaper and magazine articles were analysed according to the way they framed events in China. The period between 1900 and 1950 was divided into clusters, for which a detailed media analysis was carried out. While newspapers were analysed for the duration of the respective events (e.g. for the Xinhai Revolution October 1911 to February 1912), magazines were usually analysed for entire years because they were not published as often as newspapers and could not cover events in China as quickly as newspapers. Once individual newspaper and magazine articles and cartoons were analysed, their frames were compared to articles on China in the same newspaper or magazine, to those of the same country and to those of newspapers and magazines in the other countries. This helped to determine whether a specific frame was used only by a certain editor, correspondent or cartoonist, if it was typical of a newspaper, magazine or publications with a similar target audience or political orientation, or for all newspapers and magazines in the same country. Additionally, the frame was compared to dominant discourses that existed at the time when the events took place because these also influenced the coverage. This was done via an analysis of newspaper topics in general and

---

[36]   Charles Stangor and Mark Schaller, 'Stereotypes as Individual and Collective Representations', in Charles Stangor (ed.), *Stereotypes and Prejudice: Essential Readings* (Philadelphia, 2000), p. 69.

[37]   See also: Ross, 'Frames', pp. 31–2 (quote); Stangor and Schaller, 'Stereotypes', pp. 68–9; Eva Sabine Kuntz, *Konstanz und Wandel von Stereotypen: Deutschlandbilder in der italienischen Presse nach dem Zweiten Weltkrieg* (Frankfurt am Main, Berlin and Bern, 1997), p. 40.

[38]   Michael Meyer, 'Between Theory, Method, and Politics: Positioning of the Approaches to CDA', in Ruth Wodak and Michael Meyer (eds), *Methods of Critical Discourse Analysis* (London, Thousand Oaks and New Delhi, 2007), p. 15; Ruth Wodak, 'What CDA Is About: A Summary of Its History, Important Concepts and Its Developments', in Ruth Wodak and Michael Meyer (eds), *Methods of Critical Discourse Analysis* (London, Thousand Oaks and New Delhi, 2007), p. 3; Ruth Wodak, 'The Discourse-Historical Approach', in Ruth Wodak and Michael Meyer (eds), *Methods of Critical Discourse Analysis* (London, Thousand Oaks and New Delhi, 2007), pp. 65, 67 and 70; Ruth Wodak and Gilbert Weiss, 'Introduction: Theory, Interdisciplinarity and Critical Discourse Analysis', in Ruth Wodak and Gilbert Weiss (eds), *Critical Discourse Analysis: Theory and Interdisciplinarity* (Basingstoke, 2007), pp. 21–3.

of the political, economic, social and cultural background of the time via various sources and literature.

Newspapers were selected in such a way that they represent a variety of socio-economic profiles in their readerships. The style and content of newspapers catered to a specific target audience, causing them not only to focus on different subject matter but also to use different vocabulary in their articles. Even their layout and use of illustrations differed, for example mass papers like the *Daily Mail* and the *New York World* had far more illustrations than *The Times* or the *Manchester Guardian*, which were mostly read by the better educated middle and upper classes. Andreas Jucker distinguishes three categories of British newspapers which are based on socio-economic readership profiles: up-market, mid-market and down-market papers. Also called broadsheet papers or quality papers, up-market papers have a target audience from a high socio-economic status. Among the up-market newspapers analysed in this study are *The Times, Manchester Guardian, New York Times* and the *Neue Zürcher Zeitung*. Mid-market papers have a target audience from the lower middle class and skilled working class. Such papers include the *Atlanta Constitution, Chicago Tribune, San Francisco Chronicle, Daily Mail, Tages-Anzeiger* and *Journal de Genève*. Down-market papers, finally, have a working-class target readership. Examples of these include the *New York World*, the *Daily Express* and later the *Daily Mirror*. Of course, this is not to say that a newspaper was only read by members of one social class or by its target audience.[39]

The number and nature of newspapers in Britain changed a great deal after new machinery and technology were introduced with the Industrial Revolution. The first national newspaper was *The Times*, which was founded in 1785 as *The Daily Universal Register*. It became an extremely powerful newspaper with both the government and the public, and in the early nineteenth century developed a network of correspondents all over the world. Although it was by far the most prestigious newspaper in Britain and in 1850 had a circulation that was four times as high as that of its rivals, its leading position was soon challenged by other newspapers.[40] In the first half of the nineteenth century Britain witnessed the growth of the middle class and with it the publication of cheaper newspapers that targeted the new mass market. After 1850, adult literacy increased, which led to a further growth in newspaper readership. Moreover, the decline in average working hours together with a rise in real wages had the effect that more people bought

---

[39] Andreas Jucker, *Social Stylistics: Syntactic Variation in British Newspapers* (Berlin and New York, 1992), pp. 4–8 and 47–58. See also Tak Wing Chan and John H. Goldthorpe, 'Social Status and Newspaper Readership', *American Journal of Sociology*, 112/4 (2007): pp. 1095–134.

[40] Martin Walker, *Powers of the Press: The World's Great Newspapers* (London, Melbourne and New York, 1982), pp. 29–46; Dennis Griffiths, *Fleet Street: Five Hundred Years of the Press* (London, 2006), pp. 54–8; Political and Economic Planning, *Report on the British Press* (London, 1938), pp. 91–3.

and read newspapers, particularly those who now travelled to work by public transport. Consequently, whereas in 1851 the annual newspaper sales amounted to 85 million, in 1920 they were 5,604 million. Technological innovations like the rotary press and linotype machines as well as the abolition of several taxes and duties not only lowered the price of newspapers and increased the number of newspaper titles, but also allowed newspapers to print more issues.[41] The leading Scottish newspaper *The Scotsman*, for example, was founded in 1817 as a weekly newspaper and went daily in 1855.[42]

British newspapers catering for a mass audience with sensationalist news grew in number as newspapers became part of everyday life. Even the working classes now had access to newspapers because they tended to be read aloud in communities.[43] Around the turn of the century, various cheap daily newspapers such as the *Daily Mail* (1896), *Daily Express* (1900) and *Daily Mirror* (1903) were founded. They adhered to a lighter style of journalism that focused more on human interest stories than simply on news and also included more illustrations. The number of radical or liberal dailies, in turn, declined and only a few survived, among them the *Manchester Guardian*, the top-selling radical morning paper in Britain, and the evening newspaper *The Star*. Contrary to countries like the USA and Germany, socialist papers tended to be published only in small geographical areas and not nationwide, and so in the early twentieth century British newspapers remained mostly conservative.[44] The conservative *Daily Mail* was so successful with its mix of sensational human interest stories and only a small amount of

---

[41]   Richard D. Altick, *The English Common Reader: A Social History of the Mass Reading Public, 1800–1900* (Chicago, 1957), pp. 240–93; James Curran and Jean Seaton, *Power without Responsibility: The Press and Broadcasting in Britain*, 4th ed. (London, 1993), pp. 32–5; Political and Economic Planning, *Report*, pp. 91–2; Werner Faulstich, *Medienwandel im Industrie- und Massenzeitalter (1830–1900)* (Göttingen, 2003), pp. 25 and 32; Jürgen Wilke, *Grundzüge der Medien- und Kommunikationsgeschichte: Von den Anfängen bis ins 20. Jahrhundert* (Köln and Weimar, 2000), pp. 158–60 and 300; John M. MacKenzie, 'The Press and the Dominant Ideology of Empire', in Simon J. Potter (ed.), *Newspapers and Empire in Ireland and Britain: Reporting the British Empire, c. 1857–1921* (Dublin, 2003), p. 25.

[42]   Stephen Koss, *The Rise and Fall of the Political Press in Britain, volume 1: The Nineteenth Century* (London, 1981), p. 97; Mick Temple, *The British Press* (Maidenhead, 2008), pp. 15 and 94.

[43]   Mark Hampton, *Visions of the Press in Britain, 1850–1950* (Urbana and Chicago, 2004), pp. 19–23 and 26–8; Ernst Bollinger, *Pressegeschichte II, 1840–1903: Die goldenen Jahre der Massenpresse* (Freiburg, 1996), pp. 99–100.

[44]   Curran and Seaton, *Power*, pp. 43–4; David Ayerst, *Guardian: Biography of a Newspaper* (London, 1971), p. 266; Lucy Brown, *Victorian News and Newspapers* (Oxford, 1985), p. 72; John Goodbody, 'The Star: Its Role in the Rise of New Journalism', in Joel H. Wiener (ed.), *Papers for the Millions: The New Journalism in Britain, 1850s to 1914* (New York, Westport and London, 1988), pp. 143–63; Griffiths, *Fleet Street*, pp. 124–6; Temple, *British Press*, pp. 22–5; Kaul, *Reporting the Raj*, p. 16; Deian Hopkin, 'The Left-Wing

politics that by 1903 its circulation had risen to over one million, making it the newspaper with the largest circulation in the world. Until the 1930s the *Daily Mail* remained the newspaper with the highest circulation in Britain, when it was overtaken by the *Daily Express*.[45]

After 1900, newspapers increasingly catered to specific audiences. For example, the *Daily Mirror* targeted women but it was not as successful as hoped and was eventually turned into a very successful illustrated paper.[46] The interwar years witnessed a growth in popular journalism, stressing human interest at the expense of political and economic issues, and including more and more photographs. This made the newspapers even more accessible to readers and increased the demand for them. By the early 1920s, the British press scene was dominated by press barons like Lord Northcliffe, whose papers included the *Daily Mail* and *The Times*, his brother Lord Rothermere, who owned among other newspapers the *Daily Mirror*, and Lord Beaverbrook, owner of the *Evening Standard* and *Daily Express* etc. These men had almost complete control of their newspapers and tended to ensure that they maintained a conservative stance. They also often used the newspapers to denounce political parties or their policies.[47] By the mid-1930s, 95 morning dailies and 57.5 evening newspapers were sold per 100 families in Britain. Sunday newspapers were also very popular, selling 1.3 issues for every family in Britain each week.[48] Among the first Sunday newspapers in Britain was the *Observer*, which printed its first issues in 1791 and became one of the most prestigious Sunday publications.[49] Although local and regional newspapers continued to be printed in England, Wales, Scotland and Ireland/Northern Ireland, the Greater London area dominated the newspaper industry in Britain, and almost all the big national daily newspapers (with the notable exception of the *Manchester Guardian*) were located in London.[50] In the following tables, capital letters indicate sympathies for a particular party, small letters a general political stance:

Press and the New Journalism', in Joel H. Wiener (ed.), *Papers for the Millions: The New Journalism in Britain, 1850s to 1914* (New York, Westport and London, 1988), pp. 226–38.

45 James D. Startt, 'Good Journalism in the Era of the New Journalism: The British Press, 1902–1914', in Joel H. Wiener (ed.), *Papers for the Millions: The New Journalism in Britain, 1850s to 1914* (New York, Westport and London, 1988), pp. 276–81; Wilke, *Grundzüge*, p. 300; Hampton, *Visions*, pp. 28 and 40; Griffiths, *Fleet Street*, pp. 131–3; Political and Economic Planning, *Report*, pp. 84–5.

46 Griffiths, *Fleet Street*, pp. 143–5; Temple, *British Press*, p. 30.

47 Temple, *British Press*, pp. 33–9 and 49.

48 Political and Economic Planning, *Report*, p. 43.

49 Griffiths, *Fleet Street*, pp. 53–4; Koss, *Rise*, vol. 2, p. 35.

50 Political and Economic Planning, *Report*, pp. 47–9.

Table I.1　British Newspapers[51]

Newspaper	Founded in	Political Orientation	Circulation in 1910	Circulation in 1930	Circulation in 1950
Daily Express	1900	independent/ conservative	400,000	1,693,000	4,099,000
Daily Mail	1896	independent/ conservative	900,000	1,845,000	2,215,000
Daily Mirror	1903	independent	630,000	1,071,000	4,603,000
Evening Standard	1859	independent/ conservative	160,000	n/a	862,000*
Manchester Guardian	1821	liberal	40,000	47,000	141,000
Observer	1791	conservative	60,000**	201,000	n/a
The Star	1888	liberal	327,000	744,000	1,228,000***
The Scotsman	1817	independent	n/a	n/a	n/a
The Times	1785	independent/ conservative	45,000	187,000	258,000

Note: * Numbers for 1951; ** Numbers for 1911; *** Numbers for 1951.

The British media landscape included a wide variety of magazines and periodicals in the first half of the twentieth century, many of which had existed for decades. In 1841, *Punch*, one of the most influential humour magazines in Britain, was founded and by the early twentieth century it was one of the few remaining satirical journals whose strength lay in editorial cartoons. By this time, its editorial politics had become increasingly conservative.[52] Even more conservative than *Punch* was the *National Review*, which began publication in 1883 and remained throughout its publication a forum for conservatives.[53] The *Spectator* was founded in 1828 and became the most influential London weekly before the outbreak of the First World War. Although it changed its stance from liberal-radical to Conservative/Unionist, it remained an important publication of

---

[51]　David Butler and Anne Sloman, *British Political Facts, 1900–1975*, 4th ed. (London and Basingstoke, 1975), pp. 377–92; Political and Economic Planning, *Report*, p. 84; Kaul, *Reporting the Raj*, pp. 55–8.

[52]　R.M. Healey, 'Punch', in Sam G. Riley (ed.), *Consumer Magazines of the British Isles* (Westport, 1993), pp. 154–61; Jerold J. Savoy, 'Punch', in Alvin Sullivan (ed.), *British Literary Magazines: The Victorian and Edwardian Age, 1837–1913* (Westport and London, 1984), pp. 325–9.

[53]　Carol de Saint Victor, 'National Review, The (1883)', in Alvin Sullivan (ed.), *British Literary Magazines: The Victorian and Edwardian Age, 1837–1913* (Westport and London, 1984), pp. 242–50.

opinion and commentary.[54] A decidedly left-wing review of current affairs was the *New Statesman* (after 1931 the *New Statesman and Nation*), which published its first issue in 1913. Its founders included the Fabian Society's leaders Sidney and Beatrice Webb.[55] A different type of publication was the *Nineteenth Century and After*, founded as *Nineteenth Century* in 1877 and published as *Twentieth Century* from 1951. It was a general review that functioned as an open forum for writers and authors, and printed stories about national and international affairs (particularly imperial policies), history, literature, science, theatre and theology.[56] Other popular British publications included illustrated newspapers like the *Illustrated London News* and *The Graphic*, which originally used drawings and sketches, but after the turn of the century also increasingly printed photographs. They both targeted middle-class readers and were very popular London-based publications.[57]

Table I.2   British Magazines[58]

Magazine	Founded in	Type	Issued
Illustrated London News	1842	illustrated	weekly
National Review	1883	conservative	monthly
New Statesman	1913	socialist	weekly
Nineteenth Century and After	1877	general	monthly
Punch	1841	satirical/conservative	weekly
Spectator	1828	conservative	weekly
The Graphic	1869	illustrated	weekly

---

[54]   Lord Blake, 'Spectator', in Sam G. Riley (ed.), *Consumer Magazines of the British Isles* (Westport, 1993), pp. 197–205.

[55]   Beverly E. Smith, 'New Statesman and Society', in Sam G. Riley (ed.), *Consumer Magazines of the British Isles* (Westport, 1993), pp. 134–8; Ed Block, Jr., 'New Statesman', in Alvin Sullivan (ed.), *British Literary Magazines: The Victorian and Edwardian Age, 1837–1913* (Westport and London, 1984), pp. 262–7.

[56]   Daniel Rutenberg, 'Nineteenth Century, The', in Alvin Sullivan (ed.), *British Literary Magazines: The Victorian and Edwardian Age, 1837–1913* (Westport and London, 1984), pp. 267–75; James W. Parins and Marilyn Parins, 'Twentieth Century', in Alvin Sullivan (ed.), *British Literary Magazines: The Modern Age, 1914–1984* (Westport and London, 1986), pp. 464–7.

[57]   MacKenzie, 'The Press', p. 26.

[58]   James Willing, *Willing's Press Guide and Advertiser's Directory and Handbook, 1910* (London, 1910); Kaul, *Reporting the Raj*, pp. 56–7; Butler and Sloman, *Facts*, pp. 377–92.

As in Britain, the number and circulation of newspapers in the USA rose dramatically in the nineteenth century due to improved communication, technological inventions, improved literacy and lowered prices.[59] The *New York Times* was famous for its focus on facts and accuracy. It was founded in 1851 as the *New-York Daily Times* by Henry Jarvis Raymond and George Jones, and was renamed *New York Times* in 1869. It soon became the most important newspaper in the USA and took on an agenda-setting function for newspapers across the country.[60] The increasing number of newspapers in the nineteenth century allowed for more diversity in style and content. Thus, the *Chicago Daily Tribune* had businessmen as its target readership and championed free trade and private property. It was also deeply committed to Republican values and policies, and became one of the most influential papers in the Mid-West. During the interwar years its circulation was one of the highest in the country.[61] In the South, meanwhile, the *Atlanta Constitution* had become one of the most read dailies.[62] The West Coast was not yet as densely populated as it would become in the twentieth century, and so there were fewer newspapers than on the East Coast, and papers like the *Los Angeles Times* dominated the media landscape in their cities. Even San Francisco, which in the late nineteenth century was more important than Los Angeles, had only seven English language dailies in 1880, among them the *San Francisco Chronicle*. West Coast newspapers often dealt with different topics to East Coast papers because they were not always affected by the same issues.[63] The *Washington Post* began publication in 1877, and by the turn of the century had the largest edition of Washington newspapers. The fact that it was published in Washington DC also meant that it was read by members of Congress, presidents and employees in the administration.[64] Towards the end of the nineteenth century, tabloids like the *New York World* emerged. *The World* was owned by the newspaper baron Joseph Pulitzer and published its first issue in 1882. By 1886 its

---

[59]   Michael Emery, Edwin Emery and Nancy L. Roberts, *The Press and America: An Interpretive History of the Mass Media*, 9th ed. (Boston, 2000), pp. 97–9 and 109–18; Lindley, *20th Century American Newspapers*, pp. 9–20; Bollinger, *Pressegeschichte*, pp. 47–51 and 65–71.

[60]   Walker, *Powers*, pp. 212–23; Emery, Emery and Roberts, *The Press*, p. 108; Aurora Wallace, *Newspapers and the Making of Modern America: A History* (Westport and London), 2005, pp. 156–7 and 160.

[61]   David Paul Nord, *Communities of Journalism: A History of American Newspapers and Their Readers* (Urbana and Chicago, 2001), pp. 116–19, 137 and 249; Frank Luther Mott, *American Journalism: A History of Newspapers in the United States through 260 Years: 1690 to 1950* (New York, 1950), p. 715.

[62]   Mott, *American Journalism*, p. 456; Emery, Emery and Roberts, *The Press*, p. 164.

[63]   Ted Curtis Smythe, *The Gilded Age Press, 1865–1900* (Westport and London, 2003), pp. 91–7; Emery, Emery and Roberts, *The Press*, pp. 194 and 242.

[64]   Chalmers M. Roberts, *In the Shadow of Power: The Story of the Washington Post* (Cabin John, 1989), pp. 4 and 77.

circulation already exceeded 250,000. It changed to tabloid format (i.e. smaller size, larger headlines and more illustrations) in 1901 and continued to increase its circulation with a mix of exposés on fraud and corruption, gossip, scandals, sport, illustrations and cartoons.[65] The craze for sensations led in 1908 to the founding of the *Christian Science Monitor* which tried to counter yellow journalism by banning sensational crime and disaster news from its pages. It was popular across the USA and continued to be a prestigious paper.[66]

Table I.3   American Newspapers[67]

Newspaper	Founded in	Political Orientation	Circulation in 1910	Circulation in 1931	Circulation in 1949
Atlanta Constitution	1868	Democratic	35,454	97,848	184,782
Boston Globe	1872	Independent	178,334	142,234	116,020
Chicago Daily Tribune	1847	Independent/ Republican	150,000	838,422	985,523
Christian Science Monitor	1908	non-partisan	185,000	128,723	165,021
Los Angeles Times	1881	Independent/ Republican	53,979	171,066	404,513
New York Times	1851	Independent/ Democratic	175,000	416,995	541,269
San Francisco Chronicle	1865	Independent/ Republican	50,000	98,528	180,019
The World	1860	Independent/ Democratic	175,000	313,911	n/a
Wall Street Journal	1882	financial	12,000	51,502	99,848
Washington Post	1877	Independent	20,000	76,000	173,813

In 1815, the *North American Review and Miscellaneous Journal* was founded with the purpose of promoting American culture. It dealt with various aspects

---

[65]   Wallace, *Newspapers*, p. 12; Bollinger, *Pressegeschichte*, pp. 71–6; Mott, *American Journalism*, p. 715; David Copeland, *The Media's Role in Defining the Nation* (New York, 2010), pp. 108–9.

[66]   Leonard Ray Teel, *The Public Press, 1900–1945: History of American Journalism* (Westport and London, 2006), pp. 26–7; Mott, *American Journalism*, pp. 559–60.

[67]   N.W. Ayer & Son, *American Newspaper Annual and Directory* (Philadelphia, 1910); N.W. Ayer & Son, *Directory of Newspapers and Periodicals 1931* (Philadelphia, 1931); J. Percy H. Johnson (ed.), *N.W. Ayer & Son's Directory: Newspapers and Periodicals 1949* (Philadelphia, 1949).

of American history, politics, literature, art etc. Several of its editors had been politicians or later became politicians, and the journal had a strong impact on politics.[68] Another magazine in which politics was discussed was the *Annals of the American Academy of Political and Social Science*, which began publication in 1890.[69] *Harper's Magazine* provided its readers with a mix of articles on literature, history, science and news. By the end of the nineteenth century, it was among the most popular general periodicals in the USA, but in the following decades other magazines became more successful.[70] During the interwar years, magazines by Henry Luce were among the most widely read in the USA. Born in China to Presbyterian missionaries, Luce continued to have strong ties to China and his magazines *Time* and *Life* had a strong pro-Chinese bias. While *Time* sought to provide people with a general overview of news, *Life* was an illustrated magazine whose major focus was on photographs.[71]

Table 1.4   American Magazines[72]

Magazine	Founded in	Type	Issued
Annals of the American Academy of Political and Social Science	1889	political and social science	bi-monthly
Christian Century	1884	religion	weekly
Foreign Affairs	1922	international relations	quarterly
Harper's Magazine	1850	public affairs, literature	monthly
Life	1936	illustrated news	weekly
Nation	1865	news (left wing)	weekly
North American Review	1815	literary	quarterly
Time	1923	news	weekly

68   Daniel Straubel, 'North American Review', in Alan Nourie and Barbara Nourie (eds), *American Mass-Market Magazines* (New York, Westport and London, 1990), pp. 333–9.

69   Frank Luther Mott, *A History of American Magazines, volume 4: 1885–1905* (Cambridge, 1957), pp. 190–93.

70   James Hart, 'Harper's Magazine', in Alan Nourie and Barbara Nourie (eds), *American Mass-Market Magazines* (New York, Westport and London, 1990), pp. 149–52.

71   Jean M. Parker, 'Time', in Alan Nourie and Barbara Nourie (eds), *American Mass-Market Magazines* (New York, Westport and London, 1990), pp. 495–501; Diana A. Chlebek, 'Life', in Alan Nourie and Barbara Nourie (eds), *American Mass-Market Magazines* (New York, Westport and London, 1990), pp. 207–13; Patricia Neils, *China Images in the Life and Times of Henry Luce* (Savage, 1990).

72   Ayer, *Directory, 1910*; N.W. Ayer & Son, *Directory of Newspapers and Periodicals 1930* (Philadelphia, 1930); N.W. Ayer & Son, *Directory of Newspapers and Periodicals 1940* (Philadelphia, 1940); J. Percy H. Johnson (ed.), *N.W. Ayer & Son's Directory: Newspapers and Periodicals 1952* (Philadelphia, 1952).

Among the oldest political newspapers in Switzerland was the *Neue Zürcher Zeitung (NZZ)* which was founded in 1780. It soon became one of the most important liberal papers in the country and also the leading quality paper. The *NZZ* remained very closely connected to the *Freisinnig-Demokratische Partei der Schweiz* (Liberal-Democratic Party of Switzerland). Many editors were members of the party, one of them was even an MP and later Federal Councillor.[73] Although the number of newspapers and their circulation increased in the second half of the nineteenth century, Switzerland did not have a tabloid until 1959. Instead it had the so-called *Generalanzeiger*, which combined news, advertisements and entertainment. One of these newspapers was the *Tages-Anzeiger für Stadt und Kanton Zürich*, which was founded in 1893 by the German Wilhelm Girardet. The *Tages-Anzeiger*, as it was later called, was the first Swiss newspaper that did not support a political party, and it quickly became the newspaper with the highest circulation in Switzerland.[74]

Although Switzerland has several national languages, the majority of newspapers were printed in German. In 1930, for example, about 69 per cent of the Swiss newspapers were in German, 26 per cent in French, 4 per cent in Italian and 1 per cent in Romansch. This was fairly proportional to the distribution of native speakers in Switzerland.[75] In this study, the *Journal de Genève* was selected to represent the French-speaking Swiss press. It was first published in 1828 as an anti-reactionary bi-weekly paper and in 1850 became a daily newspaper. In the twentieth century, the *Journal de Genève* grew to be one of the leading newspapers in the French-speaking part of Switzerland.[76]

---

[73] Erich Wigger, 'Geschichtsbilder und Zukunftserwartungen: Zur Konstruktion von freisinniger Orientierung im Krisenkontext nach dem Ersten Weltkrieg in der Schweiz', in Andreas Ernst and Erich Wigger (eds), *Die neue Schweiz? Eine Gesellschaft zwischen Integration und Polarisierung (1910–1930)* (Zürich, 1996), p. 171; Thomas Maissen, 'Neue Zürcher Zeitung (NZZ)', in Stiftung Historisches Lexikon der Schweiz (ed.), *Historisches Lexikon der Schweiz*, Band 9 (Basel, 2010), p. 199.

[74] Hans Heinrich Coninx, 'Unabhängig und ein Familienunternehmen', in Werner Catrina, Roger Blum and Toni Lienhard (eds), *Medien zwischen Geld und Geist: 100 Jahre Tages-Anzeiger* (Zürich, 1993), pp. 9–11; Michael Schanne, 'Einführung in die Mediengeschichte der Schweiz', in Michael Schanne and Peter Schulz (eds), *Journalismus in der Schweiz: Fakten, Überlegungen, Möglichkeiten* (Aarau, 1993), pp. 19–28; Karl J. Lüthi, *Die Schweizer Press einst und jetzt* (Bern, 1933), pp. 12–14; Kurt Imhof, 'Vermessene Öffentlichkeit – vermessene Forschung? Vorstellung eines Projektes', in Kurt Imhof, Heinz Kleger and Gaetano Romano (eds), *Zwischen Konflikt und Konkordanz: Analyse von Medienereignissen in der Schweiz der Vor- und Zwischenkriegszeit* (Zürich, 1993), p. 44; Fritz Blaser, *Bibliographie der Schweizer Presse*, 2. Halbband (Basel, 1958), p. 1000.

[75] Karl Weber, *The Swiss Press: An Outline* (Bern, 1948), p. 20; Heiner Ritzmann-Blickenstorfer (ed.), *Historische Statistik der Schweiz* (Zürich, 1996), p. 157.

[76] Ernst Bollinger, 'Journal de Genève', in Stiftung Historisches Lexikon der Schweiz (ed.), *Historisches Lexikon der Schweiz*, Band 6 (Basel, 2007), p. 822; Fritz Blaser,

Table I.5   Swiss Newspapers[77]

Newspaper	Founded in	Political Orientation	Circulation in 1910	Circulation in 1930	Circulation in 1950
Berner Intelligenzblatt	1834	liberal	n/a	n/a	n/a
Journal de Genève	1826	liberal/ radical	n/a*	n/a	n/a
NZZ	1780	Liberal	18,100	47,500	66,600
Tages-Anzeiger	1893	independent	70,000	83,000	116,000

Note: * No newspaper directories listed the circulation of the Journal de Genève, and no official circulation numbers could be obtained from the newspaper's successor.

Several Swiss magazines are also included in the analysis. Most of them were only published for a short time and could, therefore, only be used for single chapters in this study. As a result, they do not figure on Table I.6. The three magazines that are included in the table, however, were among the most important periodicals of the time. The *Nebelspalter* was a humorous weekly magazine that presented news in a satirical manner and included many cartoons. The *Schweizer Illustrierte* and the *Weltwoche* were both illustrated newspapers written for a general audience. While the focus of the *Schweizer Illustrierte* was more on human interest, the *Weltwoche* featured more articles on politics.

Table I.6   Swiss Magazines

Name	Founded in	Type	Issued
Nebelspalter	1875	humorous/illustrated	weekly
Schweizer Illustrierte	1911	general/illustrated	weekly
Die Weltwoche	1933	news/general	weekly

The chapters are structured chronologically so that each chapter deals with political debates on and media coverage of one event or period: Chapter 1 analyses

Bibliographie der Schweizer Presse, 1. Halbband (Basel, 1956), pp. 535–6. According to Fritz Blaser, the *Journal de Genève* began publication in 1826.

77   Verband schweizerischer Annoncen-Expeditionen VSA (ed.), *Zeitungskatalog der Schweiz* (Zürich, 1950); Rudolf Mosse, *Zeitungs-Katalog Schweiz* (Basel, Zürich and Bern, 1930); Verein der Schweizerischen Presse etc. (ed.), *Jahrbuch der Schweizer Presse u. Politik 1911* (Genf, 1911); Blaser, *Bibliographie*, 1. Halbband, pp. 535–6. Numbers for the *NZZ* were provided by the *NZZ* archive (personal communication).

reactions to the Xinhai Revolution and the founding of the Chinese Republic in 1912, Chapter 2 examines perceptions of the anti-foreign agitation from the May Thirtieth Movement in 1925 to the Nanjing Incident in 1927, Chapter 3 looks at portrayals of Japanese expansion in China from the Manchurian Incident in 1931 to the Sino-Japanese War (1937–45) and Chapter 4 deals with reactions to the Communist victory in the Chinese Civil War in 1949. These events cannot be analysed in complete isolation because the frames used in press reports and cartoons reflected and affected already existing discourses on China. The chapters, therefore, not only examine a particular event but also the wider historical context in so far as it is necessary for the understanding of the frames selected by the media. Thus, the chapters include media coverage of and political debates on China in the years leading up to the event if they contributed to the popularity of a specific frame or image. For example, the way China policies had been legitimized and interests in China had been defined prior to the Xinhai Revolution formed part of a discourse on China that the press both referred to and contributed to in its coverage of the Xinhai Revolution. Their inclusion in the analysis gives us a new way of looking at the Xinhai Revolution which affects the traditional understanding of the relationship between China and the West as a single entity in the early twentieth century. Similarly, while Chapter 3 deals with Japanese expansion in China after 1931, the enemy image of the Yellow Peril can only be understood if its development is traced from its inception in each country because this affected perceptions and led to different conceptualizations of it.

A note on translation and spelling: all Swiss press articles and official documents have been translated by me. Chinese names are given with the surname first and personal name second. I used the Pinyin system of romanization with the exception of names for people and cities that are better known under their non-Mandarin names (e.g. Chiang Kai-shek, Sun Yat-sen, Hong Kong).

Chapter 1
The Dragon Throne in the Dustbin:
Press Reactions to the Xinhai Revolution

On 3 November 1911, the Qing court announced that China would, henceforth, be ruled as a constitutional monarchy. It was one of the last attempts to ensure the survival of the Qing Dynasty in the face of a rebellion which was quickly spreading across the southern provinces of China. For the British newspaper *The Times*, it was clear which country should get the laurels for this move towards democracy: Britain. The newspaper declared jubilantly: 'The [Qing] memorial states that all nations agree that the British Constitution is the mother of Constitutions. The British Constitutional monarchy has therefore been selected for adoption in China.'[1] American newspapers, however, interpreted events in China differently, announcing that the Chinese revolution should be supported because it had been caused by American thought and teaching. The *Chicago Tribune* noted: 'Americans have a special interest in the Chinese revolt because America, American ideas and institution, and American schools have played so direct though innocent a part in arousing and formulating the revolution.'[2] These two reactions demonstrate that portrayals of the Xinhai Revolution varied from nation to nation because the events in China were framed according to national interests, cultural perceptions and domestic issues. Moreover, they show that the media perceptions of China both reflected and contributed to the discursive construction of nationhood in each country: While British publications used the Qing government's reaction to portray the British constitution as the 'mother of Constitutions', American publications focused on the Xinhai Revolution to portray the USA as the mother of revolutions.

The Xinhai Revolution has surprisingly been rather neglected by Western scholars, partly because it occurred roughly a decade after the Boxer Uprising, which continues to attract a great deal of academic attention, not least because so many foreign countries were directly involved in it.[3] The Xinhai Revolution has

---

[1]   *The Times* 4.11.1911.

[2]   *Chicago Tribune* 19.11.1911.

[3]   Robert Bickers and R.G. Tiedemann (eds), *The Boxers, China, and the World* (Plymouth and Lanham, 2007); Lanxin Xiang, *The Origins of the Boxer War: A Multinational Study* (London, 2003); Ariane Knüsel, '"Western Civilization" against "Hordes of Yellow Savages": British Perceptions of the Boxer Rebellion', *Asiatische Studien*, 62/1 (2008): pp. 43–83; Hans Van de Ven, 'Robert Hart and Gustav Detring during the Boxer Rebellion', *Modern Asian Studies*, 40/3 (2006): pp. 631–62; Jane E. Elliott, *Some Did It for Civilisation – Some Did It for Their Country: A Revised View of the Boxer War* (Hong Kong, 2002);

not yet been covered to such an extent. Much of the scholarship dates back a few decades, while foreign reactions to the Revolution have hardly been analysed at all.[4] As this chapter seeks to demonstrate, however, the Xinhai Revolution and its perceptions in Western countries deserve much more scholarly attention because the Revolution occurred during a time when a great number of cultural, political and social changes occurred in many Western countries, affecting both media images and political debates about China.

Britain

Opium, Missionaries and the Boxer Uprising

In the early nineteenth century, Britain enjoyed naval supremacy. It was the first country to undergo industrial revolution, and not only became the world leader in trade with its machine-made goods but also controlled capital. As a result, Britain dominated the relations and trade between China and other nations. It was also one of the leading powers in the (illegal) opium trade, which was so lucrative that the balance of payments in British India depended upon it, accounting for up to one sixth of its total revenue.[5] Although opium was widely used in Britain in the early

---

Diana Preston, *A Brief History of the Boxer Rebellion: China's War on Foreigners, 1900* (London, 2002); Hubert Mainer and Herward Sieberg, *Der Boxerkrieg in China 1900–1901* (Hildesheim, 2001); Paul A. Cohen, *History in Three Keys: The Boxers as Event, Experience, and Myth* (New York, 1997).

[4]   For historiographical overviews see: Chün-tu Hsüeh, 'New Aspects of the 1911 Revolution', in Chün-tu Hsüeh (ed.), *The Chinese Revolution of 1911: New Perspectives* (Hong Kong, 1986), pp. 1–25; Edmund S.K. Fung, 'Post-1949 Chinese Historiography on the 1911 Revolution', *Modern China*, 4/2 (1978): pp. 181–214; Zhang Kaiyuan, 'A General Review of the Study of the Revolution of 1911 in the People's Republic of China', *The Journal of Asian Studies*, 39/3 (1980): pp. 525–31. Studies of the Xinhai Revolution include: Marius B. Jansen, 'The 1911 Revolution and United States East Asian Policy', in Etō Shinkichi and Harold Z. Schiffrin (eds), *The 1911 Revolution in China: Interpretive Essays* (Tokyo, 1984), pp. 257–65; James Reed, *The Missionary Mind and American East Asia Policy, 1911–1915* (Cambridge and London, 1983); Michael V. Metallo, 'American Missionaries, Sun Yat-sen, and the Chinese Revolution', *The Pacific Historical Review*, 47/2 (1978): pp. 261–82; Nemai Sadhan Bose, *American Attitude and Policy to the Nationalist Movement in China (1911–1921)* (Bombay and Calcutta, 1970); Eiko Woodhouse, *The Chinese Hsinhai Revolution: G.E. Morrison and Anglo-Japanese Relations, 1897–1920* (London and New York, 2004).

[5]   Simon C. Smith, *British Imperialism, 1750–1970* (Cambridge, 1989), pp. 20–21; Paul A. Van Dyke, *The Canton Trade: Life and Enterprise on the China Coast, 1700–1845* (Hong Kong, 2005), pp. 120–41 and 161–2; Ronald Findlay and Kevin O'Rourke, *Power and Plenty: Trade, War, and the World Economy in the Second Millenium* (Princeton and Oxford, 2007), pp. 346–52; Glenn Melancon, *Britain's China Policy and the Opium Crisis:*

nineteenth century, by the mid-nineteenth century it was regarded as unsuitable for Victorian citizens, and vices associated with opium smoking (e.g. immorality and indecency) were transferred onto the Chinese. The Opium Wars (1839–42 and 1856–60) were part of Britain's strategy to protect and promote the opium trade but they were disguised as forced liberation of China and Chinese society; thus, it was claimed that the Qing government was degenerate, corrupt and unable to implement reforms, and that China had to be forced to open up to free trade.[6]

In the late nineteenth century, new modes of military technology, transportation and communication were used to colonize new territories and access new markets. China was affected by this new imperialism, as France, Russia, Japan and Germany established spheres of influence, causing the British government eventually to participate in the scramble for territorial influence.[7] Following John Gallagher and Ronald Robinson, the foreign presence in China is usually described as informal imperialism in Western historiography. Accordingly, formal imperialism entailed a transfer of sovereignty and the direct administrative control of the colonized territories, while informal imperialism relied on trade, diplomacy and investment to (indirectly) control territories. Yet, one has to remember that although imperialism in China was of a co-operative nature, the actual imperial presence of the powers took on a variety of sectoral, institutional, spatial and diachronic dimensions.[8]

Balancing Drugs, Violence and National Honour, 1833–1840 (Aldershot and Burlington, 2003), pp. 17–19; Harry G. Gelber, *Opium, Soldiers and Evangelicals: England's 1840–42 War with China and Its Aftermath* (Basingstoke and New York, 2004), pp. 33–7; Hevia, *English Lessons*, pp. 50–53; Michael Greenberg, *British Trade and the Opening of China, 1800–1842* (New York and London, 1951), pp. 175–85; Jerry L. Wang, 'The Profitability of Anglo-Chinese Trade, 1861–1913', *Business History*, 35/3 (1993): p. 39.

[6]   TNA FO 17/251; FO 17/260M; FO 1080/342. See also: J.E. Hoare, *Embassies in the East: The Story of the British Embassies in Japan, China and Korea from 1850 to the Present* (Richmond, 1999), pp. 5–6 and 17–18; Hevia, *English Lessons*, pp. 4–6; Lee, *Chinas Unlimited*, pp. 25–8 and 32–8; Victor Kiernan, *The Lords of Human Kind: European Attitudes to Other Cultures in the Imperial Age* (London, 1995), p. 158.

[7]   Jürgen Osterhammel, *China und die Weltgesellschaft: Vom 18. Jahrhundert bis in unsere Zeit* (München, 1989), pp. 152–5 and 202–9; Mary H. Wilgus, *Sir Claude MacDonald, the Open Door, and British Informal Empire in China, 1895–1900* (New York and London, 1987), pp. 1–7, 20–33 and 258; Leonard K. Young, *British Policy in China: 1895–1902* (Oxford, 1970), pp. 5–6; Hevia, *English Lessons*, pp. 12–13.

[8]   John Gallagher and Ronald Robinson, 'The Imperialism of Free Trade', *The Economic History Review*, 6/1 (1953): pp. 1–15; Jürgen Osterhammel, 'Semi-Colonialism and Informal Empire in Twentieth Century China: Towards a Framework of Analysis', in Wolfgang Mommsen and Jürgen Osterhammel (eds), *Imperialism and After: Continuities and Discontinuities* (London, 1986), pp. 290–314; John Darwin, 'Britain's Empires', in Sarah Stockwell (ed.), *The British Empire: Themes and Perspectives* (Malden, Oxford and Carlton, 2008), pp. 2–3 and 14–15; David Mclean, 'Finance and "Informal Empire" before the First World War', *The Economic History Review*, new series, 29/2 (1976): pp. 291–305; Osterhammel, *China und die Weltgesellschaft*, pp. 152–71. For critics of Robinson and

Until the fall of the Qing Dynasty in 1912 Britain not only dominated foreign commercial and diplomatic relations with China but also the administration and social life in the treaty ports. British newspapers also dominated the foreign-language press in China. Britain's position in China was further strengthened by the Chinese Maritime Customs Service, which was headed by a Briton. By 1900 most of its 700 employees were also British. Founded in 1854, the Chinese Maritime Customs Service oversaw trade in the treaty ports by enforcing tariffs and collecting revenues for the Chinese government. It also charted the coast of China, established a postal system, and opened schools and colleges.[9] British commercial and geopolitical interests in China were best served by political stability, and so Britain wanted to prevent the partition of China in order to ensure that the Manchu Dynasty remained in power.[10]

Missionary societies contributed to British interests in China. After the evangelical revival in the eighteenth century, missionary philanthropy became part of the formation of a collective identity for the British middle classes, who viewed themselves as agents of civilization and reform. The relationship between British imperialism and religion was quite complex because imperialism did not always occur as a chronological process in which the arrival of missionaries was followed by merchants and then soldiers. Moreover, Britain did not consistently impose Protestantism upon all of its colonies and dependencies, and the missionaries' endeavour to expand the Empire of Christ was neither geographically nor temporally limited to the British Empire. Thus, in the early nineteenth century, British missions focused on India, Africa, the South Pacific and the West Indies, but later their main areas of activity would also include China and Islamic countries.[11]

Gallagher see: Wm. Roger Louis (ed.), *The Robinson and Gallagher Controversy* (New York and London, 1976).

[9]   Robert Bickers, 'Shanghailanders: The Formation and Identity of the British Settler Community in Shanghai, 1843–1937', *Past and Present*, 159 (1998): pp. 161–211; Jürgen Osterhammel, 'British Business in China, 1860s–1950s', in R.P.T. Davenport-Hines and Geoffrey Jones (eds), *British Business in Asia since 1860* (Cambridge and New York, 1989), pp. 191–2; Wilgus, *Sir Claude MacDonald*, pp. 18–23; Young, *British Policy*, pp. 5–7; Robert Bickers, 'Revisiting the Chinese Maritime Customs Service, 1854–1950', *The Journal of Imperial and Commonwealth History*, 36/2 (2008): pp. 221–2; Hevia, *English Lessons*, p. 72; Paul French, *Through the Looking Glass: China's Foreign Journalists from Opium Wars to Mao* (Hong Kong, 2009).

[10]   John Darwin, 'Imperialism and the Victorians: The Dynamics of Territorial Expansion', *The English Historical Review*, 112/447 (1997): pp. 619 and 631–2; Wilgus, *Sir Claude MacDonald*, pp. 24–5; Young, *British Policy*, pp. 4–5.

[11]   Alison Twells, *The Civilising Mission and the English Middle Class, 1792–1850* (Basingstoke and New York, 2009); Andrew Porter, 'An Overview, 1700–1914', in Norman Etherington (ed.), *Missions and Empire* (Oxford, 2005), pp. 40–61; Steven Maughan, '"Mighty England Do Good": The Major English Denominations and Organisation for the Support of Foreign Missions in the Nineteenth Century', in Robert A. Bickers and Rosemary Seton (eds), *Missionary Encounters: Sources and Issues* (Richmond, 1996),

Protestant missionary activity in China began with the arrival of Robert Morrison from the London Missionary Society in 1807. By 1840 more than 20 missionaries from six different missionary societies worked in China, and the number and variety of missionary societies in China increased further towards the end of the century. While their efforts to convert Chinese were not very successful, missionaries spent a great deal of time writing Christian literature in Chinese and composing writings about China and the Chinese for audiences in Britain.[12]

In the past few decades, historians have argued over Arthur Schlesinger's thesis that missionaries were agents of cultural imperialism. As Ryan Dunch and Andrew Porter point out, cultural imperialism is a problematic concept because it reduces complex interactions to a simple dichotomy, and thereby ignores indigenous choices and agency as well as the importance of how missionaries themselves were affected by their life in China and their role as inter-cultural communicators, translators and intermediaries.[13] British missionaries and churches relied upon

pp. 15–35; Jeffrey Cox, *The British Missionary Enterprise since 1700* (London and New York), 2008, pp. 9–16 and 171–2; Andrew F. Walls, 'Carrying the White Man's Burden: Some British Views of National Vocation in the Imperial Era', in William R. Hutchison and Hartmut Lehmann (eds), *Many Are Chosen: Divine Election and Western Nationalism* (Minneapolis, 1994), pp. 37–40; Andrew F. Walls, 'British Missions', in Torben Christensen and William R. Hutchison (eds), *Missionary Ideologies in the Imperialist Era: 1880–1920* (Aarhus, 1982), pp. 159–60; Eric Reinders, *Borrowed Gods and Foreign Bodies: Christian Missionaries Imagine Chinese Religion* (Berkeley, Los Angeles and London, 2004), pp. xiv and 19; Paul A. Cohen, 'Christian Missions and Their Impact to 1900', in John K. Fairbank (ed.), *The Cambridge History of China, vol. 10: Late Ch'ing, 1800–1911*, part I (Cambridge, London, New York and Melbourne, 1978), p. 547; Norman Etherington, 'Introduction', in Norman Etherington (ed.), *Missions and Empire* (Oxford, 2005), pp. 1–3.

12   Paul A. Cohen, *China and Christianity: The Missionary Movement and the Growth of Chinese Antiforeignism 1860–1870* (Cambridge, 1963), pp. 34, 64 and 67–71; Cohen, 'Christian Missions', pp. 547–8 and 552–5; R.G. Tiedemann, 'Indigenous Agency, Religious Protectorates, and Chinese Interests: The Expansion of Christianity in Nineteenth-Century China', in Dana L. Robert (ed.), *Converting Colonialism: Visions and Realities in Mission History, 1706–1914* (Grand Rapids and Cambridge, 2008), pp. 206–41; Porter, 'Overview', pp. 40–63; Jessie G. Lutz, 'China and Protestantism, 1807–1949', in Stephen Uhalley, Jr. and Xiaoxin Wu (eds), *China and Christianity: Burdened Past, Hopeful Future* (Armonk and London, 2001), pp. 180–84; Daniel H. Bays, 'The Growth of Independent Christianity in China, 1900–1937', in Daniel H. Bays (ed.), *Christianity in China: From the Eighteenth Century to the Present* (Stanford, 1996), p. 307; Andrew Porter, *Religion versus Empire? British Protestant Missionaries and Overseas Expansion, 1700–1914* (Manchester and New York, 2004), p. 207.

13   Ryan Dunch, 'Beyond Cultural Imperialism: Cultural Theory, Christian Missions, and Global Modernity', *History and Theory*, 41/3 (2002): pp. 301–25; Andrew Porter, '"Cultural Imperialism" and Protestant Missionary Enterprise, 1780–1914', *Journal of Imperial and Commonwealth History*, 25/3 (1997): pp. 367–91; Arthur Schlesinger, Jr., 'The Missionary Enterprise and Theories of Imperialism', in John K. Fairbank (ed.), *The Missionary Enterprise in China and America* (Cambridge, 1974), pp. 336–73; Paul W. Harris, 'Cultural Imperialism

the co-operation and support of British imperial authorities, yet these authorities tended to be quite critical of the missionaries.[14] This was also the case in China, as Andrew F. Walls points out: 'British official opinion often thought of missionary activity in China as an unmitigated nuisance.'[15] Indeed, British officials in China often disliked having to defend missionary interests and security since this meant that they could spend less time on commercial issues.[16] As a result, British missionaries did not influence British China policy as much as the merchants, even though some missionaries worked for the British government as translators or even consuls. This also explains why during the Boxer Uprising the focus of the British press was on the British diplomats and correspondents, not on the British missionaries in China.

Foreign missionaries in China challenged several foundations of Chinese society. Often, they did not hesitate to get involved in conflicts to protect their converts, and exploited their privileged legal status to gain excessive indemnities from Chinese officials, which resulted in higher taxes for the Chinese population. Many Chinese converts also refused to participate in traditional Chinese rituals like ancestor ceremonies or village festivals. As a result, the number of attacks on missionaries and converts rose in the 1890s, and they were increasingly blamed for economic hardship. The anti-missionary sentiment culminated in the Boxer Uprising, during which more than 30,000 Chinese converts and almost 200 foreign missionaries were killed.[17]

The Boxer movement began in 1898 in Shandong province and by 1900 had spread to the provinces Zhili, Shanxi and Henan. It was originally anti-Christian but soon targeted foreigners in general. By May 1900 the Boxers had isolated the foreigners in Beijing by destroying railway tracks and stations. On 20 June, Chinese soldiers and Boxers began the siege of the Beijing Legation Quarter, which ended on 15 August 1900 when international troops from Tianjin reached Beijing and entered the foreign legations. During the siege of the foreign legations, 66 foreigners were killed and over 150 wounded. As a consequence, allied troops carried out punitive expeditions in September and October 1900. The terms of the Boxer Protocol, which was signed on 7 September 1901 by Britain, Germany, France, Belgium, Italy, Russia, Japan, Austria-Hungary, Spain, USA,

---

and American Protestant Missionaries: Collaboration and Dependency in Mid-Nineteenth-Century China', *The Pacific Historical Review*, 60/3 (1991): pp. 309–38.

[14] Porter, 'Overview', p. 40; Cox, *The British Missionary Enterprise*, pp. 11–14.

[15] Walls, 'British Missions', p. 162.

[16] Porter, *Religion*, pp. 209–11; Dunch, 'Cultural Imperialism', p. 308.

[17] Paul A. Varg, *Missionaries, Chinese, and Diplomats: The American Protestant Missionary Movement in China, 1890–1952* (Princeton, 1958), pp. 33–41; Tiedemann, 'Indigenous Agency', pp. 229 and 235–7; Gregory, *The West*, pp. 108–16; Cohen, 'Christian Missions', pp. 566–73 and 590.

Netherlands and China, were so harsh that the Qing Dynasty could not recover and was eventually overthrown in 1912.[18]

The Boxer Uprising resulted in a great deal of negative press coverage of China in Britain because the Boxers' actions affected British citizens. What was special about the coverage of the Boxer Uprising was that neither the Foreign Office nor British newspaper editors could communicate directly with their representatives in Beijing during the siege of the foreign legations because the Boxers had cut or destroyed the telegraph cables. Among the foreigners in Beijing was *The Times*'s correspondent George Morrison. *The Times* assumed that he and the other foreigners in the capital had been killed and printed their obituaries. Worried and frustrated editors in London also increasingly relied on stereotypes associated with the Yellow Peril (covered in more detail in Chapter 3) and printed rumours about alleged Chinese atrocities.[19] Thus, the *Daily Mail* described the Chinese as the 'most diabolically cruel mob in the world',[20] and imagined how the 'four hundred millions of yellow savages [are] about to fall in some demoniac outburst of fury upon the foreigners'.[21] It eventually announced: 'white men and women are being done to death with every hideous circumstance by hordes of yellow savages.'[22] Such portrayals not only served to denigrate the Chinese but also legitimized British presence in China and the use of force against the Chinese. Various illustrations printed during the Boxer Uprising also portrayed the Boxers

---

[18]   TNA FO 405/92; 'Rear-Admiral Bruce to Admiralty', 18.8.1900, TNA FO 405/94, no. 239; 'Consul Carles to the Marquess of Salisbury', 16.8.1900, TNA FO 405/94; Claude MacDonald, 'Sir Claude MacDonald's Report on the Boxer Rebellion', in Tim Coates (ed.), *The Siege of the Peking Embassy, 1900* (London, 2000), pp. 139–283. See also: Cohen, *History*; Xiang, *Origins*; Preston, *History*, pp. 41–4.

[19]   'Acting Consul-General Warren to the Marquess of Salisbury', 24.6.1900, TNA FO 405/92; 'Acting Consul-General Warren to the Marquess of Salisbury', 20.7.1900, TNA FO 405/94; 'Statement made in the House of Commons by Mr. Brodrick, June 18, 1900', 18.6.1900, TNA FO 405/92, no. 282; 'Consul Carles to the Marquess of Salisbury', TNA FO 405/92, no. 214; 'Questions asked in the House of Commons', 24.6.1900, TNA FO 405/92, no. 351; *Daily Mail* 15.6.1900, 23.6.1900, 25.6.1900, 4.7.1900, 5.7.1900, 6.7.1900, 7.7.1900, 13.7.1900, 30.7.1900; *The Times* 15.6.1900, 18.6.1900, 25.6.1900, 27.6.1900, 17.6.1900, 17.7.1900, 31.7.1900; *Manchester Guardian* 26.6.1900. See also: Knüsel, 'Western Civilization', pp. 52–62; Xiang, *Origins*, pp. 256–65; Cohen, *History*, pp. 48–51 and 310; Hoare, *Embassies*, pp. 41–5 and 54; Jorma Ahvenainen, *The Far Eastern Telegraphs: The History of Telegraphic Communications between the Far East, Europe and America before the First World War* (Helsinki, 1981), pp. 139–44; Ariane Knuesel, 'British Diplomacy and the Telegraph in Nineteenth-Century China', *Diplomacy and Statecraft*, 18/3 (2007): pp. 528–9; T.G. Otte, 'The Boxer Uprising and British Foreign Policy: The End of Isolation', in Robert Bickers and R.G. Tiedemann (eds), *The Boxers, China, and the World* (Plymouth and Lanham, 2007), p. 161.

[20]   *Daily Mail* 23.6.1900.

[21]   *Daily Mail* 13.7.1900.

[22]   *Daily Mail* 4.7.1900.

Illustration 1.1   Paul Frenzeny, 'The Crisis in China', *Illustrated London News* (21.7.1900)

as brutal, aggressive hordes. The *Illustrated London News*, which had begun publication as the first weekly picture paper in 1842,[23] printed an illustration in which various ships were literally spilling over with Boxers, all equipped with spears and other weapons to kill foreigners (Illustration 1.1). The caption below the illustration stated: 'the hordes of "Boxers" from the inland provinces are now flocking to the coast towns and foreign settlements.'

Only a few British newspapers questioned British imperialism in China during the Boxer Uprising. The *Manchester Guardian* had been criticizing Western imperialism since the outbreak of the Boer War (1899–1902), when most British foreign correspondents wrote reports that contributed to the spread of jingoism and enthusiasm for the war in Britain. In 1900, British publications were still very much occupied with the Boer War. China did not receive the unequivocal attention of the British press and jingoism ran high in various editorial offices, affecting portrayals of the Boxer Uprising. The wave of jingoism also explains why during the Boxer Uprising the focus of the British press was not on British missionaries but on the effects of the Uprising on the British Empire, and on the Empire's contribution to the allied troops in China.[24] Sikh soldiers, for example, figured prominently in depictions of the international forces in China in the *Illustrated London News*.[25]

The Xinhai Revolution and Imperial Rivalries

After 1900, a revolutionary movement developed in China. In the 1890s, another revolutionary movement had failed to bring about substantial changes. This one, however, sought to abolish the Qing Dynasty and would turn out to be more successful.[26] In 1905, Chinese students in Japan founded the *Tongmenghui* (Alliance Society). Its leader was Sun Yat-sen (Sun Zhongshan), who had been

---

[23]   Colin Osman and Sandra S. Phillips, 'European Visions: Magazine Photography in Europe between the Wars', in Marianne Fulton (ed.), *Eyes of Time: Photojournalism in America* (Boston, Toronto and London, 1988), p. 76.

[24]   *Manchester Guardian* 19.6.1900. See also: Knüsel, 'Western Civilization'; Denis Judd and Keith Surridge, *The Boer War* (London, 2002), pp. 251–6; Stephen Badsey, 'War Correspondent in the Boer War', in John Gooch (ed.), *The Boer War: Direction, Experience and Image* (London and Portland, 2000), pp. 189–91 and 202; Stephen Badsey, 'A Print and Media War', in Craig Wilcox (ed.), *Recording the South African War: Journalism and Official History 1899–1914* (London, 1999), pp. 5–16; Andrew S. Thompson, 'The Language of Imperialism and the Meanings of Empire: Imperial Discourse in British Politics, 1895–1914', *Journal of British Studies*, 36/2 (1997): pp. 150–52 and 163; Hampton, *Visions*, pp. 57 and 136; Ayerst, *Guardian*, pp. 278–80; David Brooks, *The Age of Upheaval: Edwardian Politics, 1899–1914* (Manchester and New York, 1995), pp. 8–18; Koss, *The Rise*, vol. 1, pp. 391–400.

[25]   *Illustrated London News* 22.9.1900, 13.10.1900.

[26]   Jin Chongji, 'The 1911 Revolution and the Awakening of the Chinese Nation', in Etō Shinkichi and Harold Z. Schiffrin (eds), *The 1911 Revolution in China: Interpretive*

educated in missionary schools in Hawaii, Hong Kong and Guangzhou. Sun travelled around the globe to raise money for the revolutionary effort from overseas Chinese but also continued to organize revolutionary activities in China and Hong Kong. Anti-Manchu sentiment was widespread in 1911 when the Chinese government announced its plans for the nationalization of railway lines and the construction of another line with foreign capital (the Hukuang Loan). This caused public outrage and anti-government agitation in various provinces because railway lines interfered with *fengshui* and were associated with foreign imperialism.[27] On 9 October 1911, revolutionaries accidentally set a bomb off in Hankou. After police had found a membership list of revolutionary organizations, the revolutionaries decided to act at once and began the Xinhai Revolution on 10 October with the goal to overthrow the Qing Dynasty. The revolution spread quickly and by late November, 14 provinces had revolutionary governments. Sun Yat-sen was inaugurated as provisional President of the Republic of China on 1 January 1912 but he offered the presidency to Yuan Shikai, the commander of the imperial forces, in order to unify the country and guarantee the success of the Republic. Yuan arranged the Manchu abdication and was inaugurated as the provisional President of the Chinese Republic on 10 March 1912. More than two thousand years of imperial dynasties in China had come to an end.[28]

By 1911, the coverage of China in British publications had changed a great deal from the reports about the Boxer Uprising because journalists increasingly used the telegraph to communicate news back to the UK, and publications were able to print photographs in their reports. As a result, in 1911 British readers could not only follow the progress of the Xinhai Revolution on a daily basis, they could also see what these rebels and the cities they controlled looked like. The introduction of photographs in reports about China also marked a huge shift in British portrayals because it meant that there was less need for sketches or drawings, which were often made by artists in the UK who were without actual knowledge of China and were prone to present the Chinese in a stereotypical way, as was the case during the

---

Essays (Tokyo, 1984), pp. 3–17; Meredith Cameron, 'The Reform Movement in China 1898–1912', *History, Economics, and Political Science*, 3/1 (1931): pp. 23–87 and 100–126.

[27]   Harold Z. Schiffrin, *Sun Yat-sen and the Origins of the Chinese Revolution* (Berkeley and Los Angeles, 1968); Jin Chongji, '1911 Revolution', pp. 3–17; Clarence B. Davis, 'Railway Imperialism in China, 1895–1939', in Clarence B. Davis and Kenneth E. Wilburn, Jr. (eds), *Railway Imperialism* (London, New York and Westport, 1991), pp. 155–63; Meredith Cameron, 'Reform Movement', pp. 11–14, 23–87, 100–126 and 186–95; Danke Li, 'Popular Culture in the Making of Anti-Imperialist and Nationalist Sentiments in Sichuan', *Modern China*, 30/4 (2004): pp. 470–505.

[28]   Joseph W. Esherick, 'Founding a Republic, Electing a President: How Sun Yat-sen Became Guofu', in Etō Shinkichi and Harold Z. Schiffrin (eds), *China's Republican Revolution* (Tokyo, 1994), pp. 129–52; Marie-Claire Bergère, 'The Issue of Imperialism and the 1911 Revolution', in Etō Shinkichi and Harold Z. Schiffrin (eds), *The 1911 Revolution in China: Interpretive Essays* (Tokyo, 1984), pp. 268–71; Cameron, 'Reform Movement', pp. 195–8; Woodhouse, *Hsinhai Revolution*, pp. 48, 69–79 and 143–55.

Boxer Uprising, when the Chinese were usually depicted as the embodiment of the Yellow Peril with grotesque facial features. Nevertheless, newspapers continued to use certain frames to portray the events in China. Thus, while most agreed that the Manchu Dynasty had been corrupt, their coverage of the Xinhai Revolution did not focus so much on the revolution itself as on its effects upon the British Empire and British interests in China. With memory of the anti-foreign agitation of the Boxer Uprising still fresh, British newspapers were quick to note that the Revolution was directed against the Qing Dynasty, that foreigners were generally safe, and that foreign settlements were left alone. Some newspapers like the *Daily Mail* and the *Daily Mirror* even stressed the good behaviour of the revolutionaries towards foreigners.[29]

As the British government continued to believe that British interests were best served by a strong Chinese government, it opposed the partition of China among imperial powers and tried to prevent internal division. The Xinhai Revolution, therefore, increased worries about the future of British interests in China, particularly since Britain's share in China's external trade had been decreasing since the late nineteenth century, as shown in Table 1.1. A partition of China would have threatened to further diminish British trade with China, thereby also affecting Britain's position in China among the foreign powers and the prestige of the British Empire.

Table 1.1 Share of the British Empire in China's External Trade[30]

	Britain	Hong Kong	Dominions/Colonies	Total British Empire
1882	27.97%	31.02%	16.66%	75.65%
1892	16.39%	46.05%	9.00%	71.44%
1902	12.59%	40.95%	8.66%	61.30%
1912	10.60%	29.34%	8.49%	48.43%

It should, therefore, come as no surprise that almost all major British newspapers expressed concern about the possible partitioning of China, with the main threats to Chinese sovereignty usually defined as Russia, Germany and Japan. Various newspapers were particularly suspicious of Russian territorial interests in China. Anglo-Russian rivalry had a long tradition, resulting after 1848 in the 'Great Game'. In 1911, the British press and government feared that if the Qing Dynasty collapsed, Russia would take control of China, threatening

---

[29] *Daily Mail* 12.10.1911, 27.10.1911, 28.10.1911; *The Times* 12.10.1911; *The Scotsman* 13.10.1911; *Irish Times* 18.10.1911; *Daily Mirror* 12.10.1911; TNA FO 405/205. See also: Woodhouse, *Hsinhai Revolution*, p. 53.

[30] Data taken from TNA FO 371/18052.

British interests there. This would seriously damage British prestige in Asia, thus affecting British control over India.[31]

The fixation of British publications with imperial rivalries is also nicely shown in Illustration 1.2, a map of China by G.F. Morrell which was printed during the Xinhai Revolution in the illustrated newspaper *The Graphic*. Despite its title, 'The Great Rebellion: A Birds-Eye View on China Showing the Disaffected Regions', the map focuses not so much on the 'disaffected regions' but on the foreign gunboats which are drawn disproportionately large in the lower half of the map along with detailed lists of the French, British, German and American naval presence in the Far East that include images of the different types of gunboats. Due to Britain's naval race with Germany, the British media was obsessed with British (and German) naval strength in 1911. As Jan Rüger points out, the naval theatre was also used to celebrate imperial greatness and unity in Britain.[32] Indeed, between 1909 and 1911, illustrated newspapers like the *Graphic* or the *Illustrated London News* almost constantly printed illustrations of British and German dreadnoughts and the British fleet, including huge foldout spreads as well as colour prints that focused either on the naval race with Germany or on Britain's naval supremacy.

The detailed description in Illustration 1.2 of each nation's naval presence in China was, therefore, part of the British media's obsession with naval strength and imperial rivalries. The disproportionate size of the gunboats, however, is also a clear reminder of Britain's gunboat diplomacy of the nineteenth century and presents China as an object of foreign imperial ambitions. Finally, the map's description of the British naval presence around the China coast as by far the largest of all foreign nations stresses Britain's naval superiority and its leading position among the Western powers, once again reinforcing the image of the British Empire and the British fleet as the most powerful on earth.

The potential threats to the position and the prestige of Britain in China caused several British publications to call on the foreign powers to stay out of the Revolution and let the Chinese solve it on their own. The *Daily Mail*, for example, noted:

> Nothing short of an attack on the European settlements could justify foreign interference ... The duty of the Powers is clear. They are not called upon to

---

[31] *Manchester Guardian* 20.11.1911, 4.1.1912; *Daily Mail* 18.10.1911; *Irish Times* 18.11.1911, 4.1.1912, 10.1.1912; *Spectator* 7.2.1912; *The Scotsman* 22.12.1911, 10.1.1912, 1.2.1912. See also: M.A. Yapp, 'British Perceptions of the Russian Threat to India', *Modern Asian Studies*, 21/4 (1987): pp. 647–65; Erik Goldstein, 'Britain and the Origins of the Cold War', in Michael F. Hopkins, Michael D. Kandiah and Gillian Staerck (eds), *Cold War Britain, 1945–1964: New Perspectives* (Basingstoke, 2003), pp. 7–14; Hevia, *English Lessons*, pp. 24, 170–73 and 179–83; Dominic Lieven, 'Dilemmas of Empire, 1850–1918: Power, Territory, Identity', *Journal of Contemporary History*, 34/2 (1999): pp. 175–6.

[32] Jan Rüger, *The Great Naval Game: Britain and Germany in the Age of Empire* (Cambridge, 2007).

THE GREAT REBELLION: A BIRD'S-EYE VIEW OF CHINA SHOWING THE DISAFFECTED REGIONS

Illustration 1.2   G.F. Morrell, 'The Great Rebellion', *The Graphic* (28.10.1911)

maintain the Manchu Dynasty or take any active part against the revolutionists. This is a Chinese quarrel, and any stranger who interposes must expect the promised reward.[33]

Such a view also reflected the British government's policy of neutrality in order to protect British lives and property in China. As the Foreign Secretary, Sir Edward Grey, reminded the British Minister in China, Sir John Jordan: 'We must do what is in our power to protect British life and property when in danger, but any action we take should be strictly limited to this purpose.'[34] Nevertheless, the British government was concerned about the security of Shanghai in view of the spreading revolution, and the War Office, Admiralty and Foreign Office decided in early November that troops from Hong Kong should be ready for immediate despatch to Shanghai if necessary.[35]

Monarchic Worries

Although Britain only formally colonized Hong Kong, the British media framed events in China primarily through the prism of the British Empire. David Cannadine argues in his book *Ornamentalism* that class dominated perceptions of the Empire in Britain.[36] Press reports about China, however, demonstrate that a wide variety of aspects influenced British perceptions of the Empire, and that the class factor was almost completely absent in these perceptions. Despite worries about the possible partition of China, British newspapers were not very sympathetic towards the Qing Dynasty. After the outbreak of the Xinhai Revolution, *The Scotsman* laconically observed:

> Hopes and expectations, political, economic, and social, have been awakened which the ruling authorities are slow to fulfil, and so the people, headed by the newly-created army, appear to be taking the ripening of events into their own hands. A Chinese Republic is said to be in the birth-throes: the Dragon Throne is to pass into the dust-bin of history.[37]

---

[33] *Daily Mail* 18.10.1911.

[34] 'Sir Edward Grey to Sir J. Jordan', 16.10.1911, TNA FO 405/205. See also: 'Short Memorandum on Wuchang Revolutionaries' claim to recognition as belligerents', 26.10.1911, TNA CO 873/329.

[35] TNA ADM 116/1151.

[36] David Cannadine, *Ornamentalism: How the British Saw Their Empire* (New York, 2001). See also: Geoff Eley, 'Beneath the Skin. Or: How to Forget about Empire without Really Trying', *Journal of Colonialism and Colonial History*, 3/1 (2002), http://muse.jhu.edu/journals/journal_of_colonialism_and_colonial_history/v003/3.1eley.html (last accessed on 9.12.2011).

[37] *The Scotsman* 13.10.1911.

The *Spectator*'s stance was equally unsympathetic: 'Whatever the upshot one thing seems clear – the old régime must go.'[38] Even *The Times* was scathing in its verdict on the Qing regime:

> [T]he old Monarchy has fallen never to rise again ... It has long outlived its day. Its servants, like the servants of Solomon in the Koran, have propped up a corpse and summoned kings and princes to do it homage. They bowed down before it, says the story, so long as it stood upright. But at last the worms gnawed away the staff on which it rested, it lay prone in the dust, and the world fell into confusion.[39]

The association of decay and backwardness with China had, of course, been used by the Western media for a long time, and served not only to denigrate Chinese society and culture, but also to exalt Western society and culture. This explains why publications in Britain were very similar in their open disdain for the Qing regime and did not sympathize with the Manchu ruling class as one might have expected. In fact, the widespread criticism of the corruption of the Manchu government in the British press served as a means not only to portray the British government favourably in comparison to the Manchu government but also to justify the necessity of British informal imperialism in China as well as the presence of a British police force and soldiers in British concessions in China.[40]

However, while American newspapers enthusiastically celebrated the Xinhai Revolution, responses in the British press and in British newspapers in China were at best lukewarm. Reasons for this included concern about British interests in China being affected by a potential partitioning of China. Another reason was that the Chinese revolutionaries demanded the abolition of the Qing Dynasty and wanted to replace it with a republic. This was problematic for Britain where the monarchy was seen as crucial for the cohesion of British society. As John K. Walton points out: 'In peace and war alike, indeed, the royal family probably constituted the strongest cement for a British identity that transcended divisions, pulling in Scots, Welsh and working-class allegiances and making them visible at points of carefully orchestrated commemoration and ceremonial such as weddings, coronations and Jubilees.'[41]

When the Xinhai Revolution took place, the political system in Britain had been undergoing significant changes. By the turn of the twentieth century, a gradual

---

38   *The Spectator* 21.10.1911.

39   *The Times* 2.11.1911.

40   *The Times* 13.10.1911, 14.10.1911; *Daily Mail* 13.10.1911; *Daily Mirror* 20.11.1911; *Manchester Guardian* 13.10.1911, 25.10.1911; *Irish Times* 18.10.1911, 30.10.1911; *The Scotsman* 31.10.1911.

41   John K. Walton, 'Britishness', in Chris Wrigley (ed.), *A Companion to Early Twentieth-Century Britain* (Malden and Oxford, 2003), pp. 520–21. See also French, *Looking Glass*, p. 108.

democratization of the political system had enabled the middle and working classes to participate in the political process. This affected party politics and resulted in more distinct party profiles of the two major parties, namely the Liberal Party and the Unionist alliance (an alliance of the Conservative Party and the Liberal Unionist Party). After the Liberals formed the new government in 1906, they introduced various social reforms. Proposed bills like Welsh Disestablishment and Irish Home Rule threatened the cohesion of the United Kingdom, and after the House of Lords rejected the People's Budget in 1909, a constitutional crisis ensued that resulted in the Parliament Bill of 1911, which reduced the power of the House of Lords by removing its right to veto legislation. The constitutional crisis was so serious that in the events leading up to the Parliament Bill even the power of the monarchy was called into question.[42] Anxieties about the spread of the republican system can also be detected in Illustration 1.3, from *The Graphic*, in which areas of Republican crises are highlighted under the title: 'Republics on the Rampage: Centres of the World's Unrest.' Although the message of the illustration is that republican systems will lead to political unrest, the illustration also hints at the underlying fear that political debates in Britain could result in the replacement of the monarchy with a republican system.[43]

The challenge to the monarchy and the unity of the United Kingdom had the effect that after the coronation of King George V in 1911 the royal family resorted to the invention of a tradition with the investiture of the Prince of Wales at Caernarfon Castle in Wales.[44] Both the coronation and the investiture – which included a visit to Ireland by the royal family – received huge media attention. *The Graphic*, for example, published several issues that celebrated the coronation and the investiture.[45] According to John S. Ellis, the investiture was also an effort to reconstruct British national identity by including Celtic traditions (as opposed to only Anglo-Saxon traditions) and to reinstate the monarchy as a basis for cultural diversity in Britain. The investiture and its reconstruction of Britishness also

---

[42]   David Powell, *The Edwardian Crisis: Britain 1901–14* (Basingstoke and London, 1996), pp. 5–7, 20–28 and 48–58; Antony Taylor, *'Down with the Crown': British Anti-monarchism and Debates about Royalty since 1790* (London, 1999), pp. 183–208; Brooks, *Age*, pp. 110–40 and 151–6; G.K. Peatling, 'Home Rule for England, English Nationalism, and Edwardian Debates about Constitutional Reform', *Albion*, 35/1 (2003): pp. 71–90; David Powell, *Nationhood and Identity: The British State since 1800* (London and New York, 2002), pp. 121 and 126–7.

[43]   *The Graphic* 3.12.1910.

[44]   John S. Ellis, 'Reconciling the Celt: British National Identity, Empire, and the 1911 Investiture of the Prince of Wales', *Journal of British Studies*, 37/4 (1998): pp. 391–418; Elfie Rembold, *Die festliche Nation: Geschichtsinszenierungen und regionaler Nationalismus in Grossbritannien vor dem Ersten Weltkrieg* (Berlin and Wien, 2000), pp. 137–42. See also Eric Hobsbawm, 'Introduction: Inventing Traditions', in Eric Hobsbawm and Terence Ranger (eds), *The Invention of Tradition* (Cambridge, 1983), pp. 1–14.

[45]   *The Graphic* 20.5.1911, 15.6.1911, 17.6.1911, 21.6.1911, 24.6.1911, 27.6.1911, 30.6.1911, 15.7.1911, 22.7.1911.

REPUBLICS on the RAMPAGE : CENTRES of the WORLDS UNREST

Illustration 1.3   G.F. Morrell, 'Republics on the Rampage',
            The Graphic (3.12.1910)

demonstrate that institutional and national changes rocked the political foundations of Britain to such a degree that the monarchy was presented as guaranteeing 'unity in diversity' not only in Britain but also in the British Empire.[46]

Yet, the investiture did not succeed in putting all the debates about constitutional changes in the United Kingdom to an end, as demands for Home Rule and Welsh (and to a lesser extent Scottish) Disestablishment continued.[47] With such heightened sensitivity about the British union, positive press reactions to the Xinhai Revolution could have been interpreted as supporting Irish Home Rule, something the Unionists were deeply opposed to. Since the majority of the large newspapers in Britain were conservative, most major daily newspapers criticized the Chinese revolutionaries' demands for a republic and argued that a constitutional monarchy was a superior political system. Several English newspapers focused on the 'connecting link of the monarchy' which so far had been holding China together.[48] *The Scotsman* and *The Irish Times* also stressed that only a monarchy could preserve Chinese territorial integrity, whereas a republic would lead to chaos and the partitioning of China.[49] This is interesting as movements for national independence existed in both Scotland and Ireland. It is, therefore, no coincidence that both newspapers opposed not only the abolition of the monarchy in China but also Home Rule for Ireland.[50]

Back in China, Sir John Jordan – who also happened to be Irish – agreed with the press during the Xinhai Revolution in so far as he felt that the establishment of a republic in China would be 'a hazardous experiment, and one for which China did not seem to be at all suited'.[51] Although he remained convinced that China was not fit for a republic, Jordan noted in late December 1911 that the 'question of a monarchy or republic is one which Chinese people are best qualified to decide'.[52] Such a view was also supported by the Foreign Secretary who cabled Jordan in late December: 'We desire to see a strong and united China under whatever form of Government the Chinese people wish, and I approve your

---

[46]   Ellis, 'Reconciling the Celt'.

[47]   Powell, *Nationhood*, pp. 120 and 128–34; Rembold, *Die festliche Nation*, pp. 153 and 180–90; Peter Clarke, *Hope and Glory: Britain 1900–2000* (London, 2004), pp. 36–7 and 62–70; Brooks, *Age*, pp. 142–51.

[48]   *The Times* 16.12.1911. See also *Daily Mail* 10.1.1912; *Manchester Guardian* 19.10.1911, 8.11.1911.

[49]   *The Scotsman* 22.12.1911; *Irish Times* 4.1.1912, 5.2.1912, 13.2.1912.

[50]   For the *Scotsman*'s attitude concerning Irish Home Rule see: Richard J. Finlay, 'The Scottish Press and Empire, 1850–1914', in Simon J. Potter (ed.), *Newspapers and Empire in Ireland and Britain: Reporting the British Empire, c. 1857–1921* (Dublin, 2004), pp. 72–4.

[51]   'Sir J. Jordan to Sir Edward Grey', 14.11.1911, TNA FO 405/205.

[52]   'Sir J. Jordan to Sir Edward Grey', 25.12.1911, TNA FO 405/205.

expression of that view.'[53] Nevertheless, even he felt that a limited monarchy would be best suited for China.[54]

This point was also made by many British newspapers. At the forefront were three publications by Baron Northcliffe (Alfred Harmsworth), who exerted an immense control over his publications. While the *Daily Mail* and *The Times* questioned whether the Chinese were ready for self-government or not, claiming that the Chinese character was not suited to a republic,[55] the *Daily Mirror* was even more forthright in its argument that a republic would fail and described China as a 'bed-ridden monster infected with traditions and beliefs which abhor change in any shape or form'.[56] The *Manchester Guardian* prophesied that a Chinese republic would result in a military dictatorship,[57] which is, of course, what eventually happened under Yuan Shikai. In light of the pro-monarchical stance of the British press, it is hardly surprising that British newspapers presented Yuan Shikai – who was fairly open about his monarchical leanings – in a shining light and were rather critical of Sun Yat-sen, the ideological founder of the Chinese Republic.[58] The *Daily Mail* called Yuan 'the greatest Chinaman of the generation',[59] while *The Scotsman* declared:

> If [the revolution] should be completed without widespread disorder and shedding of blood, the transaction will redound greatly to the credit of Yuan-Shi-kai, who, more than Dr Sun Yat Sen, Wu-Ting-fang, or any of the other leaders of the Revolution, is the 'Man of the Hour' in China. It is comparatively easy to begin a rebellion, or even to carry it through successfully. But it requires a genius in statecraft and diplomacy to manipulate, by the arts of persuasion and negotiation, a venerable Eastern despotism into a brand-new democratic Republic.[60]

The Irish Times was even more overt in its bias and openly admitted that it supported Yuan because 'he will never lose his monarchical tendencies'.[61] Interestingly enough, British newspapers published for English-speaking readers in China were also jubilant at the prospect of a new monarchy but this was due more to anti-republicanism than to support of Yuan Shikai. According to Paul French, there

53   'Sir Edward Grey to Sir J. Jordan', 26.12.1911, TNA FO 405/205.
54   'Sir Edward Grey to Sir C. MacDonald', 16.1.1912, TNA FO 405/208.
55   *Daily Mail* 31.10.1911, 1.1.1912, 10.1.1912; *The Times* 16.12.1912.
56   *Daily Mirror* 17.10.1911.
57   *Manchester Guardian* 19.10.1911; 8.11.1911.
58   *The Times* 21.11.1911; *Daily Mail* 3.1.1912; *Spectator* 21.10.1911.
59   *Daily Mail* 16.10.1911.
60   *The Scotsman* 17.1.1912.
61   *Irish Times* 19.1.1912, see also 5.2.1912.

was a lot of scepticism among the British journalists in China when *The Times*'s correspondent G.E. Morrison became Yuan's personal adviser.[62]

The Fall of the Qing Dynasty – The End of Empire?

Another aspect that influenced the British media's framing of the Xinhai Revolution was the British Empire. As Chandrika Kaul points out, the press played an important part in the public debate about empire in the early twentieth century.[63] While the extent to which British culture was influenced by the British Empire has been debated by historians,[64] the press was a hugely important link between Britons and the Empire, and played a crucial part in constructing the British Empire as an imagined community. Thus, upper and middle class Britons would read about the Empire in the *Manchester Guardian, Daily Telegraph, The Graphic, Punch, Daily Mirror* or the *Illustrated London News*. Those of the lower middle and working class encountered the Empire through the *Daily Mail* or the *Daily Express*, which had pages devoted to colonial news.[65]

In the years leading up to the Xinhai Revolution, the British Empire had come under attack from various sides. The Boer War challenged traditional beliefs in British superiority, and the disastrous experiences of the British troops had the effect that the British government – wanting to avoid another imperial war – was more willing than before to enter alliances with other powers. It also focused more intently on relations with the Dominions. However, in various colonies resistance continued and riots against British rule took place.[66] As anti-imperial movements in the colonies and the Dominions' demands for self-government increased, so too did British fears for the future of the Empire and perceptions of Britain as a

---

[62]   Woodhouse, *Hsinhai Revolution*; French, *Looking Glass*, pp. 108–9 and 172.

[63]   Kaul, *Reporting the Raj*, p. 6.

[64]   See Catherine Hall, 'Culture and Identity in Imperial Britain', in Susan Stockwell (ed.), *The British Empire: Themes and Perspectives* (Malden, Oxford and Carlton, 2008), pp. 199–217; Duncan S.A. Bell, 'Empire and International Relations in Victorian Political Thought', *The Historical Journal*, 49/1 (2006): pp. 292–4; Bernard Porter, *The Absent-Minded Imperialists: Empire, Society, and Culture in Britain* (Oxford and New York, 2004).

[65]   Hampton, *Visions*, pp. 26–7 and 40; Startt, 'Good Journalism', pp. 277–81; MacKenzie, 'Press', pp. 26–31; Andrew Thompson, *The Empire Strikes Back? The Impact of Imperialism on Britain from the Mid-nineteenth Century* (Harlow, 2005), pp. 9–63; John M. MacKenzie, *Propaganda and Empire: The Manipulation of British Public Opinion, 1880–1960* (Manchester and Dover, 1984); Hall, 'Culture', pp. 200–205; Andrew S. Thompson, *Imperial Britain: The Empire in British Politics, c. 1880–1932* (Harlow, 2000), pp. 38–60. For the concept of imagined communities see Benedict Anderson, *Imagined Communities*, revised ed. (London, 1991).

[66]   Piers Brendon, *The Decline and Fall of the British Empire, 1781–1997* (London, 2007), pp. 214–27; Peter Mandler, *The English National Character: The History of an Idea from Edmund Burke to Tony Blair* (London, 2006), pp. 106–38; Thompson, 'Language', pp. 150–52.

world power in demise. Consequently, British nationalism focused increasingly on the British Empire, for example in 1904 the Empire Day was introduced as an annual celebration, and the tariff reform movement sought to restore the strength of the British Empire.[67] The coronation of King George V in 1911 was also used by the British press to celebrate the British Empire. In the weeks surrounding the coronation, *The Graphic* printed various illustrations that focused on imperial unity. Kaul has demonstrated how royal visits to India were celebrated in the British press as proof of the strength of the British Empire and British unity.[68] This was also the case in December 1911, when the King and Queen went to India where they were crowned as King-Emperor and Queen-Empress of India. Once again illustrated newspapers like *The Graphic* used the royal visit to stress the unity of the British Empire.[69]

Since control over the Dominions and the Empire had been increasingly challenged, one could also argue that Britain was wary of revolution because the spread of revolutionary ideas from China had the potential to threaten British rule over its colonies or dependencies. *The Scotsman* was keen to point out that Britain had a large interest in China because of the Indian-Chinese border, and stressed that India welcomed British rule. It wrote during King George's visit to India:

> [W]hile the other Mohammedan countries of the world seem to be tumbling
> in ruins – while conservative China itself is in revolution – India is tranquil,
> in all except in loyal rejoicing, and Delhi, a city divided between Hindu
> and Mussulman, seems filled with no other thought than to do honour to the
> Emperor-King.

The newspaper also pointed out: 'India is conscious that if the restraining, controlling, and pacifying power of the British Raj were withdrawn, it would lapse back again into social, political, and economic ruin.'[70] The fact that *The Scotsman* felt it necessary to stress the positive results of British rule and the threat

---

[67]   *The Scotsman* 1.11.1911. See also: Jim English, 'Empire Day in Britain, 1904–1958', *The Historical Journal*, 49/1 (2006): pp. 247–57; Powell, *Nationhood*, pp. 121–4; Eliza Riedi, 'Women, Gender, and the Promotion of Empire: The Victoria League, 1901–1914', *The Historical Journal*, 45/3 (2002): pp. 569–99; Thompson, *Imperial Britain*, pp. 23–4; J.G. Darwin, 'The Fear of Falling: British Politics and Imperial Decline since 1900', *Transactions of the Royal Historical Society*, fifth series, 36 (1986): pp. 30–32; Andrew S. Thompson, 'Tariff Reform: An Imperial Strategy, 1903–1913', *The Historical Journal*, 40/4 (1997): pp. 1033–54; Martin Kitchen, 'The Empire, 1900–1939', in Chris Wrigley (ed.), *A Companion to Early Twentieth-Century Britain* (Malden and Oxford, 2003), pp. 183–7.

[68]   Chandrika Kaul, 'Monarchical Display and the Politics of Empire: Prince of Wales and India 1870–1920s', *Twentieth Century British History*, 17/4 (2006): pp. 464–70.

[69]   *The Graphic* 30.12.1911; 6.1.1912; 27.1.1912, 3.2.1912.

[70]   *The Scotsman* 9.12.1911. See also 22.12.1911.

of revolution surrounding India shows that it was at least somewhat concerned about the possibility of revolution in India. Even the *Manchester Guardian*, which during the Boxer Uprising had been one of the lonely critics of British imperialism in China, now changed its stance and used the situation in China to defend British imperialism. After Russia demanded that China gave autonomy to Outer Mongolia, the paper wrote:

> In Mongolia, as in Tibet, China has been pursuing a forward policy. She needs these provinces as colonies for her surplus population, and she has as much right to them as we have to Canada or to India. For Russia to take the side of the Mongols against the Chinese is as clear an infringement of Chinese sovereignty as it would be of ours if she insisted that we must give the Indians responsible self-government after the pattern of Canada.[71]

For the *Manchester Guardian*, Russia's challenge to Chinese authority in Outer Mongolia was such a serious issue because it threatened the legitimacy of colonial rule, and therefore challenged British authority in its Empire. Thus, since the British press used issues relating to Britain and the British Empire to interpret the Xinhai Revolution, its reactions were not very favourable either to the abolition of the monarchical system or to the establishment of the Chinese Republic.

The USA

American Visions of the China Market

In the late nineteenth and early twentieth centuries, American perceptions of China were dominated by two interest groups, namely businessmen and missionaries. Following American independence in 1783, many American businessmen regarded China as an alternative that could help the USA compensate for the loss of trade with British colonies. Thus, on 22 February 1784 the *Empress of China* sailed from New York to Guangzhou, returning to New York on 11 May 1785. The Chinese goods brought on the *Empress of China* were sold in New York for a profit of $37,000 and led to the departure of more ships to China from ports on the East Coast like New York, Philadelphia, Boston, Salem and Providence. Between 1784 and 1812, approximately 400 ships sailed from the USA to Guangzhou, exchanging goods such as ginseng, sea otter and sealskin furs, sea pelts, sandalwood and sea cucumbers for tea, spices, porcelain, silk, cotton cloths, pottery and other chinoiserie items.[72] Almost all major American trade companies

---

[71]   *Manchester Guardian* 11.1.1912.

[72]   Yen-P'ing Hao, 'Chinese Teas to America: A Synopsis', in Ernest R. May and John F. Fairbank (eds), *America's China Trade in Historical Perspective* (Cambridge, 1986), pp. 11–13; William J. Brinker, 'Commerce, Culture, and Horticulture: The Beginnings of

with business in China were also involved in the opium trade. In fact, revenues from the opium trade made a considerable impact on the growth of the USA until the middle of the nineteenth century.[73]

Originally the US government's role in American trade with China was minimal. A first attempt by the American government to establish treaty relations between the USA and China failed in 1832, but another mission in 1843 resulted in the Treaty of Wangxia on 3 July 1844, which included the most-favoured nation clause. This ensured that the USA was entitled to any concession the Chinese government made in a treaty with another country. After the Treaty of Wangxia, the US government refused to assist American merchants with interventions and instead relied on the most-favoured nation clause because this allowed it to profit from the unequal treaties forced upon China by other powers without having to resort to equally aggressive measures.[74]

Although American merchants envisioned China as an El Dorado, the China trade never became as lucrative as had been hoped and trade with China was not significant for American foreign trade. Nevertheless, the perceived potential of the China market with its 400 million prospective customers fascinated businessmen and the media, and led to the founding of the American Asiatic Association in 1898, which had the goals of promoting American business interests in China and raising public awareness and interest in Far Eastern markets. Other business groups that focused on the China trade included the American China Trade Council, the National Foreign Trade Council and the Cotton Goods Export Association.[75]

Sino-American Cultural Relations', in Thomas H. Etzold (ed.), *Aspects of Sino-American Relations since 1784* (New York and London, 1978), pp. 6–14; Kailai Huang, 'Myth or Reality: American Perceptions of the China Market', in Hongshan Li and Zhaohui Hong (eds), *Image, Perception, and the Making of U.S.-China Relations* (Lanham and Cummor Hill, 1998), pp. 18–19 and 22–3; Charles R. Kitts, *The United States Odyssey in China, 1784–1990* (Lanham, New York and London, 1991), pp. 1–10. For chinoiserie see: Dawn Jacobson, *Chinoiserie* (London, 1993); Oliver Impey, *Chinoiserie: The Impact of Oriental Styles on Western Art and Decoration* (London, 1977).

[73] Michael H. Hunt, *The Making of a Special Relationship: The United States and China to 1914* (New York, 1983), pp. 7–8; Huang, 'Myth', pp. 19–20; Warren Cohen, *America's Response to China: A History of Sino-American Relations*, 4th ed. (New York and Chichester, 2000), p. 5; Mira Wilkins, 'The Impact of American Multinational Enterprise on American-Chinese Economic Relations, 1786–1949', in Ernest R. May and John F. Fairbank (eds), *America's China Trade in Historical Perspective* (Cambridge, 1986), pp. 160–62; Hao, 'Chinese Teas', pp. 21–6.

[74] 'Treaty of Wanghia (Cushing Treaty), July 3, 1844', in Department of State, *United States Relations with China: With Special Reference to the Period 1944–1949* (Washington, DC, 1949), p. 413; Hunt, *Special Relationship*, pp. 14–15 and 19; Cohen, *America's Response*, pp. 2–5 and 24–5; Huang, 'Myth', pp. 32–3; Kitts, *Odyssey*, pp. 2–4.

[75] *New York Times* 5.6.1898; *Washington Post* 15.5.1898. See also: Hunt, *Special Relationship*, pp. 8 and 11–12; Huang, 'Myth', pp. 10–29; Edward D. Graham, *American Ideas of a Special Relationship with China* (New York and London, 1988), pp. 11–12;

When in the late 1890s European and Japanese plans to partition China threatened American commercial and geopolitical interests in China, the US government looked into plans for an American sphere of influence that included the port at Samsa Bay on the Chinese coast, but it eventually decided against it. Instead, Secretary of State John Hay issued the Open Door Notes in 1899, which sought to protect China's sovereignty and bind the foreign powers in China to granting each other equal commercial privileges. On 6 September 1899, the Open Door Notes were sent to Britain, Germany and Russia, followed in November by similar notes to France, Italy and Japan. The Chinese government was not contacted by Hay until mid-November, a further indication that the Open Door Notes primarily served US interests.[76]

The Open Door Notes used the self-determinism of China as a decoy, as their real objective was to prevent further colonization of China and protect American commercial interests there.[77] This also explains why the American press mostly focused on the commercial implications of the Open Door Notes.[78] The *Chicago Tribune*, for example, described the international agreement on the Open Door as 'one of the most important commercial events of President McKinley's administration' and defined the purpose of the notes as 'guarantee[ing] that the merchants and manufacturers of the United States shall have the same rights in China, whatever the "spheres of influence," as the merchants of the countries interested'. It also described the notes as necessary for the continuing prosperity of

---

Hao, 'Chinese Teas', pp. 13, 17 and 28–31; Paul A. Varg, *The Making of a Myth: The United States and China, 1897–1912* (East Lansing, 1968), pp. 36–43; James J. Lorence, 'Organized Business and the Myth of the China Market: The American Asiatic Association, 1898–1937', *Transactions of the American Philosophical Society*, 71/4 (1981): pp. 6–11 and 16–19; Thomas J. McCormick, *China Market: America's Quest for Informal Empire, 1893–1901* (Chicago, 1967), pp. 21–52; Kang Chao, 'The Chinese-American Cotton-Textile Trade, 1830–1930', in Ernest R. May and John F. Fairbank (eds), *America's China Trade in Historical Perspective* (Cambridge, 1986), pp. 104–13.

[76]   Department of State, *United States Relations with China*, pp. 414–16; 'Hay to Conger', 19.11.1900, in Jules Davids (ed.), *American Diplomatic and Public Papers: The United States and China*, series III, volume 7 (Wilmington, 1981), p. 343. See also: David L. Anderson, *Imperialism and Idealism: American Diplomats in China, 1861–1898* (Bloomington, 1985), pp. 171–80; Cohen, *America's Response*, pp. 39–43; Raymond A. Esthus, 'The Open Door and the Integrity of China, 1899–1922: Hazy Principles for Changing Policy', in Thomas H. Etzold (ed.), *Aspects of Sino-American Relations since 1784* (New York and London, 1978), pp. 49–50; Lorence, 'Business', pp. 8–9, 15, 20–25; Lewis L. Gould, *The Presidency of William McKinley* (Lawrence, 1980), pp. 202–3; Margaret Leech, *In the Days of McKinley* (New York, 1959), pp. 481 and 515–22; McCormick, *China Market*, pp. 89–102.

[77]   David Ryan, *US Foreign Policy in World History* (London, 2000), pp. 66–9; Walter L. Hixson, *The Myth of American Diplomacy: National Identity and U.S. Foreign Policy* (New Haven and London, 2008), p. 92.

[78]   *Washington Post* 2.1.1900; *Los Angeles Times* 5.1.1900; *Boston Globe* 3.1.1900.

the USA: 'We must have our share of the vast future trade of Asia or suffer for lack of it. Now is the time to get it, when China is commercially unexplored and newly opened to the merchants of the world.'[79] A lack of sympathy for China's sovereignty could also be found in the *New York Times*, which declared pragmatically:

> Any power which chooses may, according to our contention, maltreat the Chinese as much as it chooses and carve up their inheritance to suit itself. All that we ask is that we shall hereafter be permitted to trade there, as now, on the footing of the most favored nations, which is to say, on the same footing as the conquering and partitioning power.[80]

Commercial interests also dominated American political relations with China in the twentieth century. Chinese immigration to the USA had resulted in the Chinese Exclusion Act of 1882 (see Chapter 3). After the Chinese Exclusion Act was extended in 1904, a boycott of American goods broke out on 10 May 1905, quickly spreading throughout China. The boycott lasted until 1906 and while it did not result in long-term losses for American businesses, some business and missionary organizations demanded new policies on Chinese immigration to the USA.[81] The American press tended to support such demands and many newspapers criticized the way Chinese immigrants had been treated by immigration officials. However, while the press demanded that Chinese merchants, students and travellers should be allowed to enter the USA, there was widespread agreement that Chinese workers (often pejoratively described as 'coolies' in order to invoke the image of forced labour) should remain excluded because they were regarded as a threat to white workers. Southern newspapers like the *Atlanta Constitution* in particular demanded that the Exclusion Act be changed because Southern cotton producers were extremely concerned about potential effects of the boycott on their exports to China.[82] The American government agreed with the view that trade with China

---

79   *Chicago Tribune* 1.1.1900.

80   *New York Times* 17.1.1900.

81   'Memorandum', undated, in Jules Davids (ed.), *American Diplomatic and Public Papers: The United States and China*, series III, volume 8 (Wilmington, 1981), pp. 165–7; 'Rockhill to Loomis', 6.7.1905, in Davids, *American Diplomatic and Public Papers*, series III, volume 8, pp. 167–70. See also: Guanhua Wang, *In Search of Justice: The 1905–1906 Chinese Anti-American Boycott* (Cambridge and London, 2001); Delber L. McKee, 'The Chinese Boycott of 1905–1906 Reconsidered: The Role of Chinese Americans', *The Pacific Historical Review*, 55/2 (1986): pp. 171–8 and 183–4; Sin-Kiong Wong, 'Die for the Boycott and Nation: Martyrdom and the 1905 Anti-American Movement in China', *Modern Asian Studies*, 35/3 (2001): pp. 565–7, 572–3 and 585; Shih-sham Ts'ai, 'Reaction to Exclusion: The Boycott of 1905 and Chinese National Awakening', *Historian*, 29/1 (1976): pp. 95–110; Wilkins, 'Impact', pp. 264–71; Lorence, 'Business', pp. 49–55.

82   *Atlanta Constitution* 13.5.1905, 18.5.1905, 20.5.1905, 15.6.1905; *New York Times* 16.5.1905 and 14.6.1905; *Los Angeles Times* 17.6.1905; *Washington Post* 13.6.1905 and 15.10.1905. For an example of support of continued exclusion see: George C. Perkins,

THE CHINESE BOYCOTT.

JOHN CHINAMAN. — Here's the new combination, Uncle.

Illustration 1.4   Joseph Keppler, Jr., 'The Chinese Boycott', *Puck* (28.6.1905)

was more important than the exclusion laws. President Theodore Roosevelt even wanted to improve relations with China by changing the Exclusion Act so that, with the exception of Chinese labourers, all Chinese could enter the USA, but the Foster Bill never made it through Congress.[83]

'Reasons for Continued Chinese Exclusion', *The North American Review*, July (1906): pp. 15–23.

[83]   *Atlanta Constitution* 15.6.1905. See also: David H. Burton, *William Howard Taft: Confident Peacemaker* (Philadelphia, 2004), pp. 46–8; Ralph Eldin Minger, *William Howard Taft and United States Foreign Policy: The Apprenticeship Years 1900–1908* (Urbana, Chicago and London, 1975), pp. 166–7; Donald F. Anderson, *William Howard Taft: A Conservative's Conception of the Presidency* (Ithaca and London, 1973), pp. 22–3; McKee, 'Boycott', pp. 178–89.

Illustration 1.4 is entitled 'The Chinese Boycott' and was published in the satirical magazine *Puck*. It portrays the Open Door to China as a locked safe for the USA. The exhausted Uncle Sam, who has been unsuccessfully trying to open the door to sell his 'American goods' (labels on suitcases), is offered the combination by a smug-looking Chinese ('John Chinaman') in return for 'fair treatment of China', who is saying: 'Here's the new combination, Uncle.' The exaggerated features of the Chinese (note the eyebrows and the claw-like hand) reinforced racial stereotypes that were prominent in arguments by American opponents of Chinese immigration. 'John Chinaman' was also a common derogatory term for Chinese immigrants in English-speaking countries. By portraying the Open Door as a safe, the cartoon stresses the potential profit that the USA could make from the China market. The cartoon also highlights the paradox that Americans expected access to the China market, yet refused to open the US market to Chinese workers due to their perceived racial difference from US society.

The USA as a Mentor to China

Although commercial interests continued to dominate American policies towards China in the early twentieth century, public images of China were dominated by religious interests. In the early nineteenth century, the Second Great Awakening caused evangelicals to link the birth of the American nation to the coming of the Millennium. This increased the focus on a national destiny and the notion that the USA had been chosen by God to lead the rest of the world. Public support for missionary organizations increased because it was argued that American missionaries carried out the divine mission of the entire American people. By describing China as a nation that needed the help of American missionaries to become a civilized, Westernized nation, missionary organizations portrayed their work in China as serving American self-interest and appealed to American nationalism.[84]

In 1830, Elijah Coleman Bridgman arrived as the first of many American missionaries in Guangzhou. American missionaries actively supported gunboat diplomacy because they wanted to stop restrictions imposed on missionaries by the Chinese government, and many of them worked as interpreters for diplomats

---

[84] Lian Xi, *The Conversion of Missionaries: Liberalism in American Protestant Missions in China, 1907–1932* (University Park, 1997), pp. 2–4; John K. Fairbank, 'Introduction: The Many Faces of Protestant Missions in China and the United States', in John K. Fairbank (ed.), *The Missionary Enterprise in China and America* (Cambridge, 1974), p. 7; Michael C. Lazich, *E.C. Bridgman (1801–1861): America's First Missionary to China* (Lewiston, Queenston and Lampeter, 2000), pp. 4 and 15–37; William R. Hutchison, *Errand to the World: American Protestant Thought and Foreign Missions* (Chicago and London, 1987), pp. 7–9; Varg, *Missionaries*, pp. 76–7 and 84.

and merchants, some of them even took on official positions.[85] Meanwhile in the USA, Protestant theology influenced American universities, social sciences and the press, and the evangelical revival resulted in the founding of more missionary societies and study groups. As a consequence, by 1890 there were 513 American missionaries in China, roughly 40 per cent of all the Protestant missionaries in China. There were often strong ties between local churches and missionaries, and their reports, letters and stories about their experiences in China were widely circulated back in the USA, giving them a great deal of influence on public opinion.[86]

Since missionaries needed funding, they presented China in their writings in such a way that it enticed Americans to continue donating money. Thus, missionary images of Chinese tended to focus on positive character traits and on the Chinese potential for conversion to Christianity. Moreover, the missionary movement was driven by a sense of moral duty and the belief in America's (social, political and moral) superiority, and so American missionaries relied on a paternalist perception of China as a ward of the USA in order to legitimize their presence there and to ensure public support for the missionary enterprise in China. As Christina Klein points out:

> [Missionaries] encouraged a U.S.-centered internationalism based on spreading American values and institutions and transforming other nations along American lines, initially through religious conversion and later by building schools, universities, and hospitals. With its network of congregations and settlements, the missionary movement also created a worldwide institutional infrastructure that enabled millions of Americans, especially in isolated Midwestern and rural communities, to understand themselves as participating in world affairs.[87]

---

[85]   Hunt, *Special Relationship*, pp. 19–21 and 31–2; Varg, *Missionaries*, pp. 5–13 and 85; Cohen, *America's Response*, pp. 1–2, 10–15 and 24–5; Huang, 'Myth', pp. 30–33; Harris, 'Cultural Imperialism', pp. 309–18.

[86]   Varg, *Missionaries*, pp. 13, 54–67 and 73–6; Clifton J. Phillips, 'The Student Volunteer Movement and Its Role in China Missions, 1886–1920', in John K. Fairbank (ed.), *The Missionary Enterprise in China and America* (Cambridge, 1974), pp. 91–109; Eldon J. Eisenach, 'Progressive Internationalism', in Sidney M. Milkis and Jerome M. Mileur (eds), *Progressivism and the New Democracy* (Amherst, 1999), pp. 232–3.

[87]   Christina Klein, *Cold War Orientalism: Asia in the Middlebrow Imagination, 1945–1961* (Berkeley, Los Angeles and London, 2003), p. 30. See also: Lawrence D. Kessler, '"Hands across the Sea": Foreign Missions and Home Support', in Patricia Neils (ed.), *United States Attitudes and Policies toward China: The Impact of American Missionaries* (Armonk and London, 1990), pp. 78–96; Varg, *Missionaries*, pp. 81–3 and 105–22; Isaacs, *Images*, pp. 67–8 and 124–35.

Since the Boxer Uprising was directed largely at missionaries, the reactions of American newspapers to the Uprising are interesting for their rather restrained criticism of the missionaries.[88] The *New York Times* noted:

> Evidently they [American missionaries] are not welcome to the Boxers, and probably the Boxers represent in this matter what may pass for public opinion in China. But they are there by the permission of the Chinese government. Since that Government can not or will not protect them, we must protect them ourselves, collecting afterward our damages for the Chinese failure.[89]

The reason for the muted criticism of missionaries in the American press was the widespread popularity that missionary organizations enjoyed in the USA. There were some critics who blamed the missionary movement for the Boxer Uprising. However, because of the popularity of American missionaries and their work in China, critics of the missionaries' behaviour in China remained a minority in the USA. In fact, domestic support for American missions in China even increased after the Boxer Uprising.[90]

A major difference between British and American public and media perceptions of China can be traced back to the importance of missionary interests in China. While Britons in China were predominantly businessmen and officials, who tended to have a rather negative view of the Chinese, Americans tended to be missionaries. Moreover, American missionary organizations were more influential on the media discourse about China than their British counterparts because their China images correlated not only with the government's justification of China policies but also with the discursive construction of American nationhood, as the concept of American Exceptionalism was fundamental to both of them. American Exceptionalism was based on the idea that the USA was the most civilized nation on earth and a model democracy that had been chosen by God to bring liberty, progress and self-determination to other nations.[91]

[88] *Washington Post* 7.6.1900, 22.6.1900; *Los Angeles Times* 7.1.1900; *San Francisco Chronicle* 20.7.1900; George B. Smyth, 'Causes of Anti-Foreign Feeling in China', *North American Review*, August (1900): pp. 182–97.

[89] *New York Times* 8.6.1900.

[90] Graham, *American Ideas*, p. 351; Varg, *Missionaries*, pp. 47–51.

[91] *New York Times* 5.6.1898; *Washington Post* 22.5.1898; *Chicago Tribune* 2.6.1898; Mark B. Dunnell, 'Our Policy in China', *North American Review*, October (1898): pp. 393–410; Josiah Strong, *Our Country: Its Possible Future and Its Present Crisis* (New York, 1885), pp. 166–72; John Fiske, 'Manifest Destiny', *Harper's*, 70/418 (1885): pp. 578–90. See also: Michael H. Hunt, *Ideology and U.S. Foreign Policy* (New Haven and London, 1987), pp. 29–31 and 37–42; Ryan, *US Foreign Policy*, pp. 23–6 and 40–44; Anders Stephanson, *Manifest Destiny: American Expansion and the Empire of Right* (New York, 1995); Anne R. Pierce, *Woodrow Wilson and Harry Truman: Mission and Power in American Foreign Policy* (Westport and London, 2003), pp. vii–viii; Tony Smith,

American press reports about China increasingly portrayed Sino-American relations as a friendship in which the USA adopted the role of a mentor to China. The construction of this – admittedly highly uneven – friendship can be seen in the press reactions to the Boxer Uprising. The USA was affected by the Uprising like all the other foreign powers in China, and the American Minister Conger was also in the Beijing Legations while they were under siege.[92] Most American newspapers supported American participation in the relief of the diplomats in Beijing but they were also keen to point out that the USA had no further ambitions in China and would continue to rely on the Open Door. In fact, throughout the Uprising, American newspapers stressed that the USA was unlike the other foreign powers in China because it had no territorial interests there.[93] The *Washington Post*, for example, claimed that the absence of selfish designs on the part of the USA and its moral leadership among the powers in China meant that in the future China would turn to the USA as a friend.[94] However, such a statement has to be taken with a pinch of salt. The *Washington Post*, for example, was a staunch defender of American Exceptionalism and the USA's need to increase its territory, if possible in the Pacific, in order to increase trade.[95] Commercial aspirations were probably also what the US government had in mind when Hay cabled Conger in June 1900 that he was permitted to join the other diplomats in giving the Qing government an ultimatum on suppressing the Boxer Uprising which threatened that if the Chinese government did not act, the foreign powers would act on their own.[96] Hay also reminded Conger: 'We have no policy in China except to protect with energy American interests, and especially American citizens and the legation. There must be nothing done which would commit us to future action inconsistent with your standing instructions. There must be no alliances.'[97] What seemed to matter to Hay was that after the Uprising the US government should not be tainted by collaboration with foreign imperial powers because this could have affected Sino-American commercial and diplomatic relations.

America's Mission: The United States and the Worldwide Struggle for Democracy in the Twentieth Century (Princeton, 1994), pp. 8, 25 and 42–59; Hixson, *Myth*, pp. 94–101; Frank Ninkovich, *The United States and Imperialism* (Oxford and Malden, 2001), pp. 15–19, 29–40 and 91–3; Michael Adas, *Dominance by Design: Technological Imperatives and America's Civilizing Mission* (Cambridge and London, 2006) pp. 8 and 128–82.

[92]   'Mr. Conger to Mr. Hay', 16.7.1900, in *FRUS 1900*, p. 156; 'Mr. Hay to Mr. Conger', 21.7.1900, in *FRUS 1900*, p. 156; 'Mr. Conger to Secretary of State', 11.8.1900, in *FRUS 1900*, p. 159.

[93]   *New York Times* 10.6.1900, 13.6.1900; *Washington Post* 30.6.1900 and 11.7.1900; *Chicago Tribune* 5.7.1900, 11.7.1900, 21.7.1900, 16.8.1900; *San Francisco Chronicle* 7.6.1900, 20.7.1900; *Los Angeles Times* 14.6.1900, 28.6.1900, 23.8.1900.

[94]   *Washington Post* 24.7.1900.

[95]   Roberts, *Shadow*, pp. 47–51.

[96]   'Mr. Hay to Mr. Conger', 9.6.1900, in *FRUS 1900*, p. 143.

[97]   'Mr. Hay to Mr. Conger', 10.6.1900, in *FRUS 1900*, p. 143.

As will be shown in the following chapters, the view of a special relationship between China and the USA in which the USA acted as a mentor to China, remained very influential on American perceptions of Sino-American relations until 1950. Even though many Americans used this special relationship to demonstrate that the USA had no ulterior motives in China, it was often invoked to legitimize actions that secured American commercial and geopolitical interests there. Thus, in the *North American Review*, John Barret, the former American Minister in Siam, argued that since China liked the USA more than any other country, it was the USA's duty to lead the foreign powers in the negotiations with China, and that only the USA could guarantee that the Open Door remained intact. However, at the end of the article, Barret listed all the ways in which the USA could do business with China and stated: 'In the face of these immeasurable opportunities, the improvement of which will bring vast benefits to capital and labor in America, who is willing to suggest that we shall retreat and leave China to the control of European nations?' Thus, there were clearly commercial interests involved.[98]

Illustration 1.5 from the *Los Angeles Times* shows how the Boxer Uprising was used by the US press to justify American geopolitical aspirations in China by alluding to values associated with American nationhood. In the cartoon, Uncle Sam is standing in front of Japan, Russia, France, Germany and Britain, conducting a piece entitled 'How to govern China'. Yet, instead of singing along, the foreign powers are squabbling with each other, implying that territorial ambitions affect international cooperation in China. Uncle Sam tells them to stop their bickering ('Now then, boys, attention! Stop your squabbling, all join in together and don't let's have any discord.'). Finally, attached to the USA's baton is a label with 'good offices', which portrays the USA as a friend to China.

Uncle Sam's role as the conductor of the future government of China is an almost blatant reference to American geopolitical aspirations in the Far East. It also portrays the USA as both morally and politically superior to the other powers in China. Moreover, the fact that the USA is spatially separated from the other powers reminds the viewer of the cartoon that the USA had no imperial aspirations in China. Finally, while the other powers are bickering, Uncle Sam remains calm and civilized. Thus, Uncle Sam is a perfect visualization of American Exceptionalism: he is morally superior and more civilized than the other nations, he opposes imperialism and guides the rest of the world. Note that China is not even depicted in the cartoon; it does not have to be because the cartoon's message is about the USA's role as a world leader, and not specifically about China.

American commercial interests in China continued to be legitimized as unselfish acts. In 1908, William Howard Taft became President of the USA, and made China an object of his administration's Dollar Diplomacy. As it was thought that more American investment in China would increase American influence there, the government for the first time participated in the competition

---

[98]   John Barnett, 'America's Duty in China', *North American Review*, August (1900): pp. 145–57.

THE "CONCERT OF THE POWERS" WILL SOON BEGIN IN CHINA.

Uncle Sam: "Now then, boys, attention! Stop your squabbling, all join in together and don't let's have any discord."

Illustration 1.5   'The Concert of the Powers Will Soon Begin in China',
Los Angeles Times (19.8.1900)

for foreign financing in China. Since Dollar Diplomacy also sought to protect the sovereignty of China and prevent further imperialism by other powers in China (particularly Japan), it contributed to the perception of the USA as the protector of China, thus reinforcing paternalist perceptions of China in the USA. However, the Taft Administration's Dollar Diplomacy not only failed to increase US financial presence in China and secure the Open Door in Manchuria, it also made the USA very unpopular among the other foreign nations in China who felt threatened by the USA.[99]

Nevertheless, American newspapers were very supportive of the Taft Administration's attempts at Dollar Diplomacy in China because many of them had become increasingly concerned about Russian and Japanese imperialism in Manchuria and its effects on American trade with China.[100] Interestingly, despite the Taft Administration's clear focus on commercial interests, the *Washington Post* argued that international opposition to American railway plans in China showed that the USA was China's 'one dependable, honest, and sincere friend'.[101] Thus, the American press continued to focus on the image of the USA as mentor to China or protector of Chinese sovereignty and presented the USA's motives as different from those of the other foreign powers in China. This tendency became even stronger once the Xinhai Revolution broke out.

The Xinhai Revolution as an American Achievement

In 1911, the majority of US newspapers supported the establishment of a Chinese Republic. Only a few were sceptical, among them the *Los Angeles Times*, which stated:

> It will make no difference in the commercial or political relations of China with the rest of the world whether the Manchu dynasty shall be overthrown or by concession to the rebels shall save itself. The Chinese are industrious, apt, dexterous and accustomed to frugal life. But they do not possess a single element of character out of which republican citizenship can be manufactured.[102]

In a more light-hearted fashion the *Boston Daily Globe* pointed out: 'The population of China ... was 433,553,030, so that if China becomes a Republic and follows American methods, it may take some time to count the vote.'[103] The

[99] 'The American Minister to the Secretary of State', 12.2.1912, in *FRUS 1912*, pp. 64–5. See also: Emily S. Rosenberg, *Financial Missionaries to the World: The Politics and Culture of Dollar Diplomacy, 1900–1930* (Durham and London, 2003), pp. 1–18; Walter V. Scholes and Marie V. Scholes, *The Foreign Policy of the Taft Administration* (Columbia, 1970), pp. 109–73; Hunt, *Special Relationship*, pp. 208–15; Burton, *Taft*, pp. 61–76; Anderson, *Taft*, pp. 242–58; Cohen, *America's Response*, pp. 64–7; Ninkovich, *Imperialism*, pp. 169–70 and 211–14; Esthus, 'Open Door', pp. 57–60; Minger, *Taft*, p. 164; Chi-ming Hou, *Foreign Investment and Economic Development in China, 1840–1937* (Cambridge, 1965), pp. 9, 29 and 63–5.

[100] *San Francisco Chronicle* 9.8.1909, 9.10.1909, 8.1.1910, 19.1.1910; *Washington Post* 29.8.1909, 9.1.1910, 13.1.910; *New York Times* 22.1.1910, 9.3.1910, 13.3.1910.

[101] *Washington Post* 24.10.1910.

[102] *Los Angeles Times* 1.11.1911, see also 12.11.1911.

[103] *Boston Globe* 5.12.1911.

majority of the papers, however, strongly supported the Chinese revolutionaries and their attempts to establish a republic.[104]

There are various reasons why American press reactions to the Xinhai Revolution were much more positive than those in Britain. One reason was the Progressive Movement, a middle-class urban movement that attempted to deal with the effects of modernization on society, focusing on the potential of society to improve and aiming at establishing a new moral order. The Progressive Movement was deeply influenced by Protestant values and adhered to the belief that American democracy was superior to any other forms of government.[105] As Eldon J. Eisenach points out: 'Progressive nationalism was, from the start, a kind of internationalism as well, not only in its economic analysis, but also in the later sense of seeing America as the vanguard nation leading the world in advancing social justice and political democracy.'[106] The Progressive Era began in the 1890s and ended in 1920.[107] During the time of the Xinhai Revolution and the establishment of the Chinese Republic progressive values were therefore widespread in American society. Since the Progressive Movement championed democracy and focused on the role of the USA in spreading democracy, it is little wonder that the abolition of the Qing Dynasty in favour of a republic was greeted with enthusiasm in the USA. Tai-Chi Quo from the University of Pennsylvania announced in the *Annals of the American Academy of Political and Social Science*: 'The Chinese revolution marks, in short, a great, decisive step in the onward march of human progress.'[108] The establishment of the Chinese Republic was also interpreted as largely the effect of American influence. The *Wall Street Journal*, for example, pointed out that the Chinese Republic was modelled on that of the USA and, therefore, deserved the support of Americans.[109] Various publications described the Xinhai

---

[104]   *New York Times* 31.10.1911; *Washington Post* 14.10.1911, 8.11.1911; *Wall Street Journal* 17.10.1911, 8.11.1911; *San Francisco Chronicle* 28.12.1911, 3.1.1912; *Chicago Tribune* 19.11.1911 and 26.11.1911; *Boston Globe* 16.11.1911. See also: Bose, *American Attitude*, pp. 11–14.

[105]   Alonzo L. Hamby, 'Progressivism: A Century of Change and Rebirth', in Sidney M. Milkis and Jerome M. Mileur (eds), *Progressivism and the New Democracy* (Amherst, 1999), pp. 41–5 and 60; David Traxel, *Crusader Nation: The United States in Peace and the Great War, 1898–1920* (New York, 2006), pp. 8–13; Eldon J. Eisenach, 'Introduction', in Eldon J. Eisenach (ed.), *The Social and Political Thought of American Progressivism* (Indianapolis and Cambridge, 2006), pp. x–xi and xv–xvi; Wilson Carey McWilliams, 'Standing at Armageddon: Morality and Religion in Progressive Thought', in Sidney M. Milkis and Jerome M. Mileur (eds), *Progressivism and the New Democracy* (Amherst, 1999), pp. 108–9; Michael McGerr, *A Fierce Discontent: The Rise and Fall of the Progressive Movement in America, 1870–1920* (New York, 2003), pp. 42–5.

[106]   Eisenach, 'Introduction', p. xvii.

[107]   Eisenach, 'Introduction', p. vii.

[108]   Tai-Chi Quo, 'The Chinese Revolution', *Annals of the American Academy of Political and Social Science*, 39 (1912): p. 11

[109]   *Wall Street Journal* 17.10.1911 and 5.1.1912.

Revolution as basically an American achievement, reminding their readers that many revolutionaries had been educated in missionary schools where they had come into contact with Western ideas like democracy and learned about American republicanism.[110] Many newspapers also stressed that the USA had always supported the Open Door and protected China's sovereignty, and was in return regarded by China as a friend and protector.[111]

The notion that the Xinhai Revolution had been inspired by American values is also the message of Illustrations 1.6 and 1.7, by Charles Raymond Macauley, published in the Pulitzer tabloid *The New York World*. The positive interpretation of the events in China is particularly interesting because *The World* was among the American publications that relied on Yellow Peril imagery in their reports on the Boxer Uprising. In Illustration 1.6 China has opened the door to progress, so that light illuminates its dark room with a statue labelled 'Manchu Dynasty'. Thus, China is portrayed as leaving its backwardness behind and entering a new period in which it follows in the footsteps of the USA. In Illustration 1.7 'The New China' is walking up a flight of stairs towards a beam of light which is labelled 'liberty'. Again, China is leaving behind a statue of the Manchu Dynasty. The cartoon not only can be interpreted as China modelling itself on the USA (where 'liberty' is one of the most important political concepts), but the statue could also refer to the Chinese belief in gods, implying that China is also turning its back on its heathen past.

While these cartoons focus almost exclusively on the USA's mission to spread democracy, the idea of the riches to be gained from the China markets continued to enthral some American editors. Indeed, as the *Chicago Tribune* pointed out, Americans had other reasons to support the Chinese Revolution: 'The tendency of the Chinese to cut the queue and don foreign clothes is particularly marked, and it is possible that a considerable number of inexpensive colored shirts, underclothing, celluloid collars, and made-up ties might be sold.'[112] Such comments were, however, vastly outnumbered by statements focusing on American Exceptionalism. The reason for this can be traced back to missionaries. By 1905 China had become the most important location for American missionaries, and by 1911 there were over 1800 of them there. American missionary work in China also increasingly focused on education instead of evangelization. As a result, not only the number of American missionaries in China but also the number of Chinese students in American missionary schools and colleges increased.[113]

In the early twentieth century, missionaries dominated the newspaper discourse on China in the USA because they figured both as sources and writers in newspapers. Many local newspapers could not afford a correspondent in China,

---

[110]   *Christian Science Monitor* 18.10.1911 and 3.1.1912; *Chicago Tribune* 8.11.1911 and 19.11.1911; *Atlanta Constitution* 14.10.1911.

[111]   *Wall Street Journal* 8.11.1911; *Chicago Tribune* 7.12.1911 and 8.1.1912.

[112]   *Chicago Tribune* 31.12.1911.

[113]   Varg, *Missionaries*, pp. 89–94; Reed, *Missionary Mind*, p. 18.

Illustration 1.7   C.R. Macauley, 'Into the Light', *The World* (15.1.1912)

Illustration 1.6   C.R. Macauley, 'Letting in the Light', *The World* (24.10.1911)

and consequently reprinted reports from press agencies (like the Associated Press) and big national newspapers (like the *New York Times*). In addition, American newspapers also published letters from local missionaries (every city seemed to have had one or more missionaries in China) or used missionaries who had returned from China to explain the situation there. Missionaries were, therefore, extremely influential on the way the American media portrayed China in the early twentieth century. The media's reliance on missionaries for information about China also explains why so many newspapers credited American missionaries with bringing both Christianity and Western social and political ideas to China. American missionaries felt that the Revolution and the establishment of the Chinese Republic would have a positive effect on spreading Christianity in China and that their work in China would be easier. Consequently, they portrayed the Xinhai Revolution in newspapers as proof of China's reception of Western ideas like democracy and Christianity and prophesied that the Chinese Republic would use the USA as a model for its political, social and economic institutions.[114] Missionaries and missionary organizations even tried to persuade the Taft Administration to recognize the Chinese Republic, but the Administration wanted to wait for the reactions of the other powers before granting recognition. Nevertheless, public support of the Chinese Republic was so overwhelming that on 17 April 1912 the US Senate passed a concurrent resolution of the joint resolution by the House of Representatives (passed on 29 February 1912) in which it expressed its sympathy for the Chinese provisional government. It was sent to China in order to improve Chinese support of American interests.[115]

The press coverage of the Xinhai Revolution in the USA also included reports on the reactions of Chinese Americans, where the Xinhai Revolution enjoyed massive support. Prior to the Revolution, Sun repeatedly visited Chinese communities in the USA, asking them for financial assistance for the revolutionary cause in China. There was even a National Relief Bureau in the USA, which raised money for the overthrow of the Qing Dynasty. Once reports reached the USA of the outbreak of the Xinhai Revolution in October 1911, financial contributions

---

[114] *Atlanta Constitution* 5.11.1911 and 26.11.1911; *Boston Globe* 27.11.1911; *Christian Science Monitor* 18.10.1911, 3.1.1912. See also: Murray A. Rubinstein, 'Witness to the Chinese Millenium: Southern Baptist Perceptions of the Chinese Revolution, 1911–1921', in Patricia Neils (ed.), *United States Attitudes and Policies toward China: The Impact of American Missionaries* (Armonk and London, 1990), pp. 150–54; Bose, *American Attitude*, pp. 12–13; Metallo, 'Missionaries', pp. 265–6; Lian, *Conversion*, p. 12; Varg, *Missionaries*, pp. 136–7; Kenneth Scott Latourette, *A History of Christian Missions in China*, (London, 1929), pp. 609–10.

[115] 'The Acting Secretary of State to the American Minister', 2.3.1912, in *FRUS 1912*, p. 71. See also: Bose, *American Attitude*, pp. 13, 19–21 and 26–32; Anderson, *Taft*, pp. 255–6; Metallo, 'Missionaries', p. 270, Ninkovich, *Imperialism*, p. 171; Varg, *Missionaries*, p. 137.

from Chinese communities in the USA further increased.[116] Newspapers described how Chinatowns all over the USA (New York, Boston, Chicago, San Francisco, Los Angeles, Fresno etc.) raised the flags of the revolutionaries and then the Republic, and held fundraisers and parades to celebrate the establishment of a Chinese Republic, the end of the Qing Dynasty and the election of Sun Yat-sen as provisional President of the Republic.[117] While the festivities in the Chinatowns were not as central to the press coverage of the Xinhai Revolution in the USA as the actual events in China, they contributed to the overall positive perception of the Revolution and the establishment of the Chinese Republic.

Switzerland

The Swiss and the China Market

Swiss reactions to the Xinhai Revolution differed greatly from those in Britain and the USA because Swiss interests in China were not of the same nature. As Switzerland was not a seafaring nation, the few Swiss who visited China in the seventeenth and eighteenth centuries were Jesuit missionaries. Watches were a popular gift at the Qing court and missionaries who knew how to make watches were highly sought after. As a result, several Swiss Jesuits went to Beijing and impressed the Qing court with their knowledge of watchmaking.[118] Apart from the Jesuits, there was little contact between Switzerland and China. Even during the eighteenth century, when chinoiserie was fashionable in Switzerland, Swiss watches were brought to China mostly by merchants from other countries. Swiss merchants did not arrive in greater number in China until 1822 when the Swiss brothers Edouard, Frédéric, Alphonse and Gustave Bovet founded the company

---

[116]   Sue Fawn Chung, 'The Zhigongtang in the United States, 1860–1949', in Joseph W. Esherick, Wen-hsin Yeh and Madeleine Zelin (eds), *Empire, Nation, and Beyond: Chinese History in Late Imperial and Modern Times – A Festschrift in Honor of Frederic Wakeman* (Berkeley, 2006), pp. 231–49; L. Eve Armentrout Ma, *Revolutionaries, Monarchists, and Chinatowns: Chinese Politics in the Americas and the 1911 Revolution* (Honolulu, 1990), pp. 125–55; Shehong Chen, *Being Chinese, Becoming Chinese American* (Urbana and Chicago, 2002), pp. 9–39; McKee, 'Boycott', pp. 160–70; Judy Yung, Gordon Chang and Him Mark Lai (eds), *Chinese American Voices: From the Gold Rush to the Present* (Berkeley, Los Angeles and London, 2006), pp. 104–5.

[117]   *San Francisco Chronicle* 17.10.1911; 1.11.1911, 5.11.1911; *Atlanta Constitution* 16.10.1911; *New York Times* 23.10.1911, 30.10.1911, 2.1.1912; *The World* 24.10.1911; *Los Angeles Times* 6.11.1911; *Christian Science Monitor* 1.11.1911, 2.11.1911; *Chicago Tribune* 1.12.1911, 1.1.1912, 12.1.1912, 25.1.1912; *Boston Globe* 9.1.1912.

[118]   Howard Dubois, *Die Schweiz und China* (Bern, 1978), pp. 10–12; Stephan Steinmann, 'Seldwyla im Wunderland: Schweizer im alten Shanghai (1842–1941): Eine Untersuchung ausländischer Präsenz im China der Kapitularverträge', unpublished PhD thesis (Zürich, 1998), p. 97.

Bovet Frères in London and exported watches to China with great success. Bovet Frères was soon followed by other Swiss companies specializing in watches or music boxes. However, despite the increasing attention that China received among Swiss watchmakers and the Swiss textile industry, Swiss trade with China did not take off and throughout the nineteenth century continued to rest almost solely on exports of watches and imports of Chinese raw silk.[119]

Switzerland as a national market gained importance only in the late nineteenth century with the building of railway lines, but unlike the USA and Britain, the primary trading partners of Switzerland were in Europe, so the prospect of trade with China did not make as big an impression on the Swiss and their government as it did in other countries.[120] Switzerland's failure to increase trade with China was also due to the absence of official relations between the Swiss and the Chinese governments. In the nineteenth century, Swiss consulates were established in a variety of countries with a large number of Swiss emigrants; economic or commercial interests were only of secondary importance. China was not a priority for Swiss businessmen and merchants in the Far East, and more Swiss travelled to British India and the Dutch East Indies than to China.[121] After the Treaty of Tianjin improved the conditions for foreign trade in China in 1858, the Federal Council considered the idea of establishing Swiss consulates in Shanghai and

---

[119] Max Huber, 'Bericht über die Möglichkeit der Förderung schweizerischen Exports nach China', 11.1901, BAR E 2001A 1000/45 978. See also: Yvonne Boerlin-Brodbeck, 'Chinoiserien in der deutschsprachigen Schweiz', in Paul Hugger (ed.), *China in der Schweiz: Zwei Kulturen in Kontakt* (Zürich, 2005), pp. 27–40; Jean-Pierre Voiret, 'Genf und die Verbreitung der Chinoiserie in der Schweiz', in Paul Hugger (ed.), *China in der Schweiz: Zwei Kulturen in Kontakt* (Zürich, 2005), pp. 15–20; Dubois, *Die Schweiz*, pp. 20–26; Steinmann, 'Seldwyla', pp. 17 and 98–104; Yufang Zhou, *Die Exterritorialitätsrechte der Schweiz in China (1918–1946)* (Frankfurt and Bern, 2003), pp. 41–3.

[120] 'Die Republik China und ihre Handelsaussichten', BAR E 2001A 1000/45 1055. See also: Paul Bairoch, 'La Suisse dans le contexte international aux XIX et XXe siècles', in Paul Bairoch and Martin Körner (eds), *Die Schweiz in der Weltwirtschaft* (Zürich, 1990), pp. 105–8; Jakob Tanner, 'Die Schweiz und Europa im 20. Jahrhundert: Wirtschaftliche Integration ohne politische Partizipation', in Paul Bairoch and Martin Körner (eds), *Die Schweiz in der Weltwirtschaft* (Zürich, 1990), pp. 409–10 and 413–14; Michael Bernegger, 'Die Schweiz und die Weltwirtschaft: Etappen der Integration im 19. und 20. Jahrhundert', in Paul Bairoch and Martin Körner (eds), *Die Schweiz in der Weltwirtschaft* (Zürich, 1990), pp. 430–40 and 460.

[121] Andreas Zangger, 'Von schnellem Geld und dauerhaften Bindungen: Schweizer im kolonialen Südostasien, 1860–1930', unpublished PhD thesis, University of Zurich, 2010; Matthias Schnyder, 'Das schweizerische Konsularwesen von 1798 bis 1895', *Politorbis*, 36 (2004): pp. 38–9, 45 and 52–4. There are no official numbers for Swiss residents in China in the nineteenth century. Stephan Steinman states that by 1900 there were less than 40 Swiss in Shanghai, where most Swiss lived in China: Steinmann, 'Seldwyla', pp. 17–18. The *Tages-Anzeiger*'s estimate was much higher: *Tages-Anzeiger* 27.6.1900. In 1909 the *NZZ* thought there were about 300–400: *NZZ* 4.2.1909.

Guangzhou, but eventually decided against it because Swiss citizens enjoyed the same privileges as citizens from other Western powers in China as they received consular protection from nations like Germany and the USA. As a result, in the 1860s, Swiss consulates were opened in various Asian cities but none in China, and until 1918 Switzerland had no official relations with China. Switzerland also did not participate in the scramble for spheres of influence in China in the late nineteenth century.[122] Thus, whereas Britain wanted to prevent a further loss of influence in China, and the USA had considerable commercial interests in China, neither the Swiss government nor the Swiss public were really concerned with events in China. In fact, both were largely unaware of what was going on in China. During the Boxer Uprising, for example, the Swiss government had to rely on reports from its ministers in Western capitals for information about the events in China and did not know how many Swiss citizens were affected by the anti-foreign agitation.[123]

By the turn of the century, commercial interest led various Swiss business organizations to demand diplomatic representation in China because they hoped that this would increase Swiss trade with China, but the Swiss government was still not interested.[124] The lack of economic interest in China had the effect that in the Swiss government's trade statistics until 1905, trade with China was not even registered separately but under the heading 'French India and the rest of East Asia'.[125] Not everybody agreed with the government's view. In 1909 the *NZZ* argued that Swiss-Chinese trade had not improved because of the absence of a treaty between Switzerland and China and demanded that the Swiss government change this situation:

---

[122]   *Tages-Anzeiger* 27.6.1900; 'Le Chef du Département du Commerce et des Péages, C. Fornerod, au Consul général à Leipzig, G. Hirzel-Lampe', 16.9.1858, in Commission nationale pour la publication de Documents Diplomatiques Suisses (ed.), *Documents Diplomatiques Suisses (DDS)*, vol. 1, p. 609; 'Le Consul général de Suisse à Leipzig, G. Hirzel-Lampe, au Chef du Département du Commerce et des Péages, C. Fornerud', 18.11.1858, in *DDS*, vol. 1, pp. 620–21; 'Bericht des schweizerischen Bundesrates an die h. Bundesversammlung über seine Geschäftsführung im Jahr 1859', *Bundesblatt*, 12/25 (1860): p. 77; 'Protokoll über eine in Bern den 15. Dezember 1860 abgehaltene Versammlung, behufs Beratung der schweizerischen Handelsinteressen im Orient und Ostasien', 15.12.1860, in *DDS*, vol. 1, pp. 809–17; 'Le Consul général de Suisse à Washington, J. Hitz, au Conseil fédéral', 18.9.1868, in *DDS*, vol. 2, pp. 239–41. See also: Schnyder, 'Konsularwesen', pp. 46–8; Zhou, *Exterritorialitätsrechte*, pp. 34–5 and 47–8; Dubois, *Schweiz*, pp. 21 and 24–5; Steinmann, 'Seldwyla', pp. 63 and 67–70.

[123]   'Le Ministre de Suisse à Paris, Ch. Lardy, au Président de la Confédération et Chef du Département politique, W. Hauser', 4.7.1900, in *DDS*, vol. 4, pp. 751–3.

[124]   'Bericht über die Möglichkeit der Förderung schweizerischen Exports nach China', 11.1901, BAR E 2001 A 1000/45 978. See also: Dubois, *Schweiz*, pp. 38–9.

[125]   Schweiz. Zolldepartement (ed.), *Statistik des Warenverkehrs der Schweiz mit dem Auslande im Jahre 1905* (Bern, 1906).

If one takes into account the development of China during the last ten years, and considers what a market it has become in the meantime for a majority of the European products, one cannot help but be surprised that Switzerland has until now stayed behind and has not looked after its commercial and political interests better.[126]

However, with such an opinion the *NZZ* was in the minority.

The lack of official relations and widespread commercial interest in China meant that Swiss interests in China were not used to frame events in China. The Boxer Uprising, for example, received the Swiss media's attention not because of the number of Swiss affected by it, but because of its anti-Christian and anti-foreign character. Consequently, publications like the *Journal de Genève* used the Uprising to criticize imperialism, i.e. the foreign powers' commercial interests, territorial expansion and the railway construction in China.[127] As most of the news of the Boxer Uprising reached Switzerland from abroad, several newspapers also took a stance that was similar to that of the British press, condemning the behaviour of the Boxers and portraying them as irrational fanatics.[128]

Swiss Missions and the Xinhai Revolution

While there exist a large number of studies on foreign missionaries in China, so far the influence of these missionaries on national perceptions in several countries has not been compared. While such a comparison is difficult because many missionary organizations in China were multinational, the influence of missionaries on images of China varied greatly according to each nation. Thus, although British missionaries dominated the foreign missionary presence in China during the nineteenth century, they did not greatly influence British China policy and also did not contribute significantly to the British media's coverage of events in China. In the USA, however, the arrival of American missionaries in China had the effect that American merchants increasingly lost influence over the USA's China policy as well as the frames selected by the American press in its reports about China. In Switzerland, missionaries did not receive a great deal of media attention during the Xinhai Revolution, even though two Swiss-German missions were present in China at the time of the Revolution.

---

[126]   *NZZ* 4.2.1909.

[127]   *Journal de Genève* 10.6.1900. See also: Arnd Wiedmann, *Imperialismus – Militarismus – Sozialismus: Der deutschschweizerische Protestantismus in seinen Zeitschriften und die grossen Fragen der Zeit 1900–1930* (Bern, Berlin and Frankfurt am Main, 1995), pp. 74, 81 and 108–17; Uwe Kersten, 'Die Perzeption des Imperialismus im Kleinstaat Schweiz, 1882–1904', unpublished Lizenziatsarbeit, University of Zurich, 1990, pp. 68–72.

[128]   *Tages-Anzeiger* 2.6.1900, 13.6.1900, 14.6.1900, 19.6.1900, 21.6.1900. See also Kersten, 'Perzeption', pp. 72–5.

The *Evangelische Missionsgesellschaft* in Basel, usually referred to as the Basel Mission, was founded in 1815. In 1847 the first missionaries from the Basel Mission arrived in Hong Kong, from where they ventured into China. Its area of activity was Guangdong province where it focused on converting the ethnic minority group of the Hakka.[129] Like other missionary organizations, the Basel Mission distributed publications in Switzerland and Germany in order to increase funding. These publications also included reports by missionaries in China, and in early 1911 the Basel Mission even held a course on China in Switzerland, where various missionaries spoke about their experiences in Southern China.[130] Although the Basel Mission originally did not represent a specific nation, most of its financial support and it missionaries came from southwestern Germany, not Switzerland. This might explain why, in 1900, Swiss newspaper reports on the Boxer Uprising quite often mentioned foreign missionaries in China but not specifically the Basel Mission.[131]

The second missionary organization from Switzerland in China was the *Allgemeiner Evangelisch-Protestantischer Missionsverein (Ostasien Mission)* (AEPM). It was founded in 1884 and opened its first station in China in 1895. It had missions, schools and hospitals in Shandong province, which indicates that the AEPM had a strong connection to Germany which had a sphere of influence in Shandong. In fact, the majority of AEPM missionaries were German. However, it also had quite a following in Switzerland and was supported by several women's organizations that collected money and held bazaars for it.[132]

There already exist a few studies on the Basel Mission which include reactions to the Xinhai Revolution. Willy Rüegg claims that the Basel missionaries in China openly supported the Revolution, and portrayed it as a sign of progress and spiritual liberation which had been achieved with the help of the missionaries, yet Thoralf Klein argues that not all missionaries felt this way and that, actually, quite a few either opposed the Revolution or were sceptical about its success.[133] Either way, they hardly influenced the coverage of the Xinhai Revolution in the Swiss press. This

---

[129]   Thoralf Klein, *Die Basler Mission in Guangdong (Südchina): 1859–1931* (München, 2002), pp. 107–8 and 161–5; Willy Rüegg, 'Die Chinesische Revolution in der Berichterstattung der Basler Mission', unpublished PhD dissertation, Universität Zürich, 1988, pp. 38–44.

[130]   H. Dipper (ed.), *Basler Missions-Kurs 1911* über *China: Ein Auszug für die Besucher des Kurses und für Missions-Studentenkränzchen* (Basel, 1911). See also: Klein, *Basler Mission*, pp. 41–2 and 110.

[131]   *Tages-Anzeiger* 7.6.1900, 8.6.1900, 14.6.1900, 19.6.1900. For other newspapers see Kersten, 'Perzeption', pp. 76–81; Klein, *Basler Mission*, pp. 109–11.

[132]   *'Daheim und Draußen':* Schweizerische Frauenarbeit des Allgem. evang.-protestantischen Missionsvereins für Japan und China. Festschrift zur 1. Schweiz. Ausstellung für Frauenarbeit 'Saffa', 26. August bis 30. September 1928 (Bern, 1928); W. Hückel, *Bunte Bilder aus dem heidnischen und christlichen China* (Berlin, 1925).

[133]   Rüegg, 'Revolution', pp. 61–3; Klein, *Basler Mission*, pp. 353–4.

seems quite surprising but there are several reasons for it. Firstly, missionaries did not enjoy a similar social prestige in Switzerland as they did in the highly religious American society. Secondly, the local networks of missionary organizations were much bigger in the USA than in Switzerland, in part because there were more missionaries; whereas in the USA most newspapers could print letters from 'their' local missionary in China, there were hardly any Swiss missionaries in China at the beginning of the twentieth century. Moreover, while in the USA the concept of American Exceptionalism directly linked Christianity with nationalism, and resulted in a patriotism that was deeply influenced by Christianity, this was not the case in Switzerland. Ulrich Gäbler notes that unlike the British and Americans, the Swiss did not view themselves as a people chosen by God. Partly this was because the Swiss had no common ethnic origin, religion or language.[134] Robert P. Ericksen in turn suggests that another reason for the absence of this idea in Switzerland was the lack of expansionist aspirations as well as a relative isolationist policy – as opposed to ambitions of participating in international power politics – which were both the result of Switzerland's small size.[135]

One last reason for the lack of interest on the part of the Swiss media in the experience of missionaries from the Basel Mission and the AEPM during the Xinhai Revolution was that they were perceived as German – not Swiss – societies. Although the Basel Mission was a German-Swiss organization, in the 1880s the German government decided that the Basel Mission should represent German interests and values abroad. The Swiss members of the mission committee were not happy with this decision but they were overruled by the German members. As a result, the Basel Mission was viewed as a German, not Swiss, missionary organization by the Swiss press.[136] With regard to the AEPM, it has already been pointed out that the mission was located in Shandong province, which was the German sphere of influence. This, of course, reinforced perceptions of the AEPM as a German mission. One further indication that both societies were generally seen as German societies is given by Kenneth Scott Latourette, one of the foremost experts on missions in China, who in 1929 described the AEPM and Basel Mission in his book on Christian missions in China explicitly as German societies.[137]

---

[134] Ulrich Gäbler, 'The Swiss: A Chosen People?', in William R. Hutchison and Hartmut Lehmann (eds), *Many Are Chosen: Divine Election and Western Nationalism* (Minneapolis, 1994), pp. 257–76.

[135] Robert P. Ericksen, 'Response', in William R. Hutchison and Hartmut Lehmann (eds), *Many Are Chosen: Divine Election and Western Nationalism* (Minneapolis, 1994), p. 282.

[136] Karl Rennstich, 'The Understanding of Mission, Civilisation and Colonialism in the Basel Mission', in Torben Christensen and William R. Hutchison (eds), *Missionary Ideologies in the Imperialist Era: 1880–1920* (Aarhus, 1982), pp. 94 and 98–9.

[137] Latourette, *History*, p. 576.

Domestic Issues and Barbarian Names

Whereas in Britain and the USA the domestic context influenced how events in China were portrayed in the press, in Switzerland hardly any reports about China were influenced by domestic issues. Partly this was because the Swiss media paid little attention to the Chinese Revolution in 1911.[138] Yet, even in the few articles that were printed on the Xinhai Revolution, the fact that Swiss interests in China were hardly ever mentioned is striking, not least because China became the object of Swiss commercial interests at this time.

Although Swiss trade with China decreased from 1906 to 1910, Swiss hopes for increasing trade with China resurfaced in 1911, causing the *Vorort des Schweizerischen Handels- und Industrie-Vereins*, the most important economic organization in Switzerland that represented the interests of industry, trade and finance, to demand a commercial agency in Shanghai. The *Vorort* argued that, despite the huge potential of the China market, the absence of a Swiss consul in China made it difficult to increase Swiss exports to China, because nobody was there who could negotiate or mediate business transactions. The Federal Council granted the request in December 1911 and in July 1912 the agency was opened.[139] Before his departure to Shanghai, the newly appointed Consul Matthias Winteler toured Swiss cities in order to awaken commercial interest in China. After attending a speech by Winteler, the *Journal de Genève* gushed enthusiastically: 'The relations of our country with China have until now been insignificant. ... But we could easily develop not only our exports of watches and silk, but also machines, cotton textiles, tinned goods, chocolate, condensed milk, Maggi products, bristles etc.'[140] While the *NZZ* reiterated its conviction that now was the moment for Switzerland to properly enter the China market,[141] the *Berner Intelligenzblatt* was fascinated by Winteler's view of the potential profits awaiting Swiss merchants in China: 'We can export a lot, even without having the protection of canons and gunboats behind us. On the contrary, in China our neutrality will be extremely useful because the Chinese is a man of peace.'[142] It was not only the press that was (temporarily) smitten with the potential of the China market. The Swiss representative in Tokyo, Ferdinand von Salis, also

---

[138]   See Ester Kamber, 'Medienereignishierarchien 1910–1940', in Kurt Imhof, Heinz Kleger and Gaetano Romano (eds), *Zwischen Konflikt und Konkordanz: Analyse von Medienereignissen in der Schweiz der Vor- und Zwischenkriegszeit* (Zürich, 1993), p. 360.

[139]   The consulate was closed again in 1914: 'Schreiben des Handelsdepartement an den Bundesrat', 6.12.1911, BAR E 2001 A 1000/45 1350; 'Auszug aus dem Protokoll der Sitzung des Schweizerischen Bundesrates', 10.7.1914, BAR E 2001 A 1000/45; *Journal de Genève* 4.2.1912; *Berner Intelligenzblatt* 21.12.1911. See also: Dubois, *Schweiz*, pp. 40–41; Zhou, *Exterritorialitätsrechte*, pp. 49–50; Steinmann, 'Seldwyla', pp. 72–3.

[140]   *Journal de Genève* 8.2.1912.

[141]   *NZZ* 15.2.1912.

[142]   *Berner Intelligenzblatt* 7.2.1912.

supported the establishment of a consulate in Shanghai and pointed out that soon China would 'offer an immensely rich field for commerce and industry'.[143] Yet, the fact that hardly any newspapers made the connection between Swiss commercial interests in China and the Xinhai Revolution implies that while a few individuals and organizations were indeed interested in the commercial profit, Swiss society at large was unaffected by it. In Britain and the USA the situation was different, with Britain's position in China being largely the effect of Britain's commercial and financial dominance in China in the nineteenth century, while in the USA the idea of the lucrative China market had figured prominently over the centuries, beginning in 1783 with China as a replacement for British colonies as markets for American goods, and in the 1890s as a solution to the economic crisis. In Switzerland, however, China had never occupied such a role in the economic or political debates. The *Journal de Genève* explained the lack of interest among the Swiss towards the Xinhai Revolution by stating that a car accident in the local area was much more important to the newspaper's readers than a revolution in China: 'China is so far away and all these barbarian names that one struggles with, they discourage you. After all, what do we care what the viceroy Tchant-tchet-tong has done in Ouchang!'[144]

Another reason for the absence of domestic issues as frames for covering events in China is that by far the majority of Swiss news about the Xinhai Revolution were summaries of telegraphic cables from news agencies and other newspapers, which did not make very entertaining reading. There were hardly any in-depth analyses or first person narrative accounts like in the British and American press because the Swiss newspapers at that time could not afford to have a correspondent in China and had to rely on letters from merchants in China. Consequently, many articles covering the Chinese Revolution were either directly taken from or based on reports from British, French, German, American and Italian newspapers, and therefore did not reflect Swiss interests in China so much as Swiss disinterest in China. Furthermore, the large number of telegrams and articles that reached Swiss editors from all over the world about the events in China made it sometimes hard to keep up to date with the Revolution. As the *Berner Intelligenzblatt* noted: 'The situation in China is becoming more complicated with each day.'[145]

Nevertheless, a few articles and editorials dealt with the Xinhai Revolution. Some newspapers like the *NZZ* expressed doubts about the readiness of the Chinese for a republic.[146] The Swiss representative in Japan, von Salis, was also sceptical about the success of a republic in China, noting that the majority of the Chinese had no political education whatsoever. However, he also stated: 'as flawed as the new government may be, it will still be better than the corrupt favouritism and

---

[143] 'F. Salis an den Bundespräsidenten und Vorsteher des Politischen Departementes L. Forrer', 19.2.1911, in *DDS*, vol. 5, pp. 662–3 (quote).

[144] *Journal de Genève* 17.10.1911.

[145] *Berner Intelligenzblatt* 3.1.1912.

[146] See for example *NZZ* 18.1.1912 and 1.1.1912.

Illustration 1.8　　J.F. Boscovits, 'Closing Time in China', *Nebelspalter* (17.2.1912)
Source: Scan provided by Zentralbibliothek Zürich. Reproduced with permission of
Nebelspalter.

eunuch husbandry which has been in place in Beijing for more than 50 years.'[147] This was in line with the general opinion of the Swiss press, which supported the abolition of the Qing Dynasty.[148] As the *Tages-Anzeiger* stated:

> Until a short time ago China was regarded as the gigantic model of holding on to the old and traditional, which is typical for a country and a people where ancestors are worshipped almost as gods. But the poor administration of the Manchu, the people who have been ruling in China for almost 300 years, who came to power with the Manchu Dynasty and the hatred among the Chinese people of the Manchu, have finally ended all the Chinese attachment to the old and traditional at least with respect to politics.[149]

Illustration 1.8 also expresses quite a strong disdain for the Qing Dynasty. The cartoon was printed in the satirical magazine *Nebelspalter* and is entitled 'Closing Time in China'. It shows three Chinese labelled 'Manchu Dynasty' being kicked out of the 'Inn of the Republic' by a fist swinging a stick labelled 'progress and international law'. The caption reads 'Closing Time, Gentlemen!' By comparing the Xinhai Revolution to the closing of a pub or a tavern in the evening, the revolutionaries are associated with establishing order and being in control while the Manchu Dynasty is likened to people who have to be told what to do. Note also how the figures representing the Qing Dynasty are drawn as extremely effeminate. One of them, probably a eunuch, is even wearing a pearl necklace.

The frames selected by the media in each country as a consequence of the political and commercial interests in China or the lack of such interests remained part of the dominant frames throughout the period of the Chinese Republic. Thus, British frames tended to depict China in a rather negative light, while American media portrayed China fairly positively. The Swiss press, in turn, looked at how events in China related to Swiss perceptions of democracy and imperialism. Yet, whereas in 1911 the Swiss press found other topics much more pressing and showed little interest in China, this changed in the 1920s.

---

[147] 'F. Salis an den Bundespräsidenten und Vorsteher des Politischen Departementes L. Forrer', 19.2.1912, in *DDS*, vol. 5, pp. 662(quote)–663.

[148] *Berner Intelligenzblatt* 17.10.1911; *Tages-Anzeiger* 18.10.1911; *NZZ* 9.12.1911; *Nebelspalter* 28.10.1911.

[149] *Tages-Anzeiger* 3.1.1912.

Chapter 2
The 1920s, the Red Menace and Anti-foreign Agitation in China

In October 1924, the liberal evening newspaper *The Star* published a cartoon in reaction to the anticommunist hysteria that had gripped the majority of the British press. It was drawn by David Low, one of the most famous cartoonists of that time and still regarded as one of the most influential British cartoonists of the century.[1] Low's cartoon (Illustration 2.1) described the Red Menace frenzy as 'Much Ado About Next to Nothing', a spin on William Shakespeare's *Much Ado About Nothing*. It used a tiny figure in the bottom right corner to portray the power of the Communist Party of Great Britain (CPGB) as ridiculously exaggerated by the 'Tory fabrications department' (written on the jacket of the man on the left). The cartoon also mocked the arguments of British anticommunists by including such ludicrous claims as: 'Communism will burn your home! Mortgage and all', and a very random 'Communism will abolish baths umbrellas motor cars sausage rolls etc.'. Low even included a jab at fellow cartoonists and their obsession with drawing Bolsheviks with excessive facial hair by including a poster that said 'whiskers will be compulsory under communism'.

Although antisocialist and anticommunist sentiment was also widespread in the USA and Switzerland, only the British press focused on the Red Menace in its reports on events in China in the mid-1920s. In order to explain why this was the case, this chapter looks at the perception of the Red Menace within the national contexts and analyses how they influenced the media portrayal of China from the May Thirtieth Movement, which began in 1925, to the Nanjing Incident in 1927. British, American and Swiss reactions to the May Thirtieth Movement and the Nanjing Incident have until now barely been analysed, yet they are crucial for the understanding of images of China in the West during the first half of the twentieth century. This chapter demonstrates that in the 1920s, Western perceptions of China differed greatly from nation to nation, and were not so much dictated by government policies but by various factors which included not only missionary and business organizations (on which most analyses of foreign perceptions tend to focus) but also domestic issues. Moreover, the chapter's examination of the media's usage of the Red Menace provides a new perspective for looking at anticommunism in the 1920s in the respective countries by focusing on the transnational circulation of

---

[1]   Mark Bryant, 'Low, Sir David Alexander Cecil', in Mark Bryant, *Dictionary of Twentieth-Century British Cartoonists and Caricaturists* (Aldershot and Brookfield, 2000), pp. 141–2.

Illustration 2.1 David Low, 'Much Ado About Next to Nothing', *The Star* (14.10.1924)
Source: Reproduced with permission of Solo Syndication.

the enemy image, and contributes to the history of international perceptions of the Red Menace as an enemy image that focused on the threat of the Soviet Union, socialism and/or communism. Ragnhild Fiebig-von Hase points out: 'Dislike of a country is supposedly determined not so much by concrete events, but rather by the degree of conflict believed to exist between this country and one's own.'[2] The perception of national differences, particularly political aspects, became crucial for the image of the Red Menace, yet, as this chapter seeks to demonstrate, the actual perception of the Red Menace differed from country to country. Of course, the Red Menace was not the only China image that was based on national difference. In fact, nations as imagined communities are defined by exclusion. Thus, national perceptions are based on an 'us versus them' dichotomy; some nations are perceived as friends or allies, others as enemies. Values which are used to categorize nations as enemies can be religious, ideological or ethnic/racist.[3]

Enemy images not only legitimize aggression but also reinforce domestic cultural hegemony.[4] Michael Kunczik observes: 'Creating an enemy-image is [a] propaganda trick of the trade, creating among the population a feeling of being under threat, which in turn arouses a wish for strong leadership, or at least increases the readiness to tolerate authoritarian leadership.' Enemy images like the Red Menace projected internal frustrations onto an external object and thereby unified the population.[5] In the mid-1920s, socialist and communist parties existed in Britain, Switzerland and the USA, and in all three countries labour movements gained strength. As a result, the Red Menace was invoked to focus on the socialist and/or communist internal and external threat to the nation. This reinforced specific cultural discourses which in turn contributed to the discursive construction of nationhood. Nancy Bernkopf Tucker argues: 'Self image ... provides the lens through which the public sees other peoples and governments.'[6] This chapter shows that while the British press used the Red Menace as an enemy image to justify the use of force in China and legitimize British imperialism, American and Swiss media deconstructed and disputed the claim that the events in China were proof of the Red Menace and reinterpreted them in such a way that they fit their own national interests and self-perceptions.

---

[2]   Ragnhild Fiebig-von Hase, 'Introduction', in Ragnhild Fiebig von Hase and Ursula Lehmkuhl (eds), *Enemy Images in American History* (Providence and Oxford, 1997), p. 10.

[3]   Fiebig-von Hase, 'Introduction', pp. 14–24; Donal O'Sullivan, *Furcht und Faszination: Deutsche und britische Russlandbilder, 1921–1933* (Köln, Weimar and Wien, 1996), p. 9; Anderson, *Imagined Communities*, p. 6; Philipp Sarasin, Andreas Ernst, Christoph Kübler and Paul Lang, 'ImagiNation. Eine Einleitung', in Barbara Welter (red.), *Die Erfindung der Schweiz 1848–1948: Bildentwürfe einer Nation* (Zürich, 1998), p. 22.

[4]   See Hixon, *Myth*, p. 11.

[5]   Michael Kunczik, *Images of Nations and International Public Relations* (Mahwah, 1997), p. 118, see also pp. 120–44.

[6]   Nancy Bernkopf Tucker, 'America First', in Carola McGiffert (ed.), *China in the American Political Imagination* (Washington, DC, 2003), p. 16.

Britain

The Anticommunist Hysteria of 1924

In the interwar period, Marxist groups were not as popular in Britain as socialist groups, which looked to change the system from within instead of replacing it with a revolution. The reason for this was that in the late nineteenth and early twentieth-century reform acts, the extension of the franchise and the legalization of the trade unions enabled the working class to participate in the political system in Britain. After the Labour Party was nominally founded in 1906, it took less than two decades for it to replace the Liberal Party as the second largest party in British politics.[7] The popularity of socialist thought, however, was not shared by everybody, as British reactions to the October Revolution in 1917 showed. Russia had traditionally been perceived as a threat to the British Empire due to the imperial rivalry between Britain and Russia. While the October Revolution in 1917 was celebrated by the British labour movement and socialists, conservatives regarded the Soviet Union as a socio-political threat because Britain was the most influential capitalist country and, therefore, the Soviet Union's main enemy in the war against capitalism.[8] Prime Minister Lloyd George, Secretary of War Winston Churchill and Lord Curzon (who became Foreign Secretary in 1922 after Lloyd George's government fell) in particular regarded Bolshevik anti-imperialism as a menace to the British Empire in Asia. This was not completely unrealistic because the Communist International (Comintern), which was founded in January 1919 in Moscow, sought to bring about a worldwide communist revolution for which it relied on national liberation movements. Of particular concern for Britain were the effects of the Bolshevik Revolution on the Indian national movement.[9] Nevertheless, such fears also failed to take into consideration a growing

---

[7] John Callaghan, *Socialism in Britain since 1884* (Oxford and Cambridge, 1990); Patrick Renshaw, 'Anti-Labour Politics in Britain, 1918–27', *Journal of Contemporary History*, 12/4 (1977): pp. 693–4; Keith Laybourn, *A Century of Labour: A History of the Labour Party, 1900–2000* (Stroud, 2000), pp. ix–xv and 20–30; John Davis, *A History of Britain, 1885–1939* (New York, 1999), p. 133.

[8] F.S. Northedge and Audrey Wells, *Britain and Soviet Communism: The Impact of a Revolution* (London and Basingstoke, 1982), pp. 3–4 and 142–4; Muriel E. Chamberlain, *'Pax Britannica' British Foreign Policy, 1789–1914* (London and New York, 1988), pp. 102–6; Wilgus, *MacDonald*, pp. 3–4 and 26–7; Goldstein, 'Britain', pp. 8–10; Paul Ward, *Red Flag and Union Jack: Englishness, Patriotism and the British Left, 1881–1924* (Woodbridge, 1998), pp. 155–60; Callaghan, *Socialism*, p. 91; Keith Laybourn, *The Rise of Socialism in Britain, c. 1881–1957* (Stroud, 1997), pp. 85–6.

[9] 'Manifesto of the Communist International to the Proletariat of the Entire World', in Jane Degras (ed.), *The Communist International, 1919–1943: Documents* (3 vols, London, 1971), vol. 1, p. 38. See also: Callaghan, *Socialism*, pp. 93–4 and 97; Zafar Imam, *Colonialism in East-West Relations: A Study of Soviet Policy towards India and Anglo-Soviet Relations: 1917–1947*, 2nd ed. (New Delhi, 1987), pp. 84–5; Vivekanand Shukla,

nationalism in India, as Zafar Imam notes: 'The British Government looked with alarm and suspicion at every demand the [Indian] nationalists advanced and every agitation they undertook. In them, the British detected a mysterious Bolshevik connection and failed to evaluate the nature of the growing upsurge of nationalism objectively.'[10] As the following pages show, a similar case could be made for British perceptions of Bolshevik subversion in China.

Bolshevism was perceived not only as a purely external menace in Britain but also as an internal threat connected to the British labour movement. Since the British labour movement already participated in the political system through the Labour Party, the Comintern had to rely on small revolutionary groups to form the CPGB in 1920. The CPGB was ordered to affiliate with the Labour Party to gain access to the trade unions and radicalize the British working class, but the application for affiliation was rejected in 1924. Although the CPGB subsequently tried other ways to infiltrate the trade unions and gain mass support, it had only modest success because the British labour movement was too integrated in the political processes for the CPGB to detach it from the political system, and the trade unions as well as the Labour Party remained anticommunist throughout the interwar period.[11]

The CPGB was not only too radical for the British public, many British revolutionaries also felt uncomfortable with the amount of control the Comintern had over the CPGB; not only did the Comintern use money from the Soviet state treasury to fund the CPGB, it also determined the CPGB's party line and did not tolerate any dissent from CPGB members.[12] Although the CPGB 'was never remotely close to seriously impinging upon the Labour Party's hegemony over the British left',[13] conservative hardliners in Britain viewed socialism, liberalism and

---

Soviet Revolutions and the Indian National Movement: Perceptions of Indian Media (New Delhi, 1989), pp. 219–21 and 228–9; Goldstein, 'Britain', pp. 10–12.

[10]   Imam, *Colonialism*, pp. 84–5. See also Shashi Bairathi, *Communism and Nationalism in India: A Study in Inter-relationship, 1919–1947* (Delhi, 1987), pp. 215–21.

[11]   Labour Party, *The Communist Solar System* (London, 1933). See also: Kevin McDermott and Jeremy Agnew, *The Comintern: A History of International Communism from Lenin to Stalin* (New York, 1997), pp. 105–6; Laybourn, *Rise*, pp. 87–91 and 104–8; Callaghan, *Socialism*, pp. 99–102; Davis, *History*, p. 149.

[12]   John Newsinger, 'Recent Controversies in the History of British Communism', *Journal of Contemporary History*, 41/3 (2006): pp. 557–72; Andrew Thorpe, *The British Communist Party and Moscow, 1920–1943* (Manchester, 2000), pp. 278–81; McDermott and Agnew, *Comintern*, pp. 8, 21–3 and 56; A.J. Davies, *To Build a New Jerusalem: The British Labour Movement from the 1880s to the 1990s* (London, 1992), pp. 102–9; National Council of Labour, *British Labour and Communism* (London, 1935), pp. 5–6 and 11–12; Curtis Keeble, *Britain, the Soviet Union and Russia* (Basingstoke, 2000), pp. 79–80; Andrew Thorpe, 'The Membership of the Communist Party of Great Britain, 1920–1945', *The Historical Journal*, 43/3 (2000): p. 799.

[13]   Thorpe, 'Membership', pp. 779(quote)–780.

social democracy as having the same goal as communism, namely the abolition of the existing system.[14]

In her study of American enemy images of foreign nations, Fiebig-von Hase argues: 'It is in times of social unrest, economic depression, questioned cultural identity, and war that ... external enemies are emphasised in order to create or consolidate national unity.'[15] All of this occurred in Britain after 1919: social unrest was present through strikes and unemployment, the economy suffered from debts accumulated during the war, and the decline of the British Empire challenged British cultural identity. The middle and upper classes were alarmed by what they perceived as revolutionary activity, and viewed workers, especially returning servicemen, as prone to falling for communist ideas which seemed to spread like a disease among the working class. The Conservative Party aggravated these anxieties by claiming that once the Labour Party gained power, it would be controlled by revolutionary trade unions.[16]

The Red Menace as a symbol for conservative fears of the empowerment of the working class seemed to become reality during the Polish-Soviet War, when government plans for declaring war on Russia were met with threats of a general strike by the Trades Union Congress (TUC). Russian telegrams were also intercepted in which British trade unions were asked to take action against their government's plans to interfere on Poland's side. Suddenly, the Tories' paranoia of a conspiracy to sovietize England no longer seemed so unfounded. Bolshevist agitators and agents had indeed been operating in Britain and money from Moscow was used to fund various British revolutionary movements. However, the Bolsheviks actually helped to keep the situation in Britain relatively stable because their radicalism frightened the public and the Labour Party, which would have been their key ally in the quest for revolution. Nevertheless, despite British interest in the Russian market and a Trade Agreement in 1921 between Britain and the Soviet Union, many British conservatives were convinced that communist subversion had become an internal threat to the British political system.[17]

---

[14] Markku Ruotsila, *British and American Anticommunism before the Cold War* (London, 2001), p. 174.

[15] Fiebig-von Hase, 'Introduction', p. 28.

[16] Chris Wrigley, '1919: The Critical Year', in Chris Wrigley (ed.), *The British Labour Movement in the Decade after the First World War* (Loughborough, 1979), pp. 1–13; T.O. Lloyd, *Empire, Welfare State, Europe: History of the United Kingdom 1906–2001*, 5th ed. (Oxford and New York, 2002), pp. 62–76 and 88–94; Michael Pugh, *State and Society: A Social and Political History of Britain, 1870–1997*, 2nd ed. (London, 1999), pp. 177–91; Gabriel Koureas, *Memory, Masculinity and National Identity in British Visual Culture, 1914–1930: A Study of 'Unconquerable Manhood'* (Aldershot, 2007), pp. 23–30; Ruotsila, *Anticommunism*, p. 169.

[17] Keeble, *Britain*; Northedge and Wells, *Britain*, pp. 35 and 47–8; Christine A. White, *British and American Commercial Relations with Soviet Russia, 1918–1924* (Chapel Hill and London, 1992), pp. 1, 33 and 229; Kevin Narizny, 'The Political Economy

The first minority Labour government was elected on 22 January 1924 and granted the Soviet Union de jure recognition on 1 February 1924. The move was not caused by Russophilia on the part of the Labour government, but was in line with the common practice of acknowledging foreign governments that occupied a national territory. Prime Minister Ramsay MacDonald even stressed that British socialism was different from Bolshevism, which the Labour Party rejected, and no ambassadors were exchanged. For conservatives, however, it was a damnable act. It should come as no surprise, then, that the government's organization of an Anglo-Soviet Conference drew the wrath of the conservative press.[18] By the early 1920s, newspapers had truly become a mass medium, with newspapers like the *Daily Mail*, the *Daily Mirror* and the *Daily Express* dominating the market. Their content was controlled by press barons like Lord Beaverbrook (whose newspapers included the *Evening Standard* and the *Daily Express*) and Lord Rothermere (owner of the *Daily Mail* and the *Daily Mirror*). While previously a newspaper's policy was largely defined by its editor, these press lords were almost completely in control of their papers' political stances. As their newspapers included the publications with the highest circulation, they could influence public opinion very effectively, and this is exactly what happened in 1924. Both Beaverbrook and Rothermere were conservatives – Beaverbrook had actually been a Conservative MP before his knighthood – and their opposition to British relations with Russia was adopted by their publications.[19]

While the press on its own could not topple the Labour government, the Campbell Case did. J.R. Campbell was acting editor of the communist *Workers' Weekly*, which published an open letter by Harry Pollitt from the CPGB, urging soldiers not to use their weapons in class or military wars against other workers. When charges against Campbell were dropped, rumours about Labour being soft on communism spread and fears of an imminent communist revolution grew. The Labour government was defeated in Parliament over the Campbell Case and a

---

of Alignment: Great Britain's Commitments to Europe, 1905–39', *International Security*, 27/4 (2003): p. 209; Callaghan, *Socialism*, pp. 95–6; Lloyd, *Empire*, p. 160; Ruotsila, *Anticommunism*, pp. 243–6; Laybourn, *Rise*, pp. 85–97.

[18]   J. Ramsay MacDonald, *Socialism: Critical and Constructive* (London, 1924), pp. 248–53. See also: Laybourn, *Century*, pp. 42–3; Laybourn, *Rise*, pp. 91–2; Northedge and Wells, *Britain*, pp. 38–9; Keeble, *Britain*, pp. 97–101; Stephanie Salzmann, *Great Britain, Germany and the Soviet Union: Rapallo and After, 1922–1934* (Woodbridge, 2005), pp. 7–10 and 46; Ruotsila, *Anticommunism*, pp. 193–4; Edward Hallett Carr, *Socialism in One Country, 1924–1926*, vol. 3, part 1 (London, 1964), pp. 21–8; Andrew J. Williams, *Labour and Russia: The Attitude of the Labour Party to the USSR, 1924–34* (Manchester and New York, 1989), pp. 15–17.

[19]   Curran and Seaton, *Power*, pp. 37–42; Temple, *British Press*, 33–4 and 39; Alan Wood, *The True History of Lord Beaverbrook* (London, 1965), p. 176; Koss, *The Rise and Fall*, vol. 2, p. 11.

general election was set for October 1924.[20] The conservative press tended to use the same frames as the Conservative Party during the election campaign, namely anti-socialism.[21] Election notes for Conservative candidates stated:

> Communism and Socialism are one and the same thing. The aim of Communism and Socialism is the same, but they differ as regards methods. … whoever obtains power – Socialist or Communist – this country will be ruined. It makes little difference whether we perish by the slow poison of evolutionary Socialism, or by the bloody axe of the Revolutionary Communist.[22]

This completely ignored that the Comintern did not view the Labour government as an ally or that the Labour Party had rejected applications for affiliation by the CPGB and excluded communists or limited their power.[23] Claims about the Communist control of Labour increased when, shortly before the general election, the Foreign Office and the *Daily Mail* presented an alleged message from Zinoviev, the president of the Comintern, which ordered the CPGB to infiltrate the Labour Party. The letter itself was probably a forgery but it confirmed suspicions held by the British public regarding Bolshevism, and caused the conservative *Daily Mail* to lead the campaign against communism and Soviet subversion in Britain.[24] Lord Beaverbrook described his newspapers' stance during the weeks leading up to the October 1924 general election in the following way: 'We were not fighting Mr. Ramsay MacDonald in his saner moments, but the Russian Bolshevists and the shade of Lenin. The Daily

---

[20]   *Workers' Weekly* 25.7.1924; J.R. Campbell, *My Case* (London, 1925). See also: N.D. Siederer, 'The Campbell Case', *Journal of Contemporary History*, 9/2 (1974): pp. 143–62; Northedge and Wells, *Britain*, p. 36; Davis, *History*, p. 172.

[21]   Laura Beers, *Your Britain: Media and the Making of the Labour Party* (Cambridge, 2010), pp. 51–2 and 56–7; Laura Beers, 'Counter-Toryism: Labour's Response to Anti-Socialist Propaganda, 1918–1939', in Matthew Worley (ed.), *The Foundations of the Labour Party: Identities, Cultures and Perspectives, 1900–39* (Farnham, 2009), pp. 234–6; Alan Clark, *The Tories: Conservatives and the Nation State, 1922–1997* (London, 1998), p. 39.

[22]   'Election Notes from 11 October 1924', in Unionist Central Office, *London Election Notes* (London, 1924), p. 2.

[23]   'Extracts from an ECCI Resolution on the British Labour Government and the Communist Party of Great Britain', in Degras, *The Communist International*, vol. 2, pp. 82–4; National Council of Labour, *British Labour*. See also: Narizny, 'Political Economy', p. 187; Laybourn, *Rise*, pp. 99–100.

[24]   *Daily Mail* 25.10.1924. See also: Northedge and Wells, *Britain*, pp. 42–3; William B. Husband, 'The New Economic Policy (NEP) and the Revolutionary Experiment, 1921–1929', in Gregory L. Freeze (ed.), *Russia: A History* (Oxford, 1997), p. 272; Laybourn, *Century*, p. 43; E.H. Carr, 'The Zinoviev Letter', *The Historical Journal*, 22/1 (1979): p. 209.

Express and the Sunday Express therefore exerted their whole influence in order to secure the return of an immense Conservative majority.'[25]

In the interwar period, the power of newspapers over public opinion began to be acknowledged by political parties and governments. As the extension of the franchise in 1918 had given all men over 21 and women over 30 the right to vote, papers like the *Daily Mail* and the *Daily Express* had the potential to influence the outcome of elections because they were the newspapers with the highest circulation in Britain. Moreover, they were mass-market papers and were, consequently, more influential in general election outcomes than newspapers like *The Times*, which were not aimed at the lower classes but targeted a much smaller and more elite audience. Indeed, the Conservative victory in 1924 demonstrated just how crucial the support of the press was for the electoral success of political parties.[26] During the election campaign, Conservative accusations against Labour were also taken up by cartoonists. Cartoons not only provided a visual commentary on the election campaign but had a similar effect on their audience as election posters. After all, cartoons tended to be more accessible than newspaper articles because it took little more than a glance to understand their message while it took some time to read an article. Therefore, cartoons played a considerable role in the spread of Russophobia prior to the general election.

Illustration 2.2 was drawn by Bernard Partridge, *Punch* Cartoonist from 1910 to 1945, and Illustration 2.3 by the *Daily Mirror*'s Editorial Cartoonist W.K. Haselden. Both cartoons associate Labour with the Soviet Union and imply that a victory for the Labour Party would lead to Soviet rule over Britain. In Illustration 2.2 a communist (possibly Zinoviev) is calling on Britons to 'vote for MacDonald and me'. Illustration 2.3 is entitled 'Under which flag? To-day's choice' and was printed on the day of the general election. In the cartoon, Stanley Baldwin from the Conservative Party is waving a British flag and standing in front of a poster that declares him to be in aid of Britain. On his left is Ramsay MacDonald, waving a 'red' flag in front of a poster that declares him to be supporting a (very hairy) Bolshevik. The red flag was practically ubiquitous in conservative cartoons about Labour and stressed Labour's allegiance to socialism, directing the reader's focus to the Comintern and socialism's international network. In case any readers failed to get the message, the caption of the cartoon read: 'Vote to-day for a British Government not subject to dictation from Russia!'.

Illustrations 2.2 and 2.3 are typical examples of contemporary visualizations of the Labour Party as the Red Menace: they show Labour as being under the Comintern's or the Soviet Union's control, they associate communism with dictatorship and foreign rule, and they depict communists as hairy, unhygienic creatures with facial hair and shaggy clothes, which were the opposite of the British

---

[25]   Lord Beaverbrook, *Politicians and the Press* (London, 1925), p. 87.

[26]   Davis, *History*, pp. 172–3; Northedge and Wells, *Britain*, pp. 37 and 39; Williams, *Labour*, pp. 17–18; Keeble, *Britain*, pp. 98–101; B.R. Mitchell, *British Historical Statistics* (Cambridge, New York and Melbourne, 1988), p. 796.

ON THE LOAN TRAIL.

[In a document just disclosed by the British Foreign Office (apparently after considerable delay), M. ZINOVIEFF, a member of the Bolshevist Dictatorship, urges the British Communist Party to use "the greatest possible energy" in securing the ratification of Mr. MacDONALD's Anglo-Russian Treaty, in order to facilitate a scheme for "an armed insurrection" of the British proletariat.]

Illustration 2.2   Bernard Partridge, 'On the Loan Trail', *Punch* (29.10.1924)

Source: Reproduced with permission of Punch Ltd, www.punch.co.uk.

Illustration 2.3   W.K. Haselden, 'Under which Flag? To-day's Choice',
Daily Mirror (29.10.1924)

Source: Reproduced with permission of Mirrorpix.com.

gentleman, who is depicted as an immaculately dressed, cleanly shaven aristocrat (see Illustration 2.3 top right). Sidney Strube from the *Daily Express* even drew a cartoon in which Ramsay MacDonald uses a tramp as a model for a Bolshevik in an election poster. Thus, Bolsheviks are portrayed as equal to the dregs of British society.[27] Illustration 2.3 also shows how some conservative cartoonists drew communists with simian features. These invoked traditional British portrayals of the Irish in the nineteenth century, thus reinforcing the idea of communism and socialism as a threat to British society. Such depictions were also meant to contrast with those of Stanley Baldwin, who was shown as the personification of 'Englishness'.[28] The communist was, therefore, not only turned into a political 'Other' but also a social 'Other', which represented the antithesis of core British values. In 1924, few publications criticized the anti-Soviet hysteria, among them *The Star*, for which David Low drew the cartoon that was analysed at the beginning of this chapter. Most other publications jumped on the anticommunist and anti-Labour bandwagon created by the *Daily Mail* and the *Daily Express*.

Conservatives and the 'Red International' in China

The Conservative government did not take public fears of the Red Menace lightly, and the new Home Secretary, Sir William Joynson-Hicks, started a campaign against communist subversion in Britain, which led to the arrest of the CPGB leaders in 1925.[29] While Joynson-Hicks's crusade took place, the May Thirtieth Movement broke out in China. Its occurrence at a time of rampant anticommunism in Britain had the effect that British conservatives regarded it as just another example of Soviet subversion and plans for Britain's demise. The reality, of course, was not that simple.

In July 1921, the Chinese Communist Party (CCP) was founded with the help of the Comintern's Secretary-General of the Far Eastern Bureau, Voitinsky (Grigory Naumovich Zarkhin). In 1924, the CCP entered an alliance with the strongest nationalist party in China, the Guomindang (GMD), after being ordered to do so

---

[27]   *Daily Express* 16.10.1924.

[28]   Siân Nicholas, 'The Construction of National Identity: Stanley Baldwin, "Englishness" and the Mass Media in Inter-War Britain', in Martin Francis and Ina Zweiniger-Bargielowska (eds), *The Conservatives and British Society, 1880–1990* (Cardiff, 1996), pp. 127–31; Stuart Ball, 'Democracy and the Rise of Labour: 1924 and 1929–1931', in Stuart Ball and Anthony Seldon (eds), *Recovering Power: The Conservatives in Opposition since 1867* (Basingstoke, 2005), p. 141; Beers, 'Counter-Toryism', pp. 232 and 234; Beers, *Your Britain*, pp. 60 and 66; Curtis Lewis Perry, *Apes and Angels: The Irishman in Victorian Caricature* (Newton Abbot, 1971); Roger Fischer, *Them Damned Pictures: Explorations in American Cartoon Art* (North Haven, 1996), pp. 74–93.

[29]   'Documents selected from those obtained on the arrest of the Communist leaders on the 14th and 21st October, 1925', *HCP*, 1926, Cmd. 2682. See also: Renshaw, 'Anti-Labour Politics', pp. 698–700; Keeble, *Britain*, pp. 102–8.

by the Comintern. The GMD leader, Sun Yat-sen (Sun Zhongshan), had agreed to this because he wanted to unify China and needed Russian money and advisors. In return for allowing the CCP to join the GMD, Russian agents became involved in the GMD, particularly with its military affairs and propaganda. The May Thirtieth Movement began in Shanghai, China's primary port for foreign trade, where roughly one third of the foreign investment in China was concentrated. The appalling working conditions in the factories made it easy for communists to organize the workers. At the same time, Chinese nationalism as a mass phenomenon reached new heights and focused increasingly on the presence of imperial powers in China. On 15 May 1925, a Chinese worker was killed by a Japanese foreman following a strike at a Japanese-owned cotton mill in Shanghai, setting off a string of anti-imperialist and anti-capitalist agitation by labour activists and students. When a crowd of about 2,000 tried to seize a police station in the International Settlement, Chinese and Sikh constables fired into the crowd, killing at least 11 and injuring over 40. The so-called 'Nanking Road Massacre' led to strikes and demonstrations throughout China, a general strike in Shanghai and a boycott of foreign (particularly British) goods in Hong Kong and Guangzhou, which lasted 16 months. Anti-foreign riots broke out in several British concessions, and the British and Japanese consulates in Jiujiang were destroyed.[30] The May Thirtieth Movement was largely anti-British because, for many Chinese, Britain represented

---

[30]   'ECCI Resolution on the Relations between the Chinese Communist Party and the Kuomintang', in Degras, *The Communist International*, vol. 2, pp. 5–6; 'Leitsätze zur Orientfrage', in *Thesen und Resolutionen des IV. Weltkongresses der Kommunistischen Internationale* (Hamburg, 1923), pp. 42–52; *Documents on the Shanghai Case* (Peking, 1925), pp. 3–6 and 10; 'Report on the Hong Kong-Canton Strike, March 1926', in C. Martin Wilbur and Julie Lien-ying How (eds), *Missionaries of Revolution: Soviet Advisers and Nationalist China, 1920–1927* (London and Cambridge, 1989), pp. 594–6; H.G.W. Woodhead (ed.), *China Yearbook 1928* (Nendeln, 1969 [1928]), pp. 942–51, 955 and 965. See also: Martin C. Wilbur, *The Nationalist Revolution in China, 1923–1928* (Cambridge, 1984), pp. 5–14 and 21–3; Michael Y.L. Luk, *The Origins of Chinese Bolshevism: An Ideology in the Making, 1920–1928* (Oxford, 1990); Richard W. Rigby, *The May 30 Movement: Events and Themes* (Canberra, 1980); Alexander Pantsov, *The Bolsheviks and the Chinese Revolution, 1919–1927* (Richmond, 2000), pp. 41–65; McDermott and Agnew, *Comintern*, pp. 27–39; John Fitzgerald, *Awakening China: Politics, Culture, and Class in the Nationalist Revolution* (Stanford, 1996), pp. 168–72; Edmund S.K. Fung, *The Diplomacy of Imperial Retreat: Britain's South China Policy, 1924–1931* (Hong Kong, 1991), pp. 16–21 and 34–5; Alain Roux, *Grèves et politique à Shanghai: Les disillusions (1927–1932)* (Paris, 1995), pp. 26–7 and 34–8; Harumi Goto-Shibata, *Japan and Britain in Shanghai, 1925–31* (Basingstoke and London, 1995), pp. 5 and 8–16; Hung-Ting Ku, 'Urban Mass Movement: The May Thirtieth Movement in Shanghai', *Modern Asian Studies*, 13/2 (1979): pp. 197–203 and 207; Jürgen Osterhammel, *Shanghai, 30. Mai 1925: Die chinesische Revolution* (München, 1997), pp. 12–17; John M. Caroll, *Edge of Empires: Chinese Elites and British Colonials in Hong Kong* (Cambridge and London, 2005), pp. 131–58; Kang Chao, *The Development of Cotton Textile Production in China* (Cambridge and London, 1977), pp. 92–6 and 115–20.

imperialism in China; after all, it had been the major foreign power in China during the nineteenth century. In 1925, British presence in China was still considerable with 718 British firms and 15,247 Britons (excluding troops). Only Japan and Russia had more companies and expats in China.[31]

The 1920s marked an important change in Western press coverage of China as more and more foreign reporters arrived in China. Moreover, the growth of wire services and the instalment of wireless transmitters meant that news from China could be transmitted to Western countries more quickly.[32] The domestic setting of anticommunism in Britain allowed fears of communism and socialism to be used by the conservative media and conservative politicians to frame the events in China. Accordingly, the May Thirtieth Movement was interpreted as a Soviet endeavour in order to back up claims of and measures against the Red Menace within Britain. For example, the *Daily Mail* wrote: 'the trouble in China is that there is really no Government, and consequently nothing to protect that unhappy country against Bolsheviks', and then asked its readers: 'Are we so much better off in this country?'[33] Many *Daily Mail* articles about the May Thirtieth Movement were also concerned with the effects of Bolshevism on the British Empire, ranging from statements such as: 'The British Empire is the prime object of Bolshevist hatred',[34] to jingoistic declarations like: 'The real evil-doer in China is the Soviet Government ... These dismal, long-haired criminals who are holding Russia down by terrorism and murder make the mistake of their life if they imagine that the British Empire is going to be frightened by their threats and grimaces.'[35] Once again, the physical appearance of the Communist ('long-haired') was used to imply that Communism was uncivilized and un-British.

Such a perception of the Soviet Union related to the Conservatives' interwar policy of defending the British Empire against the Soviet threat. Kevin Narizny points out: 'Ideology may have played a contributing role in the Conservatives' antipathy toward the Soviet Union, but their policies were ultimately based on a hard-nosed calculation of imperial interests.'[36] The Conservative Party's supporters came mostly from the southeast of England where finance, which depended upon the Empire, dominated the local economy. Most Liberal and Labour supporters, on the other hand, came from northern England, Scotland and Wales, i.e. areas with mines and factories that depended on European markets. Thus, for the Liberal and Labour Parties, relations with Europe were more important than with the Empire. The Conservatives, however, focused on the defence of the British Empire and the

---

[31]   Woodhead, *China Year Book 1928*, p. 4. For 1924 see: 'China Command Intelligence Diary', 7.1925, TNA FO 228/3212; H.G.W. Woodhead (ed.), *The China Year Book 1926–7* (Nendeln, 1969 [1926]), p. 30.

[32]   French, *Looking Glass*, pp. 124–7.

[33]   *Daily Mail* 18.6.1925.

[34]   *Daily Mail* 6.6.1925.

[35]   *Daily Mail* 16.6.1925.

[36]   Narizny, 'Political Economy', p. 223.

financial interests which depended upon it. As the Soviet Union seemed to pose the biggest threat to the British Empire because of its proximity to British colonies and its anti-imperialist propaganda, Russophobia was especially prominent among conservatives.[37]

The strong reactions of British conservatives and conservative publications to the events in China in 1925 were partly caused by the financial losses incurred by the May Thirtieth Movement. British cotton exports to China had declined sharply since the First World War, and the May Thirtieth Movement further damaged Britain's already deteriorating position in the Chinese textile trade: while in 1924 59.1 per cent of cotton piece goods were imported to China from Britain, in 1925 it was only 48.0 per cent. British trade with China in general also suffered severely from the anti-British boycotts. Compared to 1924, British exports to China fell by 26.1 per cent in 1925, exports from Hong Kong to China even decreased by 27.7 per cent.[38] The *Daily Express*, in particular, focused on the economic effects of the May Thirtieth Movement on the British Empire. This stance can be explained through the newspaper's owner, Lord Beaverbrook, who was an avid supporter of the Empire and later became a campaigner for the Empire Free Trade Crusade. Beaverbrook wrote in 1925: 'In the Empire, and not in Europe, our future lies, and the Daily Express has never failed to preach the Imperial doctrine in good or in bad times. The Daily Express believes that the British Empire is the greatest instrument for good that the world has ever seen.'[39] The *Daily Express*'s coverage of the May Thirtieth Movement is a great example of how the Empire dominated the newspaper's perspectives: Although the *Daily Express* mentioned Bolshevik

---

[37]   Narizny, 'Political Economy', pp. 188, 191–6, 206–7; Powell, *Nationhood*, pp. 155–6.

[38]   C.F. Remer and William B. Palmer, *A Study of Chinese Boycotts: With Special Reference to Their Economic Effectiveness* (Taipei, 1966), pp. 111–13, 119–22 and 127; Albert Feuerwerker, 'Economic Trends, 1912–49', in John K. Fairbank (ed.), *The Cambridge History of China, vol. 12: Republican China 1912–1949*, part 1 (Cambridge, 1983), pp. 125–6; Hsiao Liang-lin, *China's Foreign Trade Statistics, 1864–1949* (Cambridge, 1974), pp. 148–63; Osterhammel, 'British Business', p. 200; E.M. Gull, *British Economic Interests in the Far East* (London, 1943), pp. 106–8; Chao, *Cotton*, pp. 92–6; C.F. Remer, *Foreign Investments in China* (New York, 1933), pp. 367–72; Marguerite Dupree, 'Foreign Competition and the Interwar Period', in Mary B. Rose (ed.), *The Lancashire Cotton Industry: A History since 1700* (Preston, 1996), pp. 265, 270–73, 289; Bruce L. Reynolds, 'The East Asian "Textile Cluster" Trade, 1868–1973: A Comparative-Advantage Interpretation', in Ernest R. May and John F. Fairbank (eds), *America's China Trade in Historical Perspective* (Cambridge, 1986), pp. 144–7; Fung, *Diplomacy*, pp. 44–89; Goto-Shibata, *Japan*, p. 18; Ethel Barbara Dietrich, 'Lancashire Cotton Industry', *The American Economic Review*, 18/3 (1928): p. 469; Rigby, *May 30 Movement*, pp. 142–6; Irwin See, 'Alone against the Waking Dragon: Britain's Failure to Secure International Cooperation in China, 1925–1926', *Journal of Modern Chinese History*, 2/2 (2008): pp. 175–6.

[39]   Beaverbrook, *Politicians*, p. 126. See also: Wood, *History*.

support of the May Thirtieth Movement, it was much more interested in the economic effects of the boycott of British goods on the British Empire.[40]

Not only the British economy was affected by the May Thirtieth Movement. As Richard W. Rigby points out: 'British political interests were equally if not more important than their financial and commercial stake, for it was realised that loss of prestige in China would be a tremendous blow to British hegemony in Asia generally, and in India in particular.'[41] This explains why Prime Minister Stanley Baldwin's cabinet continued to view Bolshevism as a threat to British interests in Asia. In 1926, for example, the Under-Secretary at the Foreign Office, Sir W. Tyrell, wrote in a memorandum: 'ever since the Bolshevist regime was established in Russia its activities have been mainly directed against this country.'[42] The British media's focus on communist activity in China was also influenced by the increasing willingness of the British labour movement to resort to strikes. Between 1921 and 1925, an average of 656 labour disputes took place annually in the UK. This wave of strikes increased fears among conservatives of communist subversion. As a consequence of the perceived threat of communism to both Britain and the British Empire, most British newspapers and journals focused on the role of the Soviet Union and Chinese communists in their reports on the May Thirtieth Movement.[43] Often, the Soviet Union was described as the sole cause of the movement, like in Illustration 2.4 by Bernard Partridge from *Punch*.

In the cartoon, China is not a menacing power but a small child who is sitting on the lap of a Bolshevik. The child is throwing a temper tantrum, which the Bolshevik finds highly amusing. As it was quite common for imperial cartoons to portray colonies as children, implying that their demands should not be taken seriously, one of the cartoon's messages was to ignore Chinese demands for treaty revision and an end to (informal) imperialism. Moreover, the figure of authority in the cartoon is the Bolshevik, implying that Bolshevism instigated the anti-British agitation in China.

The view of the Soviet Union as the mastermind behind the May Thirtieth Movement was widespread in the British press, not least because most publications supported conservative politics. However, the CCP only chose to take advantage of the movement once it had already started.[44] Of course, not all newspapers

---

[40] *Daily Express* 4.6.1925, 5.6.1925, 26.6.1925, 4.7.1925, 22.8.1925.

[41] Rigby, *May 30 Movement*, p. 142.

[42] 'Memorandum by Sir W. Tyrrell', undated, in Kenneth Bourne and D. Cameron Watt (general eds), *British Documents on Foreign Affairs: Reports and Papers from the Foreign Office Confidential Print*, part II, series A, vol. 8 (Frederick, 1986), pp. 335–7.

[43] *The Times* 1.6.1925, 3.6.1925, 4.6.1925, 9.6.1925, 10.6.1925; *Daily Mail* 3.6.1925, 6.6.1925, 11.6.1925, 16.6.1925; *Manchester Guardian* 2.6.1925; *Daily Mirror* 5.6.1925, 15.6.1925.

[44] Jacques Guillermaz, *A History of the Chinese Communist Party, 1921–1949* (London, 1972), p. 85; Elizabeth Perry, *Shanghai on Strike: The Politics of Chinese Labor* (Stanford, 1993), pp. 82–4.

Illustration 2.4   Bernard Partridge, untitled, *Punch* (8.7.1925)
Source: Reproduced with permission of Punch Ltd, www.punch.co.uk.

interpreted the events in such a way. *The Times*, the *Daily Express* and the *Manchester Guardian* noted that while Bolshevik propaganda was involved in the anti-foreign movement, it was not its sole cause. Both papers blamed Chinese nationalism for the movement, yet whereas *The Times* insisted that Britain was not to be held responsible, the *Manchester Guardian* pointed out that the unequal treaties were the real cause and criticized British nationals in China who refused to adjust the extraterritoriality status: 'There are many persons who, shutting their eyes to the immense provocations that Europe has given for a century to native violence, think that all the disorders in China are to be attributed to Bolshevik agents.'[45] Such a view is surprisingly close to that of current historiography. For example Peter Zarrow argues that one should not view the May Thirtieth Movement as an isolated event but 'as part of a longer, painful process in which

_____

[45] *Manchester Guardian* 16.6.1925. See also: *The Times* 4.6.1925, 12.6.1925, 20.6.1925, 27.6.1925; *Manchester Guardian* 3.6.1925, 5.6.1925, 6.6.1925, 16.6.1925, 20.6.1925, 26.6.1925, 27.6.1925; *Daily Express* 4.7.1925.

demands for social justice and the desire for collective identity meshed to bring increasing numbers of people into the political process.'[46]

The *Manchester Guardian*'s unique stance with respect to events in China can also be explained through its owner, C.P. Scott. Unlike the newspaper barons Beaverbrook and Rothermere, Scott was not interested in personal power or aggrandizement, and he was also deeply opposed to the sensationalist style of the other publications. A final difference was that while Beaverbrook and Rothermere were Conservatives, Scott was a member of the Liberal Party. Since Scott was editor of the *Manchester Guardian* for over 50 years, he influenced the *Guardian*'s outlook tremendously. In the 1920s, the *Guardian* was one of the few papers that did not adopt a conservative stance. As a result of the different political orientation and style, the *Manchester Guardian*'s reactions to events in China also differed from those of the other papers.[47]

The Foreign Office was also aware that Chinese nationalism, not Bolshevism, caused the May Thirtieth Movement. In early 1925, the 'China Command Intelligence Diary' of the Foreign Office stated:

> Kuomintang is in touch with the Soviet government of Russia but for a specific purpose, which is to secure for China freedom from foreign control. No secret is made of the ambition, and in turning to Russia the Kuomintang is no doubt influenced by the fact that this country has been the first to renounce all treaty and other rights gained in China in the past. Kuomintang has no other interest in Russia and is very little, if at all, affected by propaganda emanating from Moscow.[48]

Similarly, in a note on the situation in China dating from 30 June 1925, the War Office described the situation in the following way:

> The Bolshevist propaganda in China, as elsewhere, is being conducted on nationalist lines. Thus, this national movement is aimed largely against the foreigners in China, and at the abolition of extra-territorial and other foreign treaty rights. Until that object is achieved, in and around foreign concessions, settlements and Treaty Ports, there is likelihood of constant, even if only intermittent, trouble, caused by Chinese agitators of Bolshevist agents ... in China there are stronger forces at work below the surface than Bolshevism. It is these stronger forces which must be considered in making plans for the future.[49]

---

[46]   Peter Zarrow, *China in War and Revolution, 1895–1949* (London and New York, 2005), pp. 208–9.

[47]   J.L. Hammond, *C.P. Scott of the Manchester Guardian* (London, 1934).

[48]   'China Command Intelligence Diary for the Period 1st December 1924 to 20th January, 1925', TNA FO 228/3212.

[49]   TNA WO 106/79.

Since it perceived Chinese nationalism to be based on demands for social reforms and an end to the unequal treaty system, the British government felt that a continuation of gunboat diplomacy would be counterproductive and that only negotiations about extraterritoriality could improve relations between Britain and China. This was rejected by the majority of the British press. Among the few voices which supported the government's policy were the *Spectator, Nineteenth Century*, the *Manchester Guardian* and the *New Statesman*, which claimed that treaty revisions would appease Chinese nationalism and make it more difficult for the Bolsheviks to take advantage of the situation.[50] As the *New Statesman* argued:

> Chinese nationalism is no more the creation of Bolsheviks than is Turkish or Egyptian or Irish nationalism. All that the Bolsheviks have done is to come into China and fan the flames of discontent – an art in which they are past-masters. But the discontent was there already, and it owed its origin mainly to the Western Powers and Japan.[51]

Nevertheless, such voices were clearly the minority in Britain, not least because domestic anticommunism had a revival in 1926 following the General Strike, which lasted from 3 May to 12 May 1926. Kenneth Morgan notes about the General Strike: 'Never before had the potential economic strength of the unions in challenging the government and the constitutional order been shown with more powerful effect.'[52] The General Strike was neither organized nor controlled by Moscow. Russian money was sent to support the strikers, but it was rejected by the General Council of the TUC. Nevertheless, the Strike damaged relations between Britain and the Soviet Union because conservatives argued that the Soviet government planned to use it to overthrow the British government. This was an unrealistic claim: most trade union leaders and Labour Party members did not support the CPGB, and the CPGB and the Comintern attacked the TUC for calling the strike off after only nine days. Moreover, while membership of the CPGB increased as a result of the General Strike to about 12,000 members in October 1926, it also decreased rapidly again and by late 1927 was back to the pre-strike level of approximately 6,000. This was nothing compared to the 3,388,000

---

50 *Nineteenth Century* November 1925; *New Statesman* 27.6.1925 and 27.7.1925; *Spectator* 11.7.1925 and 18.7.1925. For the government's view see: Rigby, *May 30 Movement*, pp. 154–62; Ku, 'Urban Mass Movement', p. 208; Fung, *Diplomacy*, pp. 35–6; Goto-Shibata, *Japan*, p. 17; Edmund S.K. Fung, 'The Sino-British Rapprochement, 1927–1931', *Modern Asian Studies*, 17/1 (1983): pp. 81–4.

51 *New Statesman* 27.6.1925.

52 Kenneth Morgan, *The Oxford History of Britain* (Oxford, 2001), p. 60. For the General Strike see: TNA PRO 30/69/1274; TNA KV 4/282. See also: Lloyd, *Empire*, pp. 125–8.

members that the Labour Party had in 1926.[53] However, even Scotland Yard used the General Strike to stress the danger of the Red Menace: 'Propaganda on a scale unequalled in the history of the world has been directed against all phases of British rule and British life, and millions of pounds have been spent to further revolutionary aims in Great Britain, her Colonies and mandated territories.'[54] Thus, not only did the General Strike reinforce fears of a domestic Red Menace, it also amplified anxieties about a communist threat to the British Empire.

Unlike conservatives, the labour movement supported the Chinese strikes that took place during the May Thirtieth Movement. On 13 June 1925, the General Council of the TUC sent the Chinese Workers' Committee a telegram in which it expressed its sympathy and support for the movement's struggle for better working conditions against international capitalism.[55] The CPGB, of course, also supported the strikes and declared in 1926: 'The Chinese coolie employed in the textile factories of Shanghai and the coal mines of Central China has been degraded below the level of slavery. This degradation of the Chinese workers will be used by the British capitalists for the further degradation of the British workers.'[56] With the Comintern's control over the CPGB such a stance is hardly surprising.

Even though Scotland Yard did not consider the Labour Party as pro-communist or even communist, the conservative press ignored the deep animosity between the Labour Party and the CPGB. Consequently, in 1925 and 1926 British perceptions of the May Thirtieth Movement as evidence for the Red Menace were considerably influenced by domestic anxieties over the growing strength of the working class and the labour movement despite

---

[53]   National Union of Conservative and Constitutional Associations, *Election Notes for Conservative Speakers and Workers: General Election 1929* (London, 1929), pp. 322–3; *Die Komintern vor dem 6. Weltkongress: Tätigkeitsbericht der Exekutive der Kommunistischen Internationale für die Zeit vom 5. bis 6. Weltkongress* (Hamburg, 1928), p. 127. See also: Thorpe, *British Communist Party*, pp. 94–5; Thorpe, 'Membership', pp. 780–81 and 793; A.N. Wilson, *After the Victorians: The World Our Parents Knew* (London, 2006), p. 259; Morgan Phillips, 'Introduction: Labour Yesterday and Today', in Herbert Tracey (ed.), *The British Labour Party: Its History, Growth Policy and Leaders*, vol. 1 (London, 1948), p. 4; Margaret Morris, 'The General Strike in Retrospect', in Chris Wigley (ed.), *The British Labour Movement in the Decade after the First World War* (Loughborough, 1979), pp. 32–3; Laybourn, *Rise*, pp. 108–10; Keeble, *Britain*, p. 105; Northedge and Wells, *Britain*, pp. 44–5; Edward Hallett Carr, *Foundations of a Planned Economy, 1926–1929*, vol. 3, part 2 (London and Basingstoke, 1976), p. 318 and 323–8.

[54]   'Aspects of the General Strike', TNA KV 4/282, part I, p. 3.

[55]   Walter Citrine (ed.), *Report of Proceedings at the 57th Annual Trades Union Congress (7–12.9.1925)* (London, 1925), pp. 314–16, 320–21, 488–9; *Documents on the Shanghai Case*, p. 13; Rigby, *May 30 Movement*, pp. 153–4.

[56]   'Resolution on China', in James Klugmann, *History of the Communist Party of Great Britain, vol. 2: The General Strike* (London, 1969), pp. 330–32.

the anticommunism of the majority of the labour movement.[57] Conservative demands for an end to relations with the Soviet Union also increased, and on 15 October 1926 a 'Clear out the Reds' demonstration was held at the Royal Albert Hall, in which Conservatives like Winston Churchill and William Joynson-Hicks participated.[58] The anti-Soviet hysteria increased when news reports about anti-British agitation in Hankou reached Britain in January 1927.

'Red Terror' in 1927

After the death of Sun Yat-sen on 12 March 1925, Chiang Kai-shek (Jiang Jieshi) took over the leadership of the GMD and introduced measures to limit Communist and Comintern influence in the GMD, resulting in a power struggle between the GMD Left under the Comintern agent Borodin and the Right under Chiang. However, Chiang did not expel the Communists from the GMD because he needed Soviet financial aid and advice in order to defeat other warlords and unite China.[59] The British government was aware of Chiang's anticommunism. In October 1926, 'Notes on China' by the General Staff of the War Office stated: 'Our chief interest in China is of a commercial nature. The British Empire wishes to see China at peace, both as regards external aggression and internal wars, so that conditions may enable us to trade there in the open market.' Stressing the possibility that the GMD could expel Soviet advisers, the notes concluded: 'Political interference by the British Empire, or by any other Power, will only serve to aggravate the present unrest and to postpone the return to normal trade conditions so essential to British interests.'[60]

Two months later, the British government declared in the December Memorandum that it was willing to revise treaties in order to undo the damage done to British trade in China. The December Memorandum's promise to abstain from gunboat diplomacy was a clear effort to appease Chinese nationalism and increase

---

[57]   TNA KV 4/282. See also: Matthew Worley, *Class against Class: The Communist Party in Britain between the Wars* (London and New York, 2002), p. 53.

[58]   *The Times*, 12.6.1926. See also: Carr, *Foundations*, vol. 3, part 2, pp. 21–2.

[59]   'Chiang Kai-shek's Speech to the Military Council', in Wilbur and How, *Missionaries of Revolution*, pp. 521–2; 'Aus dem Protokoll Nr. 22 (Sondernummer 16) der Sitzung des Politbüros des ZK der KPdSU', in Russisches Zentrum für die Archivierung und Erforschung von Dokumenten zur neuesten Geschichte (ed.), *KPdSU(B), Komintern und die national-revolutionäre Bewegung in China: Dokumente, Band 2: 1926–1927*, Teil 1 (Münster, 1998), pp. 297–8. See also: Luk, *Origins*, pp. 113 and 116–22; Tim Trampedach, 'Chiang Kaishek between Revolution and Militarism, 1926/27', in Mechthild Leutner, Roland Felber, M.L. Titarenko and A.M. Grigoriev (eds), *The Chinese Revolution in the 1920s: Between Triumph and Disaster* (London and New York, 2002), pp. 128–32; Pantsov, *Bolsheviks*, pp. 85 and 127; Dan M. Jacobs, *Borodin: Stalin's Man in China* (Cambridge and London, 1981), pp. 177 and 229–32; Wilbur, *Nationalist Revolution*, pp. 78–82.

[60]   'China', 26.10.1926, TNA WO 106/79.

British trade with China. Britain's willingness to review the unequal treaties was deeply opposed by British business communities in China, which demanded a return to gunboat diplomacy in order to protect their privileges in China. British representatives in Beijing also opposed the GMD but the Foreign Office had made up its mind. The willingness of the British government, however, was soon tested when anti-British agitation broke out in the British concession at Hankou on 3 January 1927. After the concession was occupied by the Chinese, British expats in China demanded that it be recaptured, but the British government thought that this would only exacerbate anti-British feeling in China. The government was adamant that Britain's retreat from China was not supposed to look like a defeat, and that negotiations, not military actions, were the way forward. Since Hankou was unimportant, Britain should give up rights without being forced to do so because a perceived weakness in the British Empire could motivate independence movements in the colonies. As a result, British citizens were evacuated from Hankou, Jiujiang, Yichang and Changsha, and Britain officially returned its concessions in Hankou and Jiujiang to China in February 1927.[61]

Despite its opposition to gunboat diplomacy, the British government was worried after the events in Hankou that a similar situation could arise in Shanghai, and sent 20,000 British troops to Shanghai to defend British life and property in case of further anti-foreign agitation. The reinforcement was deeply opposed by the Labour Party, the Independent Labour Party and the CPGB. When the CPGB helped organize a 'Hands off China' movement in late 1926 and 1927, the conservative press had a field day, using it to denounce Bolshevik control of left-wing politics in Britain.[62] *Punch*, for example, mocked the movement with a cartoon entitled 'Communisty Singing' (Illustration 2.5), which shows a Communist agitator conducting a crowd. Above his head is a sign 'Moscow expects', on his right is a 'Hands off China' poster, on his left a poster saying

---

[61]   TNA FO 228/3297; 'Papers respecting the agreements relative to the British Concessions at Hankow and Kiukiang', *HCP*, 1927, Cmd. 2869; Woodhead, *China Year Book 1928*, pp. 739–53. See also: French, *Looking Glass*, p. 112; Remer and Palmer, *Study*, p. 128; Jacobs, *Borodin*, pp. 227–8; Fung, *Diplomacy*, pp. 9–10, 90–120 and 194–5; Wm. Roger Louis, *British Strategy in the Far East 1919–1939* (Oxford, 1971), pp. 156–60; Robert Bickers, *Britain in China: Community, Culture and Colonialism, 1900–1949* (Manchester and New York, 1999), pp. 139–40; William C. Kirby, 'The Internationalization of China: Foreign Relations at Home and Abroad in the Republican Era', in Frederic Wakeman Jr. and Richard Louis Edmonds (eds), *Reappraising Republican China* (Oxford, 2000), pp. 188–9.

[62]   'Hands off China!', 28.1.1927, TUC Library HD 8674; TNA KV 3/327; 'Weekly Note for Speakers', 3.2.1927, TUC Library HD 8674; *Daily Mirror* 10.2.1927, 14.2.1927; *Daily Express* 7.2.1927, 22.2.1927; *The Times* 3.2.1927; *Die Komintern vor dem 6. Weltkongress*, p. 141. See also: Arnold J. Toynbee, *Survey of International Affairs, 1926* (London, 1928), pp. 374–8; Fung, *Diplomacy*, pp. 120–28; Paul Doerr, *British Foreign Policy, 1919–1939* (Manchester and New York, 1998), pp. 97–8; G.D.H. Cole, *A History of the Labour Party from 1914* (London, 1969), p. 196; Thorpe, *British Communist Party*, pp. 105–6; Williams, *Labour*, pp. 31 and 44; Carr, *Foundations*, vol. 3, part 2, pp. 341–2.

''gainst king and country'. He is singing a song based on Gilbert and Sullivan's 'For he is an Englishman' from the comic opera *H.M.S. Pinafore* but the lyrics are changed so that they are no longer patriotic and nationalistic but anti-English:

> For myself have said it / And it's much to my discredit / That I am an Englishman. / Oh I wish I'd been a Rooshian, / Or a French or Turk or Prooshian, / Or perhaps a Chinaman; / But despite my aspirations / To belong to other nations, / I remain an Englishman.

The cartoon, thus, not only discredits communism by having a communist singing a ludicrous version of a song from a comic opera, it also implies that the 'Hands off China' movement is unpatriotic and part of the Red Menace.

The conservative press of course applauded the sending of troops. The *National Review*, for example, claimed that apart from the British Shanghai Defence Force, British China policy had been made according to 'Socialist and Radical wishes' and that the agreement to return the British concession in Hankou to China 'was a complete capitulation to Canton [i.e. the Nationalist government], only comparable to the abject surrender to Sinn Fein in 1921'. The journal concluded: 'Our truckling to Moscow has immensely increased the prestige of that fell and foul Power, conspicuously in China.'[63] Thus, the British military expedition to protect British interests in China was also interpreted as an anti-Bolshevist measure in Britain since the Soviet Union was thought to be responsible for the nationalist movement in China.

In March 1927, GMD troops fought and defeated troops of the warlord Sun Chuanfang in Shanghai. GMD forces did not attack foreigners or foreign-owned property because Chiang Kai-shek wanted to avoid getting the foreign forces involved in the Chinese civil war. However, clashes between GMD troops and retreating northern troops also occurred in Nanjing. These events were far more prominent in the British press because on 24 March Chinese soldiers looted the British, American and Japanese consulates, attacked and robbed various foreigners, and killed two British citizens, one American, one Japanese, one French and one Italian. About 50 foreigners (including women and children) only managed to escape with the help of naval shelling by two US destroyers and a British cruiser. Foreign diplomats and Chiang Kai-shek's faction of the GMD blamed Russian instigation for the violence in Nanjing but the Foreign Ministers in Beijing demanded an apology and retribution from the GMD.[64]

---

[63]   *National Review* April 1927.

[64]   'Bericht von A.E. Abramovič, N.A. Fokin, T.G. Mandaljan und N.M. Nasonov', in: Russisches Zentrum für die Archivierung und Erforschung von Dokumenten zur neuesten Geschichte (ed.), *KPdSU(B), Komintern und die national-revolutionäre Bewegung in China: Dokumente, Band 2: 1926–1927*, Teil 2 (Münster, 1998), pp. 856–7; Woodhead, *China Year Book 1928*, pp. 723–35. See also: Steve Smith, 'Moscow and the Second and Third Armed Uprisings in Shanghai, 1927', in Mechthild Leutner, Roland Felber, Mikhail

COMMUNISTY SINGING.

Anti-British Leader—

"For I myself have said it
And it 's much to my discredit
That I am an Englishman.

Oh, I wish I 'd been a Rooshian,
Or a French or Turk or Prooshian,
Or perhaps a Chinaman;

But despite my aspirations
To belong to other nations,
I remain an Englishman."

[*All burst into howls of humiliation.*]

Illustration 2.5   Bernard Partridge, 'Communisty Singing', *Punch* (2.3.1927)

Source: Reproduced with permission of Punch Ltd, www.punch.co.uk.

Some British cabinet members and men on the spot demanded punitive action in order to rehabilitate Britain's position in China but the Foreign Office refused, arguing that this would only lead to more tension between China and Britain and that British forces were only supposed to be used for defensive measures. Britain's hands were also tied because the USA refused to participate in sanctions.[65] Chiang, under considerable pressure from foreign governments and Chinese collaborators, reacted with the persecution and execution of Communists and labour agitators, a raid on the Soviet embassy in Beijing, and the expulsion of all Communists from the GMD in July.[66] Nevertheless, the Nanjing Incident increased the British media's portrayal of the events in China as the work of the Red Menace. A conservative pamphlet stated: 'The Truth is that the "Reds" from Moscow have got their hands on China, and are stirring up anti-British feeling, because they want to use China as a means of smashing the British Empire in the East.'[67] Even *The Times*, which had been rather moderate in 1925, now exclaimed: 'We are dealing with anti-foreignism gone crazy through the scheming of Bolshevist agents.'[68] The *Daily Mail* spoke of 'Red terror'[69] and demanded that communists be expelled from Britain.[70] An article in the *Nineteenth Century* even declared: 'All holy wars of the past fade into insignificance beside the fanatical *Jehad* of the Red International.'[71] Not all journals agreed with such a view, but those which still supported treaty revision, like the *Spectator* and the *New Statesman*, were few. Among the big

---

L. Titarenko and Alexander M. Grigoriev (eds), *The Chinese Revolution in the 1920s: Between Triumph and Disaster* (London and New York, 2002), pp. 225–31; Guillermaz, *History*, pp. 111 and 121–2; Jonathan Fenby, *Generalissimo: Chiang Kai-Shek and the China He Lost* (London, 2005), pp. 142–4; Wilbur, *Nationalist Revolution*, pp. 90–92; Pantsov, *Bolsheviks*, p. 128; Jacobs, *Borodin*, p. 241.

[65] 'Papers relating to the Nanking Incident of 21th and 25th March, 1927', *HCP*, 1927, Cmd. 2953. See also: Fung, *Diplomacy*, pp. 137–51; Wilbur, *Nationalist Revolution*, p. 93.

[66] *Die Chinesische Frage: Auf dem 8. Plenum der Exekutive der Kommunistischen Internationale* (Hamburg, 1927), pp. 7–74; *Manchester Guardian* 12.4.1927, 14.4.1927; *The Times* 7.4.1927; Wilbur and How, *Missionaries*. See also: Wilbur, *Nationalist Revolution*, pp. 96–111; Jacobs, *Borodin*, pp. 242–5; Guillermaz, *History*, pp. 119–27; Brian G. Martin, 'The Green Gang and the Guomindang State: Du Yuesheng and the Politics of Shanghai, 1927–1937', *The Journal of Asian Studies*, 54/1 (1995): pp. 64–91; Luk, *Origins*, pp. 132–4 and 138; Hans J. van de Ven, *War and Nationalism in China, 1925–1945* (London and New York, 2003), pp. 118–19; Pantsov, *Bolsheviks*, pp. 136–48; Richard C. Thornton, *The Comintern and the Chinese Communists, 1928–1931* (Seattle and London, 1969), pp. 3–29; R.K.I. Quested, *Sino-Russian Relations: A Short History* (London and New York, 2005), pp. 97–100.

[67] *'Red' Hands off China* (London, 1927).

[68] *The Times* 5.4.1927.

[69] *Daily Mail* 23.3.1927.

[70] *Daily Mail* 9.4.1927.

[71] *Nineteenth Century* April 1927.

daily newspapers, only the *Manchester Guardian* criticized use of force in China, stating: 'The longer we maintain the treaties the harder will it be to convince the Chinese that we really intend to treat them on a footing of equality.'[72]

The revival of the Red Menace in the framing of events in China in the conservative British press in 1927 also served to justify demands for an assertive British policy towards China and the Soviet Union. Relations with the Soviet Union had been shaky ever since they had been taken up in 1924. The growing anticommunist sentiment in Britain only further increased pressure on the British government to act. In December 1926, a Foreign Office memorandum on Russia stated: 'the expulsion of the Bolshevik Mission (or missions) from this country is becoming well-nigh irresistible.' However, it cautioned: 'The ejection of the Bolsheviks from this country would be a thoroughly pleasurable proceeding, but it would be rather the satisfaction of an emotion than an act of useful diplomacy.'[73] This warning had no effect on Home Secretary Joynson-Hicks, who was on an 'anti-Bolshevik crusade'.[74] He openly blamed Moscow for the British problems in China, but – typically for the Conservatives – used China to draw attention to the Soviet threat to the British Empire: 'The whole world knows that in every part where the British Empire impinges on another country there you will find Moscovite emissaries trying to stir up mischief and quite openly as a nation pledging themselves to destroy the power of our country.'[75]

Keen to find an excuse to end relations between Britain and the Soviet Union, Joynson-Hicks must have felt like he had hit the jackpot when he heard claims that the Soviet trade agency in London was used for espionage and subversion. Although the Arcos Raid carried out on 12 May 1927 found no incriminating documents, the Cabinet decided that Anglo-Soviet relations should be over. In debates in the House of Commons Baldwin, Chamberlain and Joynson-Hicks read out several Russian telegrams which had been intercepted, turning the debate 'into an orgy of governmental indiscretion about secret intelligence for which there is no parallel in modern parliamentary history'. Their plans worked and on 26 May 1927 the British Government ended diplomatic relations with the Soviet Union. The Soviet diplomatic mission was expelled and British diplomatic staff withdrawn from Moscow.[76] However, the era of the Red Menace as an enemy

---

[72]   *Manchester Guardian* 14.4.1927. See also *New Statesman* 14.5.1927; *Spectator* 14.5.1927.

[73]   J.D. Gregory, 'Russia', TNA FO 418/66.

[74]   Christopher Andrew, 'British Intelligence and the Breach with Russia in 1927', *The Historical Journal*, 25/4 (1982): p. 959.

[75]   *The Times* 5.2.1927.

[76]   'Documents illustrating the hostile activities of the Soviet Government and Third International against Great Britain', *HCP*, 1927, Cmd. 2874; TNA HO 144/7985; 'Sir Austen Chamberlain to M. Rosengolz', 26.5.1927, TNA FO 418/67; 'Note from the Soviet Government', 28.5.1927, TNA FO 418/67. See also: Harriette Flory, 'The Arcos Raid and the Rupture of Anglo-Soviet Relations, 1927', *Journal of Contemporary History*, 12/4

image in Britain was not yet over. Communist threats to the British Empire and British interests in China remained a cause for concern for the British government, as will be shown in Chapter 4.

The USA

Anticommunism in the USA

While events in China in the mid-1920s were instrumentalized by the conservative British newspaper barons to discredit the British labour movement and increase anticommunist sentiment in Britain, in the USA the press chose different frames and did not focus on the Red Menace despite widespread anticommunist sentiment and strong public opposition to the Soviet Union. In part, this was because the American press was not dominated by a small number of newspaper barons to the degree it was in Britain. Of course, there were newspaper barons like William Randolph Hearst and Joseph Pulitzer. However, by the 1920s, many American newspaper owners gave their papers more leeway when it came to editorial policy, or insisted on objective reporting as Adolph Ochs did in the *New York Times*. Ochs wanted to establish the *New York Times* as a paper that not only focused on news but reported it as accurately and objectively as possible.[77] In the 1920s, the *New York Times* was not the only paper that refused to print sensational articles about the events in China. Even the anticommunist Robert R. McCormick of the *Chicago Tribune*, who made sure that his newspaper took a conservative stance, did not enforce an anticommunist perspective with regard to events in China.[78]

Another reason was that the political climate was different in the USA. M.J. Heale has convincingly argued that a constant fear in American society has been the enemy within. First it was personified by British spies, then Catholics and in the late nineteenth century by socialists and communists. Political radicalism was seen as un-American because of its repudiation of traditional American values that were linked to the republican system (i.e. individual liberties, private property and political democracy), and because of the importance of religion and patriotism for American society. As socialism was popular among many immigrants, socialists were considered to be foreigners or aliens, not American citizens. Thus, it was perceived as both unnatural and unpatriotic for Americans to be socialist, and organized labour as well as labour unrest were deemed the work of foreign

---

(1977): pp. 707–8; Andrew, 'British Intelligence', pp. 962–4 (quote 963); Worley, *Class*, pp. 65–6; Northedge and Wells, *Britain*, pp. 43–4; Arnold J. Toynbee, *Survey of International Affairs, 1927* (London, 1929), pp. 266–73; Keeble, *Britain*, pp. 108–10; McDermott and Agnew, *Comintern*, p. 71.

[77] Meyer Berger, *The Story of the New York Times, 1851–1951* (New York, 1951), pp. 107–18.

[78] Copeland, *The Media's Role*; Emery, Emery and Roberts, *The Press and America*.

agitators. Antisocialist and antianarchist sentiment led to the Immigration Act of 1903, which made it legal to exclude immigrants because of their political beliefs. It also prevented the naturalization of anarchists that were already in the USA. Socialism and communism continued to be perceived as a threat to the American society as industrialization spread class struggle across the USA from the eastern cities to the orchards, mines and lumber camps of the west and southwest. In 1905, the revolutionary union Industrial Workers of the World (IWW) was founded. Its members were mostly unskilled migratory workers, many of them immigrants. As the IWW often reverted to strikes to fight for worker's rights, it was associated with anarchy and revolution.[79]

During the First World War, the Wilson Administration actively mobilized patriotic sentiments: The Committee on Public Information started a propaganda campaign which presented the war as a holy mission and any kind of objection to the USA's participation in it as unpatriotic. As both the Socialist Party (founded in 1901) and the IWW opposed the war, their members were portrayed as enemies of the American Republic and were attacked by vigilante groups like the American Protective League, the Knights of Liberty, the National Security League and the American Defense Society, which policed the home front. Legal measures were also used to curb radicalism, for example the Espionage Act of 1917 and the Sedition Act of 1918 were used to silence and prosecute over 2,000 radicals and opponents of the war, and the Immigration Act of 1918 provided for the deportation of radical aliens who advocated anarchy or supported a violent overthrow of the government. As a result, subversion was associated with foreign values and foreigners.[80]

The antiradical measures could not prevent the Socialist Party's membership increasing from 20,000 in 1917 to 110,000 in 1919. In 1919, two American Communist Parties were also founded: the Communist Labor Party, which was led by John Reed, William Bross Lloyd and Benjamin Gitlow, and the Communist Party of America led by Charles Ruthenberg, Louis Fraina and Nicholas Hourwich. The propagation of revolution by the Communist Parties caused a general movement to the right by both Republicans and Democrats. Moreover, since membership in the American communist movement was dominated by immigrants, the perception increased that communism as a foreign ideology was incompatible with American

---

[79]   M.J. Heale, *American Anticommunism: Combating the Enemy Within, 1830–1970* (Baltimore and London, 1990), pp. 3–5, 9–16, 44–9 and 58–9; Peter H. Buckingham, *America Sees Red: Anti-Communism in America 1870s to 1980s* (Claremont, 1988), pp. 2–11.

[80]   Ellen Schrecker, *Many Are the Crimes: McCarthyism in America* (Princeton, 1998), pp. 53–4; Buckingham, *America*, pp. 11–20; Heale, *Anticommunism*, 49–59; Maldwyn A. Jones, *The Limits of Liberty: American History 1607–1992*, 2nd ed. (Oxford and New York, 1995), p. 370; Hixson, *Myth*, pp. 127–9.

values. As John E. Haynes points out: 'To many Americans, communism was a godless abomination.'[81]

The First World War had not only increased the opposition to socialists and syndicalism, it also introduced instruments of repression that would become useful during the Red Scare in 1919 and 1920. During these years, industrial conflict peaked. The October Revolution in Russia and an increase in communist activities in Europe also had the effect that once again radicals, especially communists, were seen as threatening the American Republic. In January 1919, a general strike was held by the Seattle shipyard workers. When they were joined on 6 February by 110 unions from the city, new fears of the Red Menace were roused. This was not completely unfounded as some of the workers indeed sympathized with Bolshevism and the IWW propagated general strikes as instruments of revolution.[82] Beginning in the spring of 1919, fears of radicalism grew after bombs exploded or were found in the mail of various public figures, officials and businessmen. Several strikes in autumn 1919 including a police strike in Boston and strikes in the steel and coal industries strengthened the belief that revolutionaries had infiltrated the labour movement and were planning to overthrow the American government. Attorney General A. Mitchell Palmer, at whose house one of the bombs had exploded, started the so-called Palmer Raids, a crusade in which he persecuted radicals with the help of J. Edgar Hoover, head of the General Intelligence Division of the Justice Department. The Palmer Raids began on 7 November 1919, mostly targeting the Union of Russian Workers but also other radicals, especially anarchists. At least 246 of these radicals were deported to Russia in December on the *Buford*, also known as the Soviet Ark. The Red Scare reached its peak during the second group of raids which took place between 2 and 5 January 1920, when over 6,000 suspected radicals, among them many members of the Communist Parties, were arrested all over the USA. In May 1920, a federal judge ruled that membership in one of the Communist Parties alone was not reason enough for deportation. The public mood also changed after it became known that many law-abiding citizens had been arrested, detained, mistreated and occasionally even died in custody.

---

[81]   John E. Haynes, *Red Scare or Red Menace? American Communism and Anticommunism in the Cold War Era* (Chicago, 1996), p. 7. See also: Hugh Wilford, 'The Communist International and the American Communist Party', in Tim Rees and Andrew Thorpe (eds), *International Communism and the Communist International 1919–43* (Manchester and New York, 1998), p. 226; Heale, *Anticommunism*, p. 65; Richard Gid Powers, *Not without Honor: The History of American Anticommunism* (New York, 1995), p. 24; Harvey Klehr, John Earl Haynes and Kyrill M. Anderson, *The Soviet World of American Communism* (New Haven and London, 1998), pp. 15–16.

[82]   Ted Morgan, *Reds: McCarthyism in Twentieth-Century America* (New York, 2003), pp. 64–9; Schrecker, *Crimes*, pp. 55–6; Heale, *Anticommunism*, pp. 60–68 and 77–8; Buckingham, *America*, pp. 19 and 21.

This together with an absence of big strikes and bombings before September 1920 turned public opinion against red-hunting.[83]

The Red Scare affected American public opinion to such a degree that communism remained an enemy image throughout the 1920s and not only proved very effective against radicalism in the USA but also practically destroyed the American Left and massively reduced the labour movement's militancy. Both Communist Parties had lost the majority of their members and were forced to go underground, the Socialist Party was weakened, the IWW was almost completely destroyed and the American Federation of Labor had become a staunch antiradical organization. Antiradicalism and anticommunism were further ingrained in US society through churches and patriotic societies like the National Security League, the National Civic Federation and the American Defense Society. Moreover, organizations such as the American Legion, the Ku Klux Klan and the Knights of Columbus had enthusiastically supported the Red Scare, and their countersubversive ideology remained active long after the Red Scare had subsided. Antiradicalism also had legal repercussions: by 1921, 35 states had passed sedition or criminal syndicalism laws allowing the prosecution of radicals.[84]

The Red Menace was employed as an enemy image by various groups for different arguments: political groups and politicians used it to discredit their political enemies, business associations relied on it to increase their influence over the government and fight against unionism, religious groups condemned the antireligious stance of communism and socialism, and various groups used it against East and Southeast European immigrants. The anticommunism of the 1920s was part of a wider social movement towards cultural hegemony which together with the isolationist policy of the USA led to a rejection of foreign influences and associated radicalism with immigrants. The idea that Anglo-Saxon purity could only be preserved by getting rid of all foreign influences led to the Immigrant Acts of 1921 and 1924, which established a quota system in which those countries where immigrants had traditionally been coming from received higher quotas than the newer immigrant countries.[85]

---

[83]   The numbers vary from author to author: Norman E. Saul, *Friends or Foes? The United States and Russia, 1921–1941* (Lawrence, 2006), pp. 6–7; Powers, *Not without Honor*, pp. 22–31; Schrecker, *Crimes*, pp. 57–60; Morgan, *Reds*, pp. 72–83; Heale, *Anticommunism*, pp. 63–76; Katherine A.S. Siegel, *Loans and Legitimacy: The Evolution of Soviet-American Relations, 1919–1939* (Lexington, 1996), p. 23.

[84]   Heale, *Anticommunism*, pp. 66–7, 73–5 and 88–9; Schrecker, *Crimes*, p. 60–64; Buckingham, *America*, pp. 11–29; Powers, *Not without Honor*, pp. 28 and 38–9; Saul, *Friends*, p. 7.

[85]   John Higham, *Strangers in the Land: Patterns of American Nativism 1860–1925*, 2nd ed. (Westport, 1963), pp. 300–330; Buckingham, *America*, pp. 31–6; Powers, *Not without Honor*, pp. 79–82; Heale, *Anticommunism*, pp. 40–41 and 80–88; Schrecker, *Crimes*, pp. 61–4; Saul, *Friends*, p. 18.

The labour movement was also largely anticommunist because many unionists were Catholic and the Catholic Church condemned communism. In 1922, American Federation of Labor leader Samuel Gompers criticized Soviet efforts to infiltrate the labour movement and opposed recognition of the Soviet Union by the USA. One year later, the American Federation of Labor expelled communist trade unionists because of their link with the Comintern. Like their British counterpart, American Communist Parties were indeed subservient to the Comintern, and followed its orders to merge by forming the aboveground American Workers' Party in 1921, which was renamed Communist Party of the USA (CPUSA) in 1929. During the 1920s, the Comintern also sent agents to the USA to assist and oversee the Communist Party, and US Communists went to Moscow to participate in Comintern conferences, worked in Comintern agencies or were trained in Comintern schools. Most of the Comintern's ideology was taken on by the American Communists, and Comintern funding was used to print pamphlets, pay professional revolutionaries and generally implement Comintern policies.[86] Harvey Klehr, John Earl Haynes and Kyrill M. Anderson point out:

> [A]t every period of the CPUSA's history, the American Communists looked to their Soviet counterparts for advice on how to conduct their own party business. … the CPUSA was never an independent political organization. There were moments when it was less strictly controlled by Moscow than at others, but there was never a time when the CPUSA made its decisions autonomously, without being obliged to answer to or – more precisely – without *wishing* to answer to Soviet authority.[87]

While the control that the Comintern had over the Communist Party had already cost it the support of many sympathizers, party unity also suffered from ethnic and regional differences. This together with the large number of foreign (i.e. non-naturalized) members made the Communist Party un-American in the eyes of many Americans.[88]

Anticommunists, Missionaries and the Red Menace in China

In light of the antiradical and anticommunist sentiment that existed in the USA in the 1920s and evidence of communist agitation in China, it is very interesting that hardly any US newspapers or magazines considered the events in China between 1925 and 1927 as proof of the growing influence of communism. A very typical

---

[86] *New York Times* 1.5.1922. See also: Klehr, Haynes and Anderson, *Soviet World*; Saul, *Friends*, pp. 18–19 and 32; Haynes, *Red Scare*, p. 10; Schrecker, *Crimes*, pp. 10–11; Wilford, 'The Communist International', p. 226; Heale, *Anticommunism*, pp. 92–5.

[87] Klehr, Haynes and Anderson, *Soviet World*, p. 4.

[88] Wilford, 'The Communist International', p. 226; Heale, *Anticommunism*, p. 90; Saul, *Friends*, pp. 18–19; Klehr, Haynes and Anderson, *Soviet World*, p. 6.

American press reaction to the anti-foreign agitation in China in the mid-1920s is the following statement from the *Christian Century* which argued: 'the Chinese government is not communist just because it accepts Soviet help.'[89] Another very prominent view was expressed by the *Chicago Tribune*, which stated: 'if there were not a strong nationalist feeling in China to work upon, the Russian propaganda would get nowhere.'[90] This is not what one would expect from the press of a society where anticommunism is rampant, let alone from a decidedly anticommunist newspaper. One explanation for the absence of Red Menace frames for the May Thirtieth Movement in the US press is that anticommunist organizations in the USA failed to instrumentalize the Red Menace in the way that the Conservative Party had in Britain. This cannot have been solely due to the fact that the US labour movement was anticommunist and, thus, not a safe haven for communists because the same was true of the labour movement in Britain. The political situation in Britain and the USA differed, however, in at least one respect: while the American Left was very weak in the mid 1920s, in Britain the Labour Party challenged the Conservative Party's leading position in British politics. Although fears of a left-wing takeover did not subside in the USA, American antiradical sentiment in the 1920s had the effect that radical groups were increasingly isolated. As a result, 'communism and anticommunism were peripheral issues to most Americans during the 1920s.' Moreover, anticommunist organizations in the USA followed no common agenda apart from being anticommunist.[91] It is, therefore, possible that because left-wing organizations were too weak to play an active part in US politics during the 1920s, the threat of socialism and communism in politics was not considered as great in the USA as in Britain, and consequently, the Red Menace was not used by the US press to frame events in China.

Another aspect which influenced the perception of the Red Menace in the USA was relations with the Soviet Union. Unlike Britain, the USA refused to recognize the Soviet Union in the 1920s. The Colby Note from August 1920, which remained fundamental for US policy towards the Soviet Union until the early 1930s, stated that the US government would not recognize the Bolshevik government because of Communism's goal of world revolution. Reasons for the non-recognition of the Soviet Union also included the refusal of the Bolshevik government to pay back loans made out to the provisional government in 1917, the seizing of American property and subversive activities in the USA.[92] However, due to the non-recognition policy adopted by the State Department, public discussion of Soviet-American relations seems to have been minimal except within business circles and was not an issue for the majority of US society.[93] As a result, the impact

---

[89]   *Christian Century* 31.3.1927.

[90]   *Chicago Tribune* 8.6.1925.

[91]   Haynes, *Red Scare*, pp. 3, 10(quote)–11; Powers, *Not without Honor*, pp. 72–9; Heale, *Anticommunism*, p. 90.

[92]   Siegel, *Loans*; Saul, *Friends*; Morgan, *Reds*, pp. 71–2.

[93]   Buckingham, *America*, pp. 36–7; Heale, *Anticommunism*, pp. 87–9.

of the Red Menace as a catchphrase in American society was limited and further explains the absence of newspaper articles linking China policy with Soviet policy, as was the case in Britain where events in China were used to demand an end of British relations with the Soviet Union. One also has to remember that for the USA the biggest rival in China after the First World War was not Russia but Japan because Japanese expansion threatened US economic presence in China and the Philippines (see Chapter 3). Britain, on the other hand, viewed Russian expansion as more problematic. Moreover, the Comintern's programme for world revolution did not affect the USA like it did the British Empire because the Philippines and Puerto Rico were not as significant for US nationalism as the British colonies – especially India – were for British nationalism.[94]

There are also local issues which contributed to the public and media's disinterest in the Red Menace as a frame for events in China. The city of Chicago, for example, was gripped by its gang wars and the underworld figure Al Capone. As a result, the *Chicago Tribune* reasserted its opposition to the Prohibition Agreement and focused its articles on organized crime in Chicago. Moreover, for years, the *Chicago Tribune*'s editor Robert McCormick was occupied with plotting the downfall of Chicago's mayor William 'Big Bill' Thompson, using the paper to accuse Thompson of corruption, inefficiency and incompetence. The *Chicago Tribune*, therefore, had two evils at hand which held greater relevance to the local readers than did the Red Menace. Indeed, until the early 1930s, Robert McCormick himself, an avid anticommunist and antisocialist, thought the repeal of the Eighteenth Amendment to be of greater importance than fighting communist subversion.[95] In the mid-1920s, the *Washington Post* was likewise preoccupied with other things, as its owner, Ned McLean was personally involved in the Teapot Dome scandal, so naturally, the newspaper's focus was on the scandal. Other topics of interest during these years were the Prohibition and the Ku Klux Klan.[96]

In areas such as the West Coast and New York, the anticommunist stance of Chinese American communities was probably another influence upon the public perception of events in China. Most Chinese immigrants in the USA sought to earn as much money as possible, and this capitalist attitude went against communist ideology. Many also sent money back to relatives in China or invested in real estate, businesses or railroads in China. This money would have been lost under a communist system that condemned the accumulation of private property. Many overseas Chinese were increasingly alienated by Sun Yat-sen's alliance with the Soviet Union and his cooperation with the CCP, and many Chinese American newspapers portrayed communism negatively.[97] As a result of all these factors, the

---

[94] See MacKenzie, *Propaganda and Empire*; Imam, *Colonialism*, pp. 46–7 and 479; Louis, 'Introduction', p. 5.

[95] Lloyd Wendt, *Chicago Tribune: The Rise of a Great American Newspaper* (Chicago, New York and San Francisco, 1979).

[96] Roberts, *Shadow*, pp. 170–82.

[97] Chen, *Being Chinese*, pp. 133–45.

US press was aware of the fact that Comintern agents were involved in the anti-foreign movement in China, but did not find it alarming.

In fact, most American newspapers and journals argued that Bolshevism played a negligible part in the movement. *Harper's Magazine* claimed: 'Ten years of even the most consummate Bolshevik propaganda cannot account for the anti-Western movements in China or elsewhere.'[98] The tabloid *The New York World* also remained unfazed by cries about Red Menace:

> No doubt Russian orators have been busy in China in late years. But the Nationalist movement had steam up before they came. It is perfectly natural for Moscow to be claiming credit for a great deed done. Moscow would claim credit for an uprising at the Pole. The Third International lives by hurrying from spot to spot to get in on the picture when the camera clicks.[99]

Several magazines pointed out the anti-Chinese bias in press reports about China. For example *Time* reminded its readers: 'all communications from that once celestial land are more or less colored.'[100] The socialist journal *The Nation* tried to be more objective: 'That the rise of anti-Christian sentiment in China should be immediately attributed to the agitation of Russian agents was inevitable. Every development in whatever corner of the world that has gone against the Western status quo during the past seven years has been laid at the gate of the Kremlin.' *The Nation* then pointed out the influence of communist ideology on Chinese students, but reminded its readers: 'Russian influence, at the most, has only served to supply a precedent for a certain line of development which other circumstances made inevitable.'[101]

The most common reaction in the US press was that the May Thirtieth Movement was a nationalistic movement against the unequal treaties, not the beginning of a communist revolution in China. This was also the view that was propagated by missionary organizations in the USA, who demanded treaty negotiations. Missionary organizations had established a very efficient network in the USA through which they managed to reach a large part of US society with their interpretation of the events which held that Chinese nationalism was awakening to fight against foreign imperialism and deserved the sympathy of the American people.[102] American missionary interests comprised a substantial share of the total interest of the USA in China. While out of 15,247 British expats

---

[98]   *Harper's* September 1927.

[99]   *The World* 23.3.1927.

[100]   *Time* 20.7.1925; see also *The World* 7.6.1925; *Nation* 6.4.1927 and 16.3.1927.

[101]   *The Nation* 17.6.1925.

[102]   NA RG 59 711.93/10; 711.93/106; 711.93/126. See also: John W. Masland, 'Missionary Influence upon American Far Eastern Policy', *The Pacific Historical Review*, 10/3 (1941): pp. 279–96; Varg, *Missionaries*, pp. 194–211; Dorothy Borg, *American Policy and the Chinese Revolution, 1925–1928* (New York, 1947), pp. 25–6 and 79–88.

in China only about 1,400 were missionaries in 1925, about half of the 9,844 Americans in China were missionaries. Thus, American missionaries were not only the largest group of foreign missionaries in China, they also influenced – if not dominated – American interests in China.[103] It has been pointed out in the previous chapter that already before the 1920s the American government and American missionary organizations portrayed China as a pupil of the USA, and thereby reinforced the belief that the USA was on a divine mission to spread democracy and progress. As liberalism increased among American missionaries, many questioned the legitimacy of Western imperialism. Missionaries were also faced with a movement against their control of schools, colleges and universities in China, demands that these schools were put under Chinese administration, and that the mandatory instruction of religion was halted. Since extraterritoriality had made missionaries unpopular in Chinese society and hindered their work, young missionaries in particular supported treaty revisions.[104] Missionary societies also acted as pressure groups both in the USA, where they mobilized public support for treaty negotiations, and in China, where they tried to influence the media discourse on China via foreign correspondents and US diplomats. They were, thus, a huge influence on American media images of China.[105]

What is striking about US press articles on China in the mid-1920s, is their focus on the missionaries: almost all newspapers analysed in this study reported the experiences of local missionaries stationed in China and printed letters they sent to their families along with photos of the missionaries. Media criticism of missionaries was very rare.[106] Missionary thinking also influenced American perceptions of the events in China to such a degree because it was central to the discursive construction of American nationhood: not only did religion play a central role in American society and culture, US foreign policy was driven by a sense of moral duty and the belief in America's (social, political and moral) superiority.[107] As a result, most newspapers stressed the USA's friendship with China and the role of the USA as a mentor of Chinese democracy. The following quote from the *New York Times* is a typical example of this:

---

[103]   Harlan P. Beach and Charles H. Fahs (eds), *World Missionary Atlas* (New York, 1925), p. 83; Woodhead, *China Year Book 1928*, p. 4; Borg, *American Policy*, p. 68; Wm. Roger Louis, 'Introduction', in Judith M. Brown and Wm. Roger Louis (eds), *The Oxford History of the British Empire, vol. 4: The Twentieth Century* (Oxford and New York, 1999), p. 17.

[104]   *New York Times* 17.3.1927; *Nation* 30.3.1927. See also: Lian, *Conversion*, pp. 12–13; Jessie Gregory Lutz, *China and the Christian Colleges, 1850–1950* (Ithaca and London, 1971), pp. 232–46; Varg, *Missionaries*, pp. 180–82, 195–8 and 202–11; Borg, *American Policy*, p. 83; Woodhead, *China Year Book 1926–7*, pp. 434 a and b.

[105]   Borg, *American Revolution*, pp. 25–6 and 70–88; Varg, *Missionaries*, p. 146.

[106]   See for example *New York Times* 31.3.1927.

[107]   Pierce, *Woodrow Wilson*, pp. 9–62; Stephanson, *Manifest Destiny*; Varg, *Missionaries*, pp. 81–5; Ryan, *US Foreign Policy*, pp. 22–9; Hixson, *Myth*, pp. 13 and 121.

What China Really Needs

Illustration 2.6   William Charles Morris, 'What China Really Needs',
Los Angeles Times (18.7.1925)

During the last quarter century or more we have taken it upon ourselves to befriend and protect the Chinese. Even should we no longer wish to do so, we cannot escape the moral responsibility that we have incurred, nor can we remain indifferent to the repercussion of Chinese troubles in other parts of the Far East.[108]

Such paternalism is also expressed in Illustration 2.6 by William Charles Morris entitled 'What China Really Needs'. It portrays an exhausted, haggard-looking China being weighed down by 'foreign impositions' that are chained to its neck, requiring support by 'the friendly hands of the nations' to stand upright. The cartoon not only criticizes the foreign powers' informal imperialism in China, it also portrays China as a helpless nation, and served as a reminder to its audience that the USA was not part of the imperial presence since it had no sphere of interest in China. Thus, the cartoon depicts China in a positive light and at the same time manages to legitimize American geopolitical interest in the Far East.

Friendship, Democracy and American Exceptionalism

National self-perception of the USA as a champion of democracy and national self-determination had been reinforced during the First World War by the Wilson Administration and propaganda campaigns. As David Reynolds points out, Wilson's argument that the USA had to fight to make the world safe for democracy justified the USA's entry into the war 'as a global crusade'.[109] This meant that any kind of action by the US government that violated the sovereignty of another democracy had to be well justified, especially following the public uproar after the US government agreed at Versailles to give the former German possession in Shandong to Japan and not China.[110] As a result, in the mid-1920s, the Red Menace as a legitimization of using force in China was not very popular in the US press. In fact, most American newspapers outright opposed using force. Illustration 2.7 by William Charles Morris depicts the USA, i.e. Uncle Sam, as ignoring ('I Can't

---

[108]   *New York Times* 27.6.1925. See also: *Washington Post* 21.6.1925, 12.7.1925, 20.7.1925; *Chicago Tribune* 31.3.1927.

[109]   David Reynolds, *From Munich to Pearl Harbor: Roosevelt's America and the Origins of the Second World War* (Chicago, 2001), p. 27.

[110]   Bruce A. Elleman, *Wilson and China: A Revised History of the Shandong Question* (Armonk and London, 2002), pp. 73–134; Noel H. Pugach, 'American Friendship for China and the Shantung Question at the Washington Conference', *The Journal of American History*, 64/1 (1977): pp. 69–70; David F. Trask, 'Sino-Japanese-American Relations during the Paris Peace Conference of 1919', in Thomas H. Etzold (ed.), *Aspects of Sino-American Relations since 1784* (New York and London, 1978), pp. 95–7; John A. Thompson, *Woodrow Wilson* (London, 2002), pp. 209–10; Hans Schmidt, 'Democracy for China: American Propaganda and the May Fourth Movement', *Diplomatic History*, 22/1 (1998): pp. 1–28.

Uncle Sam: "I Can't Hear You, Boys!"

Illustration 2.7   William Charles Morris, 'Uncle Sam: "I Can't Hear You Boys!"', *Los Angeles Times* (15.12.1926)

Hear You, Boys!') cries from Britain and Japan who are shouting: 'Let us intervene in China! We've got to make a joint demand on China and back it up by force.' As Britain and Japan were most often used both by journalists and cartoonists to negatively portray foreign imperial powers in China, the cartoon links the rejection of using force against China with American opposition to imperialism in China, while the size of the rifles is a clear condemnation of the use of force.

Instead of blaming the Red Menace for the events in China, the majority of the American press demanded treaty negotiations and argued that Soviet agitation was only successful because the imperial powers, which were usually defined as Britain, France and Japan, were unwilling to revise treaties with China.[111] The *Washington Post* wrote:

> China will not be completely independent until she is in control of her own customs and her own administration of justice. Hence the movement to gain control of customs and administration of justice is a movement toward securing a government of the people, by the people, for the people. That is a movement that commands the sympathy and moral support of every true American.[112]

By appealing to American Exceptionalism and the idea of the USA as the protector of democracy, newspapers and magazines established a link between the events in China and US nationalism that encouraged readers to take a personal interest in affairs in China and to support Chinese demands for treaty negotiations.

The refusal of the US press – including publications such as the *Washington Post*, which had been staunchly anticommunist during the Red Scare – to use the Red Menace as a frame to legitimize the use of force in China during the mid-1920s was in line with US China policy. In 1925, Nelson T. Johnson, the Chief of the Division of Far Eastern Affairs, influenced Secretary of State Frank B. Kellogg with his sympathetic view towards the Chinese and the conviction that the USA should assist China. As a result, the State Department opposed using force for reasons other than the protection of American lives and property, and instead thought that the unstable political situation required leniency on the side of the foreign powers. This policy was supported by Congress; various resolutions were introduced to the House of Representatives which demanded the recognition of the Nationalist government of Chiang Kai-shek and/or treaty negotiations. This caused the State Department to publish a statement on 27 January 1927 which asserted its willingness to enter into treaty negotiations with China concerning

---

[111]   *Chicago Tribune* 8.6.1925, 16.6.1925, 27.6.1925, 16.7.1925, 31.3.1927, 25.4.1927; *Time* 22.6.1925, 20.7.1925; *The World* 23.3.1927; *New York Times* 20.6.1925, 2.7.1925; *Los Angeles Times* 1.4.1927; *Washington Post* 6.6.1925, 12.7.1925, 20.7.1925; *Harper's* 9.1927; *Christian Century* 6.1.1927, 3.2.1927, 10.2.1927; Nicholas Roosevelt, 'Russia and Great Britain', *Foreign Affairs* (1926/1927): pp. 80–90; 'The Crux of China', *North American Review*, March–May (1927): pp. 2–4.

[112]   *Washington Post* 12.7.1925.

tariff autonomy and extraterritoriality once a representative Chinese government adequately protected foreigners.[113] The Coolidge Administration continued to stress the friendship between China and the USA even after the Nanjing Incident occurred, as the following excerpt from a speech by President Coolidge distributed by United Press demonstrates:

> The friendship of America for China has become proverbial. We feel for her the deepest sympathy in these times of her distress. We have no disposition to do otherwise than to assist and encourage every legitimate aspiration for freedom, for unity, for the cultivation of a national spirit, and the realization of a republican form of government.[114]

The only interest group that blamed the Comintern and/or the Soviet Union for the events in China and demanded an armed intervention was that of business organizations. This is hardly surprising since they were affected by the anti-foreign movement in China. Some American businessmen even suffered from the anti-British boycott in 1925/1926 because they relied on British ships or worked for international companies like the British-American Tobacco Company. As a result, US business organizations in China like the American Chambers of Commerce in Shanghai, Hankou, Tianjin, Beijing and Harbin tried to present an image of China as an El Dorado for the US economy that was threatened by Chinese nationalism and Bolshevism. They opposed further treaty negotiations and demanded an armed intervention in cooperation with other powers.[115] However, while businessmen expected that they would make less profit if the treaties between China and the

---

[113]   NA RG 59 711.93/111, 115A, 116A and 135A; 'Memorandum by the Under Secretary of State', 6.6.1925, in *FRUS 1925*, pp. 657–8; 'The Secretary of State to the Minister in China', 23.12.1926, in *FRUS 1926*, p. 663; 'The Chargé in China to the Secretary of State', 26.6.1925, in *FRUS 1925*, pp. 765–6; 'The Chargé in China to the Secretary of State', 10.7.1925, in *FRUS 1925*, pp. 778–9; 'The Minister in China to the Secretary of State', 28.12.1926, in *FRUS 1926*, p. 929. See also: Borg, *American Policy*, pp. 253–66; Russell D. Buhite, 'Nelson Johnson and American Policy toward China, 1925–1928', *The Pacific Historical Review*, 35/4 (1966): p. 455; Thomas Buckley, 'John VanAntwerp MacMurray: The Diplomacy of an American Mandarin', in Richard Dean Burns and Edward M. Bennett (eds), *Diplomats in Crisis: United States – Chinese – Japanese Relations, 1919–1941* (Santa Barbara and Oxford, 1974), pp. 38–9; L. Ethan Ellis, *Frank B. Kellogg and American Foreign Relations, 1925–1929* (New Brunswick, 1961), pp. 130–31; Shizhang Hu, *Stanley K. Hornbeck and the Open Door Policy, 1919–1937* (Westport and London, 1995), p. 78.

[114]   'The Secretary of State to the Minister in China', 27.4.1927, in *FRUS 1927*, pp. 118–19.

[115]   'Report of the Annual Meeting of the Associated American Chambers of Commerce of China, at Shanghai, October 16 and 17, 1923', undated, in *FRUS 1924*, pp. 580–94; *Chicago Tribune* 27.6.1925. See also Ellis, *Kellogg*, p. 120; Buhite, 'Johnson', p. 457; Hu, *Hornbeck*, pp. 80–81; Borg, *American Policy*, p. 429; Varg, *Missionaries*, pp. 198–9.

foreign powers were renegotiated because of higher tariffs, the general public in the USA was not directly affected by a renegotiation. Consequently, it supported treaty negotiations and viewed the US willingness to do so as a generous offer to the fledgling Chinese Republic. For example, the *Chicago Tribune* wrote: 'Our policy should express and does express the friendliness of the American people for the Chinese and our willingness to aid them, if possible, to peace and progress.'[116] The fact that the majority of the American press opposed the use of force and supported the China policy of the State Department seems to have made quite an impact on Kellogg, as he regularly sent the Minister in China, John Van Antwerp MacMurray, summaries of US press comments on US China policy.[117]

Contrary to the British Foreign Office, which followed communist agitation in China very closely and often discussed it, the State Department seems not to have considered it an important issue, even though MacMurray repeatedly mentioned communist influence in the nationalist movement in his reports. Even in 1927, when almost the entire British press jumped on the Red Menace bandwagon, the US press and the Coolidge Administration interpreted the events in China as a civil war or a revolution, not as an anti-foreign movement. For example, Kellogg rejected sanctions against Chiang's government and argued that, as long as the revolution in China went on, the USA should stay out of affairs in China and wait until things had settled down.[118] Such a view was also shared by the American media. Even after an American citizen was killed during the Nanjing Incident, media reactions remained mostly calm, some were even sympathetic. Instead of describing the Nanjing Incident as evidence of the Comintern's planned world revolution like most British papers, American publications maintained that the Nanjing Incident had not been orchestrated by the Comintern but was simply an extremely unfortunate incident in a civil war.[119] For example the *New York Times* wrote: 'It must patiently be borne in mind that when a nation passes through a social struggle many unintended events will occur that will later be keenly

---

[116]   *Chicago Tribune* 31.3.1927.

[117]   'The Secretary of State to the Minister in China', 14.4.1927, in *FRUS 1927*, pp. 194–5; 'The Consul General at Hankow to the Minister for Foreign Affairs of the Nationalist Government', 11.4.1927, in *FRUS 1927*, pp. 189–90.

[118]   NA RG 59 893.00 B/171; Letter to ambassador B. Houghton, 2.5.1927, Frank B. Kellogg Papers, roll 25; Letter to Walter Lippmann, 24.5.1927, Frank B. Kellogg Papers roll 26; 'The Chargé in China to the Secretary of State', 2.6.1925, in *FRUS 1925*, p. 740; 'The Chargé in China to the Secretary of State', 13.6.1925, in *FRUS 1925*, p. 728. See also: Borg, *American Policy*, pp. 122–53 and 423–4; Ellis, *Kellogg*, pp. 137–40; Herbert J. Wood, 'Nelson Trusler Johnson: The Diplomacy of Benevolent Pragmatism', in Richard Dean Burns and Edward M. Bennett (eds), *Diplomats in Crisis: United States – Chinese – Japanese Relations, 1919–1941* (Santa Barbara and Oxford, 1974), pp. 7–26.

[119]   *Christian Century* 7.10.1926, 2.12.1926; *New York Times* 13.3.1927, 27.3.1927, 16.4.1927.

regretted.'[120] Others pointed out that one murder was not yet reason for national hysteria. The *Christian Century* reminded its readers: 'foreigners have killed hundreds of Chinese for every foreigner who has been killed in China.'[121] Thus, despite the presence of the Red Menace as a domestic enemy image, it was hardly used by the American press to frame events in China in the mid-1920s because both American governments and American missionary organizations legitimized their interests and presence in China by constructing images of China that were directly linked with the discursive construction of nationhood and, consequently, served to reinforce perceptions of Americans that their country was on a global mission to spread democracy and progress.

Switzerland

The Red Menace in Switzerland

A comparison of British and American press reactions to those of Swiss newspapers and magazines is interesting because it highlights how crucial national interests and the conceptualization of nationhood were for the media's portrayal of the events in China. Swiss interests in China differed greatly from those of Britain and the USA. Unlike the British press, the Swiss media did not use the Red Menace as an enemy image in reference to China during the mid-1920s, even though it relied on British newspapers like *The Times*, *Daily Telegraph*, *Daily Mail*, *Morning Post*, *Westminster Gazette* and the British press agency Reuters for information about the events in China. Swiss newspapers also used French and American newspapers and press agencies. Part of this reliance on foreign sources was due to the lack of correspondents in China but, as has already been pointed out in the previous chapter, the Swiss press also generally used foreign newspapers and press agencies as sources. It is striking how the Swiss press distanced itself from the British viewpoint with regard to the events in China. For example, the *NZZ* insisted that rather than believing the British version of the events, people should know the Chinese version before they made up their minds. The *Tages-Anzeiger* in turn wrote about Chinese deaths even though most of the British newspapers wrote only about attacks on foreigners.[122] Furthermore, while almost the entire British press interpreted the events in China as evidence of the Red Menace, Swiss newspapers generally wrote in a much less sensational way, and, like American publications, described the anti-foreign incidents not as part of the Soviet Union's planned crusade against foreigners in China but as the results of a civil war.

It has been shown that the omnipresence of the Red Menace as a frame in British media reports of the May Thirtieth Movement and the Nanjing Incident

---

[120]   *New York Times* 24.3.1927.

[121]   *Christian Century* 3.2.1927.

[122]   *NZZ* 26.3.1927; *Tages-Anzeiger* 26.3.1927.

had been partly caused by the long-standing imperial rivalry between Britain and Russia. Moreover, after 1919, the British Empire became the Comintern's main target for world revolution. Neither the USA nor Switzerland had similar relations with Russia or viewed the Comintern's existence as such a threat to their foreign interests. Nevertheless, Swiss relations with Russia were fairly rocky after 1917. Switzerland had traditionally been a popular destination for Russian anarchists and revolutionaries. During the First World War, Russians emigrants in Switzerland included such prominent revolutionaries as Lenin, Karl Radek, Zinoviev and Trotsky. Switzerland, however, did not recognize the Soviet Union and so relations between those two countries deteriorated. Anticommunist sentiment in Switzerland also focused on the Swiss labour movement and sympathy demonstrations after the October Revolution as well as strikes were regarded by conservatives as evidence of communist subversion. Fears of a Bolshevik revolution were fuelled when the socialist *Sozialdemokratische Partei der Schweiz* (SPS) made the following deeply anti-capitalist appeal to the masses prior to the celebrations of the first anniversary of the October Revolution: 'The coming revolution is already reddening the skies over central Europe; the fire of redemption will cover the entire rotten blood-soaked building of the capitalist world.'[123] Needless to say, this did not go down well with Swiss anticommunists.

A general strike, which lasted from 12 to 14 November 1918 suffered from a lack of popularity among the workers and after an ultimatum was issued by the government the strike was called off. It revealed huge tensions between the labour movement and conservatives/liberals, and led to various measures to stop Bolshevik subversion in Switzerland. Swiss-Soviet relations took another turn for the worse after Vaclav Vorovsky, a Russian delegate at an international conference in Lausanne, was killed on 10 May 1923 by the Swiss Moritz Conradi who had previously lived in Russia. Not only did the Swiss government refuse to take responsibility for the murder because Vorovsky did not have diplomatic

---

[123] 'Die Zürcher Arbeiter feiern den Jahrestag der russischen Revolution', in Arbeitsgruppe für Geschichte der Arbeiterbewegung Zürich (ed.), *Schweizerische Arbeiterbewegung* (Zürich, 1975), p. 185. See also: Tobias Kaestli, *Selbstbezogenheit und Offenheit: Die Schweiz in der Welt des 20. Jahrhunderts, Zur politischen Geschichte eines neutralen Kleinstaats*, 4th ed. (Zürich, 2005), pp. 49–51 and 80–82; Dietrich Dreyer, *Schweizer Kreuz und Sowjetstern: Die Beziehungen zweier ungleicher Partner seit 1917* (Zürich, 1989), pp. 8–40 and 54; Therese Steffen, 'Gegensätzliche Partner – Die Beziehungen Schweiz-Sowjetunion 1946–1956', *Studien und Quellen*, 21 (1995): p. 46; Christine Gehrig-Straube, *Beziehungslose Zeiten: Das schweizerisch-sowjetische Verhältnis zwischen Abbruch und Wiederaufnahme der Beziehungen (1918–1946) aufgrund schweizerischen Akten* (Zürich, 1994), p. 150; Paul Schmid-Ammann, *Die Wahrheit über den Generalstreik von 1918* (Zürich, 1968), pp. 80–81, 106–48 and 176–93; Hans Ulrich Jost, 'Bedrohung und Enge', in Comité pour une Nouvelle Histoire de la Suisse (ed.), *Geschichte der Schweiz und der Schweizer* (Basel and Frankfurt am Main, 1983), pp. 765–7; Hans-Ulrich Jost, *Linksradikalismus in der deutschen Schweiz 1914–1918* (Bern, 1973), pp. 159–70; Ritzmann-Blickenstorfer, *Historische Statistik*, pp. 448–51, 502–3 and 514.

status, but the trial mutated into a trial about Bolshevism and Conradi was acquitted of the charges. It took several years of negotiations but eventually the Soviet Union and Switzerland exchanged notes on 14 April 1927. Conservatives and French-speaking newspapers in particular denounced it but Swiss business organizations and the labour movement welcomed it.[124] Thus, while Britain took up relations in 1924 with the Soviet Union, Switzerland did not do so until 1927, and so in 1925 Swiss anticommunists were less alarmed about the Red Menace as those in Britain.

The domestic situation also influenced the selection of frames. In Britain the socialist or communist threat was seen as more acute than in Switzerland or the USA because the Labour Party formed a government while in the other two countries the socialist parties remained excluded from the government. In Switzerland, conservative parties built a coalition in 1919 in order exclude the SPS from major political decisions, and in the 1920s the Swiss political landscape was dominated by the *Bürgerblock*, a loose coalition of parties that stood for conservative, agricultural and commercial interests. Thus, while there was a polarization of the political landscape that was similar to the one in Britain, in Switzerland the socialists did not manage to influence political decisions as the Labour Party did.[125]

Switzerland also had its own Communist Party, the *Kommunistische Partei der Schweiz* (KPS), which was founded on 5 March 1921. Throughout the 1920s, the

---

[124]   'Aufruf zum Streik', in: Arbeitsgruppe für Geschichte der Arbeiterbewegung Zürich (ed.), *Schweizerische Arbeiterbewegung*, pp. 186–7; 'Der schweizerische Gesandte in Berlin, H. Rüfenacht, an den Vorsteher des Politischen Departementes, G. Motta', 14.4.1927, in *DDS*, vol. 9, pp. 514–16; 'Der schweizerische Gesandte in Berlin, H. Rüfenacht, an den Vorsteher des Politischen Departementes, G. Motta', 15.4.1927, in *DDS*, vol. 9, pp. 516–17. See also: Annetta Caratsch and Michel Caillat, 'L'assassinat de Vorovsky et le procès Conradi', in Michel Caillat, Mauro Cerutti, Jean-François Fayet and Stéphanie Roulin (eds), *Histoire(s) de l'anticommunisme en Suisse/ Geschichte(n) des Antikommunismus in der Schweiz* (Zürich, 2009), pp. 109–30; Dreyer, *Schweizer Kreuz*; Schmid-Ammann, *Wahrheit*, pp. 204–311; Bernard Degen, *Abschied vom Klassenkampf: Die partielle Integration der schweizerischen Gewerkschaftsbewegung zwischen Landesstreik und Weltwirtschaftskrise (1918–1929)* (Basel, 1991), pp. 37–84; Kaestli, *Selbstbezogenheit*, pp. 84–7, 149–52 and 172; André Rauber, 'L'anticommunisme en Suisse, une quasi-doctrine d'Etat, entre phobie et manipulation de la légalité', in Michel Caillat, Mauro Cerutti, Jean-François Fayet and Stéphanie Roulin (eds), *Histoire(s) de l'anticommunisme en Suisse/Geschichte(n) des Antikommunismus in der Schweiz* (Zürich, 2009), pp. 184–5; Gehrig-Straube, *Beziehungslose Zeiten*, pp. 50–51 and 88–92.

[125]   Erich Gruner, *Die Parteien in der Schweiz*, 2nd ed. (Bern, 1977); Erich Wigger, *Krieg und Krise in der politischen Kommunikation* (Zürich, 1997), pp. 216–17; Erich Gruner, *Arbeiterschaft und Wirtschaft in der Schweiz 1880–1914: Soziale Lage, Organisation und Kämpfe von Arbeitern und Unternehmern, politische Organisation und Sozialpolitik*, vol. 3 (Zürich, 1988), pp. 35–44 and 81–91; Kaestli, *Selbstbezogenheit*, pp. 26 and 90–96; Wigger, 'Geschichtsbilder', pp. 171–3, 218 and 222; Jost, 'Bedrohung', pp. 772 and 739–40.

KPS sought to radicalize the working class but the SPS, the two biggest unions in Switzerland and the *Schweizerischer Gewerkschaftsbund* (an umbrella organization with 220,000 members in 1920, comparable to the TUC in Britain) refused to work with the KPS in a united front. Since the Swiss labour movement already participated in Swiss politics, both via the SPS and through direct democracy, it was not receptive to communist ideas or propaganda, and so the KPS remained a negligible political force.[126] The anticommunist sentiment in Switzerland was, therefore, like that in the USA, unorganized and did not dominate political debates to the same extent it did in Britain. As a result, the Swiss press – like the US press – did not make the connection between the internal threat of Communist subversion and the external threat emanating from the Soviet Union in its articles about the May Thirtieth Movement and the Nanjing Incident in China. Instead, the events were mostly portrayed as the Chinese nationalist reaction to extraterritoriality and imperialism.[127]

Swiss newspapers and magazines were – like their American counterparts – quite critical of the British portrayal of the Red Menace. For instance, the *Tages-Anzeiger* noted sceptically:

> The English cabinet carries a heavy responsibility and is burdened by great prejudices. It therefore loves the easiest explanation and believes it has found the origin of all difficulties in Moscow. In Ireland, in Egypt, in India, in China, everywhere it sees the hand of Moscow. ... It is indeed quite convenient to blame Russia for all the difficulties of the British Empire. Yet, it is also the only way not to see the real danger ....

The newspaper also argued that the real cause of the anti-foreign sentiment in China was the policy of the imperial powers.[128] This view was shared by the satirical journal *Nebelspalter* which had on one of its covers a cartoon that gloated about the problems of the foreign powers in China. In Illustration 2.8, China is drawn as a red giant in an otherwise black and white cartoon, symbolizing the Red Menace. However, a closer look reveals that the cartoon actually mocks the Red Menace discourse because the victims of China's attack are wearing military uniforms. Thus, the foreign presence in China is portrayed as a distinctively

---

[126]   Peter Huber, *Kommunisten und Sozialdemokraten in der Schweiz 1918–1935: Der Streit um die Einheitsfront in der Zürcher und Basler Arbeiterschaft* (Zürich, 1986); Peter Stettler, *Die Kommunistische Partei der Schweiz, 1921–1931* (Bern, 1980), pp. 14–45; Sozialdemokratische Partei der Schweiz (ed.), *Historisch Notizen über ihre Entstehung, ihr Wachstum und ihre Aktion* (Bern, 1928), pp. 19–20; Degen, *Abschied*, pp. 20–24; Kaestli, *Selbstbezogenheit*, pp. 99–100; Ritzmann-Blickenstorfer, *Historische Statistik*, pp. 1044–5.

[127]   *NZZ* 7.6.1925, 10.6.1925. 21.6.1925; *Journal de Genève* 13.7.1924, 20.7.1924, 24.7.1925; *Schweizer Illustrierte* 9.7.1925, 1.4.1927, 14.4.1927; *Tages-Anzeiger* 10.6.1925, 29.6.1925, 23. 3.1927.

[128]   *Tages-Anzeiger* 23.3.1927.

imperial presence that tries to subjugate the Chinese people. The cartoon's caption 'Damn – that guy is huge! How is he going to look once he gets up!' implies that China had been asleep, which in turn refers to the 'awakening China' metaphor that was used both in Switzerland and the USA to describe the growing Chinese nationalism in a positive light.

CHINA

„Verflucht — hat der Kerl eine Größe! Wie wird er erst ausfehen,
wenn er einmal auffteht!"

Illustration 2.8   René Gilsi, 'China', *Nebelspalter* (13.5.1927)
Source: Scan provided by Zentralbibliothek Zürich. Reproduced with permission of Nebelspalter.

The message of the cartoon was also similar to the opinion of the *NZZ* and the *Journal de Genève*, which in 1925 argued that the anti-foreign movement in China was a manifestation of nationalism, not Bolshevism, and that Russia simply exploited the anti-foreign sentiment caused by extraterritoriality.[129] In 1927 the *NZZ* again stressed that the problem in China was extraterritoriality and even expressed sympathy for the way the anti-foreign movement was carried out:

> The Chinese have experienced often enough that one cannot achieve much with a gentle manner. As long as the foreign powers did not feel a strong pressure or even threats, they showed no hurry whatsoever in granting even the most pressing Chinese demands which had been acknowledged as justified by everybody. Thus, they have trifled away any entitlement for patience.[130]

A possible explanation for the attitude of the Swiss press lies in the fact that Switzerland was not affected by the events in China, as it had no real interest in China; neither were many Swiss citizens directly affected by the anti-foreign movement in China. While economic interests affected British reactions to the events in China, Swiss perceptions were not dominated by commercial interests because the China market never became the object of such fascination in Switzerland as it did in the USA. In 1925 there were only 25 Swiss companies in China, which paled in comparison to 718 British and 422 American companies. Swiss trade with China was also not greatly affected by the disturbances there and so neither trade with China nor the Open Door affected images of China in the Swiss press to the degree that they did in the USA.[131]

An aspect that fundamentally shaped American images of China in the 1920s was missionary interests. In Switzerland, however, this was different because there were still hardly any Swiss missionaries in China. Moreover, they were not as affected by the anti-foreign agitation as other missions in China. The Bethlehem-Mission Immensee, for example, first sent missionaries to China in 1924 where they stayed with German missionaries in Shandong and then opened their own station in 1926 in Heilongjiang province in northern China, far away from the conflict zones in Shanghai and Guangzhou. As a result, missionaries were not treated as important sources by the Swiss press, nor did they hold similar political

---

[129]   See for example *NZZ* 21.6.1925 and 5.7.1925; *Journal de Genève* 24.7.1925.

[130]   *NZZ* 22.3.1927.

[131]   Eidgen. Oberzolldirektion (ed.), *Statistik des Warenverkehrs der Schweiz mit dem Auslande im Jahr 1924* (Bern-Bümpliz, 1925); Eidgen. Oberzolldirektion (ed.), *Statistik des Warenverkehrs der Schweiz mit dem Auslande im Jahr 1925* (Bern-Bümpliz, 1926); Eidgen. Oberzolldirektion (ed.), *Statistik des Warenverkehrs der Schweiz mit dem Auslande im Jahr 1926* (Bern-Bümpliz, 1927); Eidgen. Oberzolldirektion (ed.), *Statistik des Warenverkehrs der Schweiz mit dem Auslande im Jahr 1927* (Bern-Bümpliz, 1928); Woodhead, *China Year Book 1928*, p. 4.

power to American missionaries, who actively influenced US China policy and were constantly used as commentators by American newspapers.[132]

Sympathy for China and Criticism of Imperialism

Most American newspapers presented the events as a nationalist movement against foreign imperialism because the image of the USA as a protector of China allowed them to legitimize US interests in China and to portray the USA as the most democratic nation on earth that was on a mission to spread democracy. The Swiss media was also very critical of imperialism in China, and like their American counterparts, none of the Swiss publications analysed for this study considered Switzerland to be one of the imperial powers or even partly responsible for the situation in China. The *NZZ*, for example, argued that the main reason for the disturbances was extraterritoriality and that communist propaganda only fell on receptive ears in China because of the way the Chinese had been treated by the foreign powers.[133] Although American newspapers felt similarly about their country's involvement in China, they explicitly portrayed the USA as being on China's side. The Swiss press, however, barely mentioned the role of Switzerland in the conflict and implicitly presented Switzerland as a neutral power. This can also be seen in Illustration 2.9, a *Nebelspalter* cartoon called 'China for the Chinese'.

The title of the cartoon reminds the reader of Chinese demands for an end to foreign rule and imperialism. The cartoon is in black and white except for the dragon, which is coloured in bright yellow, symbolizing China as the Yellow Peril. China (i.e. the dragon) scares away the foreign powers, namely (from left to right) France, Britain (John Bull), Japan (Samurai), the USA (Uncle Sam) and Russia (Bolshevik). Switzerland is not present in the cartoon. While Swiss nationals in China were indeed not targeted by the May Thirtieth Movement, neither were Americans, who were portrayed in the cartoon as victims of China's rage. In fact, Switzerland enjoyed similar rights to the USA in China; Swiss nationals

---

[132]   'Daheim und Draußen'; Hückel, *Bunte Bilder*; *Journal de Genève* 13.7.1925. See also: Thoralf Klein, 'Anti-Imperialism at Grassroots: Christianity and the Chinese Revolution in Northeast Guangdong, 1919–1930', in Mechthild Leutner, Roland Felber, Mikhail L. Titarenko and Alexander M. Grigoriev (eds), *The Chinese Revolution in the 1920s: Between Triumph and Disaster* (London and New York, 2002), pp. 292–9; Ambros Rust, *Die Betlehem-Missionare Immensee* (Freiburg, 1961), pp. 84–90; Klein, *Basler Mission*; Rüegg, 'Revolution', pp. 75–9; Fritz Frei, 'L'avvicinamento alla Cina: Il caso della Società delle Missioni Estere die Betlemme, Immensee', in Pier Francesco Fumagalli, Gerardo Rigozzi and Luca Salitni (ed.), *Occidente verso la Cina* (Lugano, 2008), pp. 140–41.

[133]   *NZZ* 7.6.1925, 10.6.1925, 21.6.1925, 1.7.1925; *Schweizer Illustrierte* 18.6.1925; *Tages-Anzeiger* 26.6.1925, 29.6.1925; *Schweizerische Monatshefte für Politik und Kultur*, 6/11 (1927): pp. 665–8.

China den Chinesen

D. Baumberger

Ihr kleinen Leut', was kitzelt ihr   Paßt auf, daß es nicht, jäh ergrimmt,
das riesengroße Drachentier?   ein paar der Euren zu sich nimmt.

Illustration 2.9   Otto Baumberger, 'China for the Chinese',
Nebelspalter (17.6.1927)

Source: Scan provided by Zentralbibliothek Zürich. Reproduced with permission of Nebelspalter.

were entitled to extraterritorial privileges (Switzerland was the last country to be granted extraterritorial privileges) and Switzerland was granted the most favoured nation clause on 8 October 1919, so, legally speaking, it was part of the foreign powers.[134] Of course, Switzerland did not occupy Chinese territory nor have a sphere of interest like Britain, but in legal, political and social terms the 429 Swiss living in China in 1925 were part of the foreign presence: they were part of the foreign community in the treaty ports, their trade was subject to the same rules and regulations as all the other trade, and they were not subject to Chinese law like all the other foreigners who enjoyed extraterritorial privileges. The identification of Swiss expats with the foreign presence in China went so far that some of the Swiss residents even fought in the volunteer corps that defended the French Concession in Shanghai in 1927.[135]

While newspapers like the *NZZ* vehemently criticized extraterritoriality in China, it was of huge importance to Swiss nationals in China and the Swiss government. Thus, when the Chinese government asked Switzerland in 1924 to give up extraterritoriality, arguing that it could provide foreigners with all the guarantees they needed, the Swiss government refused to do so.[136] Why then, was the Swiss press so adamant in its portrayal of Switzerland as a neutral nation in this conflict? The answer lies in contemporary conceptualizations of anti-imperialism, neutrality and democracy as manifestations of Swiss nationhood. The late nineteenth century and early twentieth century witnessed various efforts to turn Switzerland into an imagined community by creating a national consciousness that could cope with the changing social, political and economic situation. A variety of Swiss national institutions, cultural organizations and movements were founded, which, together with paintings, books and monuments, stressed the uniqueness of Swiss history and culture.[137] Swiss press reactions to events in China were written and read within this framework.

---

[134]   'Der Chef der Abteilung für Auswärtiges des Politischen Departementes, P. Dinichert, an den schweizerischen Gesandten in Paris, A. Dunant', 13.3.1925, in *DDS*, vol. 9, pp. 25–7. See also: Zhou, *Exterritorialitätsrechte*, pp. 20–40 and 63–6.

[135]   'Protokoll der Sitzung des Bundesrates vom 31. März 1927', 31.3.1927, in *DDS*, vol. 9, pp. 489–90; Woodhead, *China Year Book 1928*, p. 4.

[136]   'Le Chef du Département politique, G. Motta, au Consul general de Suisse à Shanghaï, J. Isler', 28.2.1924, in *DDS*, vol. 8, pp. 856–8.

[137]   Jakob Tanner, '1910–1930: Konjunkturen, Kontinuitäten und Brechung zweier Jahrzehnte: Versuch einer Synopsis', in Andreas Ernst and Erich Wigger (eds), *Die neue Schweiz? Eine Gesellschaft zwischen Integration und Polarisierung (1910–1930)* (Zürich, 1996), pp. 321–2; Georg Kreis, *Der Mythos von 1291: Zur Entstehung des schweizerischen Nationalfeiertags* (Basel, 1991); Gérald Arlettaz, Pierre Pauchard, Olivier Pavillon and Ursula Gaillard, *Les Suisses dans le miroir: Les expositions nationales suisses* (Lausanne, 1991); Schweizerisches Bundesarchiv (ed.), *Expos.ch: Ideen, Interessen, Irritationen* (Bern, 2000); Kaestli, *Selbstbezogenheit*, pp. 36–8; Sarasin, Ernst, Kübler and Lang, 'ImagiNation', p. 25; Jost, 'Bedrohung und Enge', pp. 751–3; Dölf Wild, 'Auf wen schoss Wilhelm Tell? Überlegungen zu Entstehung und Gehalt der schweizerischen Staatsmythen',

A common denominator in articles about China in 1925 was criticism of imperialism. For example, the *Schweizer Illustrierte* wrote: 'Like the indigenous population in India and North Africa, the country [China] is struggling to liberate itself from the oppressing slave chains of the white powers.'[138] The quote shows how the *Schweizer Illustrierte* used the May Thirtieth Movement to make a general statement about imperialism: the magazine defined imperial powers not only as white powers (Japan also occupied territory in China) but also as slaveholders, and the anti-foreign movement as a struggle for self-determination. Switzerland was not mentioned in the article. Contrary to Britain and the USA, Switzerland never became an imperial nation, so the Swiss saw themselves as potential victims of imperial expansion rather than perpetrators. The most important north-south and east-west routes in central Europe led through Switzerland, causing a constant feeling of external menaces threatening Swiss territory, particularly during the First World War.[139] In the mid-1920s the memory of the war was still fresh and so the portrayal of the May Thirtieth Movement as an anti-imperial movement might very well have reflected these experiences. A particularly gleeful reaction to the May Thirtieth Movement was published in the *Nebelspalter*. In August 1925, the magazine printed a section on 'political medical reports' in which it stated: 'Shanghai. The English have been diagnosed with the early stages of jaundice. The disease probably has its origin in the political trouble that has developed from the shooting affair [i.e. the May Thirtieth Incident]. Well-meaning doctors decisively prescribe an instant change of air – change of climate!'[140]

Another explanation for the portrayal of Switzerland as not being a foreign power in China was the importance of neutrality for the discursive construction of Swiss national identity. Since 1815 neutrality had been the basis of Swiss foreign policy and was seen as the reason why Switzerland had survived as a sovereign nation. Many Swiss were convinced that Switzerland survived the First World War unscathed because of its neutrality. Although Swiss neutrality was criticized during the war by other powers, it had the effect that Switzerland was increasingly used as a location for international conferences, as the seat of international organizations like the Red Cross, and as a respected negotiator

---

in Silvia Ferrari, Josef Lang, Heinz Looser, Isabelle Meier, Brigitte Ruckstuhl, Dominik Siegrist, Dölf Wild, Claudia Wirthlin and Manfred Züfle, *Auf wen schoss Wilhelm Tell? Beiträge zu einer Ideologiegeschichte der Schweiz* (Zürich, 1991), p. 25.

138   *Schweizer Illustrierte* 18.6.1925.

139   Edgar Bonjour, 'Geschichte der schweizerischen Aussenpolitik in ihren Grundzügen', in Alois Riklin, Hans Haug and Hans Christoph Binswanger (eds), *Handbuch der schweizerischen Aussenpolitik* (Bern and Stuttgart, 1975), pp. 57–80; Hans Rapold, *Der Schweizerische Generalstab, Band 5: Zeit der Bewährung? Die Epoche um den Ersten Weltkrieg 1907–1924* (Basel and Frankfurt am Main, 1988), pp. 19–24 and 121–80; Max Mittler, *Der Weg zum Ersten Weltkrieg: Wie neutral war die Schweiz?* (Zürich, 2003), pp. 719–63.

140   *Nebelspalter* 7.8.1925.

in international issues.[141] All these factors further increased the importance of neutrality in Swiss national identity. Portraying Switzerland as participating in the (informal) imperialism in China would have gone against the traditional discursive construction of Switzerland as a neutral nation. Consequently, the Swiss press focused on neutrality, ignoring issues like Swiss extraterritoriality in China. For example, the *Tages-Anzeiger* declared: 'There would have to develop a general hatred of foreigners in China for our compatriots to get hurt. The Swiss as citizens of a neutral microstate do not stand in the same relationship to China as the citizens of several major powers and therefore already have less to risk.'[142] Even though the *Tages-Anzeiger* seemed not to be convinced of the total innocence of the Swiss presence in China, it claimed that Swiss neutrality absolves Switzerland from any collaboration with imperial powers.

The final reason for the sympathy expressed by the Swiss press for the May Thirtieth Movement is that the movement was portrayed as a struggle for self-determination and as such also linked to Swiss national identity. We have seen this already in the quote from the *Schweizer Illustrierte*. In 1925, the *Tages-Anzeiger* wrote: 'Despite the external fragmentation, a national independence movement has begun in almost all parts of China. It is a fight against the foreign influences, in which China stands on one side and England, America, Japan and Soviet Russia on the other.'[143] Swiss myths about the origin of Switzerland focus on a free community of peasants and shepherds in central Switzerland that fought together against foreign overlords and eventually founded a free and democratic state.[144] For the Swiss audience, democracy and self-determination were therefore extremely positive ideals that would have immediately triggered a connection with their own national history. Newspapers like the *NZZ* and the *Journal de Genève* focused on democracy and self-determination to criticize extraterritoriality in China, pointing

---

[141]   Jean-Jacques Langendorf and Pierre Streit, *Face à la guerre: L'armée et le peuple Suisse 1914–1918/1939–1945* (Gollion, 2007), pp. 132–8; Rapold, *Generalstab*, pp. 26 and 172–80; Kaestli, *Selbstbezogenheit*, pp. 34–5 and 55–60; Dietrich Schindler, 'Dauernde Neutralität', in Alois Riklin, Hans Haug and Hans Christoph Binswanger (eds), *Handbuch der schweizerischen Aussenpolitik* (Bern and Stuttgart, 1975), pp. 159–62; Mittler, *Weg*, pp. 637–46; Alois Riklin and Silvano Möckli, 'Werden und Wandel der schweizerischen Staatsidee', in Alois Riklin (ed.), *Handbuch Politisches System der Schweiz*, vol. 1 (Bern and Stuttgart, 1983), p. 27; Ulrich Im Hof, *Mythos Schweiz: Identität – Nation – Geschichte, 1291–1991* (Zürich, 1991), pp. 184–5; Paul Widmer, *Die Schweiz als Sonderfall: Grundlagen, Geschichte, Gestaltung* (Zürich, 2007), pp. 134–41; Laurent Goetschel, 'Aussenpolitik', in Ulrich Klöti, Peter Knoepfel, Hanspeter Kriesi, Wolf Linder, Yannis Papadopoulos and Pascal Sciarini (eds), *Handbuch der Schweizer Politik*, 4th ed. (Zürich, 2006), p. 603.

[142]   *Tages-Anzeiger* 26.6.1925.

[143]   *Tages-Anzeiger* 29.6.1925.

[144]   Kurt Imhof, 'Sonderfallsdiskurse und Pfadabhängigkeit: Der Fall Schweiz', in Thomas S. Eberle and Kurt Imhof (eds), *Sonderfall Schweiz* (Zürich, 2007), pp. 29–36; Wild, 'Wilhelm Tell', p. 27.

out that the Shanghai Municipal Council consisted only of foreigners even though the Chinese contributed to Shanghai's wealth and, therefore, had a right to political participation.[145] Indeed, of the nine members of the Council, at that time none were Chinese.[146] In an article in 1925, the *NZZ* criticized the system of foreign concessions which were ruled by foreign councils. The following excerpt is concerned with the Shanghai Municipal Council:

> Nobody will deny that a patriotic Chinese is justifiably complaining that he is not in control of his own house, instead in about twenty important sea ports foreign powers really exercise government. Can one wonder that the situation in Shanghai for example seems quite abnormal and unbearable to a Chinese when he sees that in this city, in which only 21,000 foreigners live next to half a million Chinese, the government of the business quarter is really in the hands of six English, one Japanese and two Americans? To a democrat as well as a nationalist it has to be an open contradiction of the two most important basic principles of political justice that an industrial community like Shanghai is governed in this way by a comparatively small body of foreign taxpayers.[147]

By addressing the reader as a democrat and a nationalist, the article emphasized the democratic foundations of Switzerland, and in this way not only expressed its sympathy for the anti-foreign movement in China but also portrayed Switzerland as a true democracy. Since the domestic situation in Switzerland was more or less under control in the 1920s due to the *Bürgerblock*, the Swiss press had no use for the Red Menace as a frame for its reports about China. Instead, it relied on political core values that were of prime importance for the discursive construction of Swiss national identity like anti-imperialism, neutrality and democracy. Thus, while the US press justified the USA's geopolitical ambitions in the Far East by claiming that the USA was a bulwark against imperialism in China, frames chosen by the Swiss press reinforced traditional images of Switzerland as a neutral island in Europe and a shelter of democracy. Yet, the valiant anti-imperialism in these articles also expresses anxieties about Swiss independence and fears that other European powers would not respect Swiss borders in times of war.

---

[145]   *Journal de Genève* 13.7.1925 and 25.3.1927; *NZZ* 22.3.1927.

[146]   Bickers, 'Shanghailanders', pp. 168–9; Nicholas R. Clifford, *Spoilt Children of Empire: Westerners in Shanghai and the Chinese Revolution of the 1920s* (Hanover and London, 1991), pp. 21–2; William W. Lockwood, Jr., 'The International Settlement at Shanghai, 1924–34', *The American Political Science Review*, 28/6 (1934): pp. 1033–4.

[147]   *NZZ* 5.7.1925.

Chapter 3

'A terror which has been truly Asiatic':
The Evolution of Yellow Peril
Imagery until 1945

During the Boxer Rebellion in 1900, the British illustrated magazine *Fun* published a cartoon by Gilbert Welby Wilkinson portraying China as a dragon from which the foreigners are protected only by a brave Japan. All the other nations are depicted as human beings, only China is an animal (Illustration 3.1). The dragon has been one of the most popular symbols of the Yellow Peril, not least because it allowed cartoonists to portray China as subhuman or being on a lower level of civilization. This chapter shows that despite being a transnational image, the Yellow Peril was defined differently in Britain, the USA and Switzerland until the Second World War. While the British press focused on China as the Yellow Peril, American and Swiss publications predominantly portrayed Japan as the Yellow Peril. Different definitions of the Yellow Peril occurred not only across nations, they also changed within nations over the years. Thus, while in Illustration 3.1, China is portrayed as the embodiment of the Yellow Peril and Japan is drawn as defending the civilized nations, in Illustration 3.2 (published in *Punch* in 1941) by E.H. Shepard, Japan is a dragon-like sea monster bearing the Emperor Hirohito's head next to sea monsters with the features of Hitler and Mussolini.

As a racial rather than a national enemy image, the Yellow Peril refers to an economic, military or social threat from China and/or Japan to the West, i.e. the white race. Although actual definitions of the Yellow Peril varied from nation to nation and changed over time, they were connected to Social Darwinist theories and fears about racial degeneration.[1] From the sixteenth century, 'race' was used by scientists to categorize human beings and describe history as having evolved from a common origin. From the eighteenth century on, it was increasingly used as a scientific concept to explain biological and cultural differences between peoples or nations. Phrenology, craniology and physiognomy among others were used to prove scientifically that non-whites were inherently primitive, immature and mentally as well as morally deficient. While most of the racial classifications

---

[1]   Heinz Gollwitzer, *Die Gelbe Gefahr: Geschichte eines Schlagworts* (Göttingen, 1962), p. 20; Jean-Pierre Lehmann, *The Image of Japan: From Feudal Isolation to World Power, 1850–1905* (London, 1978), pp. 150 and 172; Richard Austin Thompson, *The Yellow Peril, 1890–1924* (New York, 1978), pp. 36–7; John Dower, *War without Mercy: Race and Power in the Pacific War* (New York, 1986), p. 156.

Japan (to the Powers).—" All right, gentlemen; with your permission *I* will settle him."

Illustration 3.1   G. Welby Wilkinson, 'Tientsin', *Fun* (18.7.1900)

CROWDED OUT

(The story of a genuine sea-serpent washed up on a lonely beach is appearing in the daily Press.)

Illustration 3.2   E.H. Shepard, 'Crowded Out', *Punch* (4.2.1942)
Source: Reproduced with permission of Punch Ltd, www.punch.co.uk.

positioned blacks at the bottom of the racial hierarchy and whites on the top, the Chinese (who tended to be categorized as part of the 'Mongolian' group) were usually placed somewhere in-between.[2] Walter Demel has shown that until the late eighteenth century the Chinese were generally thought to have white skin. The perception that it was yellow occurred only once their culture was felt to be inferior to that of Europe.[3] The description of the Chinese as yellow, however, was not only used to debase the Chinese culture or race; it was also crucial for the concept of the Yellow Peril because it grouped all the Asians together on a (pseudo-)biological basis, namely their yellow skin.

Although the image of the East as a menace to the West goes back to Attila the Hun and Genghis Khan, the Yellow Peril's popularity coincided with the growing sense of nationalism in the second half of the nineteenth century. Since Japan was generally seen as a more capable military power than China, the military version of the Yellow Peril usually focused on an attack on the West or Western interests in East Asia by Japan or a Japanese and Chinese military alliance. Proponents of the economic Yellow Peril focused either on Japan as a competitor for Western goods or on the potential economic power of China with its population of 400 million. Social aspects of the Yellow Peril were based on Malthus and described Asian immigrants as Asian hordes invading the West in order to justify anti-Asian immigration policies. The actual phrase 'Yellow Peril' is thought to have been created after the Sino-Japanese War in France, from where it spread to Germany.[4] It received notoriousness with a drawing by Herbert Knackfuss, commissioned in 1895 by the German Kaiser Wilhelm II, which depicted European nations fighting under the name of Christianity against a Buddha (symbolizing Japan) riding a dragon (symbolizing China).[5]

---

[2]   Gregory Blue, 'Gobineau on China: Race Theory, the "Yellow Peril," and the Critique of Modernity', *Journal of World History*, 10/1 (1999): pp. 93–139; Robert Miles, *Racism* (London and New York, 2002), pp. 30–32; Michael Banton, *Racial Theories*, 2nd ed. (Cambridge, 1998), pp. 17–116; Rotem Kowner, '"Lighter than Yellow, but Not Enough": Western Discourse on the Japanese "Race", 1854–1904', *The Historical Journal*, 43/1 (2000): pp. 109–10; Dower, *War without Mercy*, p. 153.

[3]   Walter Demel, 'Wie die Chinesen gelb wurden: Ein Beitrag zur Frühgeschichte der Rassentheorien', *Historische Zeitschrift*, 255 (1992): pp. 625–55.

[4]   Baron von Falkenegg, *Japan die neue Weltmacht* (Berlin, 1905); Fritz Freiherr von der Goltz, *Die gelbe Gefahr im Licht der Geschichte* (Leipzig, 1907); Rudolf Martin, *Die Zukunft Rußlands und Japans: Die deutschen Milliarden in Gefahr* (Berlin, 1905); Von Lignitz, Friedrich Wilhelm Albrecht Victor, *Deutschlands Interessen in Ostasien und die Gelbe Gefahr* (Berlin, 1907); Alleyne Ireland, 'Commercial Aspects of the Yellow Peril', *The North American Review*, September (1900): pp. 389–400. See also: Ute Mehnert, *Deutschland, Amerika und die 'Gelbe Gefahr': Zur Karriere eines Schlagworts in der Großen Politik, 1905–1917* (Stuttgart, 1995), pp. 9–12 and 35–56; Thompson, *Yellow Peril*, pp. 27 and 31–6; Gollwitzer, *Gelbe Gefahr*, pp. 20–25 and 43–6.

[5]   Franz Herre, *Kaiser Wilhelm II.: Monarch zwischen den Zeiten* (Köln, 1993), pp. 217–18; John C.G. Röhl, *Wilhelm II.: Der Aufbau der persönlichen Monarchie 1888–*

Various aspects of the Yellow Peril have been studied before,[6] but while perceptions of Japan after Pearl Harbor have already been covered by John Dower and others,[7] this chapter focuses on the transnational circulation of Yellow Peril imagery in the USA, Britain and Switzerland between 1930 and 1945, and the impact national interests and the discursive construction of nationhood played in the actual definition of the Yellow Peril in different countries. As a result, it analyses not only reactions to Japanese expansion in Asia and to the Second World War, but also the effect of the domestic situation (i.e. Asian immigration, Limehouse fiction etc.), and the divergence between public or media perceptions of the Yellow Peril and actual policies that were carried out by the respective governments. The chapter also includes an analysis of media reactions to the Nanjing Massacre in December 1937, which according to David M. Gordon 'has become one of the symbolic events of the war, a paradigmatic example of Japanese brutality and Chinese victimization' and remains a hotly contested topic as well as a source of regular friction between China and Japan.[8]

1900 (München, 2001), pp. 840–41; Lehmann, *Image of Japan*, pp. 149–50, Gollwitzer, *Gelbe Gefahr*, pp. 42–6; Thompson, *Yellow Peril*, pp. 1–7; Mehnert, *Deutschland*, pp. 10–12, 22 and 100–123.

[6] Gollwitzer, *Gelbe Gefahr*; Mehnert, *Deutschland*; Thompson, *Yellow Peril*; William F. Wu, *The Yellow Peril: Chinese Americans in American Fiction 1850–1940* (Hamden, 1982); Jenny Clegg, *Fu Manchu and the 'Yellow Peril': The Making of a Racist Myth* (Oakhill and Stoke-on-Trent), 1994; Sepp Linhart, *'Niedliche Japaner' oder Gelbe Gefahr? Westliche Kriegspostkarten 1900–1945* (Wien and Münster, 2005); Stanford M. Lyman, 'The "Yellow Peril" Mystique: Origins and Vicissitudes of a Racist Discourse', *International Journal of Politics, Culture and Society*, 13/4 (2000): pp. 683–747.

[7] Dower, *War without Mercy*; Gerald Horne, *Race War! White Supremacy and the Japanese Attack on the British Empire* (New York and London, 2004); Christopher Thorne, 'Racial Aspects of the Far Eastern War of 1941–1945', in Michael L. Krenn (ed.), *Race and U.S. Foreign Policy from 1900 through World War II* (New York and London, 1998), pp. 257–305.

[8] David M. Gordon, 'The China-Japan War, 1931–1945', *The Journal of Military History*, 70/1 (2006): p. 154. See also: Takashi Yoshida, *The Making of the 'Rape of Nanking': History and Memory in Japan, China, and the United States* (Oxford and New York, 2006); Roger B. Jeans, 'Victims or Victimizers? Museums, Textbooks, and the War Debate in Contemporary Japan', *The Journal of Military History*, 69/1 (2005): pp. 149–95; Matthew Penney, 'Far from Oblivion: The Nanking Massacre in Japanese Historical Writing for Children and Young Adults', *Holocaust and Genocide Studies*, 22/1 (2008): pp. 25–48; James J. Orr, 'Victims and Perpetrators in National Memory: Lessons from Post-World War Two Japan', *Schweizerische Zeitschrift für Geschichte*, 57/1 (2007): pp. 42–57; Mark Eykholt, 'Aggression, Victimization, and Chinese Historiography of the Nanjing Massacre', in Joshua A. Fogel (ed.), *The Nanjing Massacre in History and Historiography* (Berkeley, Los Angeles and London, 2000), pp. 11–69.

Britain

Bushido and Fu Manchu

In the 1890s, Germany, the USA, Japan and Russia challenged Britain's leadership in East Asia. As the British Empire was too widespread for the navy to defend it effectively, Britain needed an alliance with a naval force that could protect British interests in China, limit Russian expansion and enable the British navy to focus on the Mediterranean and the Atlantic. Meanwhile, Japan had annexed Formosa as a colony but had been humiliated by the Triple Intervention in 1895, and wanted to prevent further isolation in international politics by forming an alliance with a Western power. As a result, the Anglo-Japanese Alliance was initiated in 1902.[9] The Russo-Japanese War (1904–1905) established Japan as one of the great military and political powers in East Asia and triggered Western fears of Japanese expansion. The British media, however, did not regard Japan as a threat because of the Anglo-Japanese Alliance, and because Japan had defeated Russia, Britain's main rival in Asia. In fact, the first photographs published in the *Daily Mirror* (at that time called *The Daily Illustrated Mirror*) were of the Japanese Admiral Tora Ijuin and Japanese soldiers, exemplifying the special relationship the British had with the Japanese. British writers and journalists also stressed that Japan had won the war because of its patriotism and denied that it was an aggressive power or that it had further imperialist ambitions in Asia.[10]

---

[9]   Hevia, *English Lessons*, pp. 164 and 170–83; Ian Nish, 'Britain and Japan: Long-Range Images', *Diplomacy and Statecraft*, 15/1 (2004): p. 150; Rotem Kowner, 'Between a Colonial Clash and World War Zero: The Impact of the Russo-Japanese War in a Global Perspective', in Rotem Kowner (ed.), *The Impact of the Russo-Japanese War* (Abingdon and New York, 2007), p. 8; T.G. Otte, 'The Fragmenting of the Old World Order: Britain, the Great Powers, and the War', in Rotem Kowner (ed.), *The Impact of the Russo-Japanese War* (Abingdon and New York, 2007), pp. 91–3; Akira Iriye, *Japan and the Wider World: From the Mid-Nineteenth Century to the Present* (London and New York, 1997), pp. 12–22.

[10]   *The Daily Illustrated Mirror* 7.1.1904; *The Times* 12.5.1904 and 7.1.905; *Manchester Guardian* 12.5.1905 and 2.6.1905; *The Scotsman* 30.5.1905 and 31.5.1905; Charles A'Court Repington, *The War in the Far East, 1904–1905: By the Military Correspondent of the Times* (London, 1905); Putnam Weale, *The Re-Shaping of the Far East* (London, 1905); W. Petrie Watson, *The Future of Japan* (London, 1907); Alfred Stead, *Great Japan: A Study in National Efficiency* (Houndmills, 2002 [1906]); Demetrius C. Boulger, 'The "Yellow Peril" Bogey', *Nineteenth Century and After*, 60 (1904); Bennet Burleigh, *Empire of the East or Japan and Russia at War, 1904–1905* (London, 1905). See also: Iriye, *Wider World*, pp. 12–22; Richard Connaughton, *Rising Sun and Tumbling Bear: Russia's War with Japan* (London, 2003); David Wells and Sandra Wilson, 'Introduction', in David Wells and Sandra Wilson (eds), *The Russo-Japanese War in Cultural Perspective, 1904–1905* (Basingstoke, 1999), pp. 4–13; Yitzhak Shichor, 'Ironies of History: The War and the Origins of East Asian Radicalism', in Rotem Kowner (ed.), *The Impact of the Russo-Japanese War* (Abingdon and New York, 2007), pp. 199–218; Robert Allen and John

The British obsession with Japanese patriotism goes back to the cult of *Bushidō*, which in pre-modern Japan was the code of conduct of the *bushi* (samurai) and was concerned with devotion to duty, loyalty and morality. These values were reasserted in Inazo Nitobe's *Bushido: The Soul of Japan*, which was very popular in Britain. As a result, by the turn of the twentieth century a cult of Japan and *Bushidō* existed in Britain, which adhered to the notion that the samurai spirit was a kind of chivalrous moral code that was crucial for Japan's military and social progress.[11] As a result, Japan was regarded in Britain as a civilized nation. For example, it was described as 'an apostle of civilization and peace' that introduced Western concepts to other Asian nations and helped them on the path of progress.[12] The idea of Japan as the Yellow Peril was rejected with claims that Japan was not a threat to the West but actually one of the civilized powers. One writer even went so far as to describe Japan as 'The Britain of the East'.[13] Whereas Japan was elevated to the status of a white power, Russia was degraded to a yellow power. An article in *The Times* from January 1905 described Japan as the only nation among all the Oriental nations which 'has mastered the ways of Western civilization with extraordinary completeness' but pointed out: 'we beg many racial questions when we class Russia as a white or European Power. She is herself Asiatic and yellow to an extent difficult to define with precision, but unquestionably very great.'[14]

While war scares with Japan abounded in the USA in the early twentieth century, the situation for Britain was different. Not only had the Anglo-Japanese Alliance eliminated the potential for war with Japan, Britain also faced a much closer enemy in Germany, whose naval rearmament challenged British naval superiority. In fact, many Britons were convinced that a future war would soon break out between Britain and Germany, and the illustrated press focused on the German fleet as the 'coming Armada'.[15] As a result, not Japan but China was

---

Frost, *Daily Mirror* (Cambridge, 1981), pp. 6 and 9; Otte, 'Fragmenting of the Old World Order', pp. 91–3 and 103.

[11]   Inazo Nitobe, *Bushido: The Soul of Japan* (Boston, 2001 [1900]); Colin Holmes, 'Bushido and the Samurai: Images in British Public Opinion, 1894–1914', *Modern Asian Studies*, 14/2 (1980): pp. 310–22 and 328–9; Karl F. Friday, 'Bushido or Bull? A Medieval Historian's Perspective on the Imperial Army and the Japanese Warrior Tradition', *The History Teacher*, 27/3 (1994): pp. 340–45; Lehmann, *Image of Japan*, p. 144; Anja Fleischmann, *Das Japanbild in England vom 16. bis 20. Jahrhundert* (München, 1999), p. 235; Jean-Pierre Lehmann, 'Old and New Japonisme: The Tokugawa Legacy and Modern European Images of Japan', *Modern Asian Studies*, 18/4 (1984): pp. 766–7.

[12]   Stead, *Great Japan*, pp. 469–71 (quote).

[13]   Henry Dyer, *Dai Nippon: The Britain of the East* (London, Glasgow and Dublin, 1904) (quote); Stead, *Great Japan*, p. 461; Boulger, 'Yellow Peril', pp. 30–39; Watson, *Future*, pp. 241 and 249–50; Repington, *War*. See also Lehmann, *Image of Japan*, p. 150.

[14]   *The Times* 7.1.1905. See also: *The Irish Times* 2.12.1904 and 1.5.1905; *Manchester Guardian* 5.12.1904; *Observer* 27.8.1905.

[15]   *The Graphic* 9.10.1909 (quote); *The Times* 12.5.1904; George Chesney, *The Battle of Dorking* (London, 1914). See also: I.F. Clarke, *Voices Prophesying War: Future Wars*

defined as the Yellow Peril in Britain. The Yellow Peril was often invoked to justify British imperialism and the presence of British troops in China, particularly during the Boxer Uprising (see Chapter 1).[16]

Among the earliest symbols used to represent China as the Yellow Peril was the dragon. In China, dragons were regarded as benign or even divine creatures and were associated with imperial power. Dragons figured on the imperial robes of various dynasties, and a dragon was on China's national flags during the Qing Dynasty.[17] In British chivalric romances and legends, however, dragons were evil creatures and instead the dragon slayer was celebrated.[18] As a result, British cartoonists depicted China as a dangerous dragon as early as the Opium Wars. As British dragon cartoons were generally used to justify or demand the use of force by British soldiers in China, they contained not only a menacing Chinese dragon but also a heroic British figure confronting it. Illustration 3.3, for example, was printed in *Punch* during the Boxer Uprising after rumours had spread in Britain that foreigners had been slaughtered by the Chinese Boxers. The cartoon is entitled 'The Avenger' and portrays an angelic knight fighting the Chinese dragon in the name of civilization. The fact that he is holding a shield with the St George's cross not only identifies the knight as English, it also brings to mind St George's heroic act of slaying a dragon. The cartoon, therefore, legitimizes the use of force by British troops against the Boxer rebels in China by implying that England was a chivalrous nation that adhered to a high moral code and committed a heroic act by fighting China.

The Yellow Peril gained popularity in Britain with the arrival of Chinese immigrants, even though Chinese immigration to Britain remained negligible, and by 1901 there were only 387 Chinese in Britain. They usually arrived as seamen, stewards or boatswains, and settled mostly in port cities like London, Liverpool, Bristol, Cardiff and Glasgow. By 1934, approximately 2,700 Chinese lived in Britain. As most of them were willing to work for low wages and as strike-breakers, British sailors felt that their jobs were threatened and resorted

---

1763–3749 (Oxford and New York, 1992); Michael Paris, *Warrior Nation: Images of War in British Popular Culture, 1850–2000* (London, 2000), pp. 83–100; Rüger, *Naval Game*; C.J. Bartlett, *Defence and Diplomacy: Britain and the Great Powers, 1815–1914* (Manchester and New York, 1993), pp. 99–102 and 107–12; Keith Neilson, 'The Anglo-Japanese Alliance and British Strategic Foreign Policy, 1902–1913', in Phillips Payson O'Brien (ed.), *The Anglo-Japanese Alliance, 1902–1922* (London and New York, 2004), pp. 57–9.

[16]   *Daily Mail* 4.7.1900. See also: Knüsel, 'Western Civilization'.

[17]   Roy Bates, *Chinese Dragons* (Oxford and New York, 2002); Schuyler Cammann, 'The Making of Dragon Robes', *T'oung Pao*, second series, 40/4–5 (1951): pp. 297–321; Qiguang Zhao, *A Study of Dragons, East and West* (New York, 1992), pp. 8 and 123.

[18]   Jacqueline Simpson, 'Fifty British Dragon Tales: An Analysis', *Folklore*, 89/1 (1978): pp. 79–93; Bradford B. Broughton, 'Dragon', in Bradford B. Broughton, *Dictionary of Medieval Knighthood and Chivalry* (New York and London, 1988).

THE AVENGER!

Illustration 3.3   Sir John Tenniel, 'The Avenger', *Punch* (25.7.1900)
Source: Reproduced with permission of Punch Ltd, www.punch.co.uk.

to anti-Chinese agitation. Riots broke out in London in 1908, 1911, 1916 and 1919. Anti-Chinese sentiment was also widespread among seamen in cities like Liverpool and Cardiff.[19]

Fears associated with Chinese immigration were common throughout the British Empire, and resulted not only in Chinese exclusion in countries such as Australia and Canada, but also in a transnational circulation of anti-Chinese imagery.[20] Charles H. Pearson (1830–94), for example, was a British historian, journalist and politician who had emigrated to Australia where he wrote the hugely influential though heavily debated book *National Life and Character: A Forecast*. In the book, Pearson warned that the white race would not be able to rule the world for much longer. Chinese emigration would not only affect the working conditions of white workers, it would also arrest European expansion and lead to the degeneration of the white race. *National Life and Character* reached audiences all over the world, and is therefore an interesting example of how scientific and historical knowledge about the Chinese and fears connected to racial theories circulated not only within the British Empire but also around the world.[21] Another example of how Chinese immigration in the British Empire affected perceptions of the Chinese in Britain was the issue of Chinese labourers in South African gold mines, which began in 1904. It caused nationwide anti-Chinese sentiment in Britain, and was used by the Liberal Party during the 1906 general election campaign in order to instil scepticism and fear among workers towards the Unionists and their labour policy.[22]

---

[19]   John Seed, 'Limehouse Blues: Looking for Chinatown in the London Docks, 1900–40', *History Workshop Journal*, 62 (2006): pp. 62–4 and 72–5; J.P. May, 'The Chinese in Britain, 1860–1914', in Colin Holmes (ed.), *Immigrants and Minorities in British Society* (London, Boston and Sydney, 1978), pp. 111–24; P.J. Waller, 'The Chinese', *History Today*, 35/9 (1985): p. 9; Gregor Benton and Edmund Terence Gomez, *The Chinese in Britain, 1800–Present: Economy, Transnationalism, Identity* (Basingstoke and New York, 2008), pp. 51 and 296–7; Lynn Pan, *Sons of the Yellow Emperor: A History of the Chinese Diaspora* (New York, Tokyo and London, 1994), pp. 84–5; Clegg, *Fu Manchu*, pp. 6–9 and 26–30.

[20]   Joseph Lee, 'Anti-Chinese Legislation in Australasia', *The Quarterly Journal of Economics*, 3/2 (1889): pp. 218–24. See also: David Goutor, 'Constructing the "Great Menace": Canadian Labour's Opposition to Asian Immigration, 1880–1914', *The Canadian Historical Review*, 88/4 (2007): pp. 549–76; Constance Backhouse, 'The White Women's Labor Laws: Anti-Chinese Racism in Early Twentieth-Century Canada', *Law and History Review*, 14/2 (1996): pp. 315–68; E.M. Andrews, *Australia and China: The Ambiguous Relationship* (Carlton, 1985).

[21]   Charles H. Pearson, *National Life and Character: A Forecast* (London and New York, 1893), p. 16. See also: Marilyn Lake and Henry Reynolds, *Drawing the Global Colour Line: White Men's Countries and the International Challenge of Racial Equality* (Cambridge and New York, 2009), pp. 3 and 75–94; Gollwitzer, *Gelbe Gefahr*, pp. 49–53.

[22]   *The Times* 18.2.1904, 26.4.1904, 23.6.1904, 17.1.1906, 4.5.1906; *Manchester Guardian* 11.2.1904, 28.2.1904, 24.11.1905; 'Further Correspondence relating to Affairs in the Transvaal and Orange River Colony', Parliamentary Session 1904, Paper No. Cd.

Some anti-Chinese imagery also originated in Britain and spread from there to other countries via Limehouse fiction, which had its heyday in the 1920s and 1930s and involved sensational stories about China and Chinatowns through novels, detective stories, comic books, radio shows and films. The genre was named after the Limehouse district, a slum area in the East of London frequented by sailors of various nationalities. Even though the Chinese formed a minority there, it became infamous as a location of Chinese crime through the novels of Sax Rohmer and Thomas Burke. Limehouse fiction relied on stereotypes like the opium den, which figured prominently in nineteenth-century sensational newspaper articles about gambling, opium addiction and prostitution in the Chinese underworld in East London. In Burke's stories, relationships between Chinese men and white women were often portrayed as literal versions of the Yellow Peril. Thus, a Chinese man would love an English woman or even a girl, which underlined her innocence and helplessness. Although not all the Chinese protagonists were evil, the stories focused on the racial difference of these men and used derogatory terms to describe it. Moreover, the Chinese underworld that surrounded these mixed-race couples was full of crime, opium addiction and violence. Limehouse fiction thus allowed its readers to enter a forbidden world that was fascinating and exotic but also repulsive.[23]

In 1913, Sax Rohmer (pseudonym of Arthur Sarsfield Ward) published his first story about Fu Manchu, a character who would soon embody the Yellow Peril as the archetypal Asian villain who combined Western science with Eastern magic and commanded an army of assassins to destroy Western civilization.[24] The most famous description of Fu Manchu is given in the first novel, which was a collection of short stories that had previously been serialized in British magazines:

> Imagine a person, tall, lean and feline, high-shouldered, with a brow like Shakespeare and a face like Satan, a close-shaven skull, and long, magnetic eyes of the true cat-green. Invest him with all the cruel cunning of an entire Eastern

1895, vol. LXI.213. See also: Peter Richardson, 'The Recruiting of Chinese Indentured Labour for the South African Gold-Mines, 1903–1908', *Journal of African History*, 18/1 (1977): pp. 85–108; Gary Kynoch, 'Controlling the Coolies: Chinese Mineworkers and the Struggle for Labor in South Africa, 1904–1910', *The International Journal of African Historical Studies*, 36/2 (2003): pp. 309–29; Brooks, *Age*, pp. 71–6 and 92; Lee, *Chinas*, pp. 29–33; James Thompson, '"Pictorial Lies"?: Posters and Politics in Britain c. 1880–1914', *Past and Present*, 197 (2007): pp. 177–8.

[23]   Sax Rohmer, *The Insidious Dr. Fu Manchu* (Minnesota and New York, 1997); Thomas Burke, *Limehouse Nights* (Holicong, 2003); *The Scotsman* 25.1.1897; *Manchester Guardian* 1.7.1907, 14.12.1918, 23.1.1919. See also: Seed, 'Limehouse Blues'; May, 'Chinese', pp. 113–14 and 118–19; Pan, *Sons*, pp. 85–92; Paris, *Warrior Nation*, p. 174 and 182–3; Clegg, *Fu Manchu*; Benton and Gomez, *Chinese*, pp. 302–5.

[24]   Rachel C. Lee, 'Journalistic Representations of Asian Americans and Literary Responses, 1910–1920', in King-Kok Cheung (ed.), *An Interethnic Companion to Asian American Literature* (Cambridge, New York and Melbourne, 1997), pp. 258–60; Pan, *Sons*, p. 85; Wu, *Yellow Peril*, p. 164; Dower, *War without Mercy*, p. 158.

race, accumulated in one giant intellect, with all the resources, if you will, of a wealthy government – which, however, already has denied all knowledge of his existence. Imagine that awful being, and you have a mental picture of Dr. Fu-Manchu, the yellow peril incarnate in one man.[25]

The description of Fu Manchu contrasts starkly with that of Nayland Smith, the Anglo-Saxon hero in the novels: 'lean, agile, bronzed with the suns of Burma, [he] was symbolic of the clean British efficiency which sought to combat the insidious enemy.'[26] By invoking the past duty of Smith in the service of the British Empire and describing him as 'the man who fought on behalf of the entire white race', the novels also portrayed the British Empire as the protector of the white race or Western civilization.[27] Yet, the Fu Manchu novels also contained something deeply unsettling for British readers, as Urmila Seshagiri points out: 'The recurring conflict of these thrillers – Dr. Fu-Manchu's schemes for global domination – rewrote the master narrative of modern England, inverting the British Empire's racial and political hierarchies to imagine a dystopic civilization dominated by evil Orientals.'[28] Although Smith always succeeds in preventing Fu Manchu's attempt at world domination, he never quite manages to kill him, and neither does he manage to rid London of the underworld which is teeming with evil Oriental criminals of all sorts. Fu Manchu was immensely popular in Europe and the USA. Rohmer wrote a total of 13 novels and several short stories about Fu Manchu, many of which were translated or turned into radio plays, films and comics. The fact that Rohmer eventually published his stories primarily in American publications shows how influential his stories were for the transnational circulation of Yellow Peril imagery.[29]

From Ally to Aggressor

In the decades after the Russo-Japanese War, Japan gradually increased its control over Manchuria, causing British relations with Japan to deteriorate.[30] In 1928, the

---

[25]   Rohmer, *Fu-Manchu*, p. 13.

[26]   Rohmer, *Fu-Manchu*, p. 70.

[27]   Rohmer, *Fu-Manchu*, p. 84.

[28]   Urmila Seshagiri, 'Modernity's (Yellow) Perils: Dr. Fu-Manchu and English Race Paranoia', *Cultural Critique*, 62 (2006): p. 162.

[29]   Seshagiri, 'Modernity's (Yellow) Perils', pp. 162–4; Robert G. Lee, *Orientals: Asian Americans in Popular Culture* (Philadelphia, 1999), p. 114; Pan, *Sons*, pp. 89–90; Wu, *Yellow Peril*, pp. 164–73.

[30]   TNA FO 405/269. See also: Yoshishi Tak Matsukaka, *The Making of Japanese Manchuria, 1904–1932* (Cambridge and London, 2001); Ian Nish, *Japanese Foreign Policy in the Interwar Period* (Westport and London, 2002), pp. 52–61; Louise Young, *Japan's Total Empire: Manchuria and the Culture of Wartime Imperialism* (Berkeley, Los Angeles and London, 1999), pp. 30–38.

Manchester Guardian noted: 'China is menaced by neither British nor American Imperialism, but Japanese Imperialism, although its extreme exponents have been firmly held back.'[31] The government was also concerned about its former ally's behaviour in China. In January 1930, a Foreign Office memorandum on British policy in China stated that one of its main concerns was 'to maintain the principle of the "open door" and equal opportunity for all and to see that China does not fall under the tutelage of any single Power'. Describing co-operation between the foreign powers in China as the way forward, the memorandum pointed out: 'The chief disturbing element in this respect is Japan.'[32]

Less than two years later, the Foreign Office's warning became reality. On 18 September 1931, a unit from the Kwantung Army caused an explosion on the South Manchurian Railway near Mukden (Shenyang). The Japanese military blamed it on Chinese rebels and invaded Manchuria. Chiang Kai-shek, who was busy fighting the Chinese Communists and fending off rivals, was aware that China had no chance in a war against Japan. As a result, he opted for a non-resistance policy and on 20 September 1931 appealed to the League of Nations. The Chinese felt that Japan's violation of the Open Door Policy would force powers like the USA, Britain and the Soviet Union to fight Japan as allies of China, yet the foreign powers refused to intervene on China's behalf.[33] The British government and public were relatively unfazed by the Japanese occupation of Manchuria because British interests were concentrated in southern China and because there were other pressing issues such as the replacement of the Labour government by the National government or the European banking crisis. The Foreign Office, therefore, decided to leave it to the League of Nations to deal with the Manchurian Incident. The media generally accepted Japan's need for a special sphere in Manchuria and it was even argued that Japan was defending foreign rights in China and protecting British interests there from the

---

[31]   *Manchester Guardian* 29.11.1928.

[32]   'British Policy in China', F 6720/3/10 NA RG 59.

[33]   'Note by the Secretary-General', 21.9.1931, TNA 405/269; 'Consul, Geneva, to the Marquess of Reading', received on 31.10.1931, TNA FO 405/269; 'League of Nations, twentieth meeting', 10.12.1931, TNA FO 405/269. See also: Youli Sun, *China and the Origins of the Pacific War, 1931–1941* (New York, 1993), pp. 6–39; Stephen C. Craft, 'Saving the League: V.K. Wellington Koo, the League of Nations and Sino-Japanese Conflict, 1931–39', *Diplomacy and Statecraft*, 11/3 (2000): pp. 91–5; Christopher Thorne, *The Limits of Foreign Policy: The West, the League and the Far Eastern Crisis of 1931–1933* (London, 1972), pp. 78–89 and 134–7; Sandra Wilson, *The Manchurian Crisis and Japanese Society, 1931–1933* (London and New York, 2002), pp. 23–4; Parks M. Coble, *Facing Japan: Chinese Politics and Japanese Imperialism, 1931–1937* (Cambridge and London, 1991), pp. 11–38.

Soviet Union. Only a few major daily newspapers warned of further Japanese expansion and its consequences for Britain and other nations.[34]

British supporters of Japan included the British community in China and British business organizations because they felt that Japan fought to preserve the privileges of the foreign powers. They were not the only ones: although China was only of marginal interest to British trade, the Depression had increased British fascination with the potential of the China market, and sparked hopes that British businesses could profit from Japanese expansion in China. For instance, a memorandum by the Deputy Under-Secretary of State Sir Victor Wellesley stated in 1932:

> In the persistent Chinese-Japanese struggle, British policy has oscillated between the traditional friendship with Japan and the potential attraction of the Chinese market ... The present situation in Manchuria observed solely from the standpoint of British interests, need not distress us. On the contrary, the more Manchuria develops under Japanese control the greater will be the opportunity for trade, provided that the 'door' remains open, as Japan has promised it will.

However, in a moment of almost prophetic quality, Wellesley went on: 'A genuine desire to maintain friendship with Japan does not blind me to the fact that we may be dragged by events along a path which may end in war with her.' Nevertheless, he warned of taking on 'a definite Anglo-American anti-Japanese attitude'.[35]

The British government's failure to act on behalf of China after the Manchurian Incident was criticized in Britain by liberals, socialists and the pacifist movement,

---

[34]   *Manchester Guardian* 21.9.1931; *The Times* 26.9.1931; *Spectator* 26.9.1931; *Nineteenth Century*, August 1927; 'British Policy in China', F 6720/3/10 NA RG 59; 'The Marquess of Reading to Sir F. Lindley', 29.9.1931, TNA FO 405/269; 'Memorandum by Sir J. Pratt', undated, TNA FO 405/470; 'Sino-Japanese Dispute', 22.12.1931, TNA FO 371/15507; 'The Manchurian Problem', 27.10.1931, TNA FO 371/15495; Arnold J. Toynbee, 'The Next War – Europe or Asia?', *Pacific Affairs*, 7/1 (1934): pp. 3–14. See also: Thorne, *Limits*; Anthony Best, *British Intelligence and the Japanese Challenge in Asia, 1914–1941* (Basingstoke and New York, 2002), pp. 99–101; Sandra Wilson, 'Containing the Crisis: Japan's Diplomatic Offensive in the West, 1931–1933', *Modern Asian Studies*, 29/22 (1995): pp. 353–5 and 358–9; Stephen Lyon Endicott, *Diplomacy and Enterprise: British China Policy 1933–1937* (Manchester, 1975), pp. 61–3.

[35]   'Memorandum by Sir V. Wellesley', 1.2.1932, TNA FO 405/270 (quote); 'British Policy in China', F 6720/3/10, NA RG 59; 'The Industrial and Economic position in China', TNA FO 371/18052; Kwei, Chungshu (ed.), *The Chinese Year Book, 1935–36* (Nendeln, 1968 [1935]), pp. 1079–80. See also: Ann Trotter, *Britain and East Asia 1933–1937* (London and New York, 1975), pp. 18–19; Endicott, *Diplomacy*, pp. 22–44; Remer, *Foreign Investments*, pp. 74–7; Fung, 'Rapprochement', pp. 99–103; Thorne, *Limits*, pp. 215–16; Gull, *Interests*, pp. 110 and 182–3.

which demanded that Britain lead the League of Nations against Japan.[36] The socialist weekly newspaper *New Statesman and Nation* described the Japanese defiance of the League of Nations as 'the most serious challenge that the League has ever had to face, and if it is to be ignored we may as well put the Covenant and the Kellogg Pact into the wastepaper basket, and offer the Palais des Nations to Moscow to be made into a museum.'[37] David Low, a supporter of the League of Nations,[38] drew various cartoons that criticized Japan's behaviour in China and towards the League of Nation. One of his cartoons, Illustration 3.4, is typical of British cartoons on Manchuria in that they tended to focus on the League and Japan; China was usually not pictured.[39] The cartoon presents the Japanese invasion of Manchuria as a sabotage of the League of Nations and as a disregard of the Kellogg-Briand Pact. The 'Jap War Party' is sawing off a leg of a chair on which the League of Nations is sitting, thereby preventing it from writing the rules of international law. The League's chair is labelled 'moral authority', implying that Japan is manipulating the moral authority of the League. A roll inscribed with 'Kellogg Pact' and a book labelled 'Covenant' are on the League's desk. Together with the caption, 'Will the League Stand up to Japan?', the cartoon thus clearly condemns Japan's actions but also implies that the League has to act against Japan. Note also that despite the presence of monkeys in the background, Japan is still drawn as a human – it has regular facial features and proper hands (not claws as in Yellow Peril cartoons).

After Japan withdrew from the League of Nations on 27 March 1933, the British government tried to appease all parties involved in the conflict, protect British economic interests and prestige in the Far East, and find ways to help the British economy to recover from the financial crisis. Needless to say, this became increasingly problematic. Britain's attempts to solve the crisis between Japan and China failed miserably, and British economy suffered as a result of Japanese commercial expansion, causing many British colonies to introduce import duties and quotas on Japanese textile imports in order to protect colonial markets for the Lancashire textile trade and to contain Japanese (economic) imperialism. As a result, Japan's threat to British interests in the Far East was perceived to be so great that China, Japan and Manzhouguo were ranked as the most important countries after Germany and Austria by the British Secret Intelligence Service and

---

[36]   *The Spectator* 31.10.1931; *Manchester Guardian* 26.9.1931. See also: Anthony Best, 'The Road to Anglo-Japanese Confrontation, 1931–41', in Ian Nish and Yoichi Kibata (eds), *The History of Anglo-Japanese Relations, 1600–2000, vol. 2: The Political-Diplomatic Dimension, 1931–2000* (Basingstoke, 2000), p. 28; Michael Pugh, 'Pacifism and Politics in Britain, 1931–1935', *The Historical Journal*, 23/3 (1980): pp. 641–56; Trotter, *Britain*, p. 7.

[37]   *New Statesman and Nation* 31.10.1931.

[38]   David Low, *Low's Autobiography* (London, 1956), pp. 242–4.

[39]   *Daily Express* 16.2.1933; *Evening Standard* 24.11.1932, 19.1.1933, 17.2.1933, 27.2.1933; 13.2.1935; 25.3.1935; 14.6.1935.

Illustration 3.4　David Low, 'Will the League Stand up to Japan?',
　　　　　　　　　　Evening Standard (17.11.1931)

Source: Reproduced with permission of Solo Syndication.

the most important ones by British Military Intelligence.[40] Antony Best points out: 'If one looks at the 1930s it is immediately apparent that Britain and Japan had opposing opinions over virtually every issue that springs to mind, the existence of Manzhouguo, the future of China, the legitimacy of Imperial Preference, and the naval arms limitation process being the most obvious.'[41]

On 7 July 1937 the undeclared Sino-Japanese War began when a shooting occurred between Japanese and Chinese soldiers near the Marco Polo Bridge. Chinese and Japanese troops were sent to the area, and the Japanese troops advanced quickly, occupying Beijing on 29 July 1937, Tianjin the next day, and attacking Shanghai in August. On 6 October 1937 the League of Nations passed a resolution which criticized Japanese actions in China but sanctions against Japan were still out of the question for most League members.[42] The outbreak of the Sino-Japanese War not only took the British government by surprise but also put Britain in a difficult position because it had to take sides in the conflict after efforts to establish Anglo-American cooperation and initiate communication between Japan and China failed. As if this was not enough, relations between Britain and Japan became seriously strained after the British Ambassador to China, Sir Hughe Knatchbull-Hugessen, was injured on 26 August 1937 when Japanese planes attacked his car on the way from Nanjing to Shanghai despite a Union Jack on his car that was clearly visible from the air.[43]

The British press at first remained rather unmoved by the Japanese invasion of China as it was preoccupied with Hitler's activities in Germany, the Spanish Civil War and Italy's actions in Africa. The Japanese attack on Shanghai in August 1937, however, increased opposition to Japanese actions in Britain. Various demonstrations and public meetings were held to protest against Japan. The National Council of Labour began a boycott of Japanese goods which was supported by many co-operative societies, and dockers at various British ports

---

    [40]   TNA WO 106/5392; TNA T 188/142; *Observer* 26.2.1933; *Observer* 18.10.1934. See also: Thorne, *Limits*; Trotter, *Britain*; Endicott, *Diplomacy*; Ishii Osamu, 'Markets and Diplomacy: The Anglo-Japanese Rivalries over Cotton Good Markets, 1930–36', in Ian Nish and Yoichi Kibata (eds), *The History of Anglo-Japanese Relations, 1600–2000, vol. 2: The Political-Diplomatic Dimension, 1931–2000* (Basingstoke, 2000), pp. 52–3 and 59–60.

    [41]   Best, 'Road', p. 45.

    [42]   Sun, *China*, pp. 79–91; James B. Crowley, 'A Reconsideration of the Marco Polo Bridge Incident', *The Journal of Asian Studies*, 22/3 (1963): pp. 281–91; Coble, *Facing Japan*, pp. 370–74; Aron Shai, *Origins of the War in the East: Britain, China and Japan 1937–39* (London, 1976), pp. 82–102; Craft, 'Saving the League', pp. 102–4.

    [43]   'Note on the Situation in North China', 19.11.1935, TNA WO 106/79; TNA FO 436 F7655/5727/10 and F7976/5727/10. See also: Lowe, *Great Britain*, pp. 16–24; Shai, *Origins*, pp. 24–55; Anthony Best, *Britain, Japan and Pearl Harbor: Avoiding War in East Asia, 1936–41* (London and New York, 1995), pp. 22–4 and 38–9; Endicott, *Diplomacy*, pp. 151–63; Trotter, *Britain*, pp. 189–204.

refused to unload Japanese cargoes and load Japanese ships.[44] Japan's actions in China were also covered by newsreels, which had been shown in British cinemas since 1910. In September 1937, many British newsreels showed Japanese attacks on Chinese cities like Shanghai, often with uncensored footage of Chinese bodies. A newsreel by Gaumont British News included the Reuters footage of a crying Chinese baby at the train station in Shanghai, which later became the iconic image of the Sino-Japanese War. The fact that various companies showed uncensored newsreels caused quite a few complaints, but it also increased their popularity.[45] In September 1937, *Punch* printed a cartoon by Bernard Partridge, which portrayed Japan as a military threat using Yellow Peril imagery (Illustration 3.5). The rising sun in the cartoon refers to Japan (the land of the rising sun). Hundreds of Japanese planes are flying towards the reader, implying that military danger emanating from Japan threatens the West, and that the Yellow Peril image of Asian hordes is becoming a reality. Moreover, the title of the cartoon, 'Dawn over Asia', invokes a scenario in which Japan assumes control over all of Asia, thus threatening British colonies and interests there. Finally, the dark clouds and the explosion in the right corner also hint at the destruction caused by the Japanese bombers, reminding viewers of the Japanese attack on Shanghai.

While Illustration 3.5 is testimony to the increasing public hostility towards Japan, it is not a realistic portrayal of Anglo-Japanese relations in 1937. In the cartoon war against Japan loomed on the horizon, yet the British government objected to any action that could lead to military involvement in China. It also opposed economic measures or naval action against Japan without the military cooperation of the USA because it wanted to avoid fighting a war against Japan, Germany and possibly Italy simultaneously. The press shared the government's preoccupation with Germany, and only a few publications demanded action against Japan; most agreed with the government's policies.[46] Foreign journalists in China, however, were deeply affected by the Japanese advance. Several of them

---

[44]   *The Times* 6.12.1937 and 13.12.1937; *Manchester Guardian* 6.12.1937, 7.12.1937, 13.12.1937, 8.2.1938 and 14.2.1938; *Daily Mail* 6.12.1937; National Council of Labour, *Labour: A Magazine for all Workers*, 5/2 (1937): p. 26. See also: Takao Matsumura, 'Anglo-Japanese Trade Union Relations Between the Wars', in Gordon Daniels and Chushichi Tsuzuki (eds), *The History of Anglo-Japanese Relations 1600–2000, vol. 5: Social and Cultural Perspectives* (Basingstoke and New York, 2002), pp. 270–76; Douglas Little, 'Red Scare, 1936: Anti-Bolshevism and the Origins of British Non-Intervention in the Spanish Civil War', *Journal of Contemporary History*, 23/2 (1988): pp. 291–311; Nicholas Clifford, *Retreat from China: British Policy in the Far East, 1937–1941* (London, 1967), pp. 33–4 and 47–8; Worley, *Class*, pp. 250–52.

[45]   'Japan and the World To-day', Gaumont British News, 30.9.1937; 'Scenes from the War in China', Gaumont British News, 27.9.1937. See also: Robert Herring, 'The News-Reel', in Luke McKernan (ed.), *Yesterday's News: The British Cinema Newsreel Reader* (London, 2002), p. 108.

[46]   *New Statesman and Nation* 18.12.1937. See also Shai, *Origins*, pp. 67–102 and 112–22; Lee, *Britain*, p. 87; Lowe, *Great Britain*, pp. 26–31.

DAWN OVER ASIA

Illustration 3.5   Bernard Partridge, 'Dawn over Asia', *Punch* (29.9.1937)
Source: Reproduced with permission of Punch Ltd, www.punch.co.uk.

died when Chinese planes accidentally dropped bombs on Shanghai, others were killed by Japanese snipers. Foreign reporters also ranked high on the Japanese list of most wanted foreigners and were singled out for harassment. Journalists had their equipment stolen and several newspaper offices were attacked with hand-grenades or bombs, while others became targets of (sometimes successful) assassination attempts.[47]

In December 1937, Japanese troops reached the Chinese capital and began what is commonly known as the 'Rape of Nanjing': an orgy of rape, murder and looting by Japanese soldiers. Estimates range from 50,000 to 300,000 Chinese soldiers and civilians being killed and up to 80,000 women being raped.[48] The few Westerners who remained in Nanjing formed the International Committee of the Nanjing Safety Zone. By the time the Japanese attack on Nanjing began, all British residents had left the city (they had been ordered to do so by their companies), except for one journalist who left on 15 December. This affected the coverage of events in Nanjing in the British press. Only *The Times* published an article by a British journalist; the *Daily Mail* printed articles by the American Archibald T. Steele, who also wrote for the *Chicago Daily News* and who used the wireless on the USS Oahu to transmit his article on the Japanese atrocities in Nanjing to the USA.[49] Most British newspapers, however, had correspondents in Shanghai where they had to wait for accounts of the atrocities to arrive from Nanjing. Japanese censorship also made it difficult to get news out of China, and stories, photographs and films had to be smuggled to Europe and the USA.[50] Most British publications, therefore, did not print stories about the atrocities until January and February 1938 because their correspondents could not cable their stories to Britain, but instead had to send them via airmail. This partly explains why the Nanjing Massacre never received the media echo in Britain that it did in the USA.[51] Harold Timperley, the *Manchester Guardian*'s foreign

---

[47] French, *Looking Glass*, pp. 195–200.

[48] Masahiro Yamamoto, *The History and Historiography of the Rape of Nanking* (Ann Arbor, 1998); Masahiro Yamamoto, *Nanking: Anatomy of an Atrocity* (Westport and London, 2000); Honda Katsuichi, *The Nanjing Massacre: A Japanese Journalist Confronts Japan's National Shame*, ed. Frank Gibney (Armonk and London, 1999); Zhang Kaiyuan, 'Introduction: Historical Background', in Zhang Kaiyuan (ed.), *Eyewitnesses to Massacre: American Missionaries Bear Witness to Japanese Atrocities in Nanjing* (Armonk and London, 2001), pp. xx–xxii; Suping Lu, *They Were in Nanjing: The Nanjing Massacre Witnessed by American and British Nationals* (Hong Kong, 2004), pp. 12–22. While Iris Chang's book has been fairly influential on public perceptions of the Rape of Nanjing, it has been heavily criticized by historians: Iris Chang, *The Rape of Nanking: The Forgotten Holocaust of World War II* (London, 1997).

[49] *Daily Mail* 16.12.1937; *The Times* 18.12.1937.

[50] William E. Daugherty, 'China's Official Publicity in the United States', *The Public Opinion Quarterly*, 6/1 (1942): p. 75.

[51] *Manchester Guardian* 22.1.1938, 29.1.1938, 1.2.1938, 7.2.1938, 8.2.1938, 14.2.1938; *Daily Mirror* 24.1.1938.

correspondent in Shanghai, was so outraged by the Japanese censorship that he wrote the book *What War Means*, in which he included eyewitness accounts and newspaper reports about the Japanese atrocities in Nanjing.[52]

Instead of the events in Nanjing, it was another event that caught the attention and indignation of the British media: on 12 December 1937, the Japanese fired on the HMS *Ladybird*, bombed the HMS *Scarab* and *Cricket*, and sank the USS *Panay*. The *Daily Express*, the paper with the highest circulation in Britain, printed an eyewitness account of the attack by Weldon James, a British United Press special correspondent, under the catchy title 'Bombed Lying in the Sun'. While the British government remained reluctant to act without the USA, an increasing number of editors showed signs of being fed up with Japanese attacks.[53] The *Manchester Guardian*, for example, wrote angrily: '[W]ould it not save much trouble if a special Ministry for the Conveyance of Formal Apologies were created? ... If the Japanese officers cannot distinguish the Union Jack and the White Ensign from Chinese flags at less than four hundred yards there must be something wrong with their training or their binoculars.'[54] In a similar vein, *The Times* called the Japanese attack 'hooliganism' and noted sarcastically: 'If ... the incidents were not deliberate, then it must be concluded that – save for a small civilized upper class – no Japanese can be trusted to carry firearms, even in the Emperor's service, because he is too ignorant and too irresponsible not to run amok without provocation.'[55] The *Daily Express* in turn issued a clear warning towards Japan when it stated in its editorial: 'Too many people would be interested in checking Japan if that country really MEANT trouble against the white people.'[56] The surprisingly open criticism of Japan also stemmed from a growing concern about the Japanese advance southwards, which brought Japan closer to British territories. As has been pointed out in Chapter 2, the *Daily Express*'s owner, Lord Beaverbrook, was an avid supporter of the British Empire. As a result, the *Daily Express* was alarmed about the security of Hong Kong: 'The British public seem to have sensed what British Ministers have not yet – that Japan is dynamiting her way not only through the Chinese Empire but dangerously near some other empires. Get out your map.'[57] The *Manchester Guardian* was less jingoistic but

---

[52]   *Manchester Guardian* 22.1.1938; Harold J. Timperley (ed.), *What War Means: The Japanese Terror in China* (London, 1938).

[53]   *Daily Express* 14.12.1937, 18.12.1937 (quote); *The Times* 14.12.1937, 15.12.1937; 16.12.1937; *Manchester Guardian* 14.12.1937, 16.12.1937; 28.12.1937; *New Statesman and Nation* 18.12.1937; *The Scotsman* 28.12.1937; *Spectator* 17.12.1937, 14.1.1938; Cabinet meetings on 15.12.1937 and 22.12.1937, TNA CAB 23/90. See also: Shai, *Origins*, pp. 124–36; Lee, *Britain*, pp. 89–92; Best, *Pearl Harbor*, pp. 46–8; Lowe, *Great Britain*, pp. 33–7.

[54]   *Manchester Guardian* 14.12.1937.

[55]   *The Times* 16.12.1937.

[56]   *Daily Express* 20.12.1937.

[57]   *Daily Express* 16.12.1937.

also cast a bleak future for British possessions in the Far East: 'Japan is determined to dominate China, to rule in the Far East. But her victory (assuming it is possible) will be incomplete until she has pushed from her path the Western powers who during the past century have dominated China before her.'[58]

Role Reversal

The increasing criticism of Japan contributed to a role reversal in British perceptions of Japan and China. Traditionally, British cartoonists had portrayed Japan as a noble, friendly power and China as an evil, menacing power. However, in the 1930s cartoonists switched those attributes, as can be seen in Illustration 3.6 by E.H. Shepard, in which China is the innocent victim and Japan the perpetrator. Japan is standing in military uniform in front of China, which is tied to a chair and gagged. Japan threatens: 'I'm sure you'd like to repeat after me "Asia for the Asiatics alone!"', expressing its plans to conquer the rest of Asia. Yet, the fact that it has to gag China and tie it to a chair implies that other Asiatic nations do not agree with Japan's demands, and that Japan is not overtly concerned with the desires of these other nations. The cartoon, thus, not only portrays Japan as a threat to Western interests in China (note the barricaded door which invokes the once 'open door' in China) but also describes its actions as unpopular with other Asian powers, implying that Asian nations would much rather be under Western control than Japanese control.

The British government continued to appease Japan, particularly once war broke out in Europe, and in the Craigie-Arita formula on 24 July 1939 agreed to recognize Japanese control in occupied parts of China. Public sentiment towards Japan, however, deteriorated further, and Britons named Japan after Germany as the country they liked least in a public survey in July 1939.[59] Japan, in turn, took advantage of the war in Europe and on 1 August 1940, the Japanese Foreign Minister Matsuoka Yōsuke proclaimed the Greater East Asia Co-Prosperity Sphere, according to which Japan wanted to liberate Asian nations from Western dominance so that Asia would be ruled by Asiatics. E.H. Shepard's cartoon 'Honourable Persuasion' had indeed become a reality. A month later, Japan signed the Tripartite Pact with Germany and Italy, which led to outright hostility against Japan in the British press and an increase in Yellow Peril imagery with regard

---

[58]   *Manchester Guardian* 20.12.1937 (quote); 2.12.1937, 3.12.1937, 16.12.1937, 18.12.1937, 23.12.1937, 11.2.1938; *Daily Mail* 16.12.1937; *Daily Mirror* 18.12.1937, 20.12.1937, 6.1.1938; *New Statesman and Nation* 18.12.1937; *The Times* 20.12.1937.

[59]   TNA FO 676/393; George H. Gallup, *The Gallup Poll: Public Opinion 1935–1971, vol. 1: 1935–1948* (New York, 1972), p. 167; George H. Gallup, *The Gallup International Public Opinion Polls: Great Britain 1937–1975, vol. 1: 1937–1964* (New York, 1976), p. 21. See also: Shai, *Origins*; Lee, *Britain*, pp. 17–21, 87–8 and 207–16; Best, 'Road', pp. 38–42; Clifford, 'Britain', pp. 146–52; Lowe, *Great Britain*, pp. 41–62 and 72–102; Best, *Pearl Harbor*, pp. 62–6.

HONOURABLE PERSUASION

" I'm sure you'd like to repeat after me 'Asia for the Asiatics alone !' "

Illustration 3.6   E.H. Shepard, 'Honourable Persuasion', *Punch* (12.1.1938)
Source: Reproduced with permission of Punch Ltd, www.punch.co.uk.

to Japan.[60] In spring 1941, for example, Cassandra (pseudonym of Bill Connor) described the Japanese as 'squint-eyed sons of Satan' and as 'yellow exponents of lebensraum' in the *Daily Mail*.[61] The focus on racial difference not only reminded readers of the Yellow Peril, but also portrayed the Japanese as worse enemies than the (racially equal) Germans. In their study of the *Daily Mirror*, Robert Allen and John Frost come to a similar conclusion and point out: 'The Germans were once again guilty of every crime under the sun; the Japanese were not only enemies, they were enemies with slanting eyes and yellow skin, and therefore much, much worse.'[62] The lack of racial undertones in anti-German imagery was partly due to the popularity of Anglo-Saxonism, which was based on the idea of a shared Teutonic heritage between Germans and Britons. Although in the 1930s, many British scientists rethought their views on racial difference in reaction to the dogmatic racism of Nazi Germany, race as a concept was not questioned, and Britons continued to regard those people who belonged to what were perceived as the white race favourably. This also explains why Cassandra boasted that the Japanese were not equal to 'European white men'.[63]

In August 1939, the *Daily Express* declared swaggeringly: 'Hongkong can't be surprised by anyone' and blustered:

> The Japanese will think long and ponder earnestly before they attack a British Crown Colony. It would involve them in the most serious consequences. Britain has her hands full in Europe, but she can still kick in the Far East. Retribution could follow the Japanese. An eye for an eye, a tooth for a tooth, a blockade for a blockade.[64]

---

[60]   *The Times* 4.10.1940; 'Statement by the Japanese Minister for Foreign Affairs', 1.8.1940, in *FRUS Japan*, vol. 2 (Washington, DC, 1943), p. 111. See also: Peter Duus, 'Introduction: Japan's Wartime Empire: Problems and Issues', in Peter Duus, Ramon H. Myers and Mark R. Peattie (eds), *The Japanese Wartime Empire, 1931–1945* (Princeton, 1996), pp. xxi–xxxiii; Kiyoshi Ikeda, 'Anglo-Japanese Relations, 1941–45', in Ian Nish and Yoichi Kibata (eds), *The History of Anglo-Japanese Relations, 1600–2000, vol. 2: The Political-Diplomatic Dimension, 1931–2000* (Basingstoke, 2000), pp. 116–21; Best, *Pearl Harbor*, pp. 128–35 and 195–6.

[61]   *Daily Mirror* 24.2.1941 and 28.3.1941.

[62]   Allen and Frost, *Daily Mirror*, p. 44.

[63]   *Daily Mirror* 28.3.1941 (quote); Julian S. Huxley and A.C. Haddon, *We Europeans: A Survey of 'Racial' Problems* (London, 1936); Julian Huxley, *Argument of Blood* (London, 1941). See also: Paul A. Kramer, 'Empires, Exceptions, and Anglo-Saxons: Race and Rule between the British and United States Empires, 1880–1910', *The Journal of American History*, 88/4 (2002): pp. 1315–53; Gavin Schaffer, *Racial Science and British Society, 1930–62* (Basingstoke, 2008), pp. 25–53; Nancy Stepan, *The Idea of Race in Science: Great Britain 1800–1960* (Hamden, 1984), pp. 167–9.

[64]   *Daily Express* 21.8.1939.

However, such beliefs in white supremacy and British views of the Japanese as racially inferior people were shattered by Japan's easy victories over British colonies in late 1941 and early 1942. Once the Japanese forces began their attack on Malaya on 8 December 1941, they invaded Britain's Asian colonies in a matter of months: on 25 December 1941 Hong Kong surrendered, Singapore followed on 15 February 1942, and by June 1942 Burma was almost completely under Japanese control.[65] Japan seemed to single-handedly destroy the British Empire in Asia as a real-life version of the Yellow Peril. As the *Observer* wrote in early 1942: 'Above all, for the fortunes of the British empire overseas this year is the crisis of life and death. ... In this death-grapple of the empire with Japan we have to go with open eyes into the valley of adversity.'[66]

Britain was affected by Japanese expansion in China in various ways, for example, the Japanese seized offices of the Chinese Maritime Customs Service and the British Inspector-General of the Customs, Sir Frederick Maze, was arrested in March 1942. This affected Britain's reputation and standing among the imperial powers in China because British loans to the Chinese government were secured on Customs income, and because British officials were in charge of the Customs.[67] Japan's occupation of British colonies not only humiliated the British Empire but also challenged the legitimacy of white rule over coloured peoples.[68] In Hong Kong, racial segregation similar to that in the American South had been practised until the Second World War. After occupying Hong Kong, the Japanese turned the existing racial hierarchy upside down to humiliate the whites and ridicule the notion of white supremacy. The Japanese forced the whites to march around the city while Chinese onlookers cheered, and in the Stanley Internment Camp over 2,000 white men, women and children were subjected to degrading treatment by Indian and Chinese guards. The Japanese also interned Westerners in various Chinese cities. Most British newspapers did not write much about the Japanese efforts to turn the war into a race war because they were worried that colonized peoples would side with the Japanese. As usual, the *Manchester Guardian* was among the few newspapers that did not toe the line and stated in early 1942: 'In

---

[65]   John Ferris, 'Worthy of Some Better Enemy?: The British Estimate of the Imperial Japanese Army, 1919–41, and the Fall of Singapore', *Canadian Journal of History*, 28/2 (1993): pp. 223–56; Ikeda, 'Anglo-Japanese Relations', pp. 112–34; Aron Shai, *Britain and China, 1941–47* (Basingstoke and London, 1984), pp. 1 and 11–14; Thorne, 'Racial Aspects', pp. 341–2; Dower, *War without Mercy*, pp. 99–105.

[66]   *Observer* 1.2.1942.

[67]   Maze was eventually replaced by an American, thus marking the end of the British leadership of the Customs: Donna Brunero, *Britain's Imperial Cornerstone in China: The Chinese Maritime Customs Service, 1854–1949* (London and New York, 2006), pp. 2–3, 147–57 and 206; Bickers, 'Revisiting', pp. 221–6; Lowe, *Great Britain*, pp. 38–41; Endicott, *Diplomacy*, pp. 6–8; Shai, *Origins*, pp. 176–85; Trotter, *Britain*, pp. 19–20.

[68]   A.D. Harvey, *Collision of Empires: Britain in Three World Wars, 1793–1945* (London and Rio Grande, 1992), p. 521.

this war an Asiatic Power has won sweeping and sensational victories over white armies the effect of which will not be obliterated by the turning of the tables, for the legend of white invincibility is gone.'[69]

Most other British publications simply swapped traditional perceptions of China and Japan, stripping Japan of its traditional status as a civilized power while elevating Britain's ally China to the rank of civilized nation. For instance, *The Times* wrote in 1942:

> In 1937 Japan went ahead, arrogant in her possession of the baser accomplishments of mechanized civilization, disdainful of admonitions and morality, and putting her trust in brute force. For five years, she has tortured a people who are much more than her peers in culture, and has subjected their great and honoured land to systematic dismemberment, desolation, and desecration.[70]

The lowering of Japan's status from that of a modern, Westernized nation to that of an uncivilized – if not savage – nation was also reflected in the way the British cartoons reduced the Japanese to a subhuman status: by far the most popular image for depictions of Japanese was the monkey.[71] In Illustrations 3.7 and 3.8 the Japanese are depicted as being at the same evolutionary stage as monkeys. Illustration 3.7's caption quotes *The Jungle Book*: 'Always pecking at new things are the bandar-log. This time, if I have any eyesight, they have pecked down trouble for themselves.' The Bandar-log were monkeys that raced through the jungle, destroying everything in their wake and chattering noisily, but never realizing their plans. The cartoon shows monkeys with helmets and machine guns, implying that the Japanese are foolish, ape-like people whose plans for dominating Asia will never be realized. Illustration 3.8 by Joseph Lee in turn invokes the Social Darwinist belief in the superiority of the white race with its title 'Evolution'. The cartoon depicts a British soldier trying to count Japanese prisoners of war drawn as monkeys, who are walking past him. Among the Japanese is a real monkey (third from left). The British soldier points to him and exclaims: 'I can't count that one, Sergeant. It's got a tail.' Thus, the cartoon implies that the only difference between a Japanese soldier and a monkey was that one had a uniform and the other a tail.

---

[69]   *Manchester Guardian* 10.2.1942 (quote) and 2.4.1942. See also: Horne, *Race War*.

[70]   *The Times* 7.7.1942. See also: Frank Owen, *Our Ally China* (London, 1942), p. 7 and 37; *Manchester Guardian* 20.6.1942 and 11.9.1942.

[71]   *Daily Express* 11.5.1942, 18.2.1942; *Evening Standard* 18.2.1942, 27.3.1942, 31.1.1944; *Punch* 14.1.1942; *Daily Mail* 18.2.1942, 11.3.1942. See also: Harvey, *Collision*, p. 521; John Dower, *Japan in War and Peace: Selected Essays* (New York, 1993), p. 265; Dower, *War without Mercy*, pp. 84–7.

THE MONKEY FOLK

"Always pecking at new things are the bandar-log.   This time, if I have any eyesight, they have pecked down trouble for themselves."—*The Jungle Book.*

Illustration 3.7   E.H. Shepard, 'The Monkey Folk', *Punch* (14.1.1942)

Source: Reproduced with permission of Punch Ltd, www.punch.co.uk.

SMILING THROUGH: *By* **LEE**

"I can't count that one, Sergeant. It's got a tail!"

Illustration 3.8   Joseph Lee, 'Evolution', *Evening Standard* (27.3.1944)
Source: Reproduced with permission of Solo Syndication.

Illustrations 3.9 and 3.10 were drawn by David Low. While E.H. Shepard at *Punch* was told what to draw, Low could decide both the topic and the motives of his cartoons. Illustration 3.9 predates Pearl Harbor and mocks Japan by presenting the newly appointed Japanese Prime Minister Tojo Hideki as a monkey and describing him as 'mischief', implying that he (and the Japanese navy which is saluting him) did not have to be taken seriously. Illustration 3.10 was published after the attack on Singapore and presents the Japanese air force, army and navy as monkeys feasting on 'first successes of surprise'. The caption warns them that future battles will not be won as easily. In the 1930s and 1940s, Low drew for the *Evening Standard*, yet his cartoons were also syndicated and published widely in Europe, the USA, Canada, Australia and New Zealand.[72] Even though Low did not invent the portrayal of the Japanese as monkeys, his drawings are a good example of how cartoons contributed to the transnational circulation of images because they were looked at by newspaper and magazine readers all over the world.

In Britain, the monkey was much more popular as a visual metonym for Japan than Yellow Peril imagery because the British media had traditionally associated the Yellow Peril with China. Moreover, the racial implications of Yellow Peril imagery were problematic for Britons because China fought on the side of the allies and Britain planned to regain control of its former Asian territories.[73] As a result, British newspapers and magazines preferred to portray Japan as an uncivilized power, not as the Yellow Peril. A notable exception is the book *Our Ally in China* written by Frank Owen, the editor of the *Evening Standard*. Owen ridiculed the argument of China as the Yellow Peril and instead portrayed Japan as the embodiment of the Yellow Peril, comparing Japanese savagery to that of Genghis Khan.[74]

During the war, British newspaper articles and cartoons on China usually focused on how the situation there affected the British Empire; the Chinese war effort was of little interest. As will be shown in the next chapter, this was mainly because British views of the Chinese war effort were not as rosy as those in the USA. For Britain, the USA was a much more valuable ally than China.[75] Nevertheless, some efforts were made to change traditional British perceptions of China. On 1 December 1941 *The Times* wrote: '[The Chinese] have convinced

---

[72]   Colin Seymour-Ure and Jim Schoff, *David Low* (London, 1985), pp. 58 and 63; Political and Economic Planning, *Report*, p. 175.

[73]   See also Thorne, 'Racial Aspects', p. 262.

[74]   Owen, *Ally*.

[75]   *Manchester Guardian* 9.12.1941; *The Scotsman* 9.12.1941; *Daily Mail* 24.12.1941; *Evening Standard* 29.11.1941, 9.12.1941, 1.12.1941, 29.3.1943. See also: Arthur J. Marder, *Old Friends, New Enemies: The Royal Navy and the Imperial Japanese Navy, Strategic Illusions, 1936–1941* (Oxford, 1981), p. 196; Roy Douglas, *New Alliances 1940–41* (London and Basingstoke, 1982), p. 31; Warren F. Kimball, *Forged in War: Roosevelt, Churchill, and the Second World War* (New York, 1997), pp. 119–25; Wood, *Beaverbrook*, p. 277.

THE ADMIRAL COMES ON BOARD

Illustration 3.9   David Low, 'The Admiral Comes on Board',
Evening Standard (20.10.1941)
Source: Reproduced with permission of Solo Syndication.

the countries who are fighting aggression in the west that they are worthy allies deserving of every support. China to-day finds herself standing shoulder to shoulder with Britain and America in what her people refer to with pride and hope as the A.B.C. [America Britain China] front.'[76] The *Manchester Guardian* in turn pointed out in February 1942:

> The prowess of the Chinese has destroyed, we may hope, the spirit of patronising superiority that has marked the British behaviour so often in the past; our debt to Chinese heroism in a struggle on which our life depends will compel our Governments to take serious account of the Chinese point of view.[77]

[76]   *The Times* 1.12.1941.
[77]   *Manchester Guardian* 10.2.1942.

THE NEXT COURSE DOESN'T COME SO EASILY

Illustration 3.10   David Low, 'The Next Course Doesn't Come So Easily',
Evening Standard (11.12.1941)

Source: Reproduced with permission of Solo Syndication.

The British government eventually agreed with this view and officially
abolished extraterritoriality on 11 January 1943. Although the step was applauded
by the British press, it was actually not such a significant move because Britain had
already lost its privileges when Japan occupied the coastal provinces of China, and
many British companies in China had long ago stopped relying on extraterritorial
privileges instead finding local solutions with Chinese authorities.[78]

---

[78]   TNA CAB 65/28/2; CAB 66/28/34; CAB 66/29/28; CAB 66/32/30; FO 371/31627;
FO 371/31657; F 2757/828/10 and 2767/828/10; TNA PREM 4/28/4; *The Times* 6.6.1942
and 12.1.1943; *Daily Mail* 12.2.1943; *Manchester Guardian* 12.1.1943. See also Jürgen
Osterhammel, 'China', in Judith M. Brown and Wm. Roger Louis (eds), *The Oxford History
of the British Empire, volume 4: The Twentieth Century* (Oxford and New York, 1999),
pp. 653–5; Shai, *Britain*, pp. 20–22, 38–47 and 61; Akira Iriye, *The Globalizing of America,
1913–1945* (Cambridge, 1995), pp. 191–5.

The USA

Chinese Immigration and the Yellow Peril

The image of the Yellow Peril originally circulated in the USA with respect to Chinese immigrants, who arrived on American shores in the mid-nineteenth century. Almost immediately upon their arrival, Chinese workers were singled out as unwanted immigrants and became targets of special laws and taxes. The Naturalization Act of 1790 had made only whites eligible for naturalized citizenship, and in 1854 *People vs. Hall* not only classified the Chinese as non-white but also stipulated that Chinese were not allowed to give testimonies against whites, turning them into easy targets for racist mobs and discrimination. The concentration of Chinese in specific areas led to the association of Chinatowns with crime and immorality. Soon stereotypes spread that portrayed the Chinese as morally depraved, filthy opium addicts who were incapable of progress of any kind. Scientific arguments were used to associate the Chinese body with disease and to present it as a threat to the Anglo-Saxon race. Opponents of Chinese immigration also relied on Yellow Peril imagery and spoke of yellow hordes or waves to focus on the number of Chinese immigrants and the threat they posed to white workers. In 1882, the Chinese Exclusion Act outlawed the immigration of Chinese workers to the USA for ten years. It was the first time that people were prevented from entering the USA on the basis of race. In 1892, the Exclusion Act was prolonged for a further ten years, and made permanent in 1904. Chinese immigration did not become legal again until 1943.[79] Illustration 3.11 by George Frederick Keller was published in the Californian magazine *The Wasp* in 1881 and summarizes the arguments for Chinese exclusion. It shows a dark and apocalyptic scene with a ragged Chinese version of the Statue of Liberty which is standing on a skull and holding an opium pipe, a clear warning that the Chinese would take over the USA if they were not stopped. Rays emanating from the statue's head read 'filth', 'immorality', 'disease' and 'ruin to white labor', implying that Chinese immigration would destroy American society in both a moral and physical way. Note how even the moon has slanted eyes.

---

[79]   *Chinese Immigration: The Social, Moral and Political Effect of Chinese Immigration, Policy and Means of Exclusion, Memorial of the Senate of California to the Congress of the United States, and an Address to the People of the United States* (Sacramento, 1877); American Federation of Labor, *Some Reasons for Chinese Exclusion* (Washington, DC, 1902). See also: Najia Aarim-Herjot, *Chinese Immigrants, African Americans, and Racial Anxiety in the United States, 1848–1882* (Urbana, 2003); Sucheng Chan, *Asian Americans: An Interpretive History* (Boston, 1991); Ronald Takaki, *Strangers from a Different Shore: A History of Asian Americans* (Boston, Toronto and London, 1989); John Kuo Wei Tchen, *New York before Chinatown: Orientalism and the Shaping of American Culture 1776–1882* (Baltimore and London, 2001).

Illustration 3.11   George Frederick Keller, 'A Statue for Our Harbor',
The Wasp (11.11.1881)
Source: Scan provided by The Ohio State University Billy Ireland Cartoon Library & Museum.

As the Chinese never constituted more than 0.21 per cent of the US population until 1940, they did not pose a realistic threat to white workers.[80] Nevertheless, opponents of Chinese immigration continued to stress the need for exclusion, pointing out that it would lead to racial degeneration and threatened the survival of the white race. Authors like Madison Grant and Lothrop Stoddard also used arguments that were similar to those voiced by Charles H. Pearson in 1893.[81]

American Rivalry with Japan

Even though Yellow Peril imagery spread in the USA following Chinese immigration, American perceptions of China were vastly different from American perceptions of Chinese immigrants. Americans tended to regard only those Chinese as the embodiment of the Yellow Peril who had left China for the USA. The Chinese in China were generally viewed with benevolent paternalism. One reason for this was the Yellow Peril's implication of inherent evilness, which contradicted the claims of American missionaries and the government that the Chinese were good people who could be converted to Christianity and that China could become a democratic nation with the help of the USA. Stereotypes against Chinese immigrants, however, became part of an American stock of Yellow Peril stereotypes, and spread the idea of the Yellow Peril in the USA.

Originally, Americans differentiated between Japanese immigrants in the USA, who began arriving in greater numbers from the late nineteenth century, and Japan, which was not regarded as a menace to the USA. Some scientists even tried to come up with racial theories to prove that the Japanese belonged to the white race.[82] With the Japanese victory in the Russo-Japanese War, however, Japanese-American rivalry in the Far East increased and led to fears in the USA that Japan could lead the Asian nations against the white nations. As a result, the anti-Japanese movement in the USA became stronger, and a series of war scares broke out on the West Coast. Relations with Japan eventually improved but

---

[80]   See US Department of Commerce, Bureau of the Census, *Historical Statistics of the United States Colonial Times to 1970*, part 2 (White Plains, 1989).

[81]   Madison Grant, *The Passing of the Great Race or the Racial Basis of European History* (New York, 1918); Lothrop Stoddard, *The Rising Tide of Color against White World-Supremacy* (New York, 1920). For contemporary criticism of Grant see Frank H. Hankins, *The Racial Basis of Civilization: A Critique of the Nordic Doctrine*, revised ed. (New York and London, 1931).

[82]   Sidney L. Gulick, *The White Peril in the Far East: An Interpretation of the Russo-Japanese War* (New York, London and Edinburgh, 1905), p. 155; Brooks Adams, *The New Empire* (New York, 1902), p. 189. See also David Scott, 'Diplomats and Poets: "Power and Perceptions" in American Encounters with Japan, 1860', *Journal of World History*, 17/3 (2006): pp. 319 and 321; Joseph M. Henning, 'White Mongols? The War and American Discourses on Race and Religion', in Rotem Kowner (ed.), *The Impact of the Russo-Japanese War* (New York and Milton Part, 2007), pp. 154–60; Mehnert, *Deutschland*, pp. 83–4.

various states introduced laws discriminating against Japanese immigrants, and in 1924 Japanese immigration was outlawed in the Immigration Act.[83]

During Woodrow Wilson's Presidency, US-Japanese rivalry grew because Japanese expansion in the Far East challenged Wilson's belief in the American mission to lead the world. Since support of China's sovereignty allowed the US government to oppose Japanese expansion and legitimize the American presence in the Far East, the Wilson Administration took on an increasingly protective stance over China against Japan. On 18 January 1915, Japan presented the 21 Demands to China in an attempt to turn China into a Japanese protectorate. Wilson was worried that the Demands would establish a Japanese monopoly on China's resources, and he was adamant that the USA should continue to protect Chinese interests, writing to his Secretary of State, William Jennings Bryan: 'I feel that we should be as active as the circumstances permit in showing ourselves to be champions of the sovereign rights of China, now as always.'[84] A similar tone was used by the American press in its reactions to the 21 Demands. Illustration 3.12 was drawn by John T. McCutcheon, a Pulitzer Prize-winning cartoonist who worked for the *Chicago Tribune* for over 43 years.[85] The cartoon depicts two

---

[83]   Seth Low, 'The Position of the United States among the Nations', *The Annals of the American Academy of Political and Social Science*, 26/1 (1905): pp. 5 and 10–11; James H. Wilson, 'The Settlement of Political Affairs in the Far East', *The Annals of the American Academy of Political and Social Science*, 26/1 (1905): p. 71; 'California Alien Land Tenure Law', *The American Journal of International Law, Supplement: Official Documents*, 8/3 (1914): pp. 177–9; 'Ozawa v. United States', *The American Journal of International Law*, 17/1 (1923): pp. 151–7; *New York Times* 6.8.1921 and 14.11.1922. See also: Akira Iriye, 'Japan as a Competitor, 1895–1917', in Akira Iriye (ed.), *Mutual Images: Essays in American-Japanese Relations* (Cambridge and London, 1975), pp. 73–87; Mehnert, *Deutschland*; Henning, 'White Mongols', pp. 153–4 and 162–3; Mae M. Ngai, 'The Architecture of Race in American Immigration Law: A Reexamination of the Immigration Act of 1924', *The Journal of American History*, 86/1 (1999): pp. 67–92; Tal Tovy and Sharon Halevi, 'America's First Cold War: The Emergence of a New Rivalry', in Rotem Kowner (ed.), *The Impact of the Russo-Japanese War* (Abingdon and New York, 2007), pp. 138–42 and 147; Edward S. Miller, *War Plan Orange: The U.S. Strategy to Defeat Japan, 1897–1945* (Annapolis, 1991).

[84]   'To William Jennings Bryan', 14.4.1915, in Arthur S. Link (ed.), *The Papers of Woodrow Wilson*, vol. 32 (Princeton, 1980), pp. 520–21 (quote); H.G.W. Woodhead (ed.), *The China Year Book 1920–1* (Nendeln, 1969 [1921]), pp. 683–5 and 688–9. See also: Shinkichi Etō, 'China's International Relations 1911–1931', in John K. Fairbank and Albert Feuerwerker (eds), *The Cambridge History of China, vol. 13: Republican China 1912–1949*, part 2 (Cambridge and New York, 1986), pp. 96–100; Cohen, *America's Response*, pp. 72–8; Esthus, 'Open Door', pp. 63–5 and 81–3; Clarence B. Davis, 'Financing Imperialism: British and American Bankers as Vectors of Imperial Expansion in China, 1908–1920', *The Business History Review*, 56/2 (1982): pp. 238 and 260–61; Elleman, *Wilson*, pp. 15–21; Trask, 'Sino-Japanese-American Relations', pp. 77–8.

[85]   Stephen Hess and Sandy Northrop, *American Political Cartoons: The Evolution of a National Identity, 1754–2010* (New Brunswick and London, 2011), p. 77.

Japanese soldiers breaking into the room where China is sleeping and holding it at gunpoint, claiming that they only want to protect it ('Don't be alarmed! We only want to protect you from burglars.'). The guarding lion, which is labelled 'watch dog', is completely useless against the intruders since it is a statue. The cartoon, therefore, relies on the paternalist image of China as a weak and helpless nation that has to be protected from other countries' imperialist ambitions. Yet, the safe in the bottom left corner (labelled 'the integrity of China') tells a slightly different story because it refers to the American fascination with the immense profit that could be made from the China market. Accordingly, Chinese integrity had to be protected because whoever controlled it had access to China's wealth. The cartoon, thus, highlights the discrepancy between the paternalistic and the commercial or capitalist perceptions of China in the USA, and how they could not be completely separated from each other. Finally, the cartoon also makes fun of the argument that China was the Yellow Peril: as has been shown in this chapter, the dragon was the most popular symbol for depicting China as the Yellow Peril. However, in this cartoon, the dragon has a clown nose.

During the following years, American and Japanese geopolitical ambitions continued to lead the two powers on an increasingly confrontational course over China. Things came to a head at the Peace Conference in Versailles when Japan countered China's demands for sovereignty over Shandong with several treaties and agreements made with other powers that supported Japanese claims to German privileges in Shandong. Additionally, Japan wanted a clause inserted into the League of Nations covenant that stipulated racial equality. This was opposed by the representatives of various powers, including Wilson. However, as he had to offer Japan something in order to entice it to join the League, Wilson eventually agreed to a deal in which Japan gained all of the economic and legal rights that Germany had previously enjoyed in Shandong.[86] The Shandong decision was not only extremely unpopular in China but also in the USA, where it was the most criticized provision of the entire settlement and was seen as Wilson's betrayal of China.[87] For example, the *New York Times* exclaimed: 'Four hundred million Chinamen cannot be sacrificed to the ambition of Japan. That would put Truth, not

---

[86]   Woodhead, *China Year Book 1920–1*, pp. 711–21. See also: Naoko Shimazu, *Japan, Race and Equality: The Racial Equality Proposal of 1919* (London and New York, 1998); Elleman, *Wilson*; Nish, *Japanese Foreign Policy*, pp. 18–21; Walter LaFeber, *The Clash: A History of U.S.-Japan Relations* (New York and London, 1997), pp. 114–16 and 120–25; Harold M. Vinacke, 'Woodrow Wilson's Far Eastern Policy', in Edward H. Buehrig (ed.), *Wilson's Foreign Policy in Perspective* (Bloomington, 1957), pp. 91–6 and 101–3; Noriko Kawamura, 'Wilsonian Idealism and Japanese Claims at the Paris Peace Conference', *The Pacific Historical Review*, 66/4 (1997): pp. 514, 519 and 524–5.

[87]   Elleman, *Wilson*; Pugach, 'American Friendship', pp. 69–70; Trask, 'Sino-Japanese-American Relations', pp. 95–7; Thompson, *Woodrow Wilson*, pp. 209–10; Cohen, *America's Response*, p. 79.

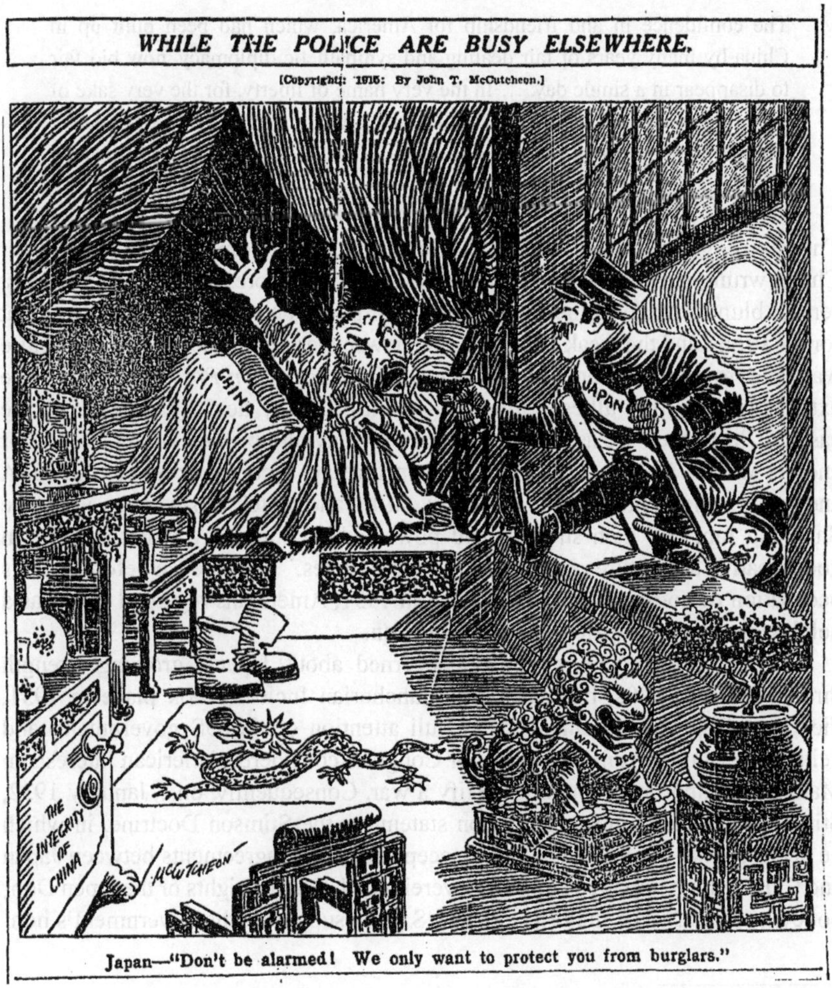
WHILE THE POLICE ARE BUSY ELSEWHERE.
(Copyright: 1915: By John T. McCutcheon.)
CHINA
JAPAN
WATCH DOG
THE INTEGRITY OF CHINA
McCUTCHEON
Japan—"Don't be alarmed! We only want to protect you from burglars."

Illustration 3.12 John T. McCutcheon, 'While the Police Are Busy Elsewhere', *Chicago Tribune* (6.5.1915)

merely in the second place, but on the scaffold.'[88] The *Washington Post*, which at first supported the League of Nations but then gave in to the non-interventionism of its owner Ned McLean,[89] used the Shandong decision to justify its opposition to the League:

---

[88] *New York Times* 4.5.1919.

[89] Chalmers, *Shadow*, pp. 147–50.

The confidence in and friendship for America, which had been built up in China by many years of fair dealing and sympathetic diplomacy, now bid fair to disappear in a single day. ... In the very name of liberty, for the very sake of preserving the world, a league is formed which has at its heart the seeds of death, because it denies truth, rewards the strong, robs the weak and blasphemes the spirit which it pretends to invoke.[90]

The *Los Angeles Times* similarly exclaimed: 'Japan's diplomatic victory over China, wrung from the western powers as the price of present peace, is the most serious blunder made by the champions of fair play who believe in equal treatment for the strong and the weak alike.'[91] Some newspapers also voiced fears of a future war. True to its non-interventionist stance, the *Washington Post* warned: 'To the extent that they [the allies] force a so-called peace by denying right, as in the case of China, they are assassinating peace and laying up stores of explosives for another war.'[92] The *Chicago Tribune* even foresaw a conflict between the USA and Japan: 'the United States must now sit by and watch Japan fatten upon the Shantung loot and gain strength and power which some day will stand her in good stead in any future clash with the United States.'[93] Thus, even before Japan's occupation of northeastern China began in 1931, Americans regarded China as a helpless nation and Japan as a predator nation.

The US government remained concerned about Japan's growing strength throughout the 1920s, but when the Manchurian Incident took place in 1931, the Great Depression demanded the full attention of the US government, and neither the Hoover Administration nor Congress considered American interests in Manchuria important enough to justify a war. Consequently, on 7 January 1932, Stimson published a non-recognition statement, the Stimson Doctrine, in which he declared that the USA would not accept treaties or agreements between Japan and China which impaired Chinese sovereignty, US treaty rights or the Open Door policy in China.[94] The majority of the US press supported the government's non-

---

[90]   *Washington Post* 4.5.1919.

[91]   *Los Angeles Times* 9.5.1919.

[92]   *Washington Post* 5.5.1919.

[93]   *Chicago Tribune* 5.5.1919.

[94]   'To the Ambassador in Japan', 7.1.1932, in *FRUS Japan*, vol. 1, p. 76; 'The Secretary of State to the Minister in Switzerland', 23.9.1931, in *FRUS 1931*, pp. 48–9; 'The Secretary of State to the Consul at Geneva', 13.10.1931, in *FRUS 1931*, pp. 183–4; 'The Secretary of State to the Consul at Geneva', 16.10.1931, in *FRUS 1931*, pp. 213–14; Henry L. Stimson, *The Far Eastern Crisis: Recollections and Observations* (New York, 1974), pp. 4–6, 41–6 and 235–7. See also: Norman A. Graebner, 'Hoover, Roosevelt, and the Japanese', in Dorothy Borg and Shumpei Okamoto (eds), *Pearl Harbor as History: Japanese-American Relations 1931–1941* (New York and London, 1973), pp. 26–9; Thorne, *Limits*, pp. 155–62; Justus D. Doenecke, *When the Wicked Rise: American Opinion-Makers and the Manchurian Crisis of 1931–1933* (London and Toronto, 1984), pp. 29–30 and

Illustration 3.13   Harold M. Talburt, 'The Light of Asia',
                     Washington Daily News (27.1.1932)
Source: Reproduced with permission of The Granger Collection, New York.

45–51; Hu, *Hornbeck*, pp. 132–40; Quincy Wright, 'The Washington Conference', *The American Political Science Review*, 16/2 (1922): pp. 285–97; Karen A.J. Miller, *Populist Nationalism: Republican Insurgency and American Foreign Policy Making, 1918–1925* (Westport and London, 1999), pp. 114–42.

intervention policy; only a minority desired a stronger reaction. Nevertheless, the public sentiment was clearly anti-Japanese. This can also be seen in the editorial cartoons published on the subject. The cartoon 'The Light of Asia' by Harold M. Talburt, for example, portrayed Japan as a huge hand that crushed a burning paper labelled 'Nine Power Treaty' and 'Kellogg Pact' (Illustration 3.13). Talburt won the Pulitzer Prize for editorial cartoons in 1933 for this cartoon.[95]

While this visualization of the Manchurian conflict was similar to British cartoons due to its focus on the League of Nations and Japan, many American cartoonists portrayed it as a conflict between a helpless China and an aggressive Japan, which robbed or beat up China, thus further stressing the USA's sympathy towards China.[96] Illustration 3.14 by Carey Orr shows the international powers in the background with a label 'world powers struggling with the depression' while Japan is forcing China at gunpoint to surrender a packet labelled 'Chinese territory' in Manchuria Alley. In Illustration 3.15 by Keith Temple, a gaunt China, worn out from 'ravages of flood and famine' is holding out a piece of paper inscribed 'signature of Japan to treaties and pacts outlawing war' to a plethora of guns, cannons, swords, bayonets and machine guns. In both cartoons, China is depicted as a helpless civilian, while Japan is associated with the military (e.g. the planes in Illustration 3.15) and violence (e.g. the exaggerated size of Japan's weapons in both cartoons).

Illustrations 3.14 and 3.15 are also great examples of the unique role editorial cartoons played in expressing and shaping public sentiment. Editorial cartoons were printed without an accompanying article and carried their own message. While non-interventionism had the effect that in the early 1930s American newspaper articles on China abstained from harsh portrayals of Japan, editorial cartoons focused on China's helplessness and portrayed Japan as a brutal aggressor.[97] One should, therefore, not mistake the initial press support for non-intervention as a decline in American sympathy for China. Yet, while it could be argued that the cartoons disclose a gap between American public perceptions and policies implemented by the government, the cartoons and the media reactions in 1931 also demonstrate that, just because Americans regarded China with paternal benevolence, this did not automatically mean that they would demand American intervention on behalf of China. Indeed, non-interventionist sentiment in Congress meant that the Roosevelt Administration's hands were tied, and that

---

[95]   *Washington Daily News* 27.1.1932. See also: Heinz-Dietrich Fischer and Erika Fischer (eds), *Editorial Cartoon Awards 1922–1997* (München, 1999), pp. 45–6.

[96]   *Washington Post* 16.10.1931, 18.10.1931, 31.12.1931, 9.1.1932, 17.1.1932, 11.2.1932, 28.2.1932, 6.1.1933, 20.5.1933; *Chicago Tribune* 23.9.1931, 28.9.1931, 30.9.1931, 1.10.1931, 7.10.1931; *Los Angeles Times* 19.11.1931, 9.1.1932, 14.2.1932, 20.2.1932, 26.2.1932; *New York Times* 14.10.1931, 15.10.1931, 18.10.1931, 20.10.1931, 21.12.1931, 9.1.1932, 29.1.1932, 2.2.1932, 25.2.1932, 10.3.1932; *Nation* 14.10.1931; *Literary Digest* 24.10.1931, 7.11.1931.

[97]   NA RG 59 711.93/275.

Illustration 3.14   Carey Orr, 'When the Cops Are Away',
Chicago Tribune (23.9.1931)

Illustration 3.15   Keith Temple, 'Another Scrap of Paper?',
Times-Picayune (13.10.1931)

Source: Scan provided by Keith Temple scrapbooks, Louisiana Research Collection, Tulane University. Reproduced with permission of the Times-Picayune.

any measures that could potentially lead to war with Japan were opposed. The press also generally rejected sanctions against Japan for fear of getting involved in the conflict.[98] The *Washington Post*, for example, wrote after the bombing of Shanghai in 1932:

> Much as Americans may detest the methods employed by Japan, and much as they may be dismayed by Japanese aggressions against China, there is no cause of war between the United States and Japan; nor would there be even if Japan should declare war against China and push the war to victory. It is not the duty of the United States to act as protector of China.[99]

Non-interventionism, therefore, caused newspapers to negate any moral compulsion to help China despite the American media's long tradition of hailing the 'special relationship' between China and the USA.

The US government's policy of non-intervention was welcomed by American businessmen who were involved in trade with Japan because Japan was the third largest export market for US business between 1932 and 1939, and the USA was Japan's most important overseas customer.[100] In January 1937, *Business Week* proclaimed:

> The industrialization of China, even under Japanese tutelage, will mean a larger market for many manufactured products from the United states. The northern [Chinese] market is gradually closing, but there are still nearly 300,000,000

---

[98]   *Los Angeles Times* 29.1.1932; *New York Times* 24.2.1932; *Washington Post* 31.1.1932, 1.2.1932; NA RG 59, Far Eastern Division, Records Relating to the Crisis in Manchuria, 1931–34, Box 1; 'From the Ambassador in Japan', 20.4.1934, in *FRUS Japan*, vol. 1, pp. 223–5; 'To the Ambassador in Japan', 28.4.1934, in *FRUS Japan*, vol. 1, pp. 231–2. See also: Dorothy Borg, *The United States and the Far Eastern Crisis of 1933–1938* (Cambridge, 1964), pp. 77–81 and 87; Graebner, 'Hoover', pp. 32–5; Doenecke, *When the Wicked Rise*, pp. 52–9; Cohen, *America's Response*, pp. 110–15; Coble, *Facing Japan*, pp. 153–62.

[99]   *Washington Post* 7.2.1932.

[100]   NA RG 59 711.93/323; *The Commercial and Financial Chronicle* 23.11.1935, 30.11.1935, 7.8.1937, 21.8.1937, 4.9.1937; *Business Week* 30.11.1935; 'Memorandum on United States Trade with China', *Memorandum*, 1/3 (1932): p. 1; 'Memorandum on Embargo or Boycott of Japan', *Memorandum*, 1/2 (1932): p. 2; 'Memorandum on the Supply of Raw Materials in Japan', *Memorandum*, 3/2 (1934); US Department of Commerce, *Historical Statistics*, pp. 903 and 905–6. See also: Peter C. Hoffer, 'American Businessmen and the Japan Trade, 1931–1941: A Case Study of Attitude Formation', *The Pacific Historical Review*, 41/2 (1972): pp. 193–4; LaFebre, *The Clash*, pp. 174–5; Mira Wilkins, 'The Role of U.S. Business', in Dorothy Borg and Shumpei Okamoto (eds), *Pearl Harbor as History: Japanese-American Relations 1931–1941* (New York and London, 1973), pp. 346–7; Lorence, 'Business', pp. 92–7; Huang, 'Myth', pp. 17–42.

Chinese in the Yangtze valley and in the south who are free to buy their imports where they will.[101]

Even after the Sino-Japanese War broke out in 1937, *Business Week* remained adamant that the USA should not get involved, reminding its readers: 'The United States has little at stake in North China, and has taken no stand at all against the extension of Japanese authority in northern China. Japan is, after all, one of this country's major foreign markets, and buys more of our cotton than any other world consumer.'[102]

Public sympathy for China increased with the publication of Pearl Buck's novel *The Good Earth* in 1931. Buck's parents were missionaries. She grew up in China and lived there as the wife of a missionary before she moved back to the USA. As an author, Buck rejected American Orientalism, but she presented herself as more Chinese than American, giving readers the idea that she was not only *the* China expert but could also give an authentic account of life in China. *The Good Earth* dealt with the lives of ordinary farmers in China and was a huge bestseller in the USA. It sold over two million copies, won the Pulitzer Prize in 1937, the Nobel Prize for literature in 1938, was turned into a Broadway show in 1933 and a film in 1937. The novel reinforced a romantic image of China, and massively increased sympathy towards China in the USA. Yet, it also perpetuated American stereotypes of Chinese culture as timeless, which was juxtaposed to modern American culture that was dominated by technology and economic insecurity caused by the Great Depression. Moreover, the novel's account of the struggles of the Chinese family with its land were comparable to popular frontier novels in the USA in which protagonists made great sacrifices in order to support their families.[103]

Japanese Brutality and a Crying Chinese Baby

The outbreak of the Sino-Japanese War increased US public support for China. A public opinion poll from 2 August 1937 revealed that 43 per cent of the interviewees sided with China, but only 2 per cent sided with Japan. When the same survey was carried out again two months later, 59 per cent sided with China and only 1 per cent with Japan.[104] One reason for the pro-Chinese stance of American society was that the Chinese government used propaganda very effectively to foster American

---

[101]   *Business Week* 9.1.1937.

[102]   *Business Week* 14.8.1937, see also 7.8.1937.

[103]   Pearl S. Buck, *The Good Earth* (New York, 1973 [1931]). See also Michael H. Hunt, 'Pearl Buck – Popular Expert on China, 1931–1949', *Modern China*, 3/1 (1977): pp. 33–64; Karen J. Leong, *The China Mystique* (London, Berkeley and Los Angeles, 2005), pp. 12–35; Robert Shaffer, 'Pearl S. Buck and the East and West Association: The Trajectory and Fate of "Critical Internationalism," 1940–1950', *Peace and Change*, 28/1 (2003): p. 1; Isaacs, *Images*, pp. 155–8; Jespersen, *American Images*, pp. 25–6.

[104]   Hadley Cantril (ed.), *Public Opinion 1935–1946* (Princeton, 1951), p. 1081.

sympathies by focusing on values like democracy that corresponded with the USA's self-perceived role as the champion of democracy. Among the main goals of Chinese propaganda were also American embargoes on Japanese goods and a reform of the Neutrality Act.[105] The clear public preference for China over Japan was shared by the press. Many American correspondents in China clearly sympathized with the Chinese, and their (pro-Chinese) eyewitness accounts were deemed more newsworthy by editors in the USA than the reports filed from Japan, which increasingly resembled Japanese government propaganda because the American correspondents stationed in Japan could not speak Japanese and had to rely on government press releases and rumours.[106] Much more important, however, was that the American media focused on Japanese brutality in China. Thus, the bombing of Shanghai in August 1937 was documented in detail in American magazines and newspapers with photographs of Americans in Shanghai as well as pictures of the destruction and of Chinese casualties.[107]

Cartoons often focused on Japanese brutality. *The Times-Picayune*, for instance, published a Keith Temple cartoon entitled 'What Ye Sow, That Shall Ye Reap', in which Japanese planes were dropping bombs labelled 'slaughter of the helpless' on China, where they exploded in 'hatred' and 'contempt of civilization'.[108] Such a framing of the Sino-Japanese War contributed to the perception of Japan as the Yellow Peril in the USA. Another example is Illustration 3.16, drawn by the *Washington Post*'s editorial cartoonist Eugene Elderman. The caption reads: 'Bushido. "The unwritten code of moral principles regulating the actions of the Japanese knighthood, or Samurai; the chivalry of Japan."' The cartoon sarcastically contrasts this definition with a smiling Japanese soldier who poses with bloody hands and a rifle on a pile of Chinese bodies lying in a pool of blood. None of the dead Chinese have weapons, implying that the Japanese are brutal murderers of innocent, helpless Chinese civilians. The victorious pose of the soldier with the Japanese flag is also a clear condemnation of Japanese imperialism.

---

[105]   Sun, *China*, pp. 136–9; Bruno Lasker and Agnes Roman, *Propaganda from China and Japan: A Case Study in Propaganda Analysis* (1938); Wilson, 'Containing the Crisis', pp. 337–52.

[106]   Ernest R. May, 'U.S. Press Coverage of Japan, 1931–1941', in Dorothy Borg and Shumpei Okamoto (eds), *Pearl Harbor as History: Japanese-American Relations 1931–1941* (New York and London, 1973), pp. 512–17 and 520–26; Stephen R. MacKinnon and Oris Friesen, *China Reporting: An Oral History of American Journalism in the 1930s and 1940s* (Berkeley, Los Angeles and London, 1987), pp. 3, 28 and 39; Daugherty, 'Publicity', pp. 70–86.

[107]   *Life* 6.9.1937.

[108]   *The Times-Picayune* 28.9.1937.

Bushido.

"The unwritten code of moral principles regulating the actions of the Japanese knighthood, or Samurai; the chivalry of Japan."

Illustration 3.16   Gene Elderman, 'Bushido', *Washington Post* (20.8.1937)

While editorial cartoons such as Illustration 3.16 were sure to trigger emotional responses in the audience, the use of very graphic photographs of Japanese atrocities in American publications meant that readers had visual testimonies of Japanese brutality and destruction in China. Illustrated newspapers and magazines had been publishing photographs since the late nineteenth century, but their use in newspapers increased massively during the interwar period due to technological advances in printing, camera design, equipment and film.[109] Vicki Goldberg points out: 'Photographs have a swifter and more succinct impact than words, an impact that is instantaneous, visceral, and intense. They share the power of images in general, which have always played havoc with the human mind and heart, and they have the added force of evident accuracy.'[110] Contrary to editorial cartoons that were drawn by hand, photographs seemed a more accurate rendering of reality, without an artist interfering between object and audience. Of course, photographs were shot in a deliberate way, with photographers choosing a certain angle, composition and focus. Moreover, photographers were influenced by the publication they worked for, and took pictures that fit their editors' definition of newsworthiness. Photographs were also edited before they were published in newspapers and magazines.[111]

In the 1930s, magazines like *Life*, *Look* and *The Digest* relied on photographs as their main source of information.[112] In 1937, they printed various issues with detailed depictions of Japanese bombings of Chinese cities. Often, photographs contained graphic images of Chinese bodies.[113] Among these pictures was Illustration 3.17, one of the most famous images of the entire Sino-Japanese War.

According to *Life*, about 136,000,000 people saw the photo of the crying Chinese baby. It was also selected by *Life* readers as one of the ten pictures of the year.[114] Christina Klein describes it as a 'classic sentimental image' which 'represented China as a weak and vulnerable infant, and appealed to an implicitly adult American viewer to extend some kind of paternal aid'.[115] Thus, one reason

---

[109] Marianne Fulton, 'Bearing Witness: The 1930s and 1950s', in Marianne Fulton (ed.), *Eyes of Time: Photojournalism in America* (Boston, Toronto and London, 1988), pp. 107–16 and 125–6; Astrid Jacobi, *Die Pressefotografie: Geschichte, Entwicklung und Ethik des Fotojournalismus* (Saarbrücken, 2007), p. 26; Vicki Goldberg, *The Power of Photography: How Photographs Changed Our Lives* (New York, London and Paris, 1991), p. 34; Allen and Frost, *Daily Mirror*, p. 26.

[110] Goldberg, *Power*, p. 7.

[111] Langton, *Photojournalism*, pp. 4–8; Jacobi, *Pressefotografie*, pp. 62–6; Goldberg, *Power*, p. 16.

[112] Fulton, 'Bearing Witness', pp. 135–7; Goldberg, *Power*, p. 34; Jacobi, *Pressefotografie*, pp. 27–8; Langton, *Photojournalism*, p. 31.

[113] *Life* 6.9.1937, 13.9.1937, 4.10.1937; *The Digest* 11.9.1937, 6.11.1937; *Literary Digest* 22.1.1938.

[114] *Life* 4.10.1937; Isaacs, *Images*, pp. 167–8.

[115] Klein, *Cold War Orientalism*, p. 176.

Illustration 3.17   H.S. Wong, 'Baby amidst Bomb Rubble', *Life* (4.10.1937)
Source: Reproduced with permission of Corbis/Specter Services.

why this picture was so popular was exactly because its message fit right into the traditional discourse on China in the USA, which described China as a weak, fledgling nation that had to be protected and supported by the USA. It is also an example of how photographs about China in the 1930s and 40s were regarded as an objective rendering of reality, but in fact achieved their effect through their use of culturally coded symbols. What makes the picture even more intriguing is that the baby was moved by the photographer Wong Hai-Sheng (also known as Newsreel Wong) and his assistant in order to be more effective.[116]

It is no surprise that Illustration 3.17, which was immensely effective in generating sympathy for the Chinese, was printed in *Life*, a magazine owned by Henry R. Luce. Luce had close ties to China. He was born in China to Presbyterian missionaries, and after studying at Yale went back to China and became a member of the Board of Trustees of Yenching University. He believed that the USA had to modernize and educate China, and made sure that *Time* and *Life* were partial in their coverage of the Sino-Japanese War. As a result, they described the Chinese war effort as heroic, and Chiang Kai-shek as a military hero and saviour of a

---

[116]   French, *Looking Glass*, pp. 190–93.

Christian and democratic China. In 1938, *Time* even made Chiang and his wife Soong Meiling 'Man and Wife of the Year'. As Luce's publications were among the most popular magazines of the time, his influence on public perceptions of China in the USA was tremendous.[117]

Part of Luce's media empire was also *March of Time*, a newsreel which was first aired in 1935. From 1932 Western newsreels regularly included news from China. It is telling that the first issue of *March of Time* dealt with the growing militarism of Japan. In September 1937, *March of Time* released 'War in China', which contained graphic images of dead and injured Chinese civilians in Shanghai as well as re-enactments that were shot in New York. The newsreel ended with footage of Americans being evacuated from Shanghai, images of the buildings they left behind, and a shot of Chiang Kai-shek and his wife, with the voice-over dramatically declaring: "Those who know China best, wonder gloomily if the end has come, not only to US hopes in China but to the ten most brilliant years of China's long struggle to achieve her national integrity."[118] Yet, it would be wrong to assume that *March of Time* was the only newsreel that contributed to American perceptions of Chinese victims and Japanese perpetrators. George H. Roeder, Jr. points out in his study that American newsreels often showed not only grieving Chinese but also Chinese victims of Japanese atrocities, including footage of a dead Chinese baby.[119]

Some newsreel footage was censored: in the early 1930s, a newsreel image of the body of a Chinese baby led to the withdrawal of the newsreel, yet newsreels of the Japanese attack on Nanjing contained graphic pictures of dead Chinese civilians, including babies. In early December 1937, the Japanese attack on the USS *Panay* was also filmed by the newsreel cameraman Norman Alley. According to Paul French, the footage of the *Panay* attack was shipped via Manila to the West Coast, from where it was flown to New York and then transported in an armoured car to the processing lab. Newsreels of the attack were shown in American theatres but Roosevelt ordered those parts removed which showed how low Japanese bombers were flying when they bombed the *Panay*, because this meant that the Japanese pilots had seen the American flags.[120] The fact that FDR

---

[117] *Time* 21.12.1936, 28.12.1936; 3.1.1938. See also: Neils, *China Images*; Jespersen, *American Images*, pp. 11–44 and 67–8; MacKinnon and Friesen, *China Reporting*, pp. 138–9; Yoshida, *Making*, pp. 39, 205 and 208; Fulton, 'Bearing Witness', pp. 131–5; Varg, *Missionaries*, p. 248; Masland, 'Missionary Influence', pp. 286–7.

[118] March of Time, 10.9.1937 (quote); 1.2.1935. See also: Raymond Fielding, *The March of Time: 1935–1951* (New York, 1978); French, *Looking Glass*, pp. 190–91.

[119] George H. Roeder, Jr., *The Censored War: American Visual Experience during World War Two* (New Haven and London, 1993), pp. 126–7.

[120] Universal Pictures, 'Bombing of U.S.S. Panay', 12.12.1937; *Los Angeles Times* 31.12.1937; *Times-Picayune* 1.12.1937; 'The Secretary of State to the Ambassador in Japan', 25.12.1937, in *FRUS Japan*, vol. 1, pp. 551–2; 'The Second Secretary of Embassy in China (Acheson) to the Secretary of State', 21.12.1937, in *FRUS Japan*, vol. 1, p. 532–

felt the need to censor newsreel coverage is testimony to the effect newsreels had on public opinion about Japan. The newspapers were also aware of this, as *The Times-Picayune* noted: 'News reels of bombs blowing children to bits, and the conception of a ruthless, arrogant power dominating the Orient, are more fundamentally provoking Americans than "incidents" and the supposed loss of prestige abroad.'[121]

Nevertheless, in accordance with government policy and widespread non-interventionism, most American newspapers tried to downplay the seriousness of the *Panay* Incident. Isolationism still dominated the sentiment concerning US policy in the Far East so much that the *Los Angeles Times* tried to convince its readers of the warm feelings of the Japanese for the USA:

> The public must remember, however, that even if the Panay was attacked intentionally and deliberately, the intention may not have been that of the Japanese government or the Japanese people. ... It seems to be evident from the attitude of the Tokio government, which apologized before apologies were asked for, and of Japanese civilians in the capital, that the Japanese people do not want the ill will of the United States and are doing their utmost to maintain friendly relations.[122]

Other voices like the *Washington Post* called on the US government to take action in order to protect American commercial and political interests in China:[123]

> The deliberate Japanese attack on the gunboat Panay ... is far too serious a matter for flag-waving or other heroics. The outrage comes as the culmination of a long line of Japanese assaults on the rights of neutrals in China. It demonstrates that the Japanese military will stick at nothing in their furious efforts to destroy the Chinese government before their own economy breaks down. ... the sinking of the [Panay] can only be regarded as emphasizing the wanton fury which is now the outstanding characteristic of Japan's policy in China.[124]

It is also interesting that while the government prevented graphic newsreel images of the Japanese attack on the *Panay*, it did not censor press reports about Japanese

---

41. See also: Manny T. Koginos, *The Panay Incident: Prelude to War* (Lafayette, 1967), pp. 25–38; Hamilton Darby Perry, *The Panay Incident: Prelude to Pearl Harbor* (Toronto, 1969); French, *Looking Glass*, p. 206; Nicholas R. Clifford, 'Britain, America, and the Far East, 1937–1940: A Failure in Cooperation', *The Journal of British Studies*, 3/1 (1963): p. 145; Shai, *Origins*, p. 126.

[121] *Times-Picayune* 26.9.1937.

[122] *Los Angeles Times* 16.12.1937. See also: *Literary Digest* 25.12.1937, 8.1.1938; *New York Times* 15.12.1937, 16.12.1937, 18.12.1937, 19.12.1937.

[123] *Washington Post* 14.12.1937, 17.12.1937, 19.12.1937.

[124] *Washington Post* 14.12.1937.

atrocities in Nanjing, which reached the USA a few days after the *Panay* Incident and further damaged the reputation of Japanese soldiers. Unlike Swiss and British journalists, American correspondents found ways to evade Japanese censorship by cabling stories of the Japanese atrocities to the United States via American ships. Arthur Menken and Archibald T. Steele used the wireless on the USS *Oahu*, and Tillman Durdin sent his article from the *Panay*. As a result, American newspapers printed very graphic first-hand accounts of the Japanese atrocities in Nanjing that described mass executions, rape and looting.[125] Letters, film footage and reports by American eyewitnesses detailing the horrific atrocities committed by the Japanese in Nanjing were also widely circulated in the USA and used by journalists as sources. They generated a huge response and helped foster the image of Japanese soldiers as brutal barbarians.[126] The following excerpts are from the *Chicago Tribune*, which published diary entries from the Associated Press correspondent Charles Yates McDaniel:

> [I] walked through streets filled with dead Chinese. Some Japanese's sense of humor – decapitated head balanced on a barricade with a biscuit in the mouth, another with a long Chinese pipe. … streets littered with dead humans and horses. Saw first Japanese car enter gate, skidding over smashed bodies. … This afternoon saw some of the [Chinese] soldiers I helped disarm dragged from houses, shot, and kicked into ditches. Tonight saw group of 500 civilians and disarmed soldiers, hands tied, marched from safety zone by Japanese carrying Chinese big swords. None returned. … My last remembrance of Nanking: Dead Chinese, dead Chinese, dead Chinese.[127]

The focus of many articles was on the horrific brutality of the Japanese.[128] The *Reader's Digest* printed an article by an eyewitness who described the atrocities as 'hellish beastliness',[129] Steele wrote in the *New York Times* of 'four days in hell',[130] and the *Nation* even spoke of a 'holocaust'.[131] *Time* focused on the sadistic nature of Japanese soldiers:

---

[125]   *Chicago Daily News* 15.12.1937; *Chicago Tribune* 16.12.1937; *Los Angeles Times* 17.12.1937; *New York Times* 16.12.1937 and 18.12.1937.

[126]   *Time* 27.12.1937. See also: Zhang, 'Introduction', pp. xx–xxii; 'Notes on the Present Situation', 21.3.1938, in Zhang Kaiyuan (ed.), *Eyewitnesses to Massacre: American Missionaries Bear Witness to Japanese Atrocities in Nanjing* (Armonk and London, 2001), p. 314; Lu, *Nanjing*, pp. 14–16; Masland, 'Missionary Influence', pp. 285–91 and 295–6; Varg, *Missionaries*, pp. 260–61; Yoshida, *Making*, p. 32; Perry, *Panay Incident*, p. 34.

[127]   *Chicago Tribune* 18.12.1937.

[128]   See for example *New York Times* 18.12.1937, 19.12.1937, 24.12.1937; *Los Angeles Times* 9.1.1938.

[129]   *Reader's Digest* July 1938.

[130]   *New York Times* 19.12.1937.

[131]   *Nation* 29.1.1938.

It was a tiresome job, lining up hundreds of [Chinese] prisoners and shooting them down batch after batch [but apparently all the Japanese] 'thoroughly enjoyed it.' Meanwhile, Chinese civilians, who had hoped that the arrival of the Japanese would mean at least a return of peace & safety, were shot down on the slightest pretext until there were scores of bodies in the streets. Houses and shops were looted, women raped and the whole city ravaged according to an immemorial custom of war.[132]

Yellow Peril imagery was often used to describe the Japanese soldiers as uncivilized savages.[133] The *New York Times* correspondent Tillman Durdin described the Japanese atrocities as 'barbaric cruelties' and stated: 'The unrestrained cruelties of the Japanese are to be compared only with the vandalism in the Dark Ages in Europe or the brutalities of medieval Asiatic conquerors.'[134] After reading this article, the American ambassador in China, Nelson T. Johnson, wrote in a letter to Stanley K. Hornbeck, the chief of the State Department's Division of Far Eastern Affairs: 'Japanese soldiers at Nanking revealed that after all they are no better than untutored oriental savages.'[135] The association of Asia with uncivilized nations was also made in the *Chicago Tribune*, which described the atrocities in Nanjing as 'a terror which has been truly Asiatic in its disregard of humanities and decencies'.[136] What is interesting about this quote is that it reveals the underlying idea that Western culture was superior to Eastern culture. Despite the atrocities and the slaughter that had been committed during the First World War on European soil, the *Chicago Tribune* adhered to the notion that Asian warfare or Asian brutality was on a whole other level to that of the West. This, of course, is exactly the type of thinking that informed Yellow Peril imagery. The ubiquity of the Yellow Peril in American thought also explains why even such a paper as the *New York Times* printed the following statement in which it portrayed Asian warfare as more brutal than Western warfare: 'Japanese soldiers subjected Nanking to treatment even worse than that which Chinese bandit hordes inflict upon captured towns.'[137]

Yet, to the chagrin of the Chinese government, war against Japan was still out of the question for the US public and press, despite strong public condemnation of the *Panay* Incident and the Nanjing atrocities. *Time* even described reactions in the USA after the *Panay* Incident as 'alarm, not that Japan would go unpunished, but that the offense might somehow involve the U.S. in a war'.[138] Nevertheless,

---

132   *Time* 28.12.1937.

133   See for example *Washington Post* 19.12.1937; *New York Times* 19.12.1937.

134   *New York Times* 9.1.1938.

135   Letter from Johnson to Hornbeck, 14.1.1938, Box 66, Nelson T. Johnson Papers.

136   *Chicago Tribune* 3.2.1938.

137   *New York Times* 19.12.1937.

138   *Time* 27.12.1937 (quote); *Los Angeles Times* 16.12.1937; *Christian Century* 5.1.1938; Gallup, *The Gallup Poll*, vol. 1, p. 85. See also: Shai, *Origins*, p. 130; Jones, *Limits*, pp. 489–90.

organizations like the League for the Protection of American Standards, the American Federation of Labour, the Committee for Industrial Organization as well as various newspapers and magazines supported boycotts of Japanese goods such as silk stockings, canned tuna, toys and light bulbs. The *Washington Post*, for example, wrote in June 1938: 'Many individuals will be stirred by the latest manifestations of Japan's barbarism to intensify their boycott of Japanese goods. And enough individual action in this direction will assuredly encourage more definite governmental protests.'[139]

The Roosevelt Administration's increasing economic pressure on Japan was supported by the public and newspapers. Americans became ever more anti-Japanese and pro-Chinese, and in May 1939, a Gallup Poll showed that 75 per cent of US society sided with China and only 1 per cent with Japan. Even the *New York Times*, whose stance on isolationism was changed in mid-1940 by its publisher Arthur Sulzberger, stated: 'American ore, American scrap iron and American gasoline are Japanese allies in this war' and called US shipments of war materials to Japan 'a dirty business'.[140] Not everybody agreed with such a view. Businessmen and isolationist publications strongly opposed the measures. The non-interventionist *Chicago Tribune*, for example, claimed that a war with Japan would serve to protect European imperialism in the Far East, and that an embargo against Japan was against the interests of the American economy because Japan was one of the best customers of the USA. It summed up its position with the statement: 'Our own China trade is not worth the life of a single American Marine.'[141]

After Japan signed the Tripartite Pact with Germany and Italy on 27 September 1940, the US government increased its financial assistance to China. Similarly, American publications grew more outspoken in their support of China, and by

---

[139]   *Washington Post* 8.6.1938 (quote), 13.7.1938; *Literary Digest* 15.1.1938; *Life* 13.9.1937; *Business Week* 9.10.1937, 16.10.1937 and 8.1.1938. See also: K. Scott Wong, *Americans First: Chinese Americans and the Second World War* (Cambridge and London, 2005), pp. 34–42; Karen J. Leong and Judy Tzu-Chun Wu, 'Filling the Rice Bowls of China: Staging Humanitarian Relief during the Sino-Japanese War', in Suchen Chang and Madeline Y. Hsu (eds), *Chinese Americans and the Politics of Race and Culture* (Philadelphia, 2008), pp. 135–6.

[140]   *New York Times* 11.1.1940 (quote), 20.6.1939, 20.7.1939; *Washington Post* 17.1.1939, 16.6.1939, 28.7.1939, 21.2.1940; Cantril, *Public Opinion 1935–1946*, p. 1082; Gallup, *The Gallup Poll*, vol. 1, pp. 177 and 168. See also: Robert Dallek, *Franklin D. Roosevelt and American Foreign Policy, 1932–1945* (New York, 1979), pp. 76–7 and 270–73; Graebner, 'Hoover', pp. 41–6; Clifford, 'Britain', pp. 146–8; Iriye, *Globalizing*, pp. 163 and 166; Liu, 'Study', pp. 33–5; Iriye, *Wider World*, pp. 76–7; Susan E. Tifft and Alex S. Jones, *The Trust: The Private and Powerful Family behind The New York Times* (Boston and New York, 1999), pp. 195–6.

[141]   *Chicago Tribune* 17.1.1939, 19.1.1939, 14.2.1939, 25.2.1939, 1.5.1939, 26.6.1939, 2.8.1939, 9.8.1939, 15.8.1939, 1.9.1939, 23.9.1939 (quote), 12.12.1939. For businessmen see Wilkins, 'Role', pp. 350–51.

August 1941 70 per cent of American society felt that the USA should take steps to keep Japan from becoming more powerful, even if this resulted in war with Japan.[142] When Japan propagated pan-Asian solidarity with the Greater East Asia Co-Prosperity Sphere in 1940, American interests and possessions in the Pacific were threatened, causing hostile press reactions.[143] Walter Lippmann, probably the most influential columnist at this time, even spoke of the Yellow Peril in its most apocalyptic form:

> The difference between a general peace and the New Order in Asia is profoundly important. What the Japanese ask us to agree to is that the hundreds of millions of peoples in Asia shall become united under the military leadership of Japan. To agree to this would be to set the stage for that war which has been the world's nightmare for two generations – a war between east and west, between the yellow peoples and the whites. … If the Chinese were conquered by Japan, and betrayed by us, and made subordinate partners in Japan's New Order with its cry of Asia for the Asiatics, the last chance would be lost of an accommodation between the east and the west. Our civilization, weakened in Europe by the fierce violence of Hitler's rebellion, would be confronted for the endless future with an insoluble, interminable struggle.[144]

On 25 July 1941, Roosevelt issued an executive order which terminated commercial and financial relations with Japan by freezing Japanese assets in the USA, resulting in a de facto oil embargo, which forced Japan either to leave China or to start a war against the USA as long as their oil reserves still lasted. On 6 September 1941 the Japanese government decided to prepare for war with the USA and the allied powers if by mid-October diplomatic measures had failed to resolve the situation. Negotiations between Nomura Kichisaburō, the Japanese Ambassador to Washington, and US Secretary of State Cordell Hull failed, and resulted on 1 December 1941 in the Japanese Imperial Conference's final decision to go to war against the USA, Britain and the Netherlands.[145]

---

[142]   *New York Times* 28.9.1940, 29.7.1941; *Washington Post* 28.9.1940, 10.10.1940; Gallup, *The Gallup Poll*, vol. 1, pp. 266, 268 and 296–7; 'Summary of the Three Power Pact between Japan, Germany, and Italy', undated, in *FRUS Japan*, vol. 2, pp. 165–6. See also: Sun, *China*, p. 146.

[143]   See for example *Washington Post* 3.12.1941.

[144]   *Washington Post* 2.12.1941.

[145]   'Executive Order No. 8832', 26.7.1941, in: *FRUS Japan*, vol. 2, p. 267; US Department of State, *Peace and War: United States Foreign Policy, 1931–1941* (Honolulu, 2003), pp. 118–22; *New York Times* 27.7.1941. See also: Noriko Kawamura, 'Emperor Hirohito and Japan's Decision to Go to War with the United States: Reexamined', *Diplomatic History*, 31/1 (2007): pp. 51–79; Graebner, 'Hoover', pp. 44–52; Sadao Asada, *From Mahan to Pearl Harbor: The Imperial Japanese Navy and the United States* (Annapolis, 2006), pp. 261–8 and 283–4; Ninkovich, *Imperialism*, pp. 227–8; Christopher

Pearl Harbor and After: Japanese Vermin, Chinese Friends

The Japanese attack on the American fleet at Pearl Harbor on 7 December 1941 occurred without a prior declaration of war and sparked a frenzy of Yellow Peril imagery in the US media. News of the attack was broadcast on the radio, ensuring that Americans all over the country were informed. Congress passed FDR's request for a declaration of war against Japan with only one dissenting vote.[146] Some publications got carried away with hatred, for example the *Los Angeles Times* wrote two days after Pearl Harbor: 'The United States knows now there can be no turning back. No one can even think of turning back. The goal is plain and every citizen must get in step. Our unity writes the death sentence of Japan.'[147] Such passions forced the *Washington Post* to admonish its readers to calm down: 'individual indignation ... may spill over into such hysterical excesses as to the wreaking of anger against the citizens in America of those countries which have loosed the forces of darkness upon the civilized world. Against all such acts the Nation must be on its guard.'[148]

Despite such warnings, suspicion of Japanese Americans as saboteurs, spies and fifth columnists grew, and on 19 February 1942 FDR signed Executive Order 9066, which allowed the US military to order the evacuation of Japanese Americans living on the West Coast. The resettlement resulted from 1942 to 1945 in the removal of about 112,000 Japanese Americans from the West Coast, initially to 15 temporary centres, and then to ten internment camps.[149] According to Wendy Ng the internment was not solely caused by Pearl Harbor but was 'a consequence of anti-Japanese sentiment from the early part of the twentieth century'.[150] While not all US newspapers and magazines supported the mass removal of Japanese Americans, editorial and public opinion on the West Coast quickly took on a stance of outright hostility towards Japanese Americans. Among the most vociferous supporters of the relocation programme was the *Los Angeles Times*, which argued

---

Thorne, *The Issue of War: States, Societies, and the Far Eastern Conflict of 1941–1945* (London, 1985), pp. 15–17; Douglas, *New Alliances*, pp. 99–109; Kimball, *Forged in War*, pp. 107–9; Akira Iriye, *Pearl Harbor and the Coming of the Pacific War* (Boston and New York, 1999); Marder, *Old Friends*, pp. 166–84.

[146] Lawrence W. Levine and Cornelia R. Levine, *The People and the President: America's Conversation with FDR* (Boston, 2002), pp. 393–5.

[147] *Los Angeles Times* 9.12.1941.

[148] *Washington Post* 9.12.1941.

[149] *Los Angeles Times* 19.2.1942. See also: Wendy Ng, *Japanese American Internment during World War II: A History and Reference Guide* (Westport, 2002), pp. 18 and 21–3; Brian Masaru Hayashi, *Democratizing the Enemy: The Japanese American Internment* (Princeton and Oxford, 2004), p. 1.

[150] Ng, *Internment*, pp. 13(quote)–14. For a slightly different view see Bruce Elleman, *Japanese-American Civilian Prisoner Exchanges and Detention Camps, 1941–45* (London and New York, 2006), pp. 2–6, 58–64 and 144–5.

that because of possible Japanese American espionage and sabotage in the USA, demands for Japanese American relocation were only the result of 'the calm common-sense of patriotic citizens who are determined there shall be no Pearl Harbor here'.[151] Even Walter Lippmann stated that because many first and second generation immigrants were American citizens, the problem arose 'that American citizenship, whether acquired by birth or by naturalization, is not an infallible guaranty of loyalty'.[152]

During the Second World War, literature and film portrayals of Chinese improved. Whereas in the interwar years Yellow Peril films with Chinese villains had been quite popular, after Pearl Harbor American films increasingly portrayed the Chinese as heroes. For example, *The Battle of China*, which was part of a series of seven documentary films about the US allies entitled *Why We Fight*, was commissioned by the War Department and directed by Frank Capra, reaching an audience of almost 4,000,000.[153] Various American organizations supported China during the war. Aid to China was also organized on a nationwide basis by the United China Relief, Inc. (UCR), which was founded in 1941 and had Henry Luce, Pearl S. Buck, John D. Rockefeller III and David O. Selznick among its original board of directors. UCR propaganda material focused on similarities between Chinese and Americans, and stressed the spread of democracy in China as well as the influence of Christianity in China, which was epitomized by Chiang and his wife.[154]

Media accounts of China often focused on Soong Meiling or, as she was usually called, Madame Chiang. Soong came from one of the most influential families in China. Her father had been a co-revolutionary of Sun Yat-sen, her sister Ching Ling married Sun in 1915, and her brother T.V. Soong was the finance minister of the Nationalist government. Born around 1898, Soong Meiling went to the USA in 1907 and remained there until 1917 when she graduated from Wellesley College. In December 1927, she married Chiang Kai-shek, and soon afterwards became

---

[151]   *Los Angeles Times* 28.1.1942 (quote), 19.2.1942, 4.3.1942, 7.3.1942, 19.5.1942. See also: Gary Y. Okihiro and Julie Sly, 'The Press, Japanese Americans, and the Concentration Camps', *Phylon*, 44/1 (1983): pp. 66–83.

[152]   *Los Angeles Times* 6.2.1942.

[153]   *The Battle of China*, dir. Frank Capra, prod. Office of War Information. See also: John Haddad, 'The Laundry Man's Got a Knife! China and Chinese America in Early United States Cinema', *Chinese America: History and Perspectives* 15 (2001): pp. 31–46; Lee, *Orientals*, pp. 117–36; Robert Fyne, *The Hollywood Propaganda of World War II* (Metuchen and London, 1994), pp. 31–72; Wong, *Americans*, pp. 77–8; Isaacs, *Images*, pp. 121 and 169–76; Sumiko Higashi, 'Melodrama, Realism, and Race: World War II Newsreels and Propaganda Film', *Cinema Journal*, 37/3 (1998): pp. 38–61.

[154]   Daugherty, 'Publicity', pp. 73–4; Kunczik, *Images*, pp. 208–9; Jespersen, *Images*, pp. 46–58, 76 and 93–5; Neils, *China Images*, pp. 60–62, 69–70 and 74; Leong and Wu, 'Rice Bowls', pp. 134–8; Masland, 'Missionary Influence', pp. 279–83 and 290–96; Varg, *Missionaries*, pp. 252–71; Riegel, 'Channels of Communication', pp. 656–7.

his adviser and translator. During the Second World War, Madame Chiang was crucial in mobilizing American support for China because the years she spent in the USA meant not only that her English sounded like that of a native speaker, but also that she picked up American mannerisms. Thus, for the American public she embodied the image of an Americanized China. In 1942, Madame Chiang visited the USA for medical treatment and afterwards toured the United States in an effort to increase American support of the Chinese Government in the war against Japan. The media was enamoured with her glamour, sharp mind and beauty, and she had such influential supporters as Henry Luce. She graced the covers of publications like *Life* and *Time*, and was described by Henry Luce's wife Claire Boothe in the *Atlanta Constitution* as the 'greatest living woman'. Luce even organized the tour in 1943, which turned her into the darling of the American public. On 18 February, she was the first Asian and the first private citizen to address both the House of Representatives and the Senate. Her speech to the House of Representatives was broadcast on the radio and her speech to the Senate was extremely well received by the media. Newsreels covered her tour in detail, and the US press hailed her as a modern Christian woman who was not only beautiful and loyal to her husband but also believed in the same values as Americans.[155]

The media's portrayal of Madame Chiang as the personification of an Americanized China epitomizes the general portrayal of China and Japan in the USA after Pearl Harbor. Since the turn of the century, US scientists had tried to prove that the Chinese and Japanese did not belong to the same race. However, whereas back then they had tried to show that the Japanese belonged to the white race and the Chinese to the Mongolian race, now the Japanese were described as an Asian race, while the psychological as well as physical qualities of the Chinese were more and more associated with those of Americans. China, thus, became 'the Oriental mirror-image of America'.[156] Already in 1931, *Time* had described the Chinese as 'peace-loving' people, and the Japanese as 'pushing, successful, militaristic neighbors'.[157] This dichotomy between the portrayal of Chinese and Japanese became even starker once the USA and China fought together on the side of the allies. In December 1941, *Time* published the article 'How to tell your friends from the Japs', in which it compared Chinese and Japanese physiognomy and characteristics so that its readers could differentiate between the Chinese (i.e. the 'friends') and the Japanese. The analysis not only included gait, physique and facial expressions, but also such random information as the choice of eyewear:

---

[155]   *Life* 30.6.1941; *Atlanta Constitution* 26.7.1942; *Time* 1.3.1943; 'News of the Day', 26.2.1943, Hearst Metrotone News; 'Madame Chiang Kai Shek speaks to Congress', 1943, Fox Movietone. See also: Laura Tyson Li, *Madame Chiang Kai-Shek: China's Eternal First Lady* (New York, 2006), pp. 181 and 193–214; Wong, *Americans First*, pp. 90–109; Jespersen, *Images*, pp. 83–4 and 92–101; Kunczik, *Images*, pp. 206–9.

[156]   Peter Schrijvers, *The GI War against Japan: American Soldiers in Asia and the Pacific during World War II* (New York, 2002), p. 145.

[157]   *Time* 28.7.1931.

'Most Chinese avoid horn-rimmed spectacles.'[158] The US Army in turn issued a *Pocket Guide to China* which outlined physical differences of Chinese and Japanese, and noted: 'OF ALL the peoples of Asia, the Chinese are most like Americans.' It also reminded its readers that the war was not about race, and that a portrayal of the Chinese as yellow played into the hands of Japanese propaganda, while notions of white superiority fell into the trap of Nazi propaganda.[159]

Japan had been described as the Yellow Peril whenever American interests were threatened by Japanese expansion. After Pearl Harbor, American fears of Japan uniting Asian nations against the West seemed to have become reality.[160] A *Time* cover by Arthur Szyk published two weeks after Pearl Harbor showed the Japanese Admiral Yamamoto as the embodiment of the Yellow Peril. His skin, his military medals and the battleship in the background are yellow, and his distorted features have an aggressive and sinister expression. Moreover, he is wearing a military uniform and is in front of a battleship whose gun ports are pointing straight at the reader, all of which hints at an intrinsically militaristic nature of the Japanese. In case any readers of *Time* failed to get the message, the caption stated: 'Japan's aggressor: Admiral Yamamoto. His was the execution of brilliant treachery.'[161] In his fireside chat of 23 February 1942, FDR also relied on typical Yellow Peril imagery when he told his audience of a possible future in which Japan would dominate the southwestern Pacific, and attack the Western Hemisphere, Africa and the Near East.[162] Even *Christian Century* jumped on the bandwagon and presented the brutality of Japanese soldiers as proof that they were a reincarnation of the original Yellow Peril: 'The atrocities committed against [Chinese] people have resurrected a pattern of horror which had been thought buried with Attila and Genghis Khan.'[163]

The enmification of Japanese Americans in US popular culture and the press was generally much more intense because the Japanese and the Chinese were constructed as polar opposites in the US media. While Japan was portrayed as the Yellow Peril in the US media, China was presented as a civilized and Christian nation. The *Los Angeles Times*, for instance, described China as 'the front-rank fighter in the "army of civilization"'.[164] A survey from 15 July 1942 showed that Americans viewed the Chinese as hardworking, honest and brave, while the

---

[158]   *Time* 22.12.1941.

[159]   War and Navy Departments (ed.), *Pocket Guide to China* (Washington, DC, 1943). See also: Wong, *Americans First*, pp. 76–9.

[160]   Dower, *War without Mercy*, p. 163. See also Saul K. Padover, 'Japanese Race Propaganda', *The Public Opinion Quarterly*, 7/2 (1943): pp. 191–204.

[161]   *Time* 22.12.1941.

[162]   Levine and Levine, *People*, p. 417.

[163]   *Christian Century* 7.7.1943.

[164]   *Los Angeles Times* 7.7.1942. See also *Life* 22.12.1941; *Time* 1.3.1943; *New York Times* 9.3.1941.

Japanese were seen as treacherous, sly and cruel.[165] The fact that until Pearl Harbor the European theatre received much more media attention than the Pacific theatre,[166] could be a reason why portrayals of Japanese were much more stereotypical than those of Germans. As the *Washington Post* explained in early 1940: 'Because there is far more power in Europe than in the Far East, because the Atlantic is much narrower than the Pacific, and because we belong to Western, not Eastern, civilization, what happens in Europe is far more important to us than what happens in eastern Asia.'[167] The *Washington Post* had been following events in Europe closely, not least because its publisher, Eugene Meyer, was Jewish and decidedly anti-fascist. In 1937, Meyer and Felix Morley, in charge of the editorial page, even went to Europe to see the situation first hand. Morley's objection to Meyer's conviction that the USA had to save Western Europe, eventually led to Morley's resignation in 1940.[168] Another reason was that, like in Britain, Social Darwinism and Anglo-Saxonism caused the US media and government propaganda to portray the Germans as racial allies, focusing their hatred on Hitler and the Nazi officials, while the Japanese were described with Yellow Peril imagery as a physically and mentally inferior and fanatical people.[169] Thus, Anne O'Hare McCormick of the *New York Times* wrote after Pearl Harbor: 'The Japanese are more fanatic than the Nazis. They have a greater indifference to death than the Russians.'[170] Various Gallup Polls also showed that the Japanese – not the Germans – were seen by Americans as the USA's main enemy, and as late as November 1944 13 per cent of interviewees in a Gallup Poll on US policies towards Japan after the war, responded that the USA should 'Kill all Japanese people'. Similarly, the use of atomic bombs on Japanese cities was supported by a staggering 85 per cent in

---

[165]   Cantril, *Public Opinion*, pp. 499 and 501.

[166]   David Reynolds, '1940: Fulcrum of the Twentieth Century?', *International Affairs*, 66/2 (1990): pp. 333–6; William L. O'Neill, *A Democracy at War: America's Fight at Home and Abroad in World War II* (London and Cambridge, 1997), pp. 15–32; Iriye, *Globalizing*, pp. 176–81; Nicholas John Cull, *Selling War: The British Propaganda Campaign against American 'Neutrality' in World War II* (Oxford and New York, 1995), pp. 97–109 and 127–34; Gerd Horten, *Radio Goes to War: The Cultural Politics of Propaganda during World War II* (Berkeley, Los Angeles and London, 2002), pp. 27–39; Alfred Haworth Jones, 'The Making of an Interventionist on the Air: Elmer Davis and CBS News, 1939–1941', *The Pacific Historical Review*, 42/1 (1973): pp. 74–93.

[167]   *Washington Post* 28.1.1940.

[168]   Roberts, *Shadow*, pp. 226, 231 and 236.

[169]   Susan D. Moeller, *Shooting War: Photography and the American Experience of Combat* (New York, 1989), pp. 159–60; Schrijvers, *GI War*, p. 147; Cull, *Selling War*, pp. 200–201; Paul P. Somers, '"Right in the Führer's Face": American Editorial Cartoons of the World War II Period', *American Journalism*, 13/3 (1996): pp. 346–7; Thorne, 'Racial Aspects', pp. 277–8; Thorne, *Issue of War*, pp. 129–30; James J. Kimble, *Mobilizing the Home Front: War Bonds and Domestic Propaganda* (College Station, 2006), pp. 84–94; Dower, *War without Mercy*, pp. 77–93.

[170]   *New York Times* 8.12.1941.

August 1945. Yellow Peril imagery must, therefore, have profoundly influenced American perceptions of Japan.[171]

According to John Dower, during the Second World War the core imagery for depicting the Japanese was taken from racial stereotypes that had been applied to non-whites for centuries and were backed up in the nineteenth century by science. They emphasized the subhuman nature of the Japanese, which had them depicted as apes and vermin; they were dehumanized and described as inherently inferior, i.e. primitive, childish, mentally deficient or mad. They were also portrayed as savage creatures which were thoroughly militaristic and irrational, not only implying that the Japanese could be killed without mercy (which resulted in a 'kill-or-be-killed' psychology in the Pacific Theatre, and instances of what Dower calls 'battlefield degeneracy', where allied troops collected Japanese gold teeth, bones, ears and skulls) but also that Western nations were democratic, rational and peaceful.[172] In Illustration 3.18 by Bruce Russell, Japan is portrayed as a gorilla-like monster that is dripping with the 'blood of defenceless civilians'. As an evil, subhuman, brutal and bloodthirsty creature that kills innocent and defenceless people, Japan is the embodiment of the Yellow Peril.

One of the most famous and beloved war correspondents of the Second World War was Ernie Pyle, who reported first from Europe and then from the Pacific Theatre. He died on 18 April 1945 in Okinawa by a Japanese sniper's bullet. Before his death, his stories reached an audience of millions. Generally known for positive reporting and a lack of racist depiction of the Japanese, Pyle noted:

> In Europe we felt that our enemies, horrible and deadly as they were, were still people. But out here I soon gathered that the Japanese were looked upon as something subhuman and repulsive; the way some people feel about cockroaches or mice. Shorty after I arrived I saw a group of Japanese prisoners in a wire-fenced courtyard, and they were wrestling and laughing and talking just like normal human beings. And yet they gave me the creeps, and I wanted a mental bath after looking at them.[173]

Pyle also wrote that marines in the Pacific called the Japanese 'Japes', a combination of 'Jap' and 'ape'.[174] The dehumanizing of the Japanese was common in the US media and served to point out their inhuman or beastly nature as well as their irrationality and fanatical behaviour. Thus, Theodore Seuss Geisel ('Dr. Seuss'), repeatedly depicted Japan as a snake in his editorial cartoons for the left-

---

[171]   Gallup, *The Gallup Poll*, vol. 1, pp. 337, 370, 388–9, 477, 508–9 and 521–2.

[172]   *New York Times* 9.12.1941; *Washington Post* 10.12.1941. See also: Dower, *War without Mercy*; Sam Keene, *Faces of the Enemy: Reflections of the Hostile Imagination* (San Francisco, 1986), p. 25.

[173]   Ernie Pyle, *Last Chapter* (New York, 1946), p. 5. See also: Dower, *War without Mercy*, p. 78; Copeland, *Media's Role*, pp. 199–201.

[174]   Pyle, *Last Chapter*, p. 23.

Japanese Print

Illustration 3.18   Bruce Russell, 'Japanese Print', *Los Angeles Times* (9.2.1942)
Source: © 1942, Los Angeles Times. Reprinted with Permission.

wing newspaper *PM*.[175] Already in 1938, *Time* wrote about the Japanese: 'Much as a hill of ants are driven by their impulses to conquer another hill, the Japanese have gone forth to war.' By equating them to ants, the article stressed their huge numbers, which related to another aspect of the Yellow Peril.[176] The *Los Angeles Times*, in turn, repeatedly referred to the Japanese as 'yellow vermin', which implied that they had to be exterminated.[177] This was also the message of various cartoons, such as Carey Orr's 'One good step deserves another', in which Japan was depicted as a spider about to be stepped on by the huge, studded boots of the USA.[178] Illustration 3.19 was the cover of a *Collier's* issue commemorating Pearl Harbor. The artist was Arthur Szyk, who also drew covers for *Time* magazine. The *Collier's* cover shows the Emperor Hirohito as a bat with huge fangs preparing to drop a bomb over Pearl Harbor on 7 December 1941.

The visualization of enemies as animals had, of course existed long before the Second World War. The spider in particular had been a very popular motif to visualize enemies as cunning, devious, greedy and revolting.[179] Yet, despite the popularity of Yellow Peril imagery in American depictions of Japan, the Yellow Peril was not an ideal image for allied propaganda due to its implications that the Chinese could potentially join the Japanese against the West, and so the Japanese were often also simply described as barbarians. This turned the war into a conflict about (democratic) civilization and gave the USA a purpose that directly related to the notion of American Exceptionalism.[180] In 1941, the *Washington Post* portrayed the Japanese soldiers 'as barbarians of the lowest order [which] embittered every civilized human being against their nation'.[181] After Pearl Harbor, the *New York Times* wrote: 'The American people, like the British, thought they had done with savagery. They go back now to the primitive business of destruction with cold anger and the deep repugnance of civilized men who have proved that they have better uses for their energies and their skills.'[182] The Chinese, in contrast, were presented as a civilized and heroic people. In 1942, Walter Lippmann described them as

---

[175]   *PM* 13.10.1941, 1.1.1942, 17.4.1942, 23.5.1942, 10.6.1942.

[176]   *Time* 3.1.1938. See also: *Los Angeles Times* 3.3.1942.

[177]   *Los Angeles Times* 21.12.1941, 28.1.1941. The *Los Angeles Times* picked the expression up from Hitler. See also: Dower, *Japan*, p. 264; Keene, *Faces*, pp. 60–64.

[178]   *Chicago Tribune* 24.4.1942.

[179]   Gerd Unverfehrt, 'Der Mensch-Tier-Vergleich: die Spinne als Zeichen', in Gerhard Langemeyer, Gerd Unverfehrt, Herwig Guratzsch and Christopf Stölzl (eds), *Bild als Waffe: Mittel und Motive der Karikatur in fünf Jahrhunderten* (München, 1984), pp. 238–49.

[180]   *New York Times* 10.12.1941, 12.12.1941; *Washington Post* 8.6.1938, 25.8.1939, 11.12.1941. See also Ryan, *US Foreign Policy*, pp. 98–102; Thorne, 'Racial Aspects', pp. 356–7; Keene, *Faces*, pp. 43–8.

[181]   *Washington Post* 7.7.1941.

[182]   *New York Times* 14.12.1941.

Illustration 3.19   Arthur Szyk, 'December 7, 1941', *Collier's* (12.12.1942)
Source: Reproduced with permission of the Arthur Szyk Society.

being 'wise with the experience of centuries of civilized life'.[183] On 10 October 1941 (a national holiday in China), the *Washington Post* called on all Americans to 'salute a country which, in defending itself against the Japanese invader, has done a valiant service for American security in the Pacific. ... Let us not forget that service as we salute a country with an unbroken history of 4000 years and a civilization which is both unique and great.'[184] In 1943, *Christian Century* wrote: 'there has been something about the heroism of the Chinese, standing almost with bare hands to defy a completely armed invader, which compels a praise that is beyond words.'[185]

The improved image of China not only had the effect that, on 11 January 1943, extraterritoriality was abolished between the USA and China, but from 1942 US media also began discussing a repeal of the Chinese Exclusion Act, arguing that China was an ally of the USA and that with the quota system there would have to be no fear of a Chinese invasion. On 21 October 1943 the House of Representatives passed the bill, the Senate followed on 26 November 1943, and FDR signed it into law on 17 December 1943. It allowed 105 Chinese to enter the USA annually, and gave Chinese the right to naturalization. The House Report not only stressed 'the tenacity and courage of the Chinese in their terrible ordeal of the last 7 years' but also noted: 'It has always been the policy of the United States to help China in her struggle against encroachment upon her independence and sovereignty and we are now brothers in arms in that cause.'[186] Thus, once again American China policies were legitimized with the image of the USA as the mentor and protector of China.

Switzerland

Anti-Imperialism and the Yellow Peril

Although Chinese and Japanese immigration was crucial to the origin and development of Yellow Peril imagery in Britain and the USA, the case of Switzerland shows that the transnational circulation of Yellow Peril imagery spread independently of Asian immigration because until 1940 less than 130 Chinese and Japanese lived in Switzerland.[187] As the Yellow Peril was based on

---

[183]   *Los Angeles Times* 8.4.1942.

[184]   *Washington Post* 10.10.1941.

[185]   *Christian Century* 7.7.1943.

[186]   'Repealing the Chinese Exclusion Laws', H. Repts. Report no. 732, 78-1, vol. 4, p. 26. See also Wong, *Americans First*, pp. 110–24; Lisa Lowe, *Immigrant Acts: On Asian American Cultural Politics* (Durham and London, 1996), pp. 19–20; Paul A. Varg, *The Closing of the Door: Sino-American Relations 1936–1946* (East Lansing, 1973), p. 51; Dong Wang, *China's Unequal Treaties: Narrating National History* (Lanham and Oxford, 2005), p. 93.

[187]   Ritzmann-Blickenstorfer, *Historische Statistik*, pp. 133 and 146.

racial theories, its popularity also depended on Social Darwinist ideas. This was the case in Switzerland, where various scientists fervently supported eugenics and craniology, and where theories of Swiss racial homogeneity culminated in the 1930s in the attempt to define a Swiss race with the *homo alpinus helveticus*.[188] Yellow Peril imagery became popular in Switzerland through Limehouse fiction, which was translated into German during the interwar period, and serialized in various Swiss magazines. However, Yellow Peril imagery was largely confined to literature and cartoons.[189]

Another factor that influenced Yellow Peril perceptions was geopolitical interest in the Far East. In the early twentieth century Britain had an alliance with Japan but had to legitimize its presence in China. Consequently, British definitions of the Yellow Peril focused on China. In the USA, on the other hand, the Yellow Peril was associated with Japan because American interests in the Far East were threatened by Japanese expansion in China. By comparison, Swiss geopolitical interests in the Far East were practically non-existent. Japan's military successes against China in 1895 and against Russia in 1905 did not lead to an influx of Yellow Peril images in Switzerland because Japan's modernization was positively compared to China, which was deemed an uncivilized nation, and because Russian autocracy and orthodoxy were seen as being the opposite of Swiss values. Furthermore, the fact that Japan as a small nation had defeated the much bigger Russia ensured Japan Swiss sympathy.[190] After the First World War, Japanese expansion in China was condemned in the Swiss press. Yet, contrary to the US press, which was pro-Chinese in its reactions to the Shandong issue, Swiss media opposed imperialism per se and showed little sympathy for or interest in China.[191]

In the 1930s, Swiss interests in the Far East were deemed unimportant, and the Swiss government was the last European government to recognize the

---

[188]   Georg Kreis, 'Der "homo alpinus helveticus": Zum schweizerischen Rassendiskurs der 30er Jahre', in Guy P. Marchal and Arram Mattioli (eds), *Erfundene Schweiz: Konstruktionen nationaler Identität* (Zürich, 1992), pp. 175–90; Patrick Kury, *Über Fremde reden: Überfremdungsdiskurs und Ausgrenzung in der Schweiz 1900–1945* (Zürich, 2003), pp. 44–55.

[189]   *Tages-Anzeiger* 21.6.1900; *Journal de Genève* 24.7.1900; *NZZ* 30.8.1919, 29.11.1927, 4.4.1935; *Schweizer Illustrierte* 25.5.1938; Sax Rohmer, *Die Mission des Dr. Fu-Mandschu* (Berlin, 1927); Paul Keller, *Japan* (St. Gallen, 1935).

[190]   Martin Hürlimann, 'Die Entwicklung der schweizerisch-japanischen Beziehungen', in Schweizerisch-Japanische Gesellschaft (ed.), *Schweiz–Japan* (Zürich, 1975), pp. 52–3; Paul Akio Nakai, 'Die Aufnahme der diplomatischen Beziehungen zwischen der Schweiz und Japan im Jahre 1864', in Comité du centenaire (ed.), *Helvetia – Nippon: 1864–1964* (Tokio, 1964), pp. 33–65; Roger Mottini, *Die Schweiz und Japan während der Meiji-Zeit (1868–1912): Begegnung, Berichterstattung und Bilder* (Bamberg, 1998), pp. 47–58, 154–9, 166–77 and 195–9; Claude Altermatt, *Les débuts de la diplomatie professionelle en Suisse (1848–1914)* (Fribourg, 1990), pp. 141–4.

[191]   *Tages-Anzeiger* 17.5.1919, 28.5.1919, 30.6.1919, 8.6.1925, 20.6.1925; *NZZ* 22.5.1919.

Nanjing government as the official Chinese government in 1933.[192] It is, therefore, quite surprising that the Japanese occupation of Manchuria in 1931 was such a hot topic in the Swiss press. The *Tages-Anzeiger*, for example, ran stories about the Manchurian Incident on its front pages until the end of September. It also immediately presented Japan as the aggressor in the conflict, often printing articles about the suffering of the Chinese civilian population, something which neither British nor American newspapers did. One of these articles stated:

> The refugees suffer from a lack of food. On the trains, where every seat is occupied, and where nobody dares to leave in order to fetch goods, fearing that they would lose their hard-fought for place, horrific scenes take place because the mothers beg heart-wrenchingly for some water for their small children who are dying of thirst.[193]

The *Journal de Genève*, in turn, argued that the Japanese sphere of influence had always been a problem, and that the Manchurian Incident simply proved that as long as the unequal treaty system was in place in China, there would not be long-lasting peace.[194]

The Manchurian Incident was also such a big issue in the Swiss media because it affected the League of Nations. After China appealed to the League, the *NZZ* euphorically declared that none of the parties involved in the Sino-Japanese conflict would be able to ignore the decision of the League without facing the gravest consequences. The *Journal de Genève* and the *Tages-Anzeiger* viewed the Sino-Japanese conflict as the most decisive test for the League of Nations, and felt that the reputation of the League depended on a strong stance against Japan. However, after Japan failed to comply with the League's demands, the *NZZ* and the *Journal de Genève* became increasingly frustrated with Japan, while the *Tages-Anzeiger* and the *Nebelspalter* criticized the League's inaction.[195] For Switzerland, the League was important because it gave small nations a voice, and so the Swiss government continued to denounce the Japanese occupation of Manchuria, yet to no avail: on 11 March 1932 the League committed itself only to a non-recognition

---

[192] 'Der Vorsteher des Politischen Departementes, G. Motta, an den schweizerischen Generalkonsul in Shanghai, J.L. Isler', 25.1.1929, in *DDS*, vol. 9, pp. 813–14; 'Le Chef du Département politique, G. Motta, au Consul général de Suisse à Shanghaï, E. Lardy', 26.1.1932, in *DDS*, vol. 10, pp. 313–14; 'Le Consul général de Suisse à Shanghaï, E. Lardy, au Chef du Département politique, G. Motta', 22.4.1932, in *DDS*, vol. 10, pp. 353–7; 'Le Consul général et Chargé d'affaires de Suisse en Chine, E. Lardy, au Chef du Département politique, G. Motta', 24.1.1933, in *DDS*, vol. 10, pp. 562–4.

[193] *Tages-Anzeiger* 22.9.1931 (quote), 19.9.1931, 25.9.1931, 29.9.1931, 24.9.1931, 25.9.1931, 29.9.1931.

[194] *Journal de Genève* 22.9.1931.

[195] *NZZ* 23.9.1931, 25.9.1931; *Journal de Genève* 25.9.1931, 27.9.1931; *Tages-Anzeiger* 23.9.1931, 25.9.1931, 26.9.1931; *Nebelspalter* 9.10.1931.

policy.[196] The lack of economic and political interest in China meant that reports on the situation in China were less prone to refer to racial stereotypes that were part of Yellow Peril imagery, but also that Swiss editors and journalists used China to make general statements about international relations. As Yellow Peril imagery would have turned the focus away from this, after 1931 there were only a few references to the Yellow Peril in the Swiss press. When one compares Swiss, British and American cartoons that were published after the Japanese occupation of Manchuria, it is quite striking how differently they visualize the event. American cartoonists viewed the USA as a mentor of China, and consequently focused on the way China was affected by the Manchurian Incident. In Britain, on the other hand, China had traditionally been perceived negatively, and the conflict was primarily interesting because it involved the League of Nations. Swiss cartoonists, though, were interested mainly in the illegality of Japan's expansion.

Of Chinese Heroes and Japanese Arsonists

In the mid-1930s, the conflict between China and Japan received less media attention in Switzerland than events in Europe and the economic crisis, but after the Marco Polo Bridge Incident in 1937, it once again became the biggest topic of both the *NZZ* and the *Tages-Anzeiger*.[197] Yet, Japanese expansion in China, and later in Asia, was not regarded as a threat to Swiss interests, so the Yellow Peril was not used as widely in the Swiss press as in the USA. For example, after the bombing of Shanghai, *Die Weltwoche* did not describe Japan as a monstrous nation but instead advised Swiss citizens to return to Switzerland.[198] Swiss interests in China were clearly not perceived as significant.

The vast majority of the Swiss press was sympathetic towards the Chinese during the Sino-Japanese War. In December 1937, reports on the situation in Nanjing made the cover of the *Tages-Anzeiger* almost on a daily basis. Once again, the newspaper focused on Chinese refugees, and the *Schweizer Illustrierte*, *Die Weltwoche* and the *Journal de Genève* printed reports and pictures of the Japanese military and the destruction the war caused in China. Some of these articles were quite blatant in guiding the sympathies of the reader. For example, in January 1938, the *Schweizer Illustrierte* had on its cover a picture of a Chinese man carrying a boy on his shoulders. The caption under the photo read: 'Horrible were the hours for the inhabitants of the Chinese city which was bombed by Japanese planes. ... The only possession which this father could save on his escape was his child. A

---

[196]   Willy Bretscher and Walther Weibel, *Der chinesisch-japanische Konflikt vor dem Völkerbund* (Zürich, 1932), pp. 99–109; Thorne, *Limits*, pp. 213–14.

[197]   Kurt Imhof, 'Kriegskommunikation im sozialen Wandel', in Kurt Imhof and Peter Schulz (eds), *Medien und Krieg – Krieg in den Medien* (Zürich, 1995), p. 128; Kamber, 'Medienereignishierarchien 1910–1940', pp. 383–6.

[198]   *Die Weltwoche* 27.8.1937; *Schweizer Illustrierte* 1.9.1937; *Die Weltwoche* 23.7.1937.

happy smile is on the father's face, while the shocked and frightened expression of the child still mirrors the fear that it had to endure.'[199] The film version of Pearl S. Buck's *The Good Earth* opened in Switzerland in late 1937 to good reviews, and Buck's stories were translated and printed in Swiss magazines, yet they alone cannot explain the Swiss press's pro-Chinese stance. The focus on Chinese refugees can be explained by Switzerland's self-image that it was a neutral nation which helped those in need. For example, *Die Weltwoche* on numerous occasions reminded its readers that they had to donate money and goods to the Red Cross and other organizations to help refugees (especially children).[200]

The fact that no Britons or Swiss were present in the Nanjing Safety Zone partly explains why there was less knowledge of the atrocities in those countries and why the media reactions were not as strong as in the USA.[201] The *Tages-Anzeiger* printed the first story about the massacres on 20 December after the Reuters correspondent had arrived in Shanghai.[202] Once accounts of the massacres reached Switzerland, the *Nebelspalter* began portraying Japanese brutality in more graphic ways. In February 1938, it published Illustration 3.20 by Gregor Rabinovitch, in which three Japanese generals look down at a sea of skulls and skeletons. The caption of the cartoon reads: 'The Japanese War Council does not declare war in order to avoid making a bad impression in the world!'

In the same issue, the *Nebelspalter* announced that Swiss salesmen had learnt from Japan's behaviour in the Far East and were now threatening housewives to buy their goods by saying: 'If you don't buy something immediately I will set your house on fire ....'[203] Indeed, the magazine had quite a field day with Japan's denial of war with China. After the League of Nations stated that Japan was conducting war against China, the *Nebelspalter* printed a cartoon in which it referred to the Swiss tradition of dyeing hard-boiled eggs for Easter celebrations. To do this, one has to place the egg in a bowl of dye by hand, which results in coloured fingers. The cartoon depicted Japan with grotesque features in a military uniform and hands dripping with blood, denying its actions by claiming 'I've just dyed eggs!'[204]

Yet, apart from the *Nebelspalter*, Swiss media tended not to be openly anti-Japanese. There are various reasons for this. Firstly, Switzerland was not directly affected by the war in the Pacific. In fact, it even profited from it by selling arms to

---

[199]   *Schweizer Illustrierte* 21.7.1937, 18.8.1937, 1.9.1937, 15.9.1937, 22.9.1937, 10.11.1937, 20.12.1937, 5.1.1938 (quote), 22.6.1938; *Tages-Anzeiger* 1.12.1937, 4.12.1937, 6.12.1937, 7.12.1937, 8.12.1937, 9.12.1937, 10.12.1937, 11.12.1937, 14.12.1937, 15.12.1937, 16.12.1937, 17.12.1937, 18.12.1937, 20.12.1937, 22.12.1937; *Die Weltwoche* 8.7.1938, 25.8.1939; *Journal de Genève* 31.1.1938.

[200]   *Die Weltwoche* 1.10.1937; 9.5.1941 and 20.3.1942; *Schweizer Illustrierte* 10.3.1943.

[201]   *NZZ* 11.1.1938.

[202]   *Tages-Anzeiger* 20.12.1937.

[203]   *Nebelspalter* 11.2.1938.

[204]   *Nebelspalter* 25.11.1938.

Rabinovitch

Der japanische Kriegsrat unterlässt die Kriegserklärung, um keinen
schlechten Eindruck auf die Welt zu machen!

Illustration 3.20   Gregor Rabinovitch, 'The Japanese War Council',
                     Nebelspalter (11.2.1938)
Source: Scan provided by Zentralbibliothek Zürich. Reproduced with permission of
Nebelspalter.

both Japan and China.[205] Another reason for the absence of Yellow Peril imagery in the Swiss press was that Switzerland continued diplomatic relations with China and Japan during the war. In 1942, Switzerland represented the interests of 20 countries in Japan and Japanese-occupied China, among them the USA and Britain.[206] Furthermore, as Switzerland was surrounded by warring parties and not greatly affected by the Sino-Japanese War, much more attention was given to the war in Europe. The constant fear of a German invasion became so dominant that even events in China were interpreted within the framework of a foreign menace threatening the nation.[207]

The lack of enmification of Japan in Swiss newspapers and magazines can also be explained by press censorship. Press censorship was common in various countries in the 1930s and during the Second World War. Due to their explicit and exaggerated nature, cartoons often underwent censorship. In Britain, the government prevented the publication of unpatriotic cartoons or cartoons that could affect Britain's relations with countries like Germany. David Low was on a few occasions asked by the editor of the *Evening Standard* to tone down his criticism of dictators (though he did not always comply). Even the Home Secretary asked Low to stop drawing cartoons that offended Hitler – to no avail. Due to his outspoken opposition to Hitler and Mussolini, Low's cartoons were banned in Germany and Italy but, ironically enough, the publication of his

---

[205] TNA FO 436 F388/34/10. See also: Peter Hug, *Schweizer Rüstungsindustrie und Kriegsmaterialhandel zur Zeit des Nationalsozialismus: Unternehmensstrategien – Marktentwicklung – politische* Überwachung (Zürich, 2002), pp. 251–4 and 312–29; Unabhängige Expertenkommission Schweiz-Zweiter Weltkrieg (ed.), *Die Schweiz, der Nationalsozialismus und der Zweite Weltkrieg: Schlussbericht* (Zürich, 2002), pp. 54–7; Jakob Tanner, '"Réduit national" und Aussenwirtschaft: Wechselwirkungen zwischen militärischer Dissuasion und ökonomischer Kooperation mit den Achsenmächten', in Philipp Sarasin and Regina Wecker (eds), *Raubgold, Reduit, Flüchtlinge: Zur Geschichte der Schweiz in Zweiten Weltkrieg* (Zürich, 1998), pp. 88–9.

[206] Zhou, *Exterritorialitätsrechte*, p. 21; Hürlimann, 'Entwicklung', p. 54; Michele Coduri, 'Argent et bons offices: Implications *économiques* de la protection des intérêts alliés en Extrême-Orient pendant la Deuxième Guerre mondiale', in Peter Hug and Martin Kloter (eds), *Aufstieg und Niedergang des Bilateralismus: Schweizerische Aussen- und Aussenwirtschaftspolitik 1930–1960: Rahmenbedingungen, Entscheidungsstrukturen, Fallstudien* (Zürich, 1999), pp. 233–57.

[207] Esther Kamber, 'Medienereignishierarchien 1930–1960: Neue Zürcher Zeitung, Tages-Anzeiger, Tagwacht, Vaterland', in Kurt Imhof, Heinz Kleger and Gaetano Romano (eds), *Konkordanz und Kalter Krieg: Analyse von Medienereignissen in der Schweiz der Zwischen- und Nachkriegszeit* (Zürich, 1996), pp. 258–66; Unabhängige Expertenkommission, *Die Schweiz*, p. 93.

cartoons in other countries increased.[208] British newsreels were also censored.[209] In the USA, censorship was introduced in 1942 with the Office of Censorship, which gave out guidelines and to which media outlets could voluntarily submit their stories for approval. The American press co-operated very well with the Office of Censorship even though the guidelines were not mandatory.[210] Swiss measures affected the press more and they were also introduced long before those in Britain and the USA. In 1934, the Swiss government introduced censorship in order to prevent claims that the Swiss press was violating the country's neutrality While it mostly targeted critical portrayals of Germany, some portrayals of Japan were also deemed problematic.[211] For example, in 1938, the Department of Foreign Affairs demanded to know from the Swiss consul in Shanghai the name of a journalist who had written an *NZZ* article criticizing Japanese warfare in China. The Department stated:

> We would be very obliged if you could find out who is the author of it, and then draw his attention to the important interest that we have in not alienating the goodwill of the Japanese government, the great majority of the Swiss established in China as well as their enterprises are situated in the regions currently occupied by the Japanese armies.[212]

Swiss journalists were not only affected by the censorship of the Swiss government, but also by that of the Japanese government in China. While American correspondents managed to evade Japanese censorship and cable stories about Japanese atrocities to the USA from US ships, Swiss correspondents were not only fewer in number than Americans, they also had no ships they could use to wire stories home and so their messages were subject to Japanese censorship like those of British journalists.

Swiss press reports about China also differed significantly from British and American reports because of the *Geistige Landesverteidigung* (i.e. spiritual defence

---

[208]   Low, *Autobiography*, pp. 249–54 and 277–80; Hugh Cudlipp, *Publish and be Damned! The Astonishing Story of the Daily Mirror* (London, 1953), pp. 175–98; Seymour-Ure and Schoff, *Low*, pp. 49–50 and 91–3.

[209]   Gerald Sanger, 'We Lived in the Presence of History: The Story of British Movietone News in the War Years', in Luke McKernan (ed.), *Yesterday's News: The British Cinema Newsreel Reader* (London, 2002), pp. 165–6.

[210]   Copeland, *Media's Role*, p. 199; Andreas Elter, *Die Kriegsverkäufer: Geschichte der US-Propaganda 1917–2005* (Frankfurt am Main, 2005), pp. 65–70.

[211]   Pascal Ihle, *Die journalistische Landesverteidigung im Zweiten Weltkrieg: Eine kommunikationshistorische Studie* (Zürich, 1997); André Lasserre, *La Suisse des années sombres: Courants d'opinion pendant la Deuxième Guerre mondiale, 1939–1945* (Lausanne, 1989), pp. 21–7.

[212]   'La Division des Affaires étrangères du Département politique au Consul general de Suisse à Shanghaï, E. Fontanel', 28.6.1938, in *DDS*, vol. 12, p. 755.

of the nation). The *Geistige Landesverteidigung* was a complex phenomenon based on a wide variety of discourses from across the political spectrum, which described Swiss nationhood and Swiss culture as a unique amalgamation of a heterogenic ethnic foundation, direct democracy, individual liberties, federalism, neutrality and political independence that had to be protected from external threats. Accordingly, the Swiss nation was based on the will of its citizens to live together as a national community (*Willensnation*), or on a common character that had evolved out of shared history and genealogical descent (*Wesensgemeinschaft*) rather than a shared racial basis.[213] The cultural nationalism of the *Geistige Landesverteidigung* and its combination of voluntary and organic nationalism became a national policy in 1938, when the Federal Council stated that the *Geistige Landesverteidigung*'s focus on Swiss cultural values was part of the national defence, and that there was no connection between race and state or language and state. Instead, it was argued that the Swiss nation was based on a common spirit and a shared love of liberty and democracy.[214]

The importance of the *Geistige Landesverteidigung* for the discursive and visual construction of Swiss nationhood had the effect that after the outbreak of the Sino-Japanese War, Swiss newspapers and magazines focused on Chinese resistance, portraying it as an act of heroic patriotism, thus linking the situation in China to that of Switzerland, where the discourse of the *Wehrbereitschaft* (i.e. the willingness to defend Swiss independence and freedom against foreign threats) was omnipresent.[215] The *NZZ* wrote:

> Entire provinces have been lost, 200 regiments annihilated or disbanded. Dozens of cities destroyed, hundreds of others suffer Japanese air terror on a daily basis, and millions of people flee the Yangzi valley from the warzone to the West. But China has a dozen other huge provinces, that no Japanese soldier has been to, it has a thousand regiments of soldiers, thousands of cities and hundreds of millions of people; the Chinese fighting spirit has not yet been

---

[213]   Unabhängige Expermenkommission, *Die Schweiz*, pp. 55, 63 and 76; Lasserre, *La Suisse*, pp. 14–15 and 20–21; Oliver Zimmer, "'A Unique Fusion of the Natural and the Man-made": The Trajectory of Swiss Nationalism, 1933–1939', *Journal of Contemporary History*, 39/1 (2004): pp. 8 and 12–17; Im Hof, *Mythos Schweiz*, pp. 252 and 254; Josef Mooser, 'Die Geistige Landesverteidigung in den 1930er Jahren: Profile und Kontexte eines vielschichtigen Phänomens der schweizerischen politischen Kultur in der Zwischenkriegszeit', *Schweizerische Zeitschrift für Geschichte*, 47 (1997): pp. 687–91 and 701–2.

[214]   'Botschaft des Bundesrates an die Bundesversammlung über die Organisation und die Aufgaben der Schweizerischen Kulturwahrung und Kulturwerbung', *Bundesblatt*, 50 (1938): pp. 985–1035.

[215]   *Die Weltwoche* 10.12.1937, 29.4.1938, 24.6.1938, 1.7.1938, 29.5.1942; *Schweizer Illustrierte* 1.6.1938, 18.8.1937, 1.9.1937, 10.11.1937; *NZZ* 15.2.1942.

broken ... the oldest national sentiment on earth is rising up furiously against its latest imperialism.[216]

The *Geistige Landesverteidigung* also led to a surge of images and sculptures which referred to historic situations where the Swiss had to defend their independence against foreign aggressors. For example, images of the *Eidgenossen* (medieval Swiss peasants) who died fighting for the Swiss Confederacy and bravely held firm against foreign oppressors, were very popular in the late 1930s and early 1940s. In 1943, the *Schweizer Illustrierte* printed an article in which Chinese resistance to Japan was compared to that of the Swiss Confederates during the early formation of Switzerland, when in the Battle of Morgarten the Swiss were vastly outnumbered by their enemy but still fought on. The article pointed out a 'curious similarity between old Switzerland and the new China', namely that the Chinese soldiers were also vastly outnumbered and yet continued to fight. The article compared the courage of the Chinese soldiers and their willingness to defend their country to that of the Swiss Confederates, and noted that the Swiss felt a deep sympathy for China and the Chinese because of the manner in which they fought against the Japanese:

> With scythes and halberds ... with crossbows against canons ... is that not the same spirit? Yes, it is the same spirit, and we experience its wonders even more when we see what it is still capable of today ... Somewhere between heaven and earth the spirit of eternal China touches the spirit of Switzerland ... Yes, it is the same spirit! And we see: where it lives, it brings about miracles of old times.[217]

The article hammered home its message with two juxtaposed images showing a Chinese soldier and an *Eidgenosse* dying in battle, again reinforcing the perceived similarity between the Swiss and the Chinese *Wehrbereitschaft* (Illustration 3.21). The article, therefore, exemplifies how the Sino-Japanese War and China's war effort received the attention of the Swiss media because they could be instrumentalized in the cause of the *Geistige Landesverteidigung*.

While the Chinese were celebrated for their resistance, the Japanese were described in *Die Weltwoche* by the Swiss journalist Lily Abegg as weak, suffering from tuberculosis and rheumatism, with bad teeth and eyes. Their physical inferiority to Europeans was explained as being caused by Japanese culture, and their willingness to commit suicide as a result of their inner imbalance.[218] *Die Weltwoche* also printed a translated version of *Time*'s 'How to tell your friends from the Japs',[219] which is another example of the transnational circulation of Yellow Peril imagery. However, apart from these few exceptions, after war broke

---

216   *NZZ* 11.2.1943.
217   *Schweizer Illustrierte* 28.7.1943.
218   *Die Weltwoche* 10.9.1937; 12.12.1941.
219   *Die Weltwoche* 13.3.1942.

Illustration 3.21   *Schweizer Illustrierte* (28.7.1943)
Source: Reproduced with permission of Ringier AG, Schweizer Illustrierte.

out in Europe, the Swiss press focused almost exclusively on the European theatre and rarely printed stories about China or Japan.[220]

Although the outbreak of the Pacific War reinforced negative perceptions of Japan in Britain, the USA and Switzerland, the Yellow Peril was not defined in the same way in each country. Britain's rivalry with Japan was of a relatively short nature due to the Anglo-Japanese Alliance, the perception of Japan as a fellow imperial power in China, and the need to legitimize British presence in China. As a result, perceptions of Japan in Britain were less influenced by the Yellow Peril than those in the USA, where the attack on Pearl Harbor had a traumatizing effect and where antipathy and animosity towards Japan had existed for decades. American publications also printed much more positive descriptions of the Chinese than British publications, because China had been traditionally portrayed positively in the American press. Swiss press reactions to events in China were of a quite different nature because the Swiss press was so focused on the threat emanating from Germany and Italy that it applied the *Geistige Landesverteidigung* to interpretations of events in the Far East, and stressed China's spirit of resistance and the plight of Chinese refugees rather than Japanese atrocities. As a result, even though the Yellow Peril was an image that circulated on a transnational level in media perceptions of China, its usage in the media varied from nation to nation because it was used to legitimize different interests and actions. Since these interests were sometimes diametrically opposed, the Yellow Peril was even used by the media in one nation to refer to Japan while, simultaneously, in another nation for China.

---

[220]   *Die Weltwoche* 6.6.1941, 10.10.1941, 31.10.1941.

Chapter 4

The Rise of the Bamboo Curtain: Perceptions of the Communist Victory in 1949

The Chinese Nationalists and the Communists began their anti-Japanese alliance in 1937 but it was an alliance only in name, and until 1945 some of the best Nationalist troops were used to blockade or fight the Communists instead of the Japanese. After the war, negotiations between Chiang Kai-shek and Mao Zedong were doomed to failure as both parties tried to gain control over territory that had previously been occupied by Japan. The Civil War between the Communists and the Nationalists raged on until the Communist victory and Chiang Kai-shek's escape to Formosa in December 1949.[1] In January 1949, the possibility of a Communist victory over the Nationalists in the Chinese Civil War caused the *Daily Mail*'s cartoonist Leslie Illingworth to draw a cartoon portraying Communism as a force not only overwhelming Nationalist China and its leader Chiang Kai-shek (the figure drowning in the bottom right corner) but also bursting through China's borders (Illustration 4.1).

The red flood or wave was used as a symbol for the Communist victory in China in newspaper articles, editorial cartoons and newsreels in Britain, the USA and Switzerland. Cold War imagery portrayed the world as being divided into two blocs of nations, one led by the USA and the other by the Soviet Union.[2] Mary Kaldor notes:

---

[1]   Odd Arne Westad, *Decisive Encounters: The Chinese Civil War, 1946–1950* (Stanford, 2003); Suzanne Pepper, 'The KMT-CCP Conflict 1945–1949', in John K. Fairbank and Albert Feuerwerker (eds), *The Cambridge History of China, vol. 13: Republican China 1912–1949*, part 2 (Cambridge, 1986), pp. 723–37 and 759–85; Odd Arne Westad, *Cold War and Revolution: Soviet-American Rivalry and the Origins of the Chinese Civil War, 1944–1946* (New York, 1993); Jun Niu, 'The Origins of the Sino-Soviet Alliance', in Odd Arne Westad (ed.), *Brothers in Arms: The Rise and Fall of the Sino-Soviet Alliance, 1945–1963* (Washington, DC, 1998), pp. 53–8; Michael Schaller, *The U.S. Crusade in China, 1938–1945* (New York, 1979), pp. 40–43.

[2]   Daniel Frei, *Assumptions and Perceptions in Disarmament* (New York, 1984), pp. 270–71; Daniel A. Neval, *'Mit Atombomben bis nach Moskau': Gegenseitige Wahrnehmung der Schweiz und des Ostblocks im Kalten Krieg 1945–1968* (Zürich, 2003), pp. 600 and 620–21.

Illustration 4.1   Leslie Illingworth, 'The Red Flood', *Daily Mail* (24.1.1949)
Source: Reproduced with permission of Solo Syndication.

> Each bloc of nations identified itself in terms of a shared social system and
> set of values, democracy or socialism, which was contrasted to an opposing
> system, totalitarianism or imperialism. Each system, at least in the imagination,
> threatened the very existence of the other. It was a struggle between good and
> evil of epic proportions.[3]

Rhetoric played a crucial role in the construction of Cold War imagery, and since
the Cold War was viewed on a global scale, it also affected perceptions and
portrayals of China in the late 1940s,[4] resulting in the transnational circulation

[3]   Mary Kaldor, *The Imaginary War: Understanding the East-West Conflict* (Oxford
and Cambridge, 1990), p. 4.

[4]   See also: Lynn Boyd Hinds and Theodore Otto Windt, Jr., *The Cold War as Rhetoric:
The Beginnings, 1945–1950* (New York and London, 1991), pp. xix, 1–2 and 5–6.

of the Red Menace as an enemy image within Western bloc powers as well as Switzerland. This is the context in which British, American and Swiss perceptions of China in 1949 have to be analysed. Despite the transnational circulation of Red Menace imagery, however, politicians, journalists and cartoonists in Britain, the USA and Switzerland also portrayed China in unique ways. Thus, whereas most scholarly works on British, American or Swiss perceptions of China in the late 1940s focus on the relations between the Chinese Nationalists, Chinese Communists, the Soviet Union and the respective country,[5] this chapter shows that despite the transnational circulation of anticommunist imagery in Western countries, domestic issues and politics were a tremendous influence on political debates about and media perceptions of China during the early Cold War.

Britain

Mao's Bible

British reactions to the Communist victory in 1949 were defined by three factors: the less than cordial relationship with the Chinese Nationalist government, hopes of increasing British trade with China, and the restoration of the Empire in Asia, which clashed with the USA's attempts to establish hegemony in the Far East.[6] Britain and China's wartime collaboration had not been a happy one. Winston Churchill regarded China as an inferior power and felt that its role in the war was greatly exaggerated by the Americans. Chiang Kai-shek, in turn, criticized the withdrawal of British troops from Burma in 1942 and demanded more British credits. Other points of disagreement were the lack of co-operation on the part of Chinese troops, Chinese demands for Hong Kong and Indian independence, and British support of Tibetan autonomy. As a result of Britain's testy relations with

[5]   Thomas D. Lutze, *China's Inevitable Revolution: Rethinking America's Loss to the Communists* (New York and Basingstoke, 2007); Simei Qing, 'American Visions of Democracy and the Marshall Mission to China', in Hongshan Li and Zhaohui Hong (eds), *Image, Perception, and the Making of U.S.-China Relations* (Lanham and Cummor Hill, 1998), pp. 257–312; David D. Perlmutter, *Picturing China in the American Press: The Visual Portrayal of Sino-American Relations in Time Magazine, 1949-1973* (Lanham, 2007); Lanxin Xiang, *Recasting the Imperial Far East: Britain and America in China, 1945–1950* (Armonk and London, 1995); Brian Porter, *Britain and the Rise of Communist China: A Study of British Attitudes, 1945–1954* (London, New York and Toronto, 1967); Shai, *Britain*; Michele Coduri, *La Suisse face à la Chine: Une continuité impossible? 1946–1955* (Louvain-la-Neuve, 2004); Regula Stämpfli, 'Die Schweiz und China, 1945–1950', *Studien und Quellen*, 13/14 (1988): pp. 163–224.

[6]   John J. Sbrega, *Anglo-American Relations and Colonialism in East Asia, 1941–1945* (New York and London, 1983), pp. 199–200 and 204–6; Neval, *Mit Atombomben*, p. 600; David Reynolds, *From World War to Cold War: Churchill, Roosevelt, and the International History of the 1940s* (Oxford, 2006), pp. 35 and 328; Xiang, *Recasting*, pp. 14 and 31.

the Chinese Nationalists, British reports about the Chinese Communists tended to be favourable even though Britain had no diplomatic contact with the CCP.[7] The Foreign Office remained fascinated with the tremendous potential of the China market and focused on the protection of British interests in China, the development of British trade with China, and non-interference in the Chinese Civil War. Thus, while the USA decided to apply economic and political pressure on the CCP, the British government settled on a policy of keeping a foot in the door, feeling that de facto relations and economic benefits would do the trick.[8]

The lack of reliable information about the Chinese Communists meant that official British views on the CCP remained extremely vague. In April 1945, a Foreign Office memorandum described the CCP in the following way: 'The Communists ... are not Communist in the usual sense of the word nor are they a political party in the usual sense.'[9] One month later, Geoffrey Hudson, who headed the Far Eastern section of the Foreign Office's Research Department, even felt

---

[7]   TNA FO 371/31527; TNA T 236/678; TNA CAB 122/1133; 'Memorandum on Present China Situation and on British and American Policies in China', 7.7.1945, TNA FO 371/46211; 'Sir H. Seymour to Mr. Bevin', 20.6.1946, TNA FO 371/53566. See also: Shian Li, 'Britain's China Policy and the Communists, 1942 to 1946: The Role of Ambassador Sir Horace Seymour', *Modern Asian Studies*, 26/1 (1992): pp. 52–60; Chen Qianping, 'Sino-British Relations and the Tibetan Crisis of 1943', in David P. Barrett and Larry N. Shyu (eds), *China in the Anti-Japanese War, 1937–1945: Politics, Culture, and Society* (New York, 2001), pp. 89–111; Shai, *Britain*; Christopher Thorne, *Allies of a Kind: The United States, Britain and the War against Japan, 1941–1945* (London, 1978), pp. 308–11 and 320; Li, *Madame Chiang*, pp. 170–81; Westad, *Decisive Encounters*, pp. 92–3; James T.H. Tang, 'From Empire Defence to Imperial Retreat: Britain's Postwar China Policy and the Decolonization of Hong Kong', *Modern Asian Studies*, 28/2 (1994): pp. 320–22.

[8]   'American Attitude towards the Communist Problems', 9.2.1945, TNA FO 371/46165; 'Mr. Wallinger to Mr. Eden', 14.2.1945, TNA FO 371/46179; 'British Foreign Policy in the Far East', 16.4.1946, TNA CAB 134/280; 'Memorandum on a Trade Mission to China', 1.6.1946, TNA FO 371/53644; 'Conclusions', 14.10.1946, TNA CAB 128/8; 'Memorandum on Present China Situation and on British and American Policies in China', 7.7.1945, TNA FO 371/46211; 'Commercial Policy in China: Interim Report', 15.1.1945, TNA FO 371/46179; 'Minute for Mr. Bevin', 18.10.1946, FO 371/53672; 'Recent Developments in the Civil War in China', 9.12.1948, TNA CAB 129/31; 'The Situation in China', CP(49)39, 4.3.1949, TNA CO 537/4829; 'Hong Kong', 25.5.1949, TNA FO 371/75872; TNA BT 11/4139; TNA T 236/678; TNA T 236/1811; *The Times* 3.9.1949; *New Statesman and Nation* 15.10.1949; *The Times* 22.10.1949; *Manchester Guardian* 23.4.1949. See also: Shai, *Britain*; Allan Bullock, *Ernest Bevin: Foreign Secretary, 1945–1951* (London, 1983), pp. 49–51; Xiang, *Recasting*; David C. Wolf, '"To Secure a Convenience": Britain Recognizes China – 1950', *Journal of Contemporary History*, 18/2 (1983): pp. 306 and 320; Steve Tsang, *The Cold War's Odd Couple: The Unintended Partnership between the Republic of China and the UK, 1950–1958* (London and New York, 2006), p. 18; Wenguang Shao, *China, Britain and Businessmen: Political and Commercial Relations, 1949–57* (Basingstoke and London, 1991): pp. 6–7 and 32–3.

[9]   'The Communist Problem in China', 24.4.1945, TNA FO 371/46167.

the need to admonish the War Office for relying too heavily on the information of journalist Gunther Stein, who had published a series of glowing articles about the CCP:

> The account of Communist military organization and operations in this paper is no doubt well founded, but the political sections appear to consist mainly of chunks of Gunther Stein. It would perhaps be better if the name of this eminent 'fellow traveller' were always attached to information derived from him.[10]

Nevertheless, in September 1946, the China Department of the Foreign Office still described Mao Zedong as 'loyal less to Marx-Leninist ideology than to the native precepts of agrarian reform and social democracy'.[11]

Yet, reports grew increasingly alarmed. In March 1948, the Foreign Office received a report from the British Embassy in Moscow, in which Mao Zedong's Christmas statement was analysed according to its ideological orthodoxy. The report stated that Mao's statement not only mirrored Lenin's objective in the early 1920s but actually used identical words, thus concluding: 'Mao not only knows his bible but works it.'[12] One month later, the China Department of the Foreign Office stated: 'Mao Tze-tung has made it clear that Chinese communism is part of the world revolution and that the ultimate aim of the Chinese Communists is the realisation in China of the full Marxist-Communist programme.'[13] Although in December 1948 the Secretary of State for Foreign Affairs, Ernest Bevin, warned that the Chinese Communists would 'adopt the policies of orthodox Communism',[14] the Cabinet remained unsure about the 'ultimate nature of Chinese Communism or of the relationship between the Chinese Communist Government and the Soviet Union', and consequently decided that a policy should be adopted which would not 'have the effect of gratuitously driving a Chinese Communist Government into the arms of the Soviet Union'.[15]

While the British government had made its mind up about Mao's true bible, the British press was still not quite sure what to make of the Chinese Communists. Conservative publications like the *National Review* rejected arguments that described them as agrarian reformers, but there was also a widely held belief that orthodox Marxism would not survive in China because it went against the Chinese sense of individualism and the importance of local autonomy, thus resulting

---

[10] Comment by G.F. Hudson from 12.6.1945 to 'Chinese "Communists"', 5.5.1945, TNA FO 371/46167.

[11] 'China', 1.9.1946, TNA FO 371/53672.

[12] 'Communism in China', 2.3.1948, TNA FO 371/69529.

[13] 'The Chinese Communists', 1.4.1948, TNA FO 405/278.

[14] 'Recent Developments in the Civil War in China', 9.12.1948, TNA CAB 129/31.

[15] 'Cabinet Meeting Conclusions', 13.12.1948, TNA CAB 128/13; 'Telegram', 20.12.1948, TNA CO 537/4829. See also Qiang Zhai, *The Dragon, the Lion, and the Eagle: Chinese-British-American Relations, 1949–1958* (Kent and London, 1994), pp. 30–32.

in a Chinese version of Communism that would eventually take over.[16] The *Manchester Guardian*, however, remained cautious and reminded its readers: 'But though Chinese Communism will be a Chinese and eccentric version there is no reason to think that it will be friendly to the West.'[17] Indeed, less than two weeks later, relations between the Chinese Communists and the British Government became extremely tense during the *Amethyst* Incident. On 20 April 1949, the HMS *Amethyst* was sailing from Shanghai to Nanjing when it was attacked by Communist forces who were preparing to cross the Yangzi. The *Amethyst* returned fire but was eventually grounded. Despite efforts by several British ships to aid the *Amethyst*, it remained trapped for several months until it managed to escape to Shanghai on 30 July. The death toll for all of the British ships involved in the *Amethyst* Incident was 45, with another 68 wounded.[18] The *Amethyst* Incident was highly problematic for the British government because Britain did not yet have official relations with the Chinese Communists, and was trying neither to offend them nor to make too many concessions to them. As a result, the government sought to keep debates on the subject civil, for example, in the preparation of the Prime Minister's statement to the House of Commons, any language that could have encouraged jingoistic behaviour was carefully avoided, and references to the inhuman conduct of the Chinese Communists were deleted.[19]

Most British publications mirrored their government's deliberate reaction. *The Times* noted: 'There can be no doubt, of course, that the firing on Amethyst was calculated and deliberate.' Yet, the paper also worried that Anglo-Chinese relations would suffer from the Incident.[20] The *Manchester Guardian*'s reaction was similar. Despite portraying the Communists as having behaved 'monstrously',[21] it stated:

> The Amethyst incident now stands in the way of attempts to find means of living together. The best course for the West is to be conspicuous by its absence while the civil war draws to its end. ... There is no time for sabre-rattling, even if we had a sabre to rattle.[22]

---

[16] *National Review* February 1947 and February 1949; *The Times* 23.4.1949, 5.5.1949; *Spectator* 7.10.1949; *Nineteenth Century* April 1948, *New Statesman and Nation* 8.1.1949; *Manchester Guardian* 30.9.1949.

[17] *Manchester Guardian* 12.4.1949.

[18] 'Cabinet Meeting Conclusions', 26.4.1949, TNA CAB 128/16. See also: Malcolm H. Murfett, *Hostage on the Yangtze: Britain, China, and the Amethyst Crisis of 1949* (Annapolis, 1991); Shao, *China*, pp. 26–9; Zhai, *Dragon*, p. 14; Wolf, 'Convenience', p. 308, Peter Lowe, *Containing the Cold War in East Asia: British Policies towards Japan, China and Korea, 1948–53* (Manchester and New York, 1997), p. 96; Xiang, *Recasting*, pp. 190–91.

[19] TNA CAB 21/1948; 'Note on Amethyst 051017', 6.7.1949, FO 371/75894.

[20] *The Times* 23.4.1949 and 27.4.1949 (quote). See also Murfett, *Hostage*, pp. 125–6.

[21] *Manchester Guardian* 27.4.1949.

[22] *Manchester Guardian* 25.4.1949.

True to its editorial policy to present news in a sensational way, the *Daily Mirror* reported details like the transport of 'thirty-six cases of blood plasma' that were used to treat injured sailors, but even it refrained from anti-Chinese statements.[23] The British crews involved in the *Amethyst* Incident were widely celebrated as heroes. For example, the *Spectator* gushed about the daring escape of the *Amethyst*: 'The gallant, resourceful and dramatic exploit of H.M. Sloop "Amethyst" has won for her commander and crew, and for the Navy whose finest (and most stylish) traditions they upheld at immense risk, the admiration of the free world.'[24] The *Daily Mail*, however, resorted to its usual jingoistic fervour and described the *Amethyst* Incident and the Communist attacks on British ships as 'Yangtse insults' that aimed to get Britain out of China.[25] It even claimed that the *Amethyst* Incident was part of a Communist conspiracy against the British Empire: 'It seems clear that the Communists in China allowed our ships to enter a trap in order to humiliate our country and murder our men.'[26]

Newsreels also showed footage of the *Amethyst* Incident. A Movietone newsreel included a voiceover describing it as 'the outrages just perpetrated by the communists in the unprovoked and deliberate shelling of British warships resulting in the murder of over forty of our men.'[27] All newsreel companies mostly relied on the same footage including the arrival of the wounded crew in Shanghai, the funeral of 23 British sailors, and the damaged ships that tried to help the *Amethyst*. Though the voiceovers differed, they all lauded the behaviour of the British Navy during the affair. The *Amethyst*'s successful escape and rejoining of the British fleet was hailed in a Movietone newsreel as 'an exploit fit to cheer the cockles of our hearts' and 'a tale which will live in British naval annals' over footage of the intact *Amethyst* and flying flag of the Royal Navy,[28] while a Pathé newsreel declared: 'No praise is too high for the heroism of these men.'[29]

After the *Amethyst* Incident, newspapers still struggled to classify the Chinese Communists. Even British journalists in China had different ideas about them. *The Times*'s correspondent in Hong Kong, for example, claimed as late as September 1949: 'in spite of the 100 per cent. pro-Soviet propaganda line which Peking radio takes at present, China has even more Titoist potentialities than Yugoslavia.'[30] Another journalist of *The Times*, however, argued less than two weeks later:

---

23   *Daily Mirror* 22.4.1949.

24   *Spectator* 5.8.1949; *Daily Mirror* 27.4.1949; *Manchester Guardian* 27.4.1949.

25   *Daily Mail* 21.4.1949, 22.4.1949, 23.4.1949, 25.4.1949, 26.4.1949 (quote).

26   *Daily Mail* 27.4.1949.

27   'Yangtze Outrage', British Movietone News, 28.4.1949.

28   'Epic of the "Amethyst"', British Movietone News, 4.8.1949 (quotes); 'Damaged Warships at Shanghai', British Movietone News, 2.5.1949; 'Shanghai Sorrow and Suspense', British Movietone News, 9.5.1949; 'Last Britons Leave', Pathé News, 9.5.1949.

29   'Yangtse Heroes', Pathé News, 2.5.1949 (quote); 'Yangtse Survivors Reach Shanghai', Gaumont British News, 2.5.1949.

30   *The Times* 3.9.1949.

'The new Government is a Communist Government pure and simple – and of an extreme type at that.'[31] The *Manchester Guardian* in turn summed up British perceptions of China with the statement: 'The idyllic picture of China as a rustic Communist democracy has slowly faded away.'[32]

Although they had different opinions regarding the Chinese Communists, British publications had become thoroughly disenchanted with the Nationalist government's corruption and ineffectiveness, and they widely agreed that corruption and ineptitude were the main reasons for the Nationalist defeat. *The Times*, for example, explained the feelings of the Chinese people to the Communists in the following way: 'They are not attracted by what they understand of their doctrines, they are not in the least interested in world revolution, but they have had their bellyful of bad government, and reckon that the new régime cannot be worse than the old.'[33] Illustration 4.2 by David Low is titled 'Asked for Trouble – and Got It'. It shows a man labelled 'corrupt old regime', who attempts to protect himself against a massive 'China red tidal wave' with an umbrella. While the association of the Communist victory with a powerful natural force like the wave was shared by many Western journalists and cartoonists, the cartoon by Low also includes a scathing criticism of the Nationalist government and actually blames it for the Communist victory.

British newsreels painted a similar picture, often including voiceovers with statements like 'China's red tide sweeps on'.[34] The voiceover of a Movietone newsreel from January 1949 stated: 'Today, communism has swept like a red tide over this ancient civilisation.' Yet, its general tone was not alarmed but rather resigned. For example, it covered the Communist occupation of Beijing and then stated: 'Life in the ancient city, indeed, is more or less reported as normal.' Moreover, it openly criticized the Nationalist regime, stating that its inefficiency had alienated outside help. Newsreels also often showed Chinese refugees but despite a dramatic score, neither the footage nor the voiceovers were anxious. Instead, the Communist control of China was presented as an inevitable outcome of the Civil War.[35] What is interesting about the newsreels is that the same footage appeared over and over again because there was only

---

[31]   *The Times* 15.9.1949.

[32]   *Manchester Guardian* 23.9.1949. See also *Manchester Guardian* 29.9.1949 and 15.10.1949.

[33]   *The Times* 22.4.1949 (quote); *Manchester Guardian* 10.3.1947; 25.4.1949; *Spectator* 11.3.1949; *Nineteenth Century* March 1948 and April 1948; *New Statesman and Nation* 28.6.1947, 26.6.1948, 19.1.1949; *National Review* February 1949.

[34]   'Yangtse Survivors Reach Shanghai', Gaumont British News, 2.5.1949; 'Reds Sweep China', Pathé News, 9.12.1948.

[35]   'China – What of Her Future?', British Movietone News, 27.1.1949. See also: 'Shanghai Awaits the Reds', British Movietone News, 16.5.1949; 'Nanking Waits for the End', Pathé News, 14.02.1949.

Illustration 4.2   David Low, 'Asked for Trouble – and Got It', *Evening Standard* (13.9.1949)

Source: Reproduced with permission of Solo Syndication.

limited footage available from China. One newsreel mentioned that it took three months for footage to reach Britain.[36]

Although British views tended not to be alarmist about the Communist expansion in China, fears of losing Hong Kong increased. Aware that Britain would not be able to defend Hong Kong against a Communist attack, Bevin described the situation in Hong Kong in December 1948 as 'living on the edge of a volcano'.[37] From early 1949, the British government no longer viewed an organized Communist attack on Hong Kong as a likely event, but its security was still deemed crucial to the resistance of Communism in Asia and for the reputation of the British Empire. As Prime Minister Clement Attlee noted at a cabinet meeting in May 1949:

> [F]ailure to meet [the] threat to the security of Hong Kong would damage very seriously British prestige throughout the Far East and South-East Asia. Moreover, the whole common front against Communism in Siam, Burma and Malaya was likely to crumble unless the peoples of those countries were convinced of [Britain's] determination and ability to resist this threat to Hong Kong.[38]

On this matter, the press agreed with the government. Even the *Manchester Guardian*, which used to be critical of Britain's imperialism in China, proudly declared in December 1946: 'At present Hong-Kong still serves as an example of good government which China can envy but cannot apparently copy.'[39] Hong Kong was not only used to uphold the image of the British Empire as the bastion of democracy and fair government, but in light of the loss of other colonies, it was increasingly hailed as an outpost of the British Empire. Thus, in 1949, the British press continually reported how the Chinese Communist advance affected Hong Kong, often describing it as representing Western influence in a region engulfed

---

[36]   'Shanghai under Red Control', Pathé News, 24.10.1949.

[37]   'Recent Developments in the Civil War in China', 9.12.1948, TNA CAB 129/31. See also: Tang, 'Empire Defence', pp. 324–5 and 328; Wolf, 'Convenience', pp. 309 and 321; Ritchie Ovendale, 'Britain, the United States, and the Cold War in South-East Asia, 1949–1950', *International Affairs*, 58/3 (1982): p. 454.

[38]   'Cabinet Meeting Conclusions', 26.5.1949, TNA CAB 128/15 (quote); 'Cabinet Meeting Conclusions', 28.4.1949, 'Memorandum on the Situation in Malaya and Hong Kong', 5.3.1949, CAB 129/33; 'Cabinet Meeting Conclusions', 5.5.1949, TNA CAB 128/15; 'Minute for Prime Minister', 12.5.1949, TNA FO 371/75872; 'Cabinet Meeting Minutes', 19.5.1949, TNA CAB 134/669; 'Memorandum on Hong Kong', 23.5.1949, CAB 129/35; 'Minute on Communist Documents Captured in Hong Kong', 25.6.1949, FO 371/75780; TNA PREM 8/1334; TNA FO 1110/194; TNA CAB 128/15. See also: Zhai, *Dragon*, p. 13; Lowe, *Containing*, pp. 94–5; Shao, *China*, p. 32.

[39]   *Manchester Guardian* 7.12.1946.

by communism.[40] For example in April 1949, the *Daily Mail* presented the British colony as a safe haven in Asia:

> Civil war and banditry, Communism and terrorism are the various afflictions in all that territory between the Bay of Bengal and the Sea of Japan. ... One tiny spot in the vast expanse is safe, peaceful, and prosperous. You can hardly find it on a small-scale map, but its importance is out of all proportion to its size. Over it flies the Union Jack, and its name is Hongkong.[41]

The *National Review* declared in an only slightly less pompous fashion: 'Hong Kong is a haven of law, order and stability in a very troubled part of the world.'[42] With the advance of the Chinese Communist troops, the British press became increasingly worried about the security of the colony. In May 1949, the *Daily Mail* noted with considerable excitement: 'For the Hongkong police force every day now may be D-Day in the battle with the Communist Fifth Column that has worked underground for months past. They are taking no chances.'[43] Newsreels on the departure of the first battalion of the Royal Leicestershire Regiment for Hong Kong were set to a score of triumphant marches in order to convey confidence and patriotism.[44] They also covered the British defence of Hong Kong in detail. As has been pointed out in the previous chapter, Britain's loss of Hong Kong to Japan in 1941 had been a traumatic event that shattered British perceptions of superiority and invincibility. The humiliation was etched deeply in national memory as a Pathé newsreel from October 1949 demonstrates: 'Hong Kong is ready. There will be no repeat of the 1941 defeat this time.'[45] For the correspondent of *The Times* however, waiting for a Communist attack was a rather tedious affair: 'All continues quiet along the Hongkong frontier. A visit there to-day revealed so little activity out of the ordinary that it verged on an anti-climax.'[46]

---

[40]   *The Times* 19.10.1949 and 27.10.1949. See also Wm. Roger Louis, 'Hong Kong: The Critical Phase, 1945–1949', *The American Historical Review*, 102/4 (1997): p. 1082.

[41]   *Daily Mail* 25.4.1949.

[42]   *National Review* May 1949.

[43]   *Daily Mail* 12.5.1949 (quote), 1.9.1949; *Daily Mirror* 6.5.1949 and 7.5.1949; *Spectator* 5.8.1949 and 7.10.1949; *Manchester Guardian* 10.9.1949.

[44]   'The "Leicesters" for Hong Kong', British Movietone News, 16.5.1949; 'The Leicester Regiment Leave for Honkong', Gaumont British News, 16.5.1949.

[45]   'Hong Kong', Pathé News, 20.10.1949 (quote); 'Hong Kong ready as Communists reach border', Gaumont British News, 20.10.1949; 'The Far East – Hong Kong Menaced', British Movietone News, 20.10.1949.

[46]   *The Times* 18.10.1949.

The Communist Virus in Asia

The British public's opinion of the Soviet Union improved when it joined the allies in the Second World War but towards the end of the war British concerns about Stalin's ambitions for a postwar settlement increased. Anglo-Soviet relations deteriorated as Soviet expansion in Eastern Europe threatened Britain's position in the Mediterranean and the Middle East, while the popularity of Communist Parties in France and Germany appeared to bring the Soviet threat to Britain's doorstep. As a consequence, Bevin stated in early March 1948 at a cabinet meeting that Soviet actions had 'showed beyond any doubt … that resolute action must be taken to counter the Soviet threat to Western civilisation'. In the same month, Britain signed the Brussels Treaty and on 4 April 1949 the North Atlantic Treaty.[47]

During the Second World War, British colonial policies were adapted to give the colonies more power after the war but the British government also planned to win back those colonial territories that had been occupied by Japan. As Winston Churchill famously declared in November 1942: 'I have not become the King's First Minister in order to preside over the liquidation of the British Empire.'[48] The re-establishment of the British Empire was, however, threatened by the USA's anti-imperialism and its dominating role in the Pacific War.[49] Anglo-American mutual suspicion continued even after the war. A cartoon by David Low uses

---

[47]   'Cabinet 19 (48) from 5.3.1948', TNA CAB 128/12 (quote); TNA CAB 128/13 and CAB 128/15. See also: Sean Greenwood, *Britain and the Cold War 1945–91* (Basingstoke, 2000); Martin A.L. Longden, 'From "Hot War" to "Cold War": Western Europe in British Grand Strategy, 1945–1948', in Michael F. Hopkins, Michael D. Kandiah and Gillian Staerck (eds), *Cold War Britain, 1945–1964: New Perspectives* (Basingstoke, 2003), pp. 112–14 and 120–26; P.M.H. Bell, *John Bull and the Bear: British Public Opinion, Foreign Policy and the Soviet Union 1941–1945* (New York, 1990); Geoffrey Warner, 'From "Ally" to Enemy: Britain's Relations with the Soviet Union, 1941–8', in Francesca Gori and Silvio Pons (eds), *The Soviet Union and Europe in the Cold War, 1943–53* (Basingstoke and London, 1996), pp. 293–8; Martin Folly, *Churchill, Whitehall and the Soviet Union, 1940–1945* (Basingstoke, 2000), pp. 116–66; Reynolds, *From World War*, pp. 249–53; Keeble, *Britain*, pp. 195–221; Gerhard Wettig, *Stalin and the Cold War in Europe: The Emergence and Development of East-West Conflict, 1939–1953* (Lanham and Boulder, 2008), pp. 46–51; Bullock, *Bevin*, pp. 129–64.

[48]   Winston Churchill, 'The End of the Beginning', speech at the Lord Mayor's Day Luncheon, 10.11.1942, in Charles Eade (comp.), *The End of the Beginning: War Speeches by the Right Hon. Winston S. Churchill C.H., M.P.*, 3rd ed. (London, Toronto etc., 1946), p. 215. See also: Thorne, *Allies*, pp. 343–5; Thorne, *Issue of War*, p. 105.

[49]   Sbrega, *Anglo-American Relations*, pp. 199–200 and 204–6; Thorne, *Allies*; Shai, *Britain*, pp. 45–8, 84–8 and 100–2; John J. Sbrega, 'The Anticolonial Policies of Franklin D. Roosevelt: A Reappraisal', *Political Science Quarterly*, 101/1 (1986): pp. 65–84; Wm. Roger Louis, *Imperialism at Bay: The United States and the Decolonization of the British Empire, 1941-1945* (Oxford, 1972), pp. 3–10; Auriol Weigold, *Churchill, Roosevelt and India: Propaganda during World War II* (New York and London, 2008).

China to portray American anti-imperialism as hypocritical due to the USA's deep involvement in the Chinese Civil War (Illustration 4.3). In the cartoon, a row of army tanks and trucks carrying armed soldiers and 'US arms & equipment' is driving past two American businessmen who are reading 'The Onesided News' and commenting: 'These British and Russian imperialists! Always trying to ruin other folks' countries!' The cartoon's caption 'It's Different with the Americans in China, of course' mocks this self-righteous view of the Americans, implying that the USA's actions in China are imperialist and American criticism of Britain biased and hypocritical. The cartoon's criticism of American involvement in the Chinese Civil War also highlights the different takes on foreign policies with regard to Asia in Britain and the USA. A final point of interest is the cartoon's depiction of the power of the press: the newspaper is shown as more influential on public opinion than actual reality. The two men are reading 'The Onesided News' and are so taken in by the newspaper's argument that they completely ignore their own surroundings, including the row of tanks and trucks that would contradict the newspaper's statement. Low's cartoon can, therefore, also be interpreted as a criticism of sensationalist or biased reporting and its effect on public opinion.

Britain had reoccupied its former possessions by September 1945, but European prestige in Southeast Asia had suffered as a result of Japan's conquest and colonial powers were faced with nationalist movements demanding self-government or independence. Since Britain lacked the military power to suppress all of the nationalist movements, it promoted moderate social reforms and economic development in the colonies in order to prevent a further spread of communism and to improve the Empire's reputation. British colonies were also prepared for self-government, and India and Pakistan were granted independence in 1947, followed by Burma and Ceylon in early 1948.[50] For the British government, the Chinese Civil War was of paramount interest for the security and stability of Southeast Asia. As a result, in early 1949 the Foreign Office instructed various Far Eastern posts to begin a covert propaganda campaign (it was officially described as 'a concerted publicity campaign ... all over Free Asia') against Chinese communism with the goal to discredit communism in Asia.[51] On 4 March 1949, Bevin presented the views of the Chiefs of Staff on the military implications of a Communist victory in China in the following way: 'The spread of Communism into Southern China will cause increased unrest and consequently an increased security commitment throughout South East Asia. ... If Communism successfully spreads into the Indian sub-continent, our whole position in South East Asia would

---

[50] 'British Foreign Policy in the Far East', 16.4.1946, TNA CAB 134/280. See also: Tsang, *Odd Couple*, pp. 5 and 11–13; Roy Douglas, *Liquidation of Empire: The Decline of the British Empire* (Basingstoke and New York, 2002), pp. 45–53; Shai, *Britain*, pp. 102–5, 124 and 138–9; Bullock, *Ernest Bevin*, pp. 31–3; Peter Weiler, 'British Labour and the Cold War: The Foreign Policy of the Labour Governments, 1945–1951', *Journal of British Studies*, 26 (1987): pp. 67–9; Louis, *Imperialism at Bay*, pp. 99–102.

[51] Note by F.R.H. Murray to A.H. Joyce, 27.4.1949, TNA FO 1110/194.

Illustration 4.3 David Low, 'It's Different with the Americans in China, of course', *Evening Standard* (13.9.1946)

Source: Reproduced with permission of Solo Syndication.

become untenable.'[52] By May 1949, the communist threat to Asia was perceived to be so serious that immediate action to strengthen resistance to communism in India, Burma, Siam, Indochina and the East Indies was deemed crucial.[53]

The British press generally shared the government's view that communism threatened Southeast Asia, and throughout 1949 focused on this issue.[54] In May, the conservative journal *National Review* pointed out: 'Recent events in China, Burma and Malaya indicate that the gravest danger to the peace and prosperity of almost every country in the Far East lies in the spread of Communism.'[55] Similarly, the *Spectator* warned of a 'coming Communist storm' that would hit India and Pakistan,[56] while *The Times* noted that the Chinese Communist armies would assist communist revolutionaries in Burma, Indo-China and other bordering countries.[57] The fear of possible communist expansion out of China also resulted in the association of communism with disease by the British press. For example, the *Spectator* described it as an infection,[58] and the *Nineteenth Century* warned that communism was 'injecting its virus further and further into the whole body of the [Chinese] State'.[59] During the Cold War, metaphors that presented communism as a disease abounded, so China was clearly interpreted within the frame of the Cold War. Yet, the focus on former British colonies was distinctly British.[60]

Punch published various cartoons about communist expansion, among them Illustrations 4.4 and 4.5 by E.H. Shepard. Illustration 4.4 has the title 'The New Hunting Ground'. It was published in June 1948 and shows a tiger labelled 'communism' with Stalin's features, creeping up on Southeast Asia. By depicting Southeast Asia as passive and Stalin/the Soviet Union as an aggressive, threatening and sneaky predator, the cartoon ignores nationalism and other issues that contributed to communism's popularity in the respective countries. Moreover, Britain or the British Empire is not depicted in the cartoon, thus evading questions regarding the legitimacy of the British Empire. This is different in Illustration 4.5, published in April 1949, which focuses on the protection of the Commonwealth from the communist threat. Britain is portrayed as a knight holding a flag with the St George's cross in a half-demolished castle, referring to the breakup of the British Empire (India and Pakistan are outside the castle, studying a note labelled

---

[52] 'The Situation in China', CP (49) 39, 4.3.1949, TNA CO 537/4829.

[53] 'Cabinet Meeting Conclusions', 9.5.1949, TNA CAB 125/15. See also: Ovendale, 'Britain', pp. 454–5.

[54] *Nineteenth Century* April 1948; *New Statesman and Nation* 26.6.1948; *National Review* May 1949; *Spectator* 10.6.1949 and 16.12.1949; *Times* 1.3.1949; *Manchester Guardian* 5.5.1949; *Scotsman* 11.1.1949; *The Economist* 28.5.1949.

[55] *National Review* May 1949.

[56] *Spectator* 10.6.1949.

[57] *The Times* 15.9.1949.

[58] *Spectator* 10.6.1949.

[59] *Nineteenth Century* April 1948.

[60] See also: Hinds and Windt, *Cold War*, pp. 11–12.

THE NEW HUNTING GROUND

Illustration 4.4   E.H. Shepard, 'The New Hunting Ground', *Punch* (30.6.1948)
Source: Reproduced with permission of Punch Ltd, www.punch.co.uk.

'Terms of Employment'). The rest of the Commonwealth nations are depicted as
animals (South Africa as a springbok, Australia as a wallaby, New Zealand as a kiwi
bird, India and Pakistan as tigers, Canada as a moose and Ceylon as an elephant).
The knight shields the animals from a dragon labelled 'communism', which is
lurking in the background and threatens the castle's walls and its inhabitants with
its flames. One message of the cartoon is, therefore, that only an alliance with
Britain through the Empire or the Commonwealth can guarantee protection from
communism. Moreover, since the dragon had traditionally been used in British
cartoons to portray China as the Yellow Peril, Illustration 4.5 also implicitly
associates the communist threat to the British Empire with the Communist victory
in China, and thereby combines the Yellow Peril with the Red Menace.

Illustration 4.5   E.H. Shepard, 'The Strengthening of the Keep',
Punch (20.4.1949)

Source: Reproduced with permission of Punch Ltd, www.punch.co.uk.

To Recognize or not Recognize Communist China

In the Moscow Declaration of December 1945, Britain had pledged not to interfere in Chinese affairs and to recognize the GMD government as the sole government of China. This remained Britain's China policy until 1949. Yet, by late 1948, the Communists had brought so much additional territory under their control that the Foreign Office began to consider recognizing the Chinese Communists in order to protect British investment in China. When the Communists took over Nanjing on 24 April 1949, the British ambassador Stevenson remained in the city with the intention of improving Britain's standing with the CCP and developing trade relations. The CCP, however, refused to recognize foreign diplomats as long as their government still had relations with the Nationalist government, and ignored the British advances.[61] Meanwhile, Britain's relations with the GMD worsened due to the GMD's blockade of Chinese port cities in June 1949, which severely damaged British trade. As a result, when Bevin and the American Secretary of State Dean Acheson held talks about their countries' policies toward China in the summer of 1949, Bevin rejected Acheson's demands for a strong stand against the Chinese Communists.[62] In August, Bevin pointed out in a memorandum to the Cabinet:

> It is easier for the United States to cut their losses in China than for the United Kingdom to do so. Their trading interests are fewer and not so deep-rooted and their communities are smaller. Moreover, the total loss of their trading interest means less to the United States than a similar loss means to the United Kingdom in our present economic and financial condition.[63]

For Bevin, the UK had to establish regional association in Southeast Asia in order to establish a 'friendly partnership between East and West' and 'prevent the spread of communism' in the area. He noted quite gleefully: 'In China, American policy has proved a total failure and shows a tendency to go into headlong retreat.'[64] When

---

[61]   TNA CAB 128/13 Cabinet 80 (48); telegram from 20.12.1948, TNA CO 537/4829; 'Recent Developments in the Civil War in China', 9.12.1948, TNA CAB 129/31; 'Memorandum on Present China Situation and on British and American Policies in China', 7.7.1945, TNA FO 371/46211. See also: Lanxin Xiang, 'The Recognition Controversy: Anglo-American Relations in China, 1949', *Journal of Contemporary History*, 27/2 (1992): pp. 330–32 and 335; Shao, *China*, p. 25; Wolf, 'Convenience', pp. 301–4 and 307.

[62]   'China Blockade', TNA PREM 8/1334 part 3; *Spectator* 24.6.1949 and 2.9.1949; *Manchester Guardian* 29.9.1949. See also: Shao, *China*, p. 36 and 44; Xiang, 'Recognition', pp. 325–6 and 336–7; Xiang, *Recasting*, pp. 180–81 and 192–3; Wolf, 'Convenience', pp. 311–12.

[63]   'China', 23.8.1949, TNA CAB 21/1947.

[64]   'The United Kingdom in South-East Asia and the Far East', 18.10.1949, TNA CAB 21/3269.

the Communists still refused to deal with Britain in October 1949, Bevin feared that further support of the Nationalist government would only damage British interests in China, and be detrimental to Britain's policy of keeping a foot in the door. Furthermore, Bevin and the Foreign Office felt that since the Communists controlled practically all of China, British recognition of the Communist government was according to the principles of international law, and might even be helpful in stoking differences between the Soviet Union and Communist China. When the Foreign Office received information that India would recognize the Communist regime before the end of December, Bevin decided that Britain should act as well because he was worried that the reputation of Britain would be damaged in Asia if it waited too long, and the impression would be given that Britain did not support Asian nationalism. He remarked rather laconically: 'It will be appreciated that recognition does not itself make the Communist authorities the rulers of China. They are that already. Recognition is no more than acceptance of a fact, which its withholding would not alter.'[65] By the time Britain recognized the People's Republic of China (PRC) on 6 January 1950, Burma, India, Pakistan and Ceylon had already done so. However, Britain did not profit from the recognition to the degree that had been hoped for because the Chinese Communists soon began to restrict British trade and British investment was eventually expropriated.[66]

In 1949, the majority of the British press favoured recognition of the CCP, not least in order to protect British enterprises, investment and influence in China.[67] After Mao proclaimed the PRC on 1 October 1949, the *Spectator* noted tersely:

> The Chinese have got rid of a Government which was bad, oppressive, corrupt and based on no coherent political faith. They have acquired a Government which is oppressive, which seems (so far) less bad and much less corrupt than its predecessor and which is based on a well-defined political faith, most of whose tenets conflict with the markedly individual outlook of the Chinese.[68]

The Times stated rather fatalistically: 'Though not all of China is yet in the hands of the Communists, there can be no doubt that, for good or for evil, this is now the

---

[65]   'Recognition of the Chinese Communist Government', 12.12.1949, TNA CAB 21/3273 (quote); 'South-East Asia and the Far East', 18.10.1949, TNA CAB 21/3269; 'Recognition of the Chinese Communist Government', 24.10.1949, TNA CAB 21/3273; 'Cabinet Meeting Conclusions', 15.12.1949, TNA CAB 128/16. See also: Porter, *Communist China*, pp. 37–8; Xiang, 'Recognition', pp. 339–40; Wolf, 'Convenience', pp. 313 and 316; Lowe, *Containing*, pp. 106–9.

[66]   'Minute from Bevin to Attlee', 23.12.1949, TNA PREM 8/1334. See also: Porter, *Communist China*, pp. 37–8; Wolf, 'Convenience', p. 318; Shao, *China*.

[67]   *Spectator* 27.5.1949, 24.6.1949, 7.10.1949; *The Times* 23.6.1949, 3.10.1949, 6.10.1949; *Manchester Guardian* 23.9.1949, 4.10.1949; *New Statesman and Nation* 8.1.1949; *Daily Mirror* 4.10.1949; *Observer* 6.2.1949.

[68]   *Spectator* 7.10.1949.

Government of nearly 500m people, the largest single homogenous racial group in the world.'[69] Although the newspaper foresaw that the relationship between Britain and a Communist China would be of a rather rocky nature, recognition was the only solution: 'There is no alternative to Communism in China today.'[70] This view was shared by the *Manchester Guardian*, which noted: 'you can only land yourself in an embarrassing and disadvantageous position by refusing to recognise regimes that have come to stay.'[71] While the press was, therefore, almost unanimously in support of the British government's recognition of the PRC, the situation in the USA was altogether different.

The USA

Siding with the Nationalists in the Civil War

American reactions to the victory of the Chinese Communists in 1949 were influenced by various factors, including fears of domestic and international communism, American support of the Chinese Nationalists in the Civil War, and traditional perceptions of democratic China as a ward of the USA. During the Second World War, the USA supported China's war effort against Japan with the lend-lease programme and the American Volunteer Group 'Flying Tigers'. In February 1942, General Joseph Stilwell was sent to China as Chief of Staff to Chiang Kai-shek and commander of all the American forces in the China, Burma and India theatre and of five Chinese divisions in Burma. He was also the general supervisor of lend-lease in China. Although Stilwell spoke fluent Chinese and had spent many years in China, he and Chiang did not get along. Stilwell criticized Chiang's military organization and the rampant corruption in the Nationalist government, while Chiang rejected Stilwell's demands for military reforms and refused to cooperate with him. Moreover, whereas Chiang wanted American help primarily for the Chinese Air Force, Stilwell was convinced that the Chinese resistance depended on improving the strength of the army. In September 1944, Chiang rejected FDR's requests that Stilwell be put in command of all Chinese forces and instead demanded Stilwell's recall, to which Roosevelt eventually acquiesced on 18 October.[72]

---

[69]   *The Times* 3.10.1949.

[70]   *The Times* 5.10.1949 (quote), 4.10.1949.

[71]   *Manchester Guardian* 23.9.1949 (quote), 4.10.1949, 11.10.1949.

[72]   Guangqiu Xu, 'The Issue of US Air Support for China during the Second World War, 1942–45', *Journal of Contemporary History*, 36/3 (2001): pp. 459–80; Barbara W. Tuchman, *Stilwell and the American Experience in China, 1911–1945* (New York, 1985), pp. 229–509; Wong, *Americans First*, pp. 61–4; Schaller, *Crusade*, pp. 71–7, 93–6 and 103–75; Cohen, *America's Response*, pp. 125–7 and 130–32.

Even though the Chinese war effort was described as heroic by the US media, Chiang's image in the USA became tarnished by his fallout with Stilwell, resulting in increasing criticism of the Nationalist government's corruption, Chiang's refusal to restructure his government despite continuing demands for more American aid, and the fact that his troops fought more against the CCP than the Japanese.[73] The frustration over Chiang and the Nationalist regime caused some Americans to become enthusiastic supporters of the Chinese Communists. Among these were also the few journalists who had access to the Communists in the late 1920s and 1930s, like Anna Louise Strong, Edgar Snow and Agnes Smedley. Of these, Edgar Snow was the most influential on American public images of the Chinese Communists. In 1936, he stayed with the Communists in Yan'an for four months. His experiences led to the publication of *Red Star over China* in 1938, in which he rendered a glowing account of the Chinese Communists as reformers. This was a different view of the Chinese Communists than had been known until then in the USA. Nevertheless, although Snow's positive portrayal of the Communists was widely read, its influence was mostly limited to liberal intellectuals.[74] Snow's stay with the Communists had been approved by Mao Zedong, who wanted more publicity for the Communists. Peter Rand argues that Mao used Snow as a 'public relations intermediary'. Snow was at the time the foreign correspondent of British and American publications, so the CCP knew that it could reach a large audience through him. Moreover, although Snow was not an outspoken communist, he openly criticized the GMD and had already prior to Yan'an been sympathetic to the CCP's goals. In fact, all of the foreign correspondents who gained access to the Communists ended up being enthusiastic supporters.[75]

Since the US government was not well informed about the Chinese Communists and uncertain about their real nature, the Chinese Communists did their utmost to cultivate American friendship, hoping to obtain American assistance in return.

---

[73] *Harper's* December 1944 and March 1946; *Nation* 13.2.1943; *New York Times* 31.10.1944. See also: Thorne, *Allies*; Steven I. Levine, 'On the Brink of Disaster: China and the United States in 1945', in Harry Harding and Yuan Ming (eds), *Sino-American Relations, 1945–1955: A Joint Reassessment of a Critical Decade* (Wilmington, 1989), pp. 9–10; MacKinnon and Friesen, *China Reporting*, pp. 111–15 and 120–21; Neils, *China Images*, pp. 93–4, 126–32 and 171–2; Tuchman, *Stilwell*, pp. 505–6; Isaacs, *Images*, pp. 179–88.

[74] Edgar Snow, *Red Star over China* (New York, 1978); Anna Louise Strong, *China's Millions* (New York, 1928). See also: Jerry Israel, '"Mao's Mr. America": Edgar Snow's Images of China', *Pacific Historical Review*, 47 (1978), pp. 111–18; Jerry Israel, 'Carl Crow, Edgar Snow, and Shifting American Journalistic Perceptions of China', in Jonathan Goldstein, Jerry Israel and Hilary Conroy (eds), *America Views China: American Images of China Then and Now* (London, Toronto and Cranbury, 1991), pp. 155–64; Neils, *China Images*, pp. 38–42 and 63–4; Isaacs, *Images*, p. 162; Thorne, *Allies*, pp. 424–5.

[75] Peter Rand, *China Hands: The Adventures and Ordeals of the American Journalists Who Joined Forces with the Great Chinese Revolution* (New York, 1995), pp. 157(quote)–68.

They gave US officials selected information which focused on the GMD's refusal to attack the Japanese, the CCP's relative independence from Moscow and its accomplishments in fighting the Japanese. As a result, US diplomats in China like John S. Service intensified their criticism of the Nationalist government and presented the Communists in a more positive light. However, after FDR replaced Stilwell with the eccentric Major General Patrick Hurley, the chances of American support for the Communists sank rapidly due to Hurley's blatant pro-Chiang stance.[76] Hurley refused to make concessions to the CCP and had dissenting members like Service transferred out of China. When Roosevelt died on 12 April 1945, Harry Truman became the new President of the United States. His Administration continued to assist Chiang, thus further deteriorating relations with the Chinese Communists. After Hurley resigned on 27 November, Truman sent General George C. Marshall to China. Despite Marshall's credentials as a military leader, the Marshall Mission was doomed to fail because he was instructed to support the GMD against the CCP, causing Chiang and Mao to harden their stances. Marshall eventually threw in the towel and asked to be recalled to the USA, where in January 1947 he became Secretary of State.[77]

---

[76] 'Memorandum by the Second Secretary of Embassy in China', 18.6.1947, in *FRUS 1947*, pp. 200–204; 'Report by the Second Secretary of Embassy in China', 22.3.1945, in *FRUS 1945*, pp. 300–301. See also: James Peck, *Washington's China: The National Security World, the Cold War, and the Origins of Globalism* (Amherst and Boston, 2006), pp. 72–5; Schaller, *Crusade*, pp. 181–91; Cohen, *America's Response*, pp. 131 and 136–42; Zhang Han Ying, 'The Marshall Mission and United States Relations with the Nationalists and Communists in China', in Priscilla Roberts (ed.), *Sino-American Relations since 1900* (Hong Kong, 1991), pp. 374–5; He Di, 'The Evolution of the Chinese Communist Party's Policy toward the United States, 1944–1949', in Harry Harding and Yuan Ming (eds), *Sino-American Relations, 1945–1955: A Joint Reassessment of a Critical Decade* (Wilmington, 1989), pp. 33–6; Zhang Baijia, 'Chinese Policies toward the United States, 1937–1945', in: Harry Harding and Yuan Ming (eds), *Sino-American Relations, 1945–1955: A Joint Reassessment of a Critical Decade* (Wilmington, 1989), pp. 21–2; Michael M. Sheng, 'America's Lost Chance in China? A Reappraisal of Chinese Communist Policy toward the United States before 1945', *The Australian Journal of Chinese Affairs*, 29 (1993): pp. 151–2.

[77] 'Economic Policies and Views of Chinese Communists', John D. Sumner Papers, China Files Box 2, Truman Library; 'Hurley to Marshall', 30.5.1945, John D. Sumner Papers, China Files Box 2, Truman Library; 'Directive by President Truman to the Supreme Commander for the Allied Powers in Japan', 15.8.1945, in *FRUS 1945*, pp. 530–31; 'The Ambassador to China (Hurley) to President Truman', 26.11.1945, in Department of State, *United States*, pp. 581–4; 'Memorandum of Conversation by George Marshall', 14.12.1945, in *FRUS 1945*, p. 770; 'President Truman to General Marshall', 15.12.1945, in *FRUS 1945*, pp. 770–73; 'Statement by the President: United States Policy toward China', 18.12.1946, in *Public Papers of the Presidents (PPP), Harry S. Truman, 1946* (Washington, 1962), pp. 499–505; Dennis Merrill (general ed.), *Documentary History of the Truman Presidency, vol. 6: The Chinese Civil War: General George C. Marshall's Mission to China, 1945–1947* (Bethesda, 1996); *Chicago Tribune* 7.8.1949; *Los Angeles Times* 7.8.1949. See also:

The US involvement in China contributed to a scandal in the USA that increased fears of communist espionage and subversion. In 1945, the journal *Amerasia* illegally received hundreds of classified State Department documents from John S. Service. The editor of *Amerasia*, Philip Jaffe, not only used Service's documents for articles in the journal but also handed them over to a Soviet spy. Although Service, Jaffe and four others were arrested on 6 June 1945, the case was closed with only Jaffe being fined because the FBI and the Office of Strategic Services had illegally searched the premises of the magazine and had placed wiretaps and bugs there without court orders.[78] The *Amerasia* case would not have ignited such anticommunist paranoia if it had not been for preexisting anticommunist sentiment. While in the early 1930s, anticommunists and anticommunist publications like the *Chicago Tribune* unleashed their wrath primarily on FDR and the New Deal, in 1939 the Nazi-Soviet Pact caused them to focus on fascism and communism as totalitarian evils Although American media portrayals of the Soviet Union improved rapidly once the USA and the Soviet Union became allies, anticommunism was not completely wiped out and by 1945 was rampant again. In a Gallup poll from 1946 a staggering 36 per cent of those questioned felt that members of the CPUSA should be killed or imprisoned.[79] After the Republicans won control of both houses in November 1946, they used anticommunism to discredit the Truman Administration, claiming that it was soft

---

Wang Chen-main, 'A Re-examination of the Instructions Used by Marshall's Mission in China (December 1945–January 1947)', in Priscilla Roberts (ed.), *Sino-American Relations since 1900* (Hong Kong, 1991), pp. 352–64; Schaller, *Crusade*, pp. 194–227 and 263–89; Westad, *Cold War*, pp. 67–8; Sheng, 'Lost Chance', pp. 155–7; Cohen, *America's Response*, pp. 145–52; Xiang, *Recasting*, pp. 18 and 20; Lutze, *Revolution*, pp. 24–5 and 36–53; Tuchman, *Stilwell*, pp. 513–15; Qing, 'American Visions', pp. 280–81 and 299–301.

[78] Gallup, *The Gallup Poll*, vol. 1; *Amerasia* 18.5.1945. See also: John Earl Haynes and Harvey Klehr, *Early Cold War Spies: The Espionage Trials That Shaped American Politics* (Cambridge and New York, 2006), pp. 25–40; Haynes, *Red Scare*, pp. 50–54; Powers, *Not without Honor*, p. 195; Hinds and Windt, *Cold War*, p. 166; Schaller, *Crusade*, p. 226.

[79] Gallup, *The Gallup Poll*, vol. 1, pp. 382, 453, 492, 523, 587, 565; George H. Gallup, *The Gallup Poll: Public Opinion 1935–1971, vol. 2: 1949–1958* (New York, 1972), p. 826; *New York Times* 18.9.1939; New York Economic State Council, *Is Your Town Red?* (New York, 1938); Elizabeth Dilling, *The Red Network: A 'Who's Who' and Handbook of Radicalism for Patriots* (Milwaukee, 1934); National Americanism Commission of the American Legion, *Isms: A Review of Alien Isms, Revolutionary Communism and Their Active Sympathizers in the United States*, 2nd ed. (Indianapolis, 1937). See also: Michael Barson and Steven Heller, *Red Scared! The Commie Menace in Propaganda and Popular Culture* (San Francisco, 2001), pp. 42–55; Hinds and Windt, *Cold War*, pp. 49–56 and 69–78; Fraser J. Harbutt, *The Cold War Era* (Malden, 2001), pp. 26–7; Powers, *Not without Honor*, pp. 191–4 and 214; Haynes, *Red Scare*, pp. 40–50; Heale, *Anticommunism*, pp. 100 and 120–35; Wendt, *Chicago Tribune*, pp. 562–74 and 598; Wilford, 'The Communist International', pp. 225–33.

on communism and had been infiltrated by communists. Truman reacted to these accusations by establishing the Loyalty Program in March 1947 but suspicions about communist subversion in the government remained.[80]

The enmification of communism also dominated US foreign policy in 1946. In his famous 'Long Telegram' of 22 February 1946, George Kennan described the threat of Soviet expansion as a threat to the USA and the West that had to be met with strong resistance. Kennan's telegram was deemed so important that copies were given to various ministers, diplomats and military personnel stationed abroad and were made required reading for high-ranking officers.[81] Another milestone in the early history of the Cold War occurred on 5 March 1946, when the former British Prime Minister Winston Churchill held his famous 'iron curtain' speech at Westminster College in Fulton, Missouri, in which he proclaimed that an iron curtain divided Europe, and that an alliance of Britain and the USA had to meet the communist threat in order to ensure the survival of democracy and Christian civilization.[82] President Harry S. Truman, in turn, declared in his message on the State of the Union in January 1947:

> Our goal is collective security for all mankind. ... The spirit of the American people can set the course of world history. If we maintain and strengthen our cherished ideals, and if we share our great bounty with war-stricken people all over the world, then the faith of our citizens in freedom and democracy will be spread over the whole earth and free men everywhere will share our devotion to those ideals.[83]

---

[80] Chamber of Commerce of the United States, *Communists within the Labor Movement: The Facts and Countermeasures* (Washington, DC, 1947); 'Defining Loyalty', in Albert Fried (ed.), *McCarthyism: The Great American Red Scare, A Documentary History* (Oxford and New York, 1997), pp. 28–30; 'Statement by the President on the Government's Employee Loyalty Program', 14.11.1947, in *PPP, Harry S. Truman, 1947* (Washington, DC, 1963), pp. 489–91; Gallup, *The Gallup Poll*, vol. 1, p. 689. See also: Heale, *Anticommunism*, pp. 122–4 and 136–49; Hinds and Windt, *Cold War*, pp. 48–9 and 165–75; Morgan, *Reds*, pp. 301–6; Haynes, *Red Scare*, pp. 65–73 and 135.

[81] 'The Chargé in the Soviet Union (Kennan) to the Secretary of State', 22.6.1946, in *FRUS 1946*, pp. 696–709. See also: Scott Lucas and Kaeten Mistry, 'Illusions of Coherence: George F. Kennan, U.S. Strategy and Political Warfare in the Early Cold War, 1946–1950', *Diplomatic History*, 33/1 (2009): pp. 47–9; John Lewis Gaddis, *Strategies of Containment: A Critical Appraisal of American National Security Policy during the Cold War*, 2nd ed. (Oxford and New York, 2005), pp. 19–25; Thomas H. Etzold, 'The Far East in American Strategy, 1948–1951', in Thomas H. Etzold (ed.), *Aspects of Sino-American Relations since 1784* (New York and London, 1978), pp. 106–8; Ryan, *US Foreign Policy*, pp. 121–2.

[82] *New York Times* 7.3.1946. See also: Hinds and Windt, *Cold War*, pp. 90–109; Reynolds, *From World War*, pp. 249 and 256–63; Harbutt, *Cold War*, pp. 29–30; Ryan, *US Foreign Policy*, p. 122.

[83] 'Annual Message to the Congress on the State of the Union', 6.1.1947, in *PPP, Harry S. Truman, 1947*, p. 12.

This was followed on 12 March 1947 by Truman's speech to the joint session of Congress, in which he outlined what later became known as the 'Truman Doctrine', describing the danger of the spread of totalitarianism, and the USA's role as the champion of the free world and protector of democracy.[84] The Truman Administration presented the containment of communism as the USA's global mission by relying on the image of the USA as the leader of the Christian world on a crusade for Western civilization and democracy against the communist, atheistic Soviet Union.[85] As a result, in the late 1940s, the notion of American Exceptionalism was directly connected to anticommunism in American political debates. This would turn out to be central to American political debates on China as well as media reactions to events in China.

The Tricky Issue of Assisting Nationalist China

In 1947, the Truman Administration regarded aid to Europe as being more important than aid to China. Hence, the European Recovery Program, better known as the Marshall Plan, was devised.[86] US support of the Chinese Nationalists, in the mean time, was increasingly being called into question due to Chiang Kai-shek's refusal to take action against corruption and military incompetence, his unwillingness to implement reforms, as well as the unpopularity of the Nationalists. While the

---

[84] 'Editorial Reaction to Current Issues', 19.3.1947, in Dennis Merrill (general ed.), *Documentary History of the Truman Presidency, vol. 8: The Truman Doctrine and the Beginning of the Cold War, 1947–1949* (Bethesda, 1996), pp. 117–19; 'Summary', undated, in Merrill, *Documentary History*, vol. 8, pp. 128–41; 'Editorial Reaction to Current Issues', 22.3.1947, in Merrill, *Documentary History*, vol. 8, pp. 142–6; 'Special Message to the Congress on Greece and Turkey: The Truman Doctrine', 12.3.1947, in *PPP, Harry S. Truman, 1947*, pp. 176–80. See also: Ryan, *US Foreign Policy*, pp. 125–9; Hinds and Windt, *Cold War*, pp. 130–49 and 155–8; Harbutt, *Cold War*, pp. 33–4; Samuel Kernell, 'The Truman Doctrine Speech: A Case Study of the Dynamics of Presidential Opinion Leadership', *Social Science History*, 1/1 (1976): pp. 20–44.

[85] 'Annual Message to the Congress on the State of the Union', 7.1.1948, in *PPP, Harry S. Truman, 1948* (Washington, DC, 1964), pp. 1–10. See also: Klein, *Cold War Orientalism*, p. 34; William Imboden, *Religion and American Foreign Policy, 1945–1960: The Soul of Containment* (New York, 2008), pp. 5 and 106–11; Michael H. Hunt, *The American Ascendancy: How the United States Gained and Wielded Global Dominance* (Chapel Hill, 2007), pp. 68–9 and 122–4.

[86] 'The Department of State Bulletin', 15.6.1947, in Dennis Merrill (general ed.), *Documentary History of the Truman Presidency, vol. 13: Establishing the Marshall Plan, 1947–1948* (Bethesda, 1996), pp. 171–3; 'Special Message to the Congress on the Marshall Plan', 19.12.1947, in *PPP, Harry S. Truman, 1947*, pp. 515–29. See also: Michael J. Hogan, *The Marshall Plan: America, Britain, and the Reconstruction of Western Europe, 1947–1952* (Cambridge and New York, 1987), pp. 26–45; John Lewis Gaddis, *The Cold War: A New History* (New York, 2005), pp. 31–4; Ryan, *US Foreign Policy*, pp. 130–34; Harbutt, *Cold War*, pp. 34–6 and 57.

Joint Chiefs of Staff emphasized that the threat of Soviet expansion in Asia would become very real if China turned communist, the National Security Council argued that the continuation of unconditional support for Chiang would leave the USA with no alternative for action, thus strengthening the influence of the Soviet Union on the CCP and increasing anti-American sentiment in Chinese society. However, when the Truman Administration sought to limit American involvement in China, it was faced with claims from the China Lobby (politicians, businessmen and missionaries) that the Chinese Civil War had been unnecessarily prolonged because the USA had not given the Nationalists enough arms and credits. The China Lobby not only criticized the Truman Administration for failing Nationalist China, it also jeopardized Congressional support for the Marshall Plan by threatening to vote against it unless Chiang received US support. As if this was not enough pressure, the American public also continued to support Chiang, causing the Truman Administration to fear that its popularity would suffer if it stopped assisting the Chinese Nationalists. As a result, Truman eventually asked Congress for $570 million for China, of which $400 million were granted in the China Aid Act of April 1948.[87]

Once the Republicans lost control of Congress in 1948, they looked to win back political power by focusing on anticommunist policies and Soviet espionage in the government, and they struck gold with the Alger Hiss Case. Alger Hiss had been a political advisor of the Far Eastern Division of the State Department from 1939 to 1944 and director of the Office of Special Political Affairs from 1945 to 1947. In 1948, Whitaker Chambers, a former communist, claimed that Alger Hiss was a Soviet agent and had given him official documents for the Soviets. Hiss denied the charges and was supported in this by Under Secretary of State Dean Acheson; even

---

[87] 'The Consul General at Chanchun (Clubb) to the Secretary of State', 28.8.1947, in *FRUS 1947*, pp. 263–6; 'Memorandum by Mr. Philip Sprouse to General Wedemeyer', undated, in *FRUS 1947*, pp. 741–59; 'Memorandum by the First Secretary of Embassy in China (Ludden)', 31.7.1947, in *FRUS 1947*, pp. 693–5; 'Study of the Military Aspects of United Sates Policy towards China', undated, in *FRUS 1947*, pp. 838–48; 'Special Message to the Congress on the Need for Assistance to China', 18.2.1948, in *PPP, Harry S. Truman, 1948*, pp. 144–6; 'China Aid Act of 1948', in Department of State, *United States*, pp. 991–4; 'Memorandum by the Policy Planning Staff', 7.9.1948, in *FRUS 1948*, pp. 146–85; 'Draft Report by the National Security Council on United States Policy toward China', 2.11.1948, in *FRUS 1948*, pp. 185–7. See also: John H. Feaver, 'The China Aid Bill of 1948: Limited Assistance as a Cold War Strategy', *Diplomatic History*, 5/2 (1981): pp. 107–20; John F. Melby, 'The Origins of the Cold War in China', *Pacific Affairs*, 41/1 (1968): pp. 25–9; Cohen, *America's Response*, pp. 158–61; Schaller, *Crusade*, pp. 299–301; Westad, *Decisive Encounters*, pp. 160–61 and 186–7; Peck, *Washington's China*, pp. 25, 32 and 63–7; Xiang, *Recasting*, pp. 162–3; Thomas J. Christensen, *Useful Adversaries: Grand Strategy, Domestic Mobilization, and Sino-American Conflict, 1947–1958* (Princeton, 1996), pp. 80–82; Lawrence K. Rosinger, 'China Policy and the 1948 Elections', *Far Eastern Survey*, 17/20 (1948): pp. 234–6; Ernest R. May, 'When Marshall Kept the U.S. out of War in China', *Journal of Military History*, 66/4 (2002): pp. 1008–10.

Harry Truman condemned the charges. Yet, eventually it was proven that Hiss had indeed been a Soviet spy. The Alger Hiss case was just what the Republicans had been waiting for: it established that Soviet spies had infiltrated the government, it discredited the Truman Administration and it increased anticommunist paranoia about communist subversion in the USA.[88]

The Truman Administration's goal of limiting American assistance of Chiang Kai-shek was made impossible by the anticommunist atmosphere that suffused political debates in the USA in the late 1940s. It is important to differentiate between various strands of anticommunism. Some anticommunists focused on the Soviet Union as the communist adversary of the USA. For them, communism was a global threat and the Communist victory in China was seen as yet another milestone in the Soviet Union's quest for communist world domination. Other anticommunists focused on domestic communist subversion. In this case, China figured mostly as a passive player, with the main interest being communist subversives in the Truman Administration. In both strands, anticommunism was linked to the discursive construction of American nationhood. What made American involvement in China even trickier was that American anticommunism was also based on the idea that the USA could defeat communism because of American Exceptionalism. Moreover, American support of Nationalist China had for decades been linked to American Exceptionalism, meaning that enormous pressure was on the Truman Administration to conform to the discursive constructions of American nationhood by fighting communism and supporting the Chinese Nationalists.

When Dean Acheson became Secretary of State in January 1949, he faced the wrath of the China Lobby because the expiration of the China Aid Bill in April coincided with the Truman Administration's efforts to increase support for military aid to Europe and the ratification of the North Atlantic Treaty Organization (NATO). In February, 51 members of Congress signed a letter to Truman in which they demanded that the US government's China policy be reviewed. Senator Pat McCarran also introduced a bill calling for further aid to China, which threatened to affect Congressional approval of the military aid programme for Europe.[89] At the forefront of the Truman Administration-bashing papers was the *Chicago Tribune*. Its publisher Robert McCormick had for decades been a fervent anticommunist. Lloyd Wendt describes McCormick's influence on his paper in the 1940s in the following way: 'McCormick's every editorial thought ... became orders and instructions to a growing editorial staff. These orders were translated into type and art and appeared in more than a million Tribunes, seven days a week, 52 weeks a year.' As a result of McCormick's anticommunist paranoia, in

---

[88]   *Chicago Tribune* 20.6.1949 and 8.7.1949. See also: Powers, *Not without Honor*, pp. 221–5; Heale, *Anticommunism*, pp. 143–7; Haynes and Klehr, *Cold War Spies*, pp. 60–135; Morgan, *Reds*, pp. 241–53.

[89]   Cohen, *America's Response*, pp. 161 and 163–4; Christensen, *Useful Adversaries*, pp. 80–84.

the late 1940s, the *Chicago Tribune* championed the Republican quest to detect communist subversion in the Truman Administration.[90] In April 1949, the paper criticized Acheson's opposition to the McCarran Bill, accusing him of being pro-communist and questioning his commitment to containment:

> Not only has Mr. Acheson liquidated the No. 1 Roosevelt war aim, but he has rendered ridiculous his and Mr. Truman's policy of 'containing' Communist aggression. ... Mr. Acheson, during his earlier service in the state department, was identified with the pro-Communist faction in the department. This may explain why he is so willing to throw in the towel in China.[91]

The *Chicago Tribune* also referred to Soviet spy cases in the USA and pointed out that Alger Hiss, who was under indictment for perjury when the article appeared, had been Acheson's principal assistant in 1944. By linking domestic fears of communist subversion to fears of the global communist threat, it used the Republicans' strategy to accuse the State Department of being pro-communist, and supported the China Lobby's allegations that the State Department had handed China to the Soviet Union and thereby negated the USA's reason to enter the war with Japan.[92] Stating that 'a pro-Russian faction in the state department ... paved the way for the Communist victory in China', it concluded: 'Thus the state department has been and is dominated by pro-Russian and pro-English influence. ... Congress should withhold all appropriations until the department has been Americanized.'[93] What is particularly interesting about this last quote is that it demonstrates how in the discursive construction of nationhood, American Exceptionalism was intrinsically connected to the global defeat of communism. By 1949, however, it was clear that the Communists would win the Chinese Civil War. Yet, rather than admitting that maybe American Exceptionalism was not going to result in a global victory over communism, the *Chicago Tribune* chose to 'de-Americanize' the Truman Administration and absolve the 'real' USA of any responsibility in the Communist victory in China in order to maintain the image of the USA as valiant victor against communism.

In its criticism of US China policy, the *Chicago Tribune* found an unlikely ally in the *New York Times* which, despite its opposition to further aid for Chiang Kai-shek, condemned that the USA did not care as much about China as it did about European countries:

> As a people, and as a government representing that people, we are essentially Europe-minded, not Far-East-minded. ... The brave words that we have uttered about resisting the flood of communism and of helping free peoples

---

[90]   Wendt, *Chicago Tribune*, pp. 564–5, 613 (quote), 692.
[91]   *Chicago Tribune* 19.4.1949.
[92]   *Chicago Tribune* 19.4.1949, 22.4.1949, 9.5.1949, 10.8.1949, 15.8.1949.
[93]   *Chicago Tribune* 9.5.1949.

to remain free have given way to an embarrassed silence when the freedom of China is at stake.[94]

In July 1949, the Senate ratified the NATO treaty and began debating Marshall Plan extensions and military aid for Europe as part of the Military Assistance Program, which was eventually approved by Congress in August.[95] Among the most vociferous critics of NATO was – not surprisingly – the *Chicago Tribune*, which blamed the Roosevelt and Truman Administrations for focusing US aid on Europe and ignoring China, and accused the State Department (particularly Acheson) of being a British vassal that formulated US China policy according to British wishes, describing the State Department as 'his majesty's undersecretariat of state for the North American colonies'.[96]

Yet, despite criticism of US China policy, many American publications presented a damning verdict on the Nationalist government, opposing further financial support of it because it was corrupt and inefficient.[97] The *New York Times* criticized that Chiang had not implemented any large-scale reforms and had not found a solution to China's inflation.[98] The *Los Angeles Times* claimed that, so far, money given to China had 'all gone down the drain', and that further loans would not make a difference in the outcome of the Civil War.[99] This was quite a surprising stance given the Republican outlook dictated by its political editor Kyle Palmer and publisher Norman Chandler.[100] The *Washington Post*, in turn, accused the Chinese Nationalist regime of staging 'perhaps the worst orgy of corruption in Chinese history'[101] and prophesied a rather bleak future for a Nationalist China under Chiang: 'Chiang Kai-shek, whatever his merits in the days before the Sino-Japanese war, ha[s] lost his touch completely.'[102] Owen Lattimore, who had been a political advisor to the GMD in 1941 and 1942, and director of Pacific operations for the US Office of War Information, stated in the *Nation*: 'If America is unpopular in present-day China, it is because it tried to support a government that Chinese of all classes had come to despise.'[103] Walter Lippmann likewise pointed out that

---

[94]   *New York Times* 24.4.1949; see also 13.7.1949.

[95]   Reynolds, *From World War*, p. 317; Gaddis, *The Cold War*, p. 35; Christensen, *Useful Adversaries*, pp. 93–5.

[96]   *Chicago Tribune* 27.8.1949, see also 27.3.1949, 19.4.1949, 23.4.1949, 29.4.1949, 9.5.1949, 16.5.1949, 19.5.1949, 29.5.1949, 1.6.1949, 25.6.1949, 19.7.1949, 25.8.1949, 27.8.1949, 1.6.1949, 16.11.1949.

[97]   *Harper's* July 1947; *Los Angeles Times* 10.9.1949; *Nation* 30.6.1949.

[98]   *New York Times* 23.1.1949.

[99]   *Los Angeles Times* 28.4.1949, 6.8.1949 quote, 26.8.1949.

[100]   See Marshall Berges, *The Life and Times of Los Angeles: A Newspaper, a Family and a City* (New York, 1984).

[101]   *Washington Post* 28.4.1949.

[102]   *Washington Post* 28.4.1949.

[103]   *Nation* 30.6.1949. See also: Haynes and Klehr, *Cold War Spies*, pp. 40–41.

the Nationalist government had no popular support and that US assistance had been and would be useless because of the regime's corruption.[104] The opposition to further financial support of Chiang Kai-shek's government that was voiced in American newspapers and magazines, however, should not be interpreted as support for the Chinese Communists.

The Red Flood as a Global Catastrophe

In March 1949, John K. Fairbank, Professor at Harvard and one of the foremost China experts, warned that the situation in Asia should not be judged purely in the Cold War framework: 'We should have learned by now that the one sure path to American defeat is to judge the local regime in each area not on its merits, but solely by its attitude toward us and the Russians.'[105] Despite his efforts, the Cold War's bipolar world order deeply influenced the press coverage of the Chinese Communist victory in the USA because of the domestic increase in anticommunism and the Truman Administration's use of anticommunism to justify containment policies. Thus, various American publications spoke of the 'bamboo curtain' which descended or was about to descend on China, and thereby likened the situation in the Far East with that of Eastern Europe and the Iron Curtain.[106]

In early 1949, practically all American newspapers and magazines argued that communism would spread from China throughout Asia. Among the most outspoken publications was the *New York Times*, which on 21 April 1949 stated: 'there can be no doubt that further Communist successes in China must further shrink the free world and tip the balance of power in the Far East in favor of the Soviet bloc. That is a bitter fruit to grow out of our victory in the Pacific, for which we paid so dearly.'[107] Four days later, the Chinese Civil War was described as an event of apocalyptic proportions:

> While the Western World watches in stunned and helpless silence, the Communist armies are spreading out in China at a pace that no purely Chinese-led armies have ever attained before, and the tramp of their victory-flushed soldiery proclaims the rise of the red sun over the most populous country on

---

[104]   *Washington Post* 12.1.1949, 26.4.1949, 19.9.1949, 12.9.1949.

[105]   John K. Fairbank, 'Competition with Communism, Not Containment', *Foreign Policy Reports*, March 15 (1949): p. 6.

[106]   *Christian Science Monitor* 3.3.1939; *Time* 14.3.1949, 27.6.1949, 7.11.1949; *New York Times* 10.2.1949, 12.2.1949, 2.4.1949, 4.5.1949, 13.12.1949; *Washington Post* 11.4.1949.

[107]   *New York Times* 21.4.1949 (quote), 21.1.1949, 24.1.1949, 25.4.1949, 26.4.1949, 15.5.1949; *Los Angeles Times* 8.6.1949, *Washington Post* 6.6.1949, 22.8.1949, 29.8.1949; *Christian Century* 5.1.1949.

earth. ... This is a cataclysmic development which casts long shadows not only over Asia but over the whole world.[108]

In case some readers had missed the point, the newspaper hammered home its argument the next day:

> The Communist victories in China do not affect China alone. They threaten to take all Eastern Asia out of the orbit of the free world and in so doing reduce still further the breathing space which that world needs for its survival. What is more, they enlist in the Communist cause a new and unexpectedly effective fighting force which is expanding the frontiers of Soviet domination and tipping again in favor of Soviet Russia the world balance of power and strategic advantage which the North Atlantic Treaty was intended to restore.[109]

The *New York Times* reinforced its message with various maps on communist expansion in Asia. In May 1949, it published an image of a globe detailing communist influence in Asia, thus presenting communist expansion as a global threat emanating from the Soviet Union in all directions except Alaska. This perspective was reinforced by the title 'The Communist Shadow over the Far East', implying eventual Soviet control over all of the Far East. The globe, however, clearly indicated that communism not only affected the Far East but threatened the entire world, including the USA.[110]

The alarm expressed in the *New York Times* and many American newspapers and magazines often caused them to describe the Communist victory in China as a natural catastrophe. In late 1948, *Time*'s summary of a week's progress in the Chinese Civil War was: 'The Communists were overrunning China like lava.'[111] The metaphor of running lava for the Communist advance in China implied that communism was an unstoppable, destructive and deadly threat. Most American publications relied not on volcanic but aquatic metaphors and wrote of the 'red flood', 'red tide' and 'red wave' emanating from China. Even newsreels had titles such as 'red tide sweeps China'. The most original aquatic metaphor for the communist threat was probably 'huge whirlpool of Communist agitation', courtesy of Polyzoides in the *Los Angeles Times*.[112] The wave had been part of Yellow Peril imagery in the USA since the arrival of Chinese immigrants in the USA, and was therefore well established as an enemy image of the Chinese. The American obsession with communism had the effect that aquatic metaphors were omnipresent as descriptions for the Communist victory in China, portraying it as

---

[108] *New York Times* 25.4.1949.

[109] *New York Times* 26.4.1949.

[110] *New York Times* 15.5.1949.

[111] *Time* 6.12.1948.

[112] *Los Angeles Times* 19.8.1949. See also 'Americans Flee as Red Tide Sweeps China', Warner Pathé, Film ID 1522.44.

a scenario of apocalyptic proportions. As the columnist Stewart Alsop declared in August 1949:

> American policy in the Far East can now have only one primary aim. The aim must be to stop the threatened absorption of all Asia into the Soviet sphere. Even Japan and the Philippines will be in immediate danger if the Communist tide washes out of China into Indo-China, Siam, Malaya, Burma and Indonesia. The disaster in China will thus become a world catastrophe.[113]

For the *Washington Post*, the Communist victory in China was a catastrophe: 'The passage of China under the domination of Russian communism means not merely that we have by our own fault lost an ancient friend. In our position as the spearhead of world resistance to communism we have suffered an extreme disadvantage.'[114] Interestingly enough, the *Washington Post* was at the forefront of publications criticizing the hunt for communist spies in the USA. It staunchly defended Alger Hiss in the trial, which began in late 1948, and was itself even accused of being soft on communism.[115] Consequently, the political stance of a paper alone did not account for its reaction to events in China.

What made the Communist victory in China such a tremendous disaster for many US publications across the political spectrum was that they had previously linked China to the discursive construction of US identity and used it to legitimize US aspirations in Asia. This also explains why a paper such as the *New York Times*, generally regarded as the leading publication for objective and high-quality coverage of foreign news in the USA, published a decidedly sensationalist syndicated cartoon by Tom Little (Illustration 4.6), which exemplifies the revival of the Yellow Peril in the USA with respect to China. Little's cartoon contains typical Yellow Peril imagery such as the dragon and the masses of Chinese, which are loyally following the banner of 'communism' directly into the mouth of a dragon labelled 'China'. The title of the cartoon ('According to Tradition') invokes historical events where Chinese hordes were seen as a threat to the West, for example the Boxer Uprising or Chinese immigration to the USA. The cartoon visualizes China's retreat from capitalism to communism by having the Chinese walk away from the viewer into the mouth of the dragon, whose smoking nostrils, fangs and claws are further indications of the aggressive nature that China is expected to develop against the West once it has fully joined the communist camp.

In light of this rather hysterical reaction, it is interesting that prior to mid-1949, the real nature of the Chinese Communists was still debated by various publications. In 1948, the Subcommittee on National and International Movements of the Committee on Foreign Affairs stated: 'Chinese communism is regular communism. Its doctrines follow those of Lenin and Stalin. Its leaders are

---

[113] *Los Angeles Times* 8.6.1949.
[114] *Washington Post* 18.11.1949.
[115] Roberts, *Shadow*, pp. 273–9.

Illustration 4.6   Tom Little, 'According to Tradition', *New York Times* (5.6.1949)

Moscow-trained. Its policies and actions, its strategies and tactics, are Communist. The Chinese Communists have followed faithfully every zigzag of the Kremlin's line for a decade.'[116] Nevertheless, newspapers like the *Los Angeles Times* and the *Washington Post* thought that there was a possibility of Titoism in China.[117] Other papers, such as the *Chicago Tribune*, thundered against such a view, consistently presenting the Chinese Communists as 'Soviet Russia's Communist agents in China'.[118] This, of course, is not highly surprising, given the Republican stance of the paper. Neither should it by now be shocking that the *New York Times* joined the club and prophesied that a communist China would be 'a new Communist tyranny ready to deliver their country to the masters of the Kremlin'.[119] It also interpreted the Communist victory in China as evidence of the USA's failed China policy and a victory for the Soviet Union.[120]

The most dominant reaction in the US media to the Chinese Communist victory, however, was summarized by the *Los Angeles Times* in May 1949, when it announced: 'China has been lost.' As the reason for the USA's loss of China it named FDR's willingness to sacrifice his allies for the alliance with Russia.[121] The idea of having lost China is, as Chen Jian accurately points out, America-centred and negates any agency on the part of the Chinese Communists.[122] It also presupposes that the USA had once possessed China, which is very interesting considering the strongly anti-imperialist stance the USA had adopted with regard to China against other foreign powers since the late nineteenth century. Yet, one has to bear in mind that the US government had spent $3 billion on the Chinese Nationalist government, and had relied on idealistic images of China as a ward of the USA or as the Asiatic equivalent of the USA in order to legitimize US policies and geopolitical ambitions. The previous chapters have shown that since the turn of the century, American journalists, missionaries and government officials had been describing the USA as a mentor to China and thereby linked American Exceptionalism to China's modernization and democratization. The Communist victory in 1949 was, therefore, also such a traumatic experience because it went against the discursive construction of American nationhood.

Some historians have claimed that, due to the mutual suspicion between the CCP and the Soviet Union in the late 1940s, the USA could have established

---

[116] Subcommittee on National and International Movements of the Committee on Foreign Affairs, 'Communism in China', in *Report: The Strategy and Tactics of World Communism*, Supplement III (Washington, DC, 1948), p. III.

[117] *Los Angeles Times* 17.6.1949; *Washington Post* 28.2.1949.

[118] *Chicago Tribune* 22.4.1949.

[119] *New York Times* 21.4.1949; see also 11.12.1949.

[120] *New York Times* 24.1.1949; 18.4.1949, 21.4.1949, 23.4.1949, 25.4.1949, 26.4.1949, 15.5.1949.

[121] *Los Angeles Times* 5.5.1949.

[122] Chen Jian, 'The Myth of America's "Lost Chance" in China: A Chinese Perspective in Light of New Evidence', *Diplomatic History*, 21/1 (1997): p. 77.

friendly relations with the Communists and, drawn the CCP away from the Soviet Union. However, nowadays the 'Lost Chance' thesis is generally refuted. Chen, for example, argues that the CCP was not interested in Western recognition in 1949, while Laxing Xiang contends that both Acheson and Truman adopted a tough stance against the CCP and were not committed to the idea of establishing a Chinese Tito. Michael Sheng in turn points out that the CCP was not a proxy of the Soviet Union but an ally, even though the Soviet Union was clearly in the more powerful position. Moreover, Sheng argues that the CCP's rejection of the USA was also caused by the pro-USA stance of the GMD and the CCP's view of the bipolar world order, which further induced the CCP to side with the Soviet Union.[123]

In an effort to counter increasing accusations of having lost China, the State Department published a White Paper on China in August 1949, yet ironically it had the opposite effect. In the publication, Acheson signed a letter of transmittal portraying the Chinese Communists in a very negative way and not reflecting his own views. Most people – including journalists – only read this letter and not the rest of the book, which contained a great deal of evidence of the Nationalists' corruption and the CCP's nationalism.[124] As a result, the press tended to interpret the White Paper as a confession by the Truman Administration to its failure to fight communism in China. True to form, the *Chicago Tribune* not only concluded that China had been delivered into communist hands by the Roosevelt and Truman Administrations, but also that 'Roosevelt was out to communize the world'.[125] The *Washington Post*'s reactions to the White Paper were outright scathing: 'Never can there have been such a story of monumental stupidity, military incompetence, and political venality and myopia as is threaded through the crowded pages of this White Paper.' Yet, its criticism was directed as much against the USA as against the Chinese Nationalists:

> In the postwar story of China the United States sought to co-operate with moral turpitude (Government corruption) and a moth-eaten administration. It was this decay that ... the United States tried to make a functioning and victorious

---

[123]   Chen, 'Myth', p. 77; Xiang, 'Recognition', p. 319; Sheng, 'Lost Chance', p. 142; Michael Sheng, 'The United States, the Chinese Communist Party, and the Soviet Union, 1948–1950: A Reappraisal', *Pacific Historical Review*, 63 (1994): pp. 525–7; Warren I. Cohen, 'Symposium: Rethinking the Lost Chance in China', *Diplomatic History*, 21/1 (1997): pp. 71–5.

[124]   Dean Acheson, 'Letter of Transmittal', in Department of State, *United States*, pp. III–XVII; 'Memorandum of Meeting with the President', 27.6.1949, in Memoranda of Conversations File, 1949–1953, Box 65, Dean G. Acheson Papers, Truman Library; *Nation* 13.8.1949 and 3.9.1949; *Time* 15.8.1949. See also: Christensen, *Useful Adversaries*, pp. 96–7; Gallup, *Gallup Poll*, vol. 2, p. 852; Cohen, *America's Response*, p. 165.

[125]   *Chicago Tribune* 9.8.1949.

regime, though none of the American representatives entertained the slightest notion that that regime had any popular support.[126]

However, not all journalists blamed the Truman Administration for having lost China. Walter Lippmann viewed Chiang's defeat as the USA's defeat but he blamed Chiang and not the American government for it.[127] In the *Nation*, Owen Lattimore accused the China Lobby of ignoring the actual situation in China: 'The cry for all-out aid to Chiang Kai-shek cited the welfare of China less and less every time it was repeated, and the moral satisfaction of an active, gunpowder-and-human-blood front against Russia more and more.' And he concluded: 'The White Paper is primarily significant as evidence of the increasing ruthlessness of political warfare within the United States.'[128] Despite its own slating of the White Paper, the *Washington Post* also criticized the Republicans for their reactions and accused them of using 'Chiang as a stick with which to spank Harry Truman'.[129] It also condemned Republican demands for more aid to Chiang, exclaiming: 'It is time the sinogogues of the GOP stopped playing politics and think-of-a-number strategy about arms to China, and explored with the Administration the general outline of a policy toward China based on antiaggression instead of intervention.'[130] Likewise, the liberal journalist Marquis Childs, who was regarded as an eminence in domestic as well as international politics, stated in his column: 'One thing the White Paper does document on the testimony of men of varying views – most of the aid sent to China from this country since the end of the war has been wasted.'[131] The *Washington Post* grew increasingly impatient with the China Lobby and noted in September 1949: 'the decay in China cannot be honestly ascribed to lack of funds. The advocates of bigger and better aid conspicuously neglect to mention the 300 million dollars in gold bullion which Chiang Kai-shek has taken with him to Formosa.'[132] By October the newspaper had had enough and declared: 'The time is overdue to disembarrass ourselves of Chiang Kai-shek, so that a truly American policy can be developed.'[133]

Since American reactions to events in China were highly emotional, the issue of recognition was extremely tricky. In early 1949, the US government opposed recognition of Communist China not only for ideological reasons but also because such a step would have required the abandonment of Chiang Kai-shek.[134] Nevertheless, the State Department tried to establish contacts with the

---

126   *Washington Post* 8.8.1949.
127   *Los Angeles Times* 10.9.1949, 14.9.1949.
128   *Nation* 3.9.1949.
129   *Washington Post* 8.8.1949.
130   *Washington Post* 25.8.1949.
131   *Washington Post* 11.8.1949.
132   *Washington Post* 13.9.1949.
133   *Washington Post* 10.10.1949.
134   Peck, *Washington's China*, p. 93.

Chinese Communists, and so the American Ambassador in China, John Leighton Stuart, met Huang Hua, Zhou Enlai's assistant in May and June 1949. A meeting between Stuart, Mao and Zhou, however, was rejected by Acheson who feared that the American public would react badly to such news. Not only the US public but also various politicians rejected contact or trade with the Chinese Communists, and in June 1949 21 Senators wrote to Acheson expressing their opposition to such actions.[135] The issue of recognition was also problematic due to domestic anticommunism, the Truman Administration's use of anticommunism to legitimize US policies, and the public and media's opposition to recognizing Communist China. When news of the detention of the American Consul in Mukden, Angus I. Ward, by the Chinese Communists reached the USA in November 1949, it was even more difficult for Truman to justify recognition. Ward had been put under house arrest by the Chinese Communists in November 1948 after he refused to hand over the American consulate's radio transmitter. He was eventually charged with espionage and detained until December 1949.[136] A Warner Pathé newsreel covering Ward's release dwelt on Ward's solitary confinement and contained various shots of menacing Chinese Communist soldiers.[137] The media was, thus, a key influence on American public perceptions of China, and long-term media images of China turned out to be a huge problem for the Truman Administration in 1949 because they influenced political debates considerably.

Switzerland

Anticommunism and the Geistige Landesverteidigung

Like in Britain and the USA, anticommunism was widespread in Switzerland after 1945. During the Second World War, the *Geistige Landesverteidigung* was very effective in mobilizing nationalist sentiment in Switzerland but the defeat of Nazi Germany in 1945 meant that a new enemy would need to be found in order for the *Geistige Landesverteidigung* to continue its unifying effect. This enemy turned out to be communism. Domestic anticommunism had never really disappeared

---

[135] *Time* 4.7.1949; *Washington Post* 28.6.1949. See also: Christensen, *Useful Adversaries*, pp. 79 and 85–90; Chen, 'Myth', pp. 79–81; Westad, *Decisive Encounters*, p. 306; Xiang, 'Recognition', p. 329; Cohen, *America's Response*, pp. 164–5.

[136] *New York Times* 17.10.1949, 18.11.1949, 27.11.1949, 3.12.1949, 13.12.1939, 30.12.1949; *Washington Post* 6.10.1949, 16.11.1949, 18.11.1949; *Chicago Tribune* 16.11.1949; Gallup, *Gallup Poll*, vol. 2, pp. 831, 868 and 881. See also: Chen Jian, 'The Ward Case and the Emergence of Sino-American Confrontation, 1948–1950', *The Australian Journal of Chinese Affairs*, 30 (1993): pp. 149–70; Christensen, *Useful Adversaries*, pp. 97–104; Chen, 'Myth', pp. 78 and 81; Peck, *Washington's China*, pp. 93–6; Sheng, 'United States', p. 529.

[137] 'Chinese Reds Free Angus Ward', 1949, Warner Pathé, Film ID 2284.20.

since the 1930s and soon after the Second World War, various organizations again mobilized their members against communism (e.g. *Schweizerischer Vaterländischer Verband, Entente Internationale Anticommuniste, Redressement National*). The focus of the *Geistige Landesverteidigung* on the communist threat not only led to domestic stabilization but also resulted in measures against communist propaganda and subversion, such as the confiscation of Soviet propaganda and a law against speeches being made by communist foreigners.[138] Anticommunism was also present in the media. In May 1948, for example, the magazine *Schweizer Rundschau* published an entire issue on communism. In the editorial, it stated: 'Communism is standing as an arch enemy in front of the gates of countries, brains and hearts. It threatens peoples, states, society, every single one of us, even the worker. [Communism] means misery, slavery, desperation and extermination.'[139]

After 1945, the *Geistige Landesverteidigung* contributed to the idealization of neutrality in Switzerland.[140] In a nationwide survey from 1946, over 90 per cent of the participants felt that Switzerland should maintain neutrality. Arguments for neutrality included that it had been important for Switzerland in the past, that it helped prevent war, that it fostered peace within the nation, that it was important for Switzerland's humanitarian role in the world, and that it helped protect Swiss independence.[141] Although the dogmatization of neutrality had a unifying effect on Swiss society, it limited Switzerland's foreign policy because it

---

[138]   Kurt Imhof, 'Wiedergeburt der geistigen Landesverteidigung: Kalter Krieg in der Schweiz', in Kurt Imhof, Heinz Kleger and Gaetano Romano (eds), *Konkordanz und Kalter Krieg: Analyse von Medienereignissen in der Schweiz der Zwischen- und Nachkriegszeit* (Zürich, 1996), pp. 178–236 and 242–7; Boris Burri, 'Notrechtliches Vorgehen gegen die Kommunisten: Der Umgang der Schweizer Behörden mit ausländischer Propaganda nach dem Zweiten Weltkrieg (1945–1953)', *Schweizerische Zeitschrift für Geschichte*, 54/2 (2004): pp. 161–6; Kurt Imhof, 'Das kurze Leben der geistigen Landesverteidigung: Von der "Volksgemeinschaft" vor dem Krieg zum Streit über die "Nachkriegsschweiz" im Krieg', in Kurt Imhof, Heinz Kleger and Gaetano Romano (eds), *Konkordanz und Kalter Krieg: Analyse von Medienereignissen in der Schweiz der Zwischen- und Nachkriegszeit* (Zürich, 1996), pp. 19–84; Jakob Tanner, 'Switzerland and the Cold War: A Neutral Country between the "American Way of Life" and "Geistige Landesverteidigung"', in Joy Charnley and Malcolm Pendler (eds), *Switzerland and War* (Bern, 1999), pp. 113–18; Neval, *Mit Atombomben*, pp. 270–74, 598–604 and 628; Sébastien Farré, 'Justice, interdictions et répression anticommuniste (1936–1945)', in Michel Caillat, Mauro Cerutti, Jean-François Fayet and Stéphanie Roulin (eds), *Histoire(s) de l'anticommunisme en Suisse/Geschichte(n) des Antikommunismus in der Schweiz* (Zürich, 2009), pp. 195–208.

[139]   *Schweizer Rundschau*, 48/2 (1948): p. 73.

[140]   Peter Hug, 'Verhinderte oder verpasste Chancen? Die Schweiz und die Vereinten Nationen, 1943–1947', in Georg Kreis (ed.), *Die Schweiz im internationalen System der Nachkriegszeit 1943–1950* (Basel, 1996), pp. 92–6.

[141]   Verein Volksumfrage unter dem Patronat der neuen Helvetischen Gesellschaft, *Die Schweiz hält durch* (Zürich, 1948), pp. 173–5.

meant Switzerland did not join organizations concerned with collective military defence, like the Brussels Pact or NATO, as well as organizations like the European Council. As a result, Switzerland tried to position itself between the two blocs by taking up relations with the Soviet Union in 1946 and signing a treaty concerning the exchange of goods in 1948, and joining the Organization for European Economic Cooperation in the same year. Switzerland eventually integrated itself into the Western bloc and reduced economic relations with the Eastern bloc, but the 'splendid isolation' mentality propagated by the *Geistige Landesverteidigung*'s elevation of Swiss neutrality meant that Switzerland entered a period of isolationism.[142]

The Return of the Yellow Peril

Contrary to the British and US press, events in the Far East were of only minor importance for Swiss newspapers in the late 1940s because the issue of Swiss neutrality and Switzerland's position between the power constellations of the early Cold War led the Swiss press to focus primarily on the situation in Europe, the USA and the Soviet Union. Articles about China were also often interpreted within the framework of the Cold War. Between 1945 and 1949, *Nebelspalter* cartoons about China, for example, almost always included Joseph Stalin to imply that the Soviet Union controlled events in China. Similarly, the *Tages-Anzeiger*, described the Chinese Civil War as a fight between American and Russian interests.[143] The lack of interest in China shown by the Swiss press reflected that of the Swiss government. Due to its neutrality during the Second World War, Switzerland did not relinquish extraterritoriality in China like Britain and the USA, which as allies of China were compelled to do so as a sign of goodwill. The Swiss government only relinquished extraterritoriality on 13 March 1946, after the majority of the other treaty powers had done so. The Swiss press, Swiss businessmen and officials

---

[142]   Tanner, 'Cold War', p. 116; Daniel Trachsler, *Neutral zwischen Ost und West? Infragestellung und Konsolidierung der schweizerischen Neutralitätspolitik durch den Beginn des Kalten Krieges, 1947–1952* (Zürich, 2002); Gehrig-Straube, *Beziehungslose Zeiten*; Steffen, 'Gegensätzliche Partner', pp. 60–75; Dreyer, *Schweizer Kreuz*, pp. 48–60; Kaestli, *Selbstbezogenheit*; Daniel Möckli, 'The Long Road to Membership: Switzerland and the United Nations', in Jürg Martin Gabriel and Thomas Fischer (eds), *Swiss Foreign Policy, 1945–2002* (Basingstoke, 2003), pp. 48–52; Kurt R. Spillmann, Andreas Wenger, Christoph Breitenmoser and Marcel Gerber, *Schweizer Sicherheitspolitik seit 1945: Zwischen Autonomie und Kooperation* (Zürich, 2001), pp. 34–46; Manfred Linke, 'Zwischen Bilateralismus und Multilateralismus: Die schweizerische Aussenpolitik 1944–1950', in Georg Kreis (ed.), *Die Schweiz im internationalen System der Nachkriegszeit 1943–1950* (Basel, 1996), pp. 60–66; Katharina Bretscher-Spindler, *Vom Heissen zum Kalten Krieg: Vorgeschichte und Geschichte der Schweiz im Kalten Krieg 1943–1968* (Zürich, 1997), pp. 99–103 and 146–8.

[143]   *Tages-Anzeiger* 22.7.1945. See also Kamber, 'Medienereignishierarchien 1930–1960', pp. 267–70.

in China were also very outspoken in their criticism of Nationalist corruption and the miserable condition of the Chinese economy.[144]

During the Chinese Civil War, the Swiss government remained a passive observer of the events in China and sought to avoid getting involved. For example, it opposed arms sales to China in 1946 because it was worried that the Civil War could eventually become an object of international attention and draw Switzerland into an international conflict.[145] Switzerland's position was, therefore, very different from that of the USA, which actively supported the Nationalists, and was much more like that of Britain, which also avoided getting drawn into the Civil War. Since there were no clear sympathies towards either of the two warring parties in the Chinese Civil War, Chinese stereotypes made a comeback in the Swiss press between 1945 and 1949. This is particularly noteworthy in the numerous cartoons about China published in the *Nebelspalter* that portrayed the Chinese Civil War as a new instance of the Yellow Peril. The cartoons tended to portray the situation in China with such well established stereotypes as the dragon or facial features associated with the Chinese. It is also telling that the colours yellow and red dominated the cartoons, further demonstrating how Yellow Peril and Red Menace imagery dominated.[146] For instance, Illustration 4.7 by the Bil Spira was published in January 1949, after the Civil War had been raging for several years and it had become more or less clear that a Communist victory was inevitable. Yet, rather than trying to depict what was actually going on in the Chinese Civil War or what it was all about, the cartoon relied on the stereotype that the Chinese all looked alike and portrayed the Civil War as a killing orgy in which all Chinese soldiers were stock characters with yellow skin, slanted eyes and buck teeth without any signs of which warring party they belonged to. The ironic title of the cartoon 'Land des Lächelns' (literally: 'land of the smile') referred to what was seen to be a curious habit of the Chinese to smile in situations where Westerners would not. *Das Land des Lächelns* was also the name of a popular operetta by Franz Lehár of which the English title is 'the land of smiles'. The message seemed to be that for Swiss readers, the Chinese Civil War was of no interest except for racist amusement, and the Chinese were reduced once more to the racial and cultural Other. Yellow Peril stereotypes also made a comeback in British and American cartoons, but those cartoons usually focused on the threat of communism to Asia or the world. Such an ideological meaning is completely missing from Illustration 4.7. The complete lack of interest in the suffering of the Chinese Civil War victims in the cartoon becomes even more puzzling when

---

[144]   *Weltwoche* 22.10.1948. See also: *NZZ* 2.4.1949 and 30.4.1949; *Schweizer Illustrierte* 19.1.1949; *Tages-Anzeiger* 25.9.1949; *Weltwoche* 10.5.1946; *Nebelspalter* 13.1.1949. See also: Stämpfli, 'Schweiz und China', pp. 166–7 and 174–5; Coduri, *La Suisse*, pp. 50–55.

[145]   BAR E 2001 E 1967/113 154. See also: Coduri, *La Suisse*; Stämpfli, 'Schweiz und China', pp. 168–9.

[146]   *Nebelspalter* 6.1.1949, 20.1.1949, 17.2.1949, 28.7.1949, 15.9.1949.

Land des Lächelns

Illustration 4.7   Bil Spira, 'Land of the Smile', *Nebelspalter* (6.1.1949)
Source: Scan provided by Zentralbibliothek Zürich. Reproduced with permission of Nebelspalter.

one takes into account that during the Second World War, the artist of the cartoon had himself been interned in Buchenwald and Theresienstadt and had personally experienced the pain and horror inflicted by war.[147]

Switzerland had even less contact with the CCP prior to 1949 than Britain or the USA, which meant that there was very little reliable information available about the Chinese Communists. Although by 1949 Swiss officials in China were convinced that the CCP would win the Civil War, they were not sure how strong Soviet control over the CCP was.[148] This was also an issue the Swiss press was concerned about. Already in 1946, the *Weltwoche* tried to assess the exact nature of the Chinese Communists. While it was fairly convinced that they were not orthodox Marxists, it worried that their victory would lead to communist expansion in Asia.[149] Three years later, the *NZZ* viewed the Communist victory in China as part of the 'indirect Soviet-Russian expansion in the Far East'.[150] One can, therefore, see that there was a tendency among British, American and Swiss publications to describe the Chinese Communists as unorthodox Marxists. Yet, whereas British and American correspondents relied on quite damning verdicts on the Chinese Communists, the sparse information that Swiss newspapers had access to, meant that for them the exact nature of the Chinese Communists remained elusive, and they often had to resort to generalized statements about the CCP. Contrary to the British and American press, there were also hardly any in-depth analyses of the Chinese Communists in the Swiss press. One of the most alarmist reports about the Chinese Communists in the Swiss press was printed in 1948 in the *Schweizer Rundschau*. It claimed that the Communists acted contrary to their portrayal and upheld a reign of terror which spread hunger and poverty. The author was a Chinese missionary, and thus personally affected by the increasingly hostile treatment of missionary organizations by the Communists.[151]

Like their British and American counterparts, Swiss newspapers published reports of a 'communist flood' in the Far East. In addition, the *Tages-Anzeiger* described the spread of communism as a monster with equally horrific consequences as a natural catastrophe: 'Everywhere in Asia the Moscow-inspired communism is lifting its head.'[152] Much like the flood and the wave that had been long established as part of Yellow Peril imagery, the monster had been present in Swiss newspaper articles and editorial cartoons as a visualization of the Yellow Peril. Reports about the Communist victory were, therefore, in all three countries drenched in a mixture of traditional Yellow Peril and Red Menace imagery (e.g. the flood was described as communist, the monster as inspired by Moscow). The

---

[147]   Bil Spira, *Die Legende vom Zeichner*, edited by Konstantin Kaiser and Vladimir Vertlib (Wien, 1997).

[148]   Stämpfli, 'Schweiz und China', pp. 167–70.

[149]   *Weltwoche* 10.5.1946.

[150]   *NZZ* 29.5.1949.

[151]   *Schweizer Rundschau* 48/2 (1948): pp. 178–82.

[152]   *Tages-Anzeiger* 24.9.1949.

popularity of the Red Menace can be explained by the fact that neither Britain, the USA nor Switzerland were part of the Eastern bloc. As Britain and the USA were (ideological) opponents of the Soviet Union in the Cold War, their culture was permeated with Red Menace imagery. In the USA this was even more so because of the paranoia related to domestic communist subversion. Switzerland, on the other hand, was not officially part of the Western bloc although it sympathized with the West. While a military alliance with Western nations was out of the question for the Swiss government, the use of Red Menace imagery enabled the Swiss media to present Swiss nationhood as part of the West. Moreover, metaphors such as 'communist flood' were ubiquitous because Red Menace imagery allowed newspapers and magazines to interpret events in China within the framework of the Cold War, which was understood by their readers. Thus, even in Switzerland, where there was no huge interest in Chinese affairs, Cold War imagery ensured that reports on the situation in China would be read by the Swiss audience with interest. The *NZZ*, for example, stressed that the big winner of the Communist victory in China was the Soviet Union, which could not only celebrate an ideological but also a geographical success while the West lost prestige.[153] The *Tages-Anzeiger* also attested to the Chinese Communists' total spiritual dependence on Moscow:

> The founding of the Chinese People's Republic ... is an event of prime importance not only for China but for the entire Far East, because the first powerful Soviet state has been created which thinks it is destined to lead the Asiatic peoples and bring them the 'salvation' of Communism. This poses a threat to the free nations of Asia as well as those of Europe and the Americas, which, apart from the change in the military-strategic balance of power, would have to expect most serious economic setbacks from Asia's slide into communism ....[154]

Although Switzerland was supposed to be a neutral country, the Swiss press clearly sided with the Western bloc. British, American and Swiss media reactions to the Communist victory in 1949, therefore, demonstrate not only that the Red Menace as a frame for the events in China circulated on a transnational level, but also that it was a prime example of the way the Western bloc was visually and verbally constructed as a unity against communism in the emerging Cold War.

Yet, while the red wave circulated transnationally as a media image of the Communist victory in 1949, the effects of the wave were interpreted differently in each nation. In Britain, the wave was primarily a threat to Asia, while in the USA and Switzerland it was described as a global catastrophe because those countries experienced strong domestic anticommunist sentiment in the mid-to-late 1940s. Switzerland was not greatly affected by a Communist victory in China or communist expansion in Asia, and so for the Swiss media, the most pressing international issues were the preservation of Swiss neutrality within the changing

---

153   *NZZ* 11.10.1949 and 15.10.1949.
154   *Tages-Anzeiger* 15.10.1949.

situation in Europe, and Switzerland's need to reposition itself between the two emerging blocs of the Cold War through economic cooperation with Western nations. Consequently, Swiss newspapers and magazines sympathized with the Western bloc by portraying the Communist victory as part of a worldwide Red Menace but printed hardly any in-depth analyses of the Civil War.

A further factor influencing Swiss press reports about the Chinese Communists were plans for future economic relations with China. Despite Switzerland's neutrality in the Second World War, Swiss trade with China suffered during the war because commercial routes between Switzerland and China were disrupted. Japan also confiscated goods of Swiss companies in China, and storage buildings were bombed, burned or looted. Nevertheless, Swiss businesses continued to be enchanted by the China market, and 32 Swiss firms in China founded the Swiss Merchants Association, which later became the *Vereinigung Schweizer Handelskammern*. The postwar situation for the Swiss economy looked quite bleak because many traditional markets had either diminished or were temporarily closed to Swiss goods, and so measures were taken to improve commercial relations with China.[155] However, not everybody believed in the promise of the China market. By May 1949, the Swiss Consul General in Shanghai, Adalbert Koch, noted on the future of foreign trade in China: 'Judging from the experiences so far, the future prospects of the role and interests of the white man in a red China ... are not exceedingly rosy.'[156]

The *Nebelspalter*, with its usual lack of respect for the – admittedly negligible – Swiss interests in China published in July 1949 the cartoon 'The White Man in China' by the cartoonist Peter Bachmann (Illustration 4.8). It is an almost perfect visualization of Koch's view. The cartoon foresees the expulsion of Western businessmen from China and contrasts the era of the unequal treaties to the contemporary situation, juxtaposing the former domination of the (traditionally clad) Chinese by Western businessmen with the contemporary Communist rule, in which a Communist soldier forces the Western businessman to leave, which suggests that this is not an altogether unjustified occurrence. The difference in size between the Chinese man and the businessman in the picture on the left-hand side, and the pistol in the pocket of the White businessman refer to gunboat diplomacy and the subjugation of the Chinese by the imperial powers. From such a standpoint, the role reversal (depicted by the switching of sizes between the Westerner and the Chinese) is not such a tragic incident. Nevertheless, the use of the colour red to visualize the Communist victory in China (the entire right-hand image is coloured in red except for the businessman) invokes the Red Menace and, therefore, portrays the defeat of the businessman in China as a defeat for the West in the Cold War.

---

[155]   BAR E 2001 D 1968/154 391. See also: Coduri, *La Suisse*, pp. 44–8 and 56–60; Stämpfli, 'Schweiz und China', pp. 180–89.

[156]   'Report by A. Koch', 3.5.1949, BAR E 2001 E 1967/113 154.

Der weiße Mann in China

Einst...   und jetzt

Illustration 4.8   Peter Bachmann, 'The White Man in China',
Nebelspalter (7.7.1949)
Source: Scan provided by Zentralbibliothek Zürich. Reproduced with permission of
Nebelspalter.

Media reactions to the Swiss recognition of Communist China are also interesting because they were deeply influenced by economic interests. Since the Swiss government was convinced that the Communists would be in power for some time, the government concluded that a Swiss recognition should happen sooner rather than later. There were several reasons for this, including the protection of Swiss businessmen in Shanghai, the improvement of commercial relations between China and Switzerland, and the hope that recognition would enable Switzerland to take on the role of a mediator between Eastern and Western powers due to its neutral status, thus increasing Switzerland's international prestige.[157] Swiss plans to recognize China did not go down well in the USA, where John Carter Vincent had already warned Switzerland on 29 June 1949 not to recognize a Communist regime in China and avoid direct contact with members of such a government. Yet, the Swiss government was also aware of Britain's stance towards the Communists.[158] Therefore, the Federal Council decided on 7 October 1949 to recognize the Communist government as the official Chinese government once 20 or 30 other countries had recognized it. According to Michele Coduri, even though anticommunism was widespread in Switzerland, it did not affect the Federal Council's decision to recognize the Communist regime because China was not a big issue at that time and because Swiss public sentiment did not have a major impact on foreign policy. The Federal Councillor Max Petitpierre also supported recognition because he felt that it would protect Swiss missionaries in China, particularly since some of them had been imprisoned.[159] Eventually, it was decided that Swiss recognition would follow that of Britain. In December 1949, the British minister in Berne informed the Swiss government that Britain had set the date for 2 January 1950. The Swiss government subsequently assured Britain that Swiss recognition would promptly follow the British one, and on 17 January Switzerland became the fifth Western nation to recognize the PRC.[160]

The recognition was met with relative indifference in the Swiss press. For example, the *NZZ* and the *Journal de Genève* printed the Federal Council's official message without further comments, and a couple of days later published short announcements that Nationalist China had ended relations with Switzerland.[161] Only the *Tages-Anzeiger* printed a response to the Swiss recognition of the PRC. It found nothing out of the ordinary with the Federal Council's actions and stated that it was unclear whether economic relations between the PRC and Switzerland had improved, but that Switzerland had important economic interests in China.

---

[157]   BAR E 2001 E 1967/113 154. See also: Stämpfli, 'Schweiz und China', pp. 192–3 and 199–200.

[158]   Stämpfli, 'Schweiz und China', p. 192; Coduri, *La Suisse*, pp. 103–6.

[159]   Coduri, *La Suisse*, pp. 108–12.

[160]   BAR E 2001 E 1967/113 154. See also: Coduri, *La Suisse*, pp. 114–19; Wolf, 'Convenience', p. 318; Stämpfli, 'Schweiz und China', p. 196; Linke, 'Bilateralismus', p. 65.

[161]   *Journal de Genève* 18.1.1950 and 20.1.1950; *NZZ* 17.1.1950 and 20.1.1950.

Like the Swiss government, the newspaper viewed Switzerland's recognition of Communist China in a pragmatic way.[162] The Swiss situation was, therefore, relatively similar to that of Britain, where the government and the press supported British recognition of Communist China because it was thought that this action could protect economic interests in China. Furthermore, as in Britain, various Swiss papers argued that the Nationalists' corruption had been a major reason for the Communist victory. Indeed, in 1949, the *Nebelspalter* had a field day with cartoons about Nationalist corruption, and after the founding of the PRC, the *NZZ* printed a series of articles by its correspondent Walter Bosshard from Formosa. Bosshard painted a bleak picture of Nationalist China's future and portrayed Chiang Kai-shek as a lonely, bitter man.[163] Thus, although Swiss sympathies were not with the Communists, neither were they with the Nationalists. Instead, China was utilized by the Swiss press and the government to reposition Switzerland between the two blocs in the Cold War.

---

[162] *Tages-Anzeiger* 18.1.1950.

[163] *NZZ* 10.1.1950.

Conclusion

figured in political debates about China. Businesss interests, on the other hand, received more media attention. Although British missionaries dominated the foreign missionary presence in China until the early twentieth century, they did not greatly influence British China policy and also did not contribute significantly to the British media's coverage of events in China. During the Boxer uprising, for example, the British press relied on stereotypes such as the Yellow Peril to legitimize the British presence in China and the use of force against the Chinese

Contrary to general assumptions regarding 'China and the West', media images and political debates about China were not only different in each nation between 1900 and 1950 but they also changed over time because they were influenced by such factors as geopolitical and economic interests, domestic issues, the presence of missionaries in China, portrayals of China and the Chinese in film and literature etc.

The previous chapters demonstrated that national interests in China did not remain static but changed over the years because alliances affected media images and political debates about China, for example the Anglo-Japanese Alliance in the case of Britain in the early twentieth century, the alliance between Britain, the USA and China during the Second World War, and the Western bloc which included Britain, the USA and – to a lesser degree – Switzerland in the early Cold War. Such alliances contributed to the transnational circulation of China images either by generating new images or by focusing on existing images that depicted China in a particular way. Thus, in the Second World War, Japan was portrayed as the Yellow Peril and China as the helpless victim in all three nations because Britain and the USA fought on the side of the allies, while Switzerland was neutral but feared an invasion by the axis powers.

Despite their transnational circulation, China images were always slightly different in each country. Thus, as Chapter 3 has shown, although all three nations referred to Japan as the Yellow Peril and China as the innocent victim, the American press presented China as the Asian equivalent of the USA, relying on the traditional representation of China as the USA's ward. In Britain, references to China were less glowing due to the long history of negative China portrayals in the British press and the need to justify Britain's imperial presence there. Swiss publications also condemned Japanese actions and reported China's plight but the main focus was on the courage of the Chinese soldiers and China's will to resist Japanese domination because Switzerland itself was surrounded by the axis powers and the Swiss press, therefore, sought to instil courage and bravery in its readers in case of a German attack.

While Britain, the USA and Switzerland had missionaries in China, these did not influence press portrayals and political debates equally in each country. A number of studies have been written on the foreign missionary presence in China but none compare the influence of missionaries on national perceptions. In Britain and Switzerland, missionary organizations in China were not regarded as major national interests by either the press or politicians. Missionaries were also only occasionally used as sources by journalists from these countries and hardly ever figured in political debates about China. Business interests, on the other hand, received more media attention. Although British missionaries dominated the foreign missionary presence in China during the nineteenth century, they did not greatly influence British China policy and also did not contribute significantly to the British media's coverage of events in China. During the Boxer Uprising, for example, the British press relied on stereotypes such as the Yellow Peril to legitimize the British presence in China and the use of force against the Chinese. Such an image was problematic for British missionaries because it depicted the Chinese as inherently evil, which was not an ideal prerequisite for conversion to Christianity. In Switzerland, the experiences of missionaries did not receive a great deal of media attention because the majority of Swiss missionaries in China belonged to three missions, of which two were Swiss-German but were perceived as German, while the third opened its first stations in the 1920s in Manchuria, where it was far away from many of the main events of that decade.

American newspapers and magazines, however, constantly told their readers about the experiences of American missionaries in China, and often printed letters or statements of local missionaries who were in China or had recently returned from China. One reason why American missionaries had such a tremendous influence upon the US media coverage of events in China was that they successfully used American Exceptionalism to legitimize their presence in China. American businessmen, in contrast, turned China into an object that was there to be exploited by the foreign nations and described it as an El Dorado that could bring massive fortune to Americans. Such an image contrasted sharply with that of the missionary organizations which portrayed China as a pupil of the USA that had to be nurtured and protected from foreign imperialism. The American government also referred to American Exceptionalism to legitimize its China policies, and presented the USA as different from the other foreign powers in China, namely without territorial ambitions and as a champion of democracy. As this was crucial for the discursive construction of American nationhood, business organizations increasingly lost influence over the American media's portrayal of events in China. Yet, the cultivation of the image of the USA as mentor of China by the American government and American missionary organizations had the consequence that in 1949 the Communist victory was a huge shock. Whereas the British government received a great deal of press support for the decision to recognize Communist China and the Swiss press showed hardly any interest in the Swiss recognition, for the American press the issue was out of the question due to the traditional instrumentalization of China in the discursive construction of American nationhood in media and politics.

Another aspect that has so far been overlooked in accounts of relations between China and Western nations is the importance of domestic issues on perceptions of China, even though they often played a crucial role in the media's framing of events in China and political debates about China. Thus, press reactions in Britain to the Xinhai Revolution and the abdication of the Manchu Dynasty were hugely influenced by concerns about the power of the British monarchy and Britain's hold over its Empire, while in the USA they were heavily influenced by the Progressive Movement. The fact that the May Thirtieth Movement was preceded by a period of Russophobia during the General Election in Britain also caused a large part of the British media to rely on the Red Menace to frame events in China. Swiss publications, in turn, used the *Geistige Landesverteidigung*'s focus on resistance against a foreign aggressor to frame reports about the Sino-Japanese War after 1937. Finally, in the late 1940s, domestic anti-communism among Republicans massively influenced the portrayal of the Chinese Civil War and the Chinese Communist victory in American publications and led to Republican accusations of communist subversion in the Truman Administration and claims that the Administration had handed China over to the Communists.

An analysis of media portrayals of China reveals that articles about China not only contained a great deal of information about national self-perceptions but that they also contributed to the discursive construction of nationhood. Thus, the portrayal of China in American newspapers and magazines tended to depict the USA as a mentor of China, and thereby contributed to the belief in American Exceptionalism, which held that the USA was on a divine mission to spread democracy and progress. British representations of China tended to portray Britain as a strong and – more importantly – unified power that could count on the support of its colonies and dominions. British conservative newspapers also used reports about China to describe the British Empire as a righteous and strong global power. The Swiss media, finally, often used events in China to portray Switzerland as a neutral and democratic country that abhorred imperialism.

Typical examples of the way the discursive construction of nationhood affected the transnational circulation of images are press reactions to the May Thirtieth Movement and the Nanjing Incident. Although Britain, the USA and Switzerland all witnessed anticommunist sentiment in the 1920s, the Red Menace was only for the British press the primary choice for framing events in China because in the USA and Switzerland the discursive construction of nationhood rendered such a frame problematic. American newspapers and magazines presented the anti-foreign agitation in China as a (righteous) nationalist movement against foreign imperialism that deserved the sympathy of American readers. Such a positive portrayal allowed the American press to stress that the USA had no territorial interest in China and was different from all the other nations in China. Moreover, this frame contributed to the concept of American Exceptionalism by stressing that the USA had to protect those who could not defend themselves against imperialism. Swiss newspapers and magazines also did not use the Red Menace to frame the May Thirtieth Movement, focusing instead on democracy, neutrality and anti-imperialism because these concepts were of prime importance for the discursive construction Swiss national identity and traditional images of Switzerland as a bastion of democracy and neutrality.

Of course, not all newspapers and magazines relied on the same frame to interpret events in China. Some newspapers were under the almost complete control of their owner. This was particularly the case in Britain with the conservative newspaper barons Lord Beaverbrook, Lord Northcliffe and Lord Rothermere. Although there existed newspaper dynasties in the USA, American owners generally gave their editors more leeway and dictated their papers' stance to a lesser degree than did their British counterparts. Since the political orientation of a newspaper's owner was almost always the decisive factor in the way events in China were framed in Britain, the liberal *Manchester Guardian* and the socialist *New Statesman* were among the few publications taking a critical view of British imperialism in China. Most British newspapers and magazines sympathized with the Conservative Party and portrayed events in China in such a way that they justified British imperialism and reinforced pride in the British Empire. This sometimes took on quite a jingoistic form and often included Yellow Peril imagery, to distract from or ridicule Chinese demands for an end to Britain's informal imperialism in China.

The situation in the USA was different because American Exceptionalism had a unifying effect on the framing of events in China. Consequently, the portrayal of events in China tended to be relatively similar across political party lines, and until the 1930s, the American press focused on the image of the USA as protector of China against imperialist ambitions of other countries and on the role of the USA as the champion of democracy. In the 1930s, however, portrayals of the situation in the Far East began to diverge on the issue of intervention or non-intervention on China's behalf against Japan. After the outbreak of the Sino-Japanese War, newspapers like the *Washington Post* or the *New York Times* increasingly supported intervention while the *Chicago Tribune* steadfastly maintained that it was not the USA's job to help China out. After the Second World War, newspapers across the political spectrum blamed the Truman Administration for the Communist victory in China, even though some of them openly criticized the (Republican) hunt for communist spies in the USA itself. The discursive construction of American nationhood, thus, meant that frames chosen by US editors superseded party lines and led to a more or less homogenous press reaction to events in China.

Since the Swiss press often framed events in China in order to make statements about Swiss national identity, the situation was relatively similar to that of the USA. In Switzerland, newspapers were much less aligned with political parties than in the USA or in Britain, and the political orientation of a paper did not really influence the framing of events in China. Moreover, Switzerland's multi-party government made it harder to blame specific parties for political problems. Furthermore, the Swiss press did not link domestic issues to events in China. This would have certainly led to a more politically nuanced reaction among the newspapers. Instead, Swiss publications focused on topics like democracy and neutrality, i.e. concepts that were supported by parties and publications across the political spectrum because they related to the discursive construction of Swiss nationhood. Already in the 1920s, Swiss press reactions focused on these issues to show Swiss support for the anti-foreign movement in China and to portray Switzerland as one of the most democratic nations on earth and as a non-imperial power. Similarly, in the 1930s the *Geistige Landesverteidigung* was hugely influential in the portrayal of China in practically all Swiss publications, and in the late 1940s, anticommunism dominated the framing of events in China because it enabled editors to portray Switzerland as part of the Western bloc in the Cold War.

The relationship between the press and the respective government's China policy is another interesting aspect. Since press reactions to events in China were influenced by such factors as domestic issues, existing stereotypes and national self-images, newspapers and magazines did not always refer explicitly to government policies in their reports on China. However, whenever British, American or Swiss nationals in China were affected by the events, publications tended to use it as an opportunity to comment on government policies. Thus, during the Boxer Uprising many British and American publications pointed out that their government's China policy was correct. Yet, events in China were also exploited by the press to criticize governmental policies. For example, the conservative *Daily Mail* used the May Thirtieth Movement to denounce the Soviet Union and claim that the events in China proved that the British government had to expel all Bolsheviks from Britain. The *Manchester Guardian*, in turn, argued that Britain's China policy was to blame for the anti-British boycott in China and that the situation would only improve for Britons in China once Britain agreed to renegotiate the unequal treaties. In the USA, such criticism was rare because the American government ensured press support for its China policies by presenting them in such a way that they neatly fit in with American Exceptionalism. This made it quite difficult for newspapers and magazines to criticize American China policy because it would have also meant challenging assumptions associated with American Exceptionalism. Only when the American government's China policy diverged from the message of American Exceptionalism did the US press criticize the government. For example, after Japan was granted the former German privileges in Shandong province in 1919, the Wilson Administration faced the wrath of numerous newspapers and magazines which claimed that the government had acted treacherously and had abandoned China. In the late 1940s, the Truman Administration was also criticized for abandoning China, when it became clear that the Communists would win the Chinese Civil War. In both instances, the media was furious because the American government had failed to act as a guardian of China, which in the past had been used as legitimization for US China policies. In the case of Switzerland, media interest in the government's China policy was negligible even after Switzerland had established official relations with China in 1918. As a result, Swiss newspapers framed events in China mostly in such a way that they contributed to the discursive construction of nationhood.

Both the Red Menace and the Yellow Peril were used to justify discrimination and/or war and enjoyed transnational circulation in the first half of the twentieth century. They are also typical examples of the way values and beliefs that challenged national self-images were discursively excluded. Thus, in Britain, the USA and Switzerland, the Red Menace was used by the press as a frame to portray communists as unpatriotic and as traitors. Use of the Red Menace also demonstrates that fears of social unrest and economic crises resulted in the creation or increasing use of enemy images onto which aspects of social problems were projected. In this respect, the Red Menace was part of the wider process of the discursive construction of nationhood that portrayed a country like the USA as racially, culturally and politically homogenous. In Britain, the Red Menace was also very efficiently instrumentalized by the conservative press in the 1920s to discredit the labour movement and the Labour Party. Yet, there were also national differences in the interpretation of the Red Menace. In 1949, for example, the red wave circulated transnationally as a media image of the Chinese Communist victory, but the effects of the wave were interpreted differently in each nation. In Britain, the wave was primarily portrayed as a threat to Asia, while in the USA and Switzerland it was described as a global catastrophe.

The Yellow Peril was often used to legitimize the discrimination of the Chinese. In the USA, for example, it was invoked to demand Chinese and later Japanese exclusion. In Britain, it was used to legitimize the presence of British troops in China and their involvement in armed conflicts against Chinese, be it in the Boxer Uprising, the anti-British agitation in 1925 or the Chinese takeover of Hankou in 1927. Because Britain had a larger presence in China than the USA or Switzerland, it more often faced Chinese demands for an end to imperialism. As a result, China was more regularly portrayed as the Yellow Peril in Britain than in the USA or Switzerland because this allowed the press to present the Chinese demands as unworthy of consideration. In Swiss publications, the Yellow Peril was very popular, particularly among editorial cartoonists. As Switzerland had no clearly defined interests in China and as Swiss trade with China was much smaller than that of Britain or the USA, Swiss newspapers and magazines remained largely indifferent to events in China. As a result, Swiss cartoons of China and the Chinese often contained stock characters that were part of Yellow Peril imagery.

Another aspect of the transnational circulation of images is the diachronic change of images. It has been shown that the Yellow Peril was invoked at different times for different nations. Thus, during the Boxer Uprising it tended to refer to China but by the Second World War it was used to portray Japan as a threat to Western nations. After Japan's defeat by the allies, the label was switched back to China. This process did not take place in the same way in each nation because the perception of the Yellow Peril was influenced by various factors such as geopolitical interests in the Far East, Chinese and/or Japanese immigration, stereotypes of Chinese and/or Japanese from novels and films etc. Thus, in Britain the Anglo-Japanese Alliance and the need to justify British presence in China resulted in the depiction of China as the Yellow Peril until the 1930s, when Japanese interests increasingly clashed with those of Britain and caused a perceptive shift from China to Japan as the Yellow Peril. In the USA, Japan was regarded as the Yellow Peril because Japan seemed to threaten geopolitical aspirations in Asia, and because American missionary organizations spread positive images of the Chinese. As the Swiss press was prone to use stereotypes, it is no surprise that Yellow Peril imagery was very popular and used rather indiscriminately for both Chinese and Japanese in various magazines. The outbreak of the Cold War, however, had the effect that in all three nations the press tended to portray China as the Yellow Peril.

Since Britain and the USA belonged to the Western bloc and Switzerland – despite being neutral – sympathized with it, the victory of the Chinese Communists led to an outpouring of Yellow Peril portrayals of China, particularly in Switzerland. Among these images was the dragon, which has figured prominently in British, American and Swiss portrayals of the Yellow Peril. Between 1900 and 1950, editorial cartoons often portrayed the Western nations as human beings that fought the Chinese dragon, implying that it was an evil creature that had to be killed by righteous (white) knights. Even today, China continues to be portrayed as a dragon to signify a menace to or competition for the West. Countless books about the Chinese economy or about China as a global power refer to it as a dragon in order to invoke the image of China as a threat to the West. The dragon is also still the most popular symbol for China in British, American and Swiss editorial cartoons. Thus, even though the era of informal imperialism in China has long been over, images of China that were constructed by the press during this period are still used today by newspapers and magazines to frame events in China.

Bibliography

Manuscript Sources

Acheson, Dean G., Papers held at the Harry S. Truman Library, Independence, MO.

BAR E2001: Papers from the Eidgenössische Politische Departement, held at the Bundesarchiv in Berne, Switzerland.

Johnson, Nelson T., Papers held at the Library of Congress, Washington, DC.

NA RG 59: General Records of the State Department, held at the National Archives, College Park, MD.

Sumner, John D., Papers held at the Harry S. Truman Library, Independence, MO.

TNA ADM: Records of the Admiralty, Naval Forces, Royal Marines, Coastguard, and related bodies, held at the National Archives, Kew.

TNA CAB: Records of the Cabinet Office, held at the National Archives, Kew.

TNA CO: Records of the Colonial Office, Commonwealth and Foreign and Commonwealth Offices, Empire Marketing Board, and related bodies, held at the National Archives, Kew.

TNA FO: Records created and inherited by the Foreign Office, held at the National Archives, Kew.

TNA PREM: Records of the Prime Minister's Office, held at the National Archives, Kew.

TNA T: Records created and inherited by HM Treasury, held at the National Archives, Kew.

TNA WO: Records created or inherited by the War Office, Armed Forces, Judge Advocate General, and related bodies, held at the National Archives, Kew.

TUC Library: Trades Union Congress Library, London.

Printed Primary Sources

Newspapers and Periodicals

Amerasia
Annals of the American Academy of Political and Social Science
Atlanta Constitution
Berner Intelligenzblatt
Boston Globe
Bundesblatt
Business Week

Chicago Tribune
Christian Science Monitor
Collier's
Daily Express
Daily Mail
Daily Mirror
Die Weltwoche
Evening News
Evening Standard
Far Eastern Survey
Foreign Affairs
Foreign Policy Reports
Harper's
Hartford Courant
Illustrated London News
Journal de Genève
Life
Literary Digest
Los Angeles Times
Manchester Guardian
Memorandum
Nation
National Review
Nebelspalter
Neue Zürcher Zeitung
New Statesman/New Statesman and Nation
New York Times
Nineteenth Century and After
North American Review
Observer
PM
Public Opinion Quarterly
Puck
Punch
Reader's Digest
San Francisco Chronicle
Schweizer Illustrierte
Schweizer Rundschau
Schweizerische Monatshefte für Politik und Kultur
Spectator
Tages-Anzeiger
The Commercial and Financial Chronicle
The Digest
The Graphic

The Irish Times
The Scotsman
The Star
The Times
The Times-Picayune
The Wasp
The World
Time
Wall Street Journal
Washington Daily News
Washington Post
Workers' Weekly

Newsreels and Films

British Movietone News
Fox Movietone
Gaumont British News
Hearst Metrotone News
March of Time
Pathé News
Universal Pictures
Warner Pathé
The Battle of China, directed by Frank Capra, produced by the Office of War Information (1944).

Published Documents, Document Collections and Books

Adams, Brooks, *The New Empire* (New York, 1902).
American Federation of Labor, *Some Reasons for Chinese Exclusion* (Washington, DC, 1902).
Arbeitsgruppe für Geschichte der Arbeiterbewegung Zürich (ed.), *Schweizerische Arbeiterbewegung* (Zürich, 1975).
Ayer, N.W. & Son, *American Newspaper Annual and Directory* (Philadelphia, 1910).
——, *Directory of Newspapers and Periodicals 1930* (Philadelphia, 1930).
——, *Directory of Newspapers and Periodicals 1931* (Philadelphia, 1931).
——, *Directory of Newspapers and Periodicals 1940* (Philadelphia, 1940).
Barnett, John, 'America's Duty in China', *North American Review* (August 1900): 145–57.
Beach, Harlan P. and Charles H. Fahs (eds), *World Missionary Atlas* (New York, 1925).
Beaverbrook, Lord, *Politicians and the Press* (London, 1925).

Bil Spira, *Die Legende vom Zeichner*, edited by Konstantin Kaiser and Vladimir Vertlib (Wien, 1997).

'Botschaft des Bundesrates an die Bundesversammlung über die Organisation und die Aufgaben der Schweizerischen Kulturwahrung und Kulturwerbung', *Bundesblatt*, 50 (1938): 985–1035.

Boulger, Demetrius C., 'The "Yellow Peril" Bogey', *Nineteenth Century and After*, 60 (1904).

Bourne, Kenneth and D. Cameron Watt (general eds), *British Documents on Foreign Affairs: Reports and Papers from the Foreign Office Confidential Print*, part II, series A, volume 8 (Frederick, 1986).

Buck, Pearl S., *The Good Earth* (New York, 1973 [1931]).

Burke, Thomas, *Limehouse Nights* (Holicong, 2003).

Burleigh, Bennet, *Empire of the East or Japan and Russia at War, 1904–1905* (London, 1905).

'California Alien Land Tenure Law', *The American Journal of International Law, Supplement: Official Documents*, 8/3 (1914): 177–9.

Campbell, J.R., *My Case* (London, 1925).

Cantril, Hadley (ed.), *Public Opinion 1935–1946* (Princeton, 1951).

Chamber of Commerce of the United States, *Communists within the Labor Movement: The Facts and Countermeasures* (Washington, DC, 1947).

Chesney, George, *The Battle of Dorking* (London, 1914).

Chinese Immigration: The Social, Moral and Political Effect of Chinese Immigration, Policy and Means of Exclusion, Memorial of the Senate of California to the Congress of the United States, and an Address to the People of the United States (Sacramento, 1877).

Churchill, Winston, 'The End of the Beginning', speech at the Lord Mayor's Day Luncheon, 10.11.1942, in Charles Eade (comp.), *The End of the Beginning: War Speeches by the Right Hon. Winston S. Churchill C.H., M.P.*, third edition (London, Toronto etc., 1946).

Citrine, Walter (ed.), *Report of Proceedings at the 57th Annual Trades Union Congress (7–12.9.1925)* (London, 1925).

'Daheim und Draußen': Schweizerische Frauenarbeit des Allgem. evang.-protestantischen Missionsvereins für Japan und China, Festschrift zur 1. Schweiz. Ausstellung für Frauenarbeit 'Saffa', 26. August bis 30. September 1928 (Bern, 1928).

Davids, Jules (ed.), *American Diplomatic and Public Papers: The United States and China*, series III, volume 7 (Wilmington, 1981).

—— (ed.), *American Diplomatic and Public Papers: The United States and China*, series III, volume 8 (Wilmington, 1981).

DDS vol. 1: Commission nationale pour la publication de Documents Diplomatiques Suisses (ed.), *Documents Diplomatiques Suisses, volume 1 (1848–1865)* (Bern, 1990).

DDS vol. 2: Commission nationale pour la publication de Documents Diplomatiques Suisses (ed.), *Documents Diplomatiques Suisses, volume 2 (1866–1872)* (Bern, 1985).

DDS vol. 4: Commission nationale pour la publication de Documents Diplomatiques Suisses (ed.), *Documents Diplomatiques Suisses, volume 4 (1890–1903)* (Bern, 1994).

DDS vol. 5: Commission nationale pour la publication de Documents Diplomatiques Suisses (ed.), *Documents Diplomatiques Suisses, volume 5 (1904–1914)* (Bern, 1983).

DDS vol. 8: Commission nationale pour la publication de Documents Diplomatiques Suisses (ed.), *Documents Diplomatiques Suisses, volume 8 (1920–1924)* (Bern, 1988).

DDS vol. 9: Commission nationale pour la publication de Documents Diplomatiques Suisses (ed.), *Documents Diplomatiques Suisses, volume 9 (1925–1929)* (Bern, 1980).

DDS vol.10: Commission nationale pour la publication de Documents Diplomatiques Suisses (ed.), *Documents Diplomatiques Suisses, volume 10 (1930–1933)* (Bern, 1982).

DDS vol. 12: Commission nationale pour la publication de Documents Diplomatiques Suisses (ed.), *Documents Diplomatiques Suisses, volume 12 (1937–1938)* (Bern, 1994).

Degras, Jane (ed.), *The Communist International, 1919–1943: Documents* (3 vols, London, 1971).

Department of State, *United States Relations with China: With Special Reference to the Period 1944–1949* (Washington, DC, 1949).

Die Chinesische Frage: Auf dem 8. Plenum der Exekutive der Kommunistischen Internationale (Hamburg, 1927).

Die Komintern vor dem 6. Weltkongress: Tätigkeitsbericht der Exekutive der Kommunistischen Internationale für die Zeit vom 5. bis 6. Weltkongress (Hamburg, 1928).

Dilling, Elizabeth, *The Red Network: A 'Who's Who' and Handbook of Radicalism for Patriots* (Milwaukee, 1934).

Dipper, H. (ed.), *Basler Missions-Kurs 1911 über China: Ein Auszug für die Besucher des Kurses und für Missions-Studentenkränzchen* (Basel, 1911).

Documents on the Shanghai Case (Peking, 1925).

Dunnell, Mark B., 'Our Policy in China', *North American Review*, October (1898): 393–410.

Dyer, Henry, *Dai Nippon: The Britain of the East* (London, Glasgow and Dublin, 1904).

Eidgen. Oberzolldirektion (ed.), *Statistik des Warenverkehrs der Schweiz mit dem Auslande im Jahr 1924* (Bern-Bümpliz, 1925).

—— (ed.), *Statistik des Warenverkehrs der Schweiz mit dem Auslande im Jahr 1925* (Bern-Bümpliz, 1926).

—— (ed.), *Statistik des Warenverkehrs der Schweiz mit dem Auslande im Jahr 1926* (Bern-Bümpliz, 1927).

—— (ed.), *Statistik des Warenverkehrs der Schweiz mit dem Auslande im Jahr 1927* (Bern-Bümpliz, 1928).

Fairbank, John K., 'Competition with Communism, Not Containment', *Foreign Policy Reports*, March 15 (1949): 6–12.

Fiske, John, 'Manifest Destiny', *Harper's*, 70/418 (1885): 578–90.

Fried, Albert (ed.), *McCarthyism: The Great American Red Scare, A Documentary History* (Oxford and New York, 1997).

FRUS 1900: *Papers Relating to the Foreign Relations of the United States, with the Annual Message of the President, Transmitted to Congress December 3, 1900* (Washington, DC, 1902).

FRUS 1912: *Papers Relating to the Foreign Relations of the United States, with the Annual Message of the President, Transmitted to Congress December 3, 1912* (Washington, DC, 1919).

FRUS 1924: *Papers Relating to the Foreign Relations of the United States 1924*, volume I (Washington, DC, 1939).

FRUS 1925: *Papers Relating to the Foreign Relations of the United States 1925*, volume I (Washington, DC, 1940).

FRUS 1926: *Papers Relating to the Foreign Relations of the United States 1926*, volume I (Washington, DC, 1941).

FRUS 1927: *Papers Relating to the Foreign Relations of the United States 1927*, volume II (Washington, DC, 1942).

FRUS 1931: *Papers Relating to the Foreign Relations of the United States 1931*, volume III (Washington, DC, 1946).

FRUS 1945: *Foreign Relations of the United States Diplomatic Papers 1945*, volume VII: The Far East, China (Washington, DC, 1969).

FRUS 1946: *Foreign Relations of the United States 1946*, volume VI: Eastern Europe; The Soviet Union (Washington, DC, 1969).

FRUS 1947: *Foreign Relations of the United States 1947*, volume VII: The Far East, China (Washington, DC, 1972).

FRUS 1948: *Foreign Relations of the United States 1948*, volume VIII: The Far East, China (Washington, DC, 1973).

FRUS Japan, vol. 1: *Papers Relating to the Foreign Relations of the United States, Japan: 1931–1941*, volume 1 (Washington, DC, 1943).

FRUS Japan, vol. 2: *Papers Relating to the Foreign Relations of the United States, Japan: 1931–1941*, volume 2 (Washington, DC, 1943).

Gallup, George H., *The Gallup International Public Opinion Polls: Great Britain 1937–1975, volume 1: 1937–1964* (New York, 1976).

——, *The Gallup Poll: Public Opinion 1935–1971, volume 1: 1935–1948* (New York, 1972).

——, *The Gallup Poll: Public Opinion 1935–1971, volume 2: 1949–1958* (New York, 1972).

Grant, Madison, *The Passing of the Great Race or the Racial Basis of European History* (New York, 1918).

Gulick, Sidney L., *The White Peril in the Far East: An Interpretation of the Russo-Japanese War* (New York, London and Edinburgh, 1905).

Hankins, Frank H., *The Racial Basis of Civilization: A Critique of the Nordic Doctrine*, revised edition (New York and London, 1931).

HCP (House of Commons Papers): Accessed via House of Commons Parliamentary Papers Online, ProQuest. www.proquest.com (June 2009).

House of Representatives, 'Repealing the Chinese Exclusion Laws', H. Repts, Report no. 732, 78-1, vol. 4.

Huxley, Julian, *Argument of Blood* (London, 1941).

Huxley, Julian S. and A.C. Haddon, *We Europeans: A Survey of 'Racial' Problems* (London, 1936).

Ireland, Alleyne, 'Commercial Aspects of the Yellow Peril', *The North American Review* (September 1900): 389–400.

Johnson, J. Percy H. (ed.), *N.W. Ayer & Son's Directory: Newspapers and Periodicals 1949* (Philadelphia, 1949).

—— (ed.), *N.W. Ayer & Son's Directory: Newspapers and Periodicals 1952* (Philadelphia, 1952).

Keller, Paul, *Japan* (St. Gallen, 1935).

Kellog, Frank B., Frank B. Kellog Papers: 1916–1937, Microfilm edition by the Minnesota Historical Society Library and Archives, M 332.

Kwei Chungshu (ed.), *The Chinese Year Book 1935–1936* (Nendeln, 1968[1935]).

Labour Party, *The Communist Solar System* (London, 1933).

Link, Arthur S. (ed.), *The Papers of Woodrow Wilson*, volume 32 (Princeton, 1980).

Low, David, *Low's Autobiography* (London, 1956).

Low, Seth, 'The Position of the United States among the Nations', *The Annals of the American Academy of Political and Social Science*, 26/1 (1905).

MacDonald, Claude, 'Sir Claude MacDonald's Report on the Boxer Rebellion', in Tim Coates (ed.), *The Siege of the Peking Embassy, 1900* (London, 2000).

MacDonald, J. Ramsay, *Socialism: Critical and Constructive* (London, 1924).

Martin, Rudolf, *Die Zukunft Rußlands und Japans: Die deutschen Milliarden in Gefahr* (Berlin, 1905).

Merrill, Dennis (general ed.), *Documentary History of the Truman Presidency, volume 6: The Chinese Civil War: General George C. Marshall's Mission to China, 1945–1947* (Bethesda, 1996).

—— (general ed.), *Documentary History of the Truman Presidency, volume 8: The Truman Doctrine and the Beginning of the Cold War, 1947–1949* (Bethesda, 1996).

—— (general ed.), *Documentary History of the Truman Presidency, volume 13: Establishing the Marshall Plan, 1947–1948* (Bethesda, 1996).

Mosse, Rudolf, *Zeitungs-Katalog Schweiz* (Basel, Zürich and Bern, 1930).

National Americanism Commission of the American Legion, *Isms: A Review of Alien Isms, Revolutionary Communism and Their Active Sympathizers in the United States*, second edition (Indianapolis, 1937).

National Council of Labour, *British Labour and Communism* (London, 1935).

——, *Labour: A Magazine for all Workers*, 5/2 (1937).

National Union of Conservative and Constitutional Associations, *Election Notes for Conservative Speakers and Workers: General Election 1929* (London, 1929).

New York Economic State Council, *Is Your Town Red?* (New York, 1938).

Nitobe, Inazo, *Bushido: The Soul of Japan* (Boston, 2001 [1900]).

Owen, Frank, *Our Ally China* (London, 1942).

'Ozawa v. United States', *The American Journal of International Law*, 17/1 (1923): 151–7.

Pearson, Charles H., *National Life and Character: A Forecast* (London and New York, 1893).

Perkins, George C., 'Reasons for Continued Chinese Exclusion', *The North American Review* (July 1906): 15–23.

Political and Economic Planning, *Report on the British Press* (London, 1938).

Public Papers of the Presidents, *Harry S. Truman, 1946* (Washington, DC, 1962).

——, *Harry S. Truman, 1947* (Washington, DC, 1963).

——, *Harry S. Truman, 1948* (Washington, DC, 1964).

Pyle, Ernie, *Last Chapter* (New York, 1946).

Quo, Tai-Chi, 'The Chinese Revolution', *Annals of the American Academy of Political and Social Science*, 39 (1912): 11–17.

'Red' Hands off China (London, 1927).

Repington, Charles A'Court, *The War in the Far East, 1904–1905: By the Military Correspondent of the Times* (London, 1905).

Rohmer, Sax, *Die Mission des Dr. Fu-Mandschu* (Berlin, 1927).

——, *The Insidious Dr. Fu Manchu* (Minnesota and New York, 1997).

Roosevelt, Nicholas, 'Russia and Great Britain', *Foreign Affairs* (1926/1927): 80–90.

Rosinger, Lawrence K., 'China Policy and the 1948 Elections', *Far Eastern Survey*, 17/20 (1948): 233–8.

Russisches Zentrum für die Archivierung und Erforschung von Dokumenten zur neuesten Geschichte (ed.), *KPdSU(B), Komintern und die national-revolutionäre Bewegung in China: Dokumente, Band 2: 1926–1927*, Teil 1 (Münster, 1998).

—— (ed.), *KPdSU(B), Komintern und die national-revolutionäre Bewegung in China: Dokumente, Band 2: 1926–1927*, Teil 2 (Münster, 1998).

Schweiz. Zolldepartement (ed.), *Statistik des Warenverkehrs der Schweiz mit dem Auslande im Jahre 1905* (Bern, 1906).

Smyth, George B., 'Causes of Anti-Foreign Feeling in China', *North American Review* (August 1900): 182–97.

Snow, Edgar, *Red Star over China* (New York, 1978).

Stead, Alfred, *Great Japan: A Study in National Efficiency* (Houndmills, 2002 [1906]).

Stoddard, Lothrop, *The Rising Tide of Color against White World-Supremacy* (New York, 1920).

Strong, Anna Louise, *China's Millions* (New York, 1928).

Strong, Josiah, *Our Country: Its Possible Future and Its Present Crisis* (New York, 1885).

Subcommittee on National and International Movements of the Committee on Foreign Affairs, 'Communism in China', in *Report: The Strategy and Tactics of World Communism*, Supplement III (Washington, DC, 1948).

Thesen und Resolutionen des IV. Weltkongresses der Kommunistischen Internationale (Hamburg, 1923).

Timperley, Harold J. (ed.), *What War Means: The Japanese Terror in China* (London, 1938).

Toynbee, Arnold J., *Survey of International Affairs, 1926* (London, 1928).

——, *Survey of International Affairs, 1927* (London, 1929).

——, 'The Next War – Europe or Asia?', *Pacific Affairs*, 7/1 (1934): 3–14.

US Department of Commerce, Bureau of the Census, *Historical Statistics of the United States Colonial Times to 1970*, part 2 (White Plains, 1989).

US Department of State, *Peace and War: United States Foreign Policy, 1931–1941* (Honolulu, 2003).

Unionist Central Office, *London Election Notes* (London, 1924).

Verband schweizerischer Annoncen-Expeditionen VSA (ed.), *Zeitungskatalog der Schweiz* (Zürich, 1950).

Verein der Schweizerischen Presse etc. (ed.), *Jahrbuch der Schweizer Presse u. Politik 1911* (Genf, 1911).

Verein Volksumfrage unter dem Patronat der neuen Helvetischen Gesellschaft, *Die Schweiz hält durch* (Zürich, 1948).

Von der Goltz, Fritz Freiherr, *Die gelbe Gefahr im Licht der Geschichte* (Leipzig, 1907).

Von Falkenegg, Baron, *Japan die neue Weltmacht* (Berlin, 1905).

Von Lignitz, Friedrich Wilhelm Albrecht Victor, *Deutschlands Interessen in Ostasien und die Gelbe Gefahr* (Berlin, 1907).

War and Navy Departments (ed.), *Pocket Guide to China* (Washington, DC, 1943).

Watson, W. Petrie, *The Future of Japan* (London, 1907).

Wilbur, C. Martin and Julie Lien-ying How (eds), *Missionaries of Revolution: Soviet Advisers and Nationalist China, 1920–1927* (London and Cambridge, 1989).

Willing, James, *Willing's Press Guide and Advertiser's Directory and Handbook, 1910* (London, 1910).

Wilson, James H., 'The Settlement of Political Affairs in the Far East', *The Annals of the American Academy of Political and Social Science*, 26/1 (1905): 61–74.

Woodhead, H.G.W. (ed.), *The China Year Book 1920–1* (Nendeln, 1969 [1921]).

—— (ed.), *The China Year Book 1926–7* (Nendeln, 1969 [1926]).

—— (ed.), *The China Year Book 1928* (Nendeln, 1969 [1928]).

Secondary Sources

Aarim-Herjot, Najia, *Chinese Immigrants, African Americans, and Racial Anxiety in the United States, 1848–1882* (Urbana, 2003).

Adas, Michael, *Dominance by Design: Technological Imperatives and America's Civilizing Mission* (Cambridge and London, 2006).

Ahvenainen, Jorma, *The Far Eastern Telegraphs: The History of Telegraphic Communications between the Far East, Europe and America before the First World War* (Helsinki, 1981).

Allen, Robert and John Frost, *Daily Mirror* (Cambridge, 1981).

Altermatt, Claude, *Les débuts de la diplomatie professionelle en Suisse (1848– 1914)* (Fribourg, 1990).

Althusser, Louis, 'Ideology and Ideological State Apparatuses: On Ideology', in Hazard Adams and Leroy Searle (eds), *Critical Theory since 1965* (Tallahassee, 1986).

Altick, Richard D., *The English Common Reader: A Social History of the Mass Reading Public, 1800–1900* (Chicago, 1957).

Anderson, Benedict, *Imagined Communities*, revised edition (London, 1991).

Anderson, David L., *Imperialism and Idealism: American Diplomats in China, 1861–1898* (Bloomington, 1985).

Anderson, Donald F., *William Howard Taft: A Conservative's Conception of the Presidency* (Ithaca and London, 1973).

Andrew, Christopher, 'British Intelligence and the Breach with Russia in 1927', *The Historical Journal*, 25/4 (1982): 957–64.

Andrews, E.M., *Australia and China: The Ambiguous Relationship* (Carlton, 1985).

Appleby, Joyce, Lynn Hunt and Margaret Jacob, *Telling the Truth about History* (London and New York, 1994).

Arkush, R. David and Leo O. Lee (eds), *Land without Ghosts: Chinese Impressions of America from the Mid-Nineteenth Century to the Present* (Berkeley, 1989).

Arlettaz, Gérald, Pierre Pauchard, Olivier Pavillon and Ursula Gaillard, *Les Suisses dans le miroir: Les expositions nationales suisses* (Lausanne, 1991).

Asada, Sadao, *From Mahan to Pearl Harbor: The Imperial Japanese Navy and the United States* (Annapolis, 2006).

Ayerst, David, *Guardian: Biography of a Newspaper* (London, 1971).

Backhouse, Constance, 'The White Women's Labor Laws: Anti-Chinese Racism in Early Twentieth-Century Canada', *Law and History Review*, 14/2 (1996): 315–68.

Badsey, Stephen, 'A Print and Media War', in Craig Wilcox (ed.), *Recording the South African War: Journalism and Official History 1899–1914* (London, 1999).

——, 'War Correspondent in the Boer War', in John Gooch (ed.), *The Boer War: Direction, Experience and Image* (London and Portland, 2000).

Bairathi, Shashi, *Communism and Nationalism in India: A Study in Inter-relationship, 1919–1947* (Delhi, 1987).

Bairoch, Paul, 'La Suisse dans le contexte international aux XIX et XXe siècles', in Paul Bairoch and Martin Körner (eds), *Die Schweiz in der Weltwirtschaft* (Zürich, 1990).

Ball, Stuart, 'Democracy and the Rise of Labour: 1924 and 1929–1931', in Stuart Ball and Anthony Seldon (eds), *Recovering Power: The Conservatives in Opposition since 1867* (Basingstoke, 2005).

Bantimaroudis, Philemon and Hyun Ban, 'Covering the Crisis in Somalia: Framing Choices by The New York Times and The Manchester Guardian', in Stephen D. Reese, Oscar H. Gandy, Jr. and August E. Grant (eds), *Framing Public Life: Perspectives on Media and Our Understanding of the Social World* (Mahwah and London, 2001).

Banton, Michael, *Racial Theories*, second edition (Cambridge, 1998).

Barson, Michael and Steven Heller, *Red Scared! The Commie Menace in Propaganda and Popular Culture* (San Francisco, 2001).

Bartlett, C.J., *Defence and Diplomacy: Britain and the Great Powers, 1815–1914* (Manchester and New York, 1993).

Bates, Roy, *Chinese Dragons* (Oxford and New York, 2002).

Bays, Daniel H., 'The Growth of Independent Christianity in China, 1900–1937', in Daniel H. Bays (ed.), *Christianity in China: From the Eighteenth Century to the Present* (Stanford, 1996).

Beers, Laura, 'Counter-Toryism: Labour's Response to Anti-Socialist Propaganda, 1918–1939', in Matthew Worley (ed.), *The Foundations of the Labour Party: Identities, Cultures and Perspectives, 1900–39* (Farnham, 2009).

——, *Your Britain: Media and the Making of the Labour Party* (Cambridge, 2010).

Bell, Allan, 'The Discourse Structure of News Stories', in Allan Bell and Peter Garrett (eds), *Approaches to Media Discourse* (Oxford and Malden, 1998).

Bell, Duncan S.A., 'Empire and International Relations in Victorian Political Thought', *The Historical Journal*, 49/1 (2006): 281–98.

Bell, P.M.H., *John Bull and the Bear: British Public Opinion, Foreign Policy and the Soviet Union 1941–1945* (New York, 1990).

Benton, Gregor and Edmund Terence Gomez, *The Chinese in Britain, 1800–Present: Economy, Transnationalism, Identity* (Basingstoke and New York, 2008).

Berger, Meyer, *The Story of the New York Times, 1851–1951* (New York, 1951).

Bergère, Marie-Claire, 'The Issue of Imperialism and the 1911 Revolution', in Etō Shinkichi and Harold Z. Schiffrin (eds), *The 1911 Revolution in China: Interpretive Essays* (Tokyo, 1984).

Berges, Marshall, *The Life and Times of Los Angeles: A Newspaper, a Family and a City* (New York, 1984).

Bernegger, Michael, 'Die Schweiz und die Weltwirtschaft: Etappen der Integration im 19. und 20. Jahrhundert', in Paul Bairoch and Martin Körner (eds), *Die Schweiz in der Weltwirtschaft* (Zürich, 1990).

Berry, Nicholas O., *Foreign Policy and the Press: An Analysis of The New York Times' Coverage of U.S. Foreign Policy* (New York, Westport and London, 1990).

Best, Anthony, *Britain, Japan and Pearl Harbor: Avoiding War in East Asia, 1936–41* (London and New York, 1995).

——, 'The Road to Anglo-Japanese Confrontation, 1931–41', in Ian Nish and Yoichi Kibata (eds), *The History of Anglo-Japanese Relations, 1600–2000, volume 2: The Political-Diplomatic Dimension, 1931–2000* (Basingstoke, 2000).

——, *British Intelligence and the Japanese Challenge in Asia, 1914–1941* (Basingstoke and New York, 2002).

Bickers, Robert, 'Shanghailanders: The Formation and Identity of the British Settler Community in Shanghai, 1843–1937', *Past and Present*, 159 (1998): 161–211.

——, *Britain in China: Community, Culture and Colonialism, 1900–1949* (Manchester and New York, 1999).

——, 'Revisiting the Chinese Maritime Customs Service, 1854–1950', *The Journal of Imperial and Commonwealth History*, 36/2 (2008): 221–6.

Bickers, Robert and R.G. Tiedemann (eds), *The Boxers, China, and the World* (Plymouth and Lanham, 2007).

Blake, Lord, 'Spectator', in Sam G. Riley (ed.), *Consumer Magazines of the British Isles* (Westport, 1993).

Blaser, Fritz, *Bibliographie der Schweizer Presse*, 1. Halbband (Basel, 1956).

——, *Bibliographie der Schweizer Presse*, 2. Halbband (Basel, 1958).

Block, Ed Jr., 'New Statesman', in Alvin Sullivan (ed.), *British Literary Magazines: The Victorian and Edwardian Age, 1837–1913* (Westport and London, 1984).

Blue, Gregory, 'Gobineau on China: Race Theory, the "Yellow Peril," and the Critique of Modernity', *Journal of World History*, 10/1 (1999): 93–139.

Bödeker, Hans Erich, 'Ausprägung der Historischen Semantik', in Hans Erich Bödeker (ed.), *Begriffsgeschichte, Diskursgeschichte, Metapherngeschichte* (Göttingen, 2002).

——, 'Reflexionen über Begriffsgeschichte als Methode', in Hans Erich Bödeker (ed.), *Begriffsgeschichte, Diskursgeschichte, Metapherngeschichte* (Göttingen, 2002).

Boerlin-Brodbeck, Yvonne, 'Chinoiserien in der deutschsprachigen Schweiz', in Paul Hugger (ed.), *China in der Schweiz: Zwei Kulturen in Kontakt* (Zürich, 2005).

Bollinger, Ernst, *Pressegeschichte II, 1840–1903: Die goldenen Jahre der Massenpresse* (Freiburg, 1996).

——, 'Journal de Genève', in Stiftung Historisches Lexikon der Schweiz (ed.), *Historisches Lexikon der Schweiz*, Band 6 (Basel, 2007).

Bonjour, Edgar, 'Geschichte der schweizerischen Aussenpolitik in ihren Grundzügen', in Alois Riklin, Hans Haug and Hans Christoph Binswanger (eds), *Handbuch der schweizerischen Aussenpolitik* (Bern and Stuttgart, 1975).

Borg, Dorothy, *American Policy and the Chinese Revolution, 1925–1928* (New York, 1947).

——, *The United States and the Far Eastern Crisis of 1933–1938* (Cambridge, 1964).

Bose, Nemai Sadhan, *American Attitude and Policy to the Nationalist Movement in China (1911–1921)* (Bombay and Calcutta, 1970).

Brendon, Piers, *The Decline and Fall of the British Empire, 1781–1997* (London, 2007).

Bretscher, Willy and Walther Weibel, *Der chinesisch-japanische Konflikt vor dem Völkerbund* (Zürich, 1932).

Bretscher-Spindler, Katharina, *Vom Heissen zum Kalten Krieg: Vorgeschichte und Geschichte der Schweiz im Kalten Krieg 1943–1968* (Zürich, 1997).

Brinker, William J., 'Commerce, Culture, and Horticulture: The Beginnings of Sino-American Cultural Relations', in Thomas H. Etzold (ed.), *Aspects of Sino-American Relations since 1784* (New York and London, 1978).

Brooks, David, *The Age of Upheaval: Edwardian Politics, 1899–1914* (Manchester and New York, 1995).

Broughton, Bradford B., 'Dragon', in Bradford B. Broughton, *Dictionary of Medieval Knighthood and Chivalry* (New York and London, 1988).

Brown, Lucy, *Victorian News and Newspapers* (Oxford, 1985).

Brunero, Donna, *Britain's Imperial Cornerstone in China: The Chinese Maritime Customs Service, 1854–1949* (London and New York, 2006).

Brunner, Otto, Werner Conze and Reinhart Koselleck (eds), *Geschichtliche Grundbegriffe: Historisches Lexikon zur politisch-sozialen Sprache in Deutschland* (7 vols, Stuttgart, 1972–97).

Bryant, Mark, 'Low, Sir David Alexander Cecil', in Mark Bryant, *Dictionary of Twentieth-Century British Cartoonists and Caricaturists* (Aldershot and Brookfield, 2000).

Buckingham, Peter H., *America Sees Red: Anti-Communism in America 1870s to 1980s* (Claremont, 1988).

Buckley, Thomas, 'John VanAntwerp MacMurray: The Diplomacy of an American Mandarin', in Richard Dean Burns and Edward M. Bennett (eds), *Diplomats in Crisis: United States – Chinese – Japanese Relations, 1919–1941* (Santa Barbara and Oxford, 1974).

Buhite, Russell D., 'Nelson Johnson and American Policy toward China, 1925–1928', *The Pacific Historical Review*, 35/4 (1966): 451–65.

Bullock, Allan, *Ernest Bevin: Foreign Secretary, 1945–1951* (London, 1983).

Burri, Boris, 'Notrechtliches Vorgehen gegen die Kommunisten: Der Umgang der Schweizer Behörden mit ausländischer Propaganda nach dem Zweiten Weltkrieg (1945–1953)', *Schweizerische Zeitschrift für Geschichte*, 54/2 (2004): 158–72.

Burton, David H., *William Howard Taft: Confident Peacemaker* (Philadelphia, 2004).

Butler, David and Anne Sloman, *British Political Facts, 1900–1975*, fourth edition (London and Basingstoke, 1975).

Callaghan, John, *Socialism in Britain since 1884* (Oxford and Cambridge, 1990).

Cameron, Meredith E., 'The Reform Movement in China 1898–1912', *History, Economics, and Political Science*, 3/1 (1931): 1–224.

Cammann, Schuyler, 'The Making of Dragon Robes', *T'oung Pao*, second series, 40/4–5 (1951): 297–321.

Cannadine, David, *Ornamentalism: How the British Saw Their Empire* (New York, 2001).

Caratsch, Annetta and Michel Caillat, 'L'assassinat de Vorovsky et le procès Conradi', in Michel Caillat, Mauro Cerutti, Jean-François Fayet and Stéphanie Roulin (eds), *Histoire(s) de l'anticommunisme en Suisse/Geschichte(n) des Antikommunismus in der Schweiz* (Zürich, 2009).

Carr, E.H., *Socialism in One Country, 1924–1926*, volume 3, part 1 (London, 1964).

——, *Socialism in One Country, 1924–1926*, volume 3, part 2 (London, 1964).

——, *Foundations of a Planned Economy, 1926–1929*, volume 3, part 2 (London and Basingstoke, 1976).

——, 'The Zinoviev Letter', *The Historical Journal*, 22/1 (1979): 209–10.

Carrol, John M., *Edge of Empires: Chinese Elites and British Colonials in Hong Kong* (Cambridge and London, 2005).

Chamberlain, Muriel E., *'Pax Britannica' British Foreign Policy, 1789–1914* (London and New York, 1988).

Chan, Sucheng, *Asian Americans: An Interpretive History* (Boston, 1991).

Chan, Tak Wing and John H. Goldthorpe, 'Social Status and Newspaper Readership', *American Journal of Sociology*, 112/4 (2007): 1095–134.

Chang, Iris, *The Rape of Nanking: The Forgotten Holocaust of World War II* (London, 1997).

Chao, Kang, *The Development of Cotton Textile Production in China* (Cambridge and London, 1977).

——, 'The Chinese-American Cotton-Textile Trade, 1830–1930', in Ernest R. May and John F. Fairbank (eds), *America's China Trade in Historical Perspective* (Cambridge, 1986).

Chen, Jian, 'The Ward Case and the Emergence of Sino-American Confrontation, 1948–1950', *The Australian Journal of Chinese Affairs*, 30 (1993): 149–70.

——, 'The Myth of America's "Lost Chance" in China: A Chinese Perspective in Light of New Evidence', *Diplomatic History*, 21/1 (1997): 77–86.

Chen, Qianping, 'Sino-British Relations and the Tibetan Crisis of 1943', in David P. Barrett and Larry N. Shyu (eds), *China in the Anti-Japanese War, 1937–1945: Politics, Culture, and Society* (New York, 2001).

Chen, Shehong, *Being Chinese, Becoming Chinese American* (Urbana and Chicago, 2002).

Chlebek, Diana A., 'Life', in Alan Nourie and Barbara Nourie (eds), *American Mass-Market Magazines* (New York, Westport and London, 1990).

Christensen, Thomas J., *Useful Adversaries: Grand Strategy, Domestic Mobilization, and Sino-American Conflict, 1947–1958* (Princeton, 1996).

——, 'The Zhigongtang in the United States, 1860–1949', in Joseph W. Esherick, Wen-hsin Yeh and Madeleine Zelin (eds), *Empire, Nation, and Beyond: Chinese History in Late Imperial and Modern Times – A Festschrift in Honor of Frederic Wakeman* (Berkeley, 2006).

Chung, Sue Fawn, 'The Zhigongtang in the United States, 1860–1949', in Joseph W. Esherick, Wen-hsin Yeh and Madeleine Zelin (eds), *Empire, Nation, and Beyond: Chinese History in Late Imperial and Modern Times – A Festschrift in Honor of Frederic Wakeman* (Berkeley, 2006).

Clark, Alan, *The Tories: Conservatives and the Nation State, 1922–1997* (London, 1998).

Clarke, I.F., *Voices Prophesying War: Future Wars 1763–3749* (Oxford and New York, 1992).

Clarke, Peter, *Hope and Glory: Britain 1900–2000* (London, 2004).

Clegg, Jenny, *Fu Manchu and the 'Yellow Peril': The Making of a Racist Myth* (Oakhill and Stoke-on-Trent, 1994).

Clifford, Nicholas R., 'Britain, America, and the Far East, 1937–1940: A Failure in Cooperation', *The Journal of British Studies*, 3/1 (1963): 137–54.

——, *Retreat from China: British Policy in the Far East, 1937–1941* (London, 1967).

——, *Spoilt Children of Empire: Westerners in Shanghai and the Chinese Revolution of the 1920s* (Hanover and London, 1991).

Coble, Parks M., *Facing Japan: Chinese Politics and Japanese Imperialism, 1931–1937* (Cambridge and London, 1991).

Coduri, Michele, 'Argent et bons offices: Implications économiques de la protection des intérêts alliés en Extrême-Orient pendant la Deuxième Guerre mondiale', in Peter Hug and Martin Kloter (eds), *Aufstieg und Niedergang des Bilateralismus: Schweizerische Aussen- und Aussenwirtschaftspolitik 1930–1960: Rahmenbedingungen, Entscheidungsstrukturen, Fallstudien* (Zürich, 1999).

——, *La Suisse face à la Chine: Une continuité impossible? 1946–1955* (Louvain-la-Neuve, 2004).

Cohen, Paul A., *China and Christianity: The Missionary Movement and the Growth of Chinese Antiforeignism 1860–1870* (Cambridge, 1963).

——, 'Christian Missions and Their Impact to 1900', in John K. Fairbank (ed.), *The Cambridge History of China, volume 10: Late Ch'ing, 1800–1911*, part I (Cambridge, London, New York and Melbourne, 1978).

——, *History in Three Keys: The Boxers as Event, Experience, and Myth* (New York, 1997).

Cohen, Warren, 'Symposium: Rethinking the Lost Chance in China', *Diplomatic History*, 21/1 (1997): 71–5.

——, *America's Response to China: A History of Sino-American Relations*, fourth edition (New York and Chichester, 2000).

Cole, G.D.H., *A History of the Labour Party from 1914* (London, 1969).

Coninx, Hans Heinrich, 'Unabhängig und ein Familienunternehmen', in Werner Catrina, Roger Blum and Toni Lienhard (eds), *Medien zwischen Geld und Geist: 100 Jahre Tages-Anzeiger* (Zürich, 1993).

Connaughton, Richard, *Rising Sun and Tumbling Bear: Russia's War with Japan* (London, 2003).

Copeland, David, *The Media's Role in Defining the Nation* (New York, 2010).

Cox, Jeffrey, *The British Missionary Enterprise since 1700* (London and New York, 2008).

Craft, Stephen C., 'Saving the League: V.K. Wellington Koo, the League of Nations and Sino-Japanese Conflict, 1931–39', *Diplomacy and Statecraft*, 11/3 (2000): 91–112.

Crowley, James B., 'A Reconsideration of the Marco Polo Bridge Incident', *The Journal of Asian Studies*, 22/3 (1963): 277–91.

Cudlipp, Hugh, *Publish and be Damned! The Astonishing Story of the Daily Mirror* (London, 1953).

Cull, Nicholas John, *Selling War: The British Propaganda Campaign against American 'Neutrality' in World War II* (Oxford and New York, 1995).

Curran, James and Jean Seaton, *Power without Responsibility: The Press and Broadcasting in Britain*, fourth edition (London, 1993).

Dallek, Robert, *Franklin D. Roosevelt and American Foreign Policy, 1932–1945* (New York, 1979).

Danielian, Lucig, 'Interest Groups in the News', in J. David Kennamer (ed.), *Public Opinion, the Press, and Public Policy* (Westport, 1992).

Darwin, John, 'The Fear of Falling: British Politics and Imperial Decline since 1900', *Transactions of the Royal Historical Society*, fifth series, 36 (1986): 27–43.

——, 'Imperialism and the Victorians: The Dynamics of Territorial Expansion', *The English Historical Review*, 112/447 (1997): 614–42.

——, 'Britain's Empires', in Sarah Stockwell (ed.), *The British Empire: Themes and Perspectives* (Malden, Oxford and Carlton, 2008).

Daugherty, William E., 'China's Official Publicity in the United States', *The Public Opinion Quarterly*, 6/1 (1942): 70–86.

Davies, A.J., *To Build a New Jerusalem: The British Labour Movement from the 1880s to the 1990s* (London, 1992).

Davis, Clarence B., 'Financing Imperialism: British and American Bankers as Vectors of Imperial Expansion in China, 1908–1920', *The Business History Review*, 56/2 (1982): 236–64.

——, 'Railway Imperialism in China, 1895–1939', in Clarence B. Davis and Kenneth E. Wilburn, Jr. (eds), *Railway Imperialism* (London, New York and Westport, 1991).

Davis, John, *A History of Britain, 1885–1939* (New York, 1999).

De Saint Victor, Carol, 'National Review, The (1883)', in Alvin Sullivan (ed.), *British Literary Magazines: The Victorian and Edwardian Age, 1837–1913* (Westport and London, 1984).

Degen, Bernard, *Abschied vom Klassenkampf: Die partielle Integration der schweizerischen Gewerkschaftsbewegung zwischen Landesstreik und Weltwirtschaftskrise (1918–1929)* (Basel, 1991).

Demel, Walter, 'Wie die Chinesen gelb wurden: Ein Beitrag zur Frühgeschichte der Rassentheorien', *Historische Zeitschrift*, 255 (1992): 625–55.

Dietrich, Ethel Barbara, 'Lancashire Cotton Industry', *The American Economic Review*, 18/3 (1928): 468–76.

Dirks, Nicholas B., Geoff Eley and Sherry B. Ortner, 'Introduction', in Nicholas B. Dirks, Geoff Eley and Sherry B. Ortner (eds), *Culture/Power/History: A Reader in Contemporary Social Theory* (Princeton, 1994).

Doenecke, Justus D., *When the Wicked Rise: American Opinion-Makers and the Manchurian Crisis of 1931–1933* (London and Toronto, 1984).

Doerr, Paul, *British Foreign Policy, 1919–1939* (Manchester and New York, 1998).

Dorogi, Thomas Laszlo, *Tainted Perceptions: Liberal-Democracy and American Popular Images of China* (Lanham, 2001).

Douglas, Roy, *New Alliances 1940–41* (London and Basingstoke, 1982).

——, *Liquidation of Empire: The Decline of the British Empire* (Basingstoke and New York, 2002).

Dower, John, *War without Mercy: Race and Power in the Pacific War* (New York, 1986).

——, *Japan in War and Peace: Selected Essays* (New York, 1993).

Dreyer, Dietrich, *Schweizer Kreuz und Sowjetstern: Die Beziehungen zweier ungleicher Partner seit 1917* (Zürich, 1989).

Dubois, Howard, *Die Schweiz und China* (Bern, 1978).

Dunch, Ryan, 'Beyond Cultural Imperialism: Cultural Theory, Christian Missions, and Global Modernity', *History and Theory*, 41/3 (2002): 301–25.

Dupree, Marguerite, 'Foreign Competition and the Interwar Period', in Mary B. Rose (ed.), *The Lancashire Cotton Industry: A History since 1700* (Preston, 1996).

Duus, Peter, 'Introduction: Japan's Wartime Empire: Problems and Issues', in Peter Duus, Ramon H. Myers and Mark R. Peattie (eds), *The Japanese Wartime Empire, 1931–1945* (Princeton, 1996).

Eder, Franz X. (ed.), *Historische Diskursanalysen: Genealogie, Theorie, Anwendungen* (Wiesbaden, 2006).

Eisenach, Eldon J., 'Progressive Internationalism', in Sidney M. Milkis and Jerome M. Mileur (eds), *Progressivism and the New Democracy* (Amherst, 1999).

——, 'Introduction', in Eldon J. Eisenach (ed.), *The Social and Political Thought of American Progressivism* (Indianapolis and Cambridge, 2006).

Eley, Geoff, 'Beneath the Skin. Or: How to Forget about Empire without Really Trying', *Journal of Colonialism and Colonial History*, 3/1 (2002), http://muse.

jhu.edu/journals/journal_of_colonialism_and_colonial_history/v003/3.1eley.
html (last accessed on 9.12.2011).

Elleman, Bruce A., *Wilson and China: A Revised History of the Shandong Question* (Armonk and London, 2002).

——, *Japanese-American Civilian Prisoner Exchanges and Detention Camps, 1941–45* (London and New York, 2006).

Elliott, Jane E., *Some Did It for Civilisation – Some Did It for Their Country: A Revised View of the Boxer War* (Hong Kong, 2002).

Ellis, John S., 'Reconciling the Celt: British National Identity, Empire, and the 1911 Investiture of the Prince of Wales', *The Journal of British Studies*, 37/4 (1998): 391–418.

Ellis, L. Ethan, *Frank B. Kellogg and American Foreign Relations, 1925–1929* (New Brunswick, 1961).

Elter, Andreas, *Die Kriegsverkäufer: Geschichte der US-Propaganda 1917–2005* (Frankfurt am Main, 2005).

Emery, Michael, Edwin Emery and Nancy L. Roberts, *The Press and America: An Interpretive History of the Mass Media*, ninth edition (Boston, 2000).

Endicott, Stephen Lyon, *Diplomacy and Enterprise: British China Policy 1933–1937* (Manchester, 1975).

English, Jim, 'Empire Day in Britain, 1904–1958', *The Historical Journal*, 49/1 (2006): 247–76.

Entman, Robert M., *Projections of Power: Framing News, Public Opinion, and U.S. Foreign Policy* (Chicago and London, 2004).

——, 'Foreword', in Karen Callaghan and Frauke Schell (eds), *Framing American Politics* (Pittsburgh, 2005).

——, 'Framing: Toward Clarification of a Fractured Paradigm', in Anders Hansen (ed.), *Mass Communication Research Methods*, volume 3 (London, Thousand Oaks, New Delhi and Singapore, 2008).

Ericksen, Robert P., 'Response', in William R. Hutchison and Hartmut Lehmann (eds), *Many Are Chosen: Divine Election and Western Nationalism* (Minneapolis, 1994).

Esherick, Joseph W., 'Founding a Republic, Electing a President: How Sun Yat-sen Became Guofu', in Etō Shinkichi and Harold Z. Schiffrin (eds), *China's Republican Revolution* (Tokyo, 1994).

Esthus, Raymond A., 'The Open Door and the Integrity of China, 1899–1922: Hazy Principles for Changing Policy', in Thomas H. Etzold (ed.), *Aspects of Sino-American Relations since 1784* (New York and London, 1978).

Etherington, Norman, 'Introduction', in Norman Etherington (ed.), *Missions and Empire* (Oxford, 2005).

Etō, Shinkichi, 'China's International Relations 1911–1931', in John K. Fairbank and Albert Feuerwerker (eds), *The Cambridge History of China, volume 13: Republican China 1912–1949*, part 2 (Cambridge and New York, 1986).

Etzold, Thomas H., 'The Far East in American Strategy, 1948–1951', in Thomas H. Etzold (ed.), *Aspects of Sino-American Relations since 1784* (New York and London, 1978).

Eykholt, Mark, 'Aggression, Victimization, and Chinese Historiography of the Nanjing Massacre', in Joshua A. Fogel (ed.), *The Nanjing Massacre in History and Historiography* (Berkeley, Los Angeles and London, 2000).

Fairbank, John K., 'Introduction: The Many Faces of Protestant Missions in China and the United States', in John K. Fairbank (ed.), *The Missionary Enterprise in China and America* (Cambridge, 1974).

Fairclough, Norman, *Media Discourse* (London, 2002).

Farré, Sébastien, 'Justice, interdictions et répression anticommuniste (1936–1945)', in Michel Caillat, Mauro Cerutti, Jean-François Fayet and Stéphanie Roulin (eds), *Histoire(s) de l'anticommunisme en Suisse/Geschichte(n) des Antikommunismus in der Schweiz* (Zürich, 2009).

Faulstich, Werner, *Medienwandel im Industrie- und Massenzeitalter (1830–1900)* (Göttingen, 2003).

Feaver, John H., 'The China Aid Bill of 1948: Limited Assistance as a Cold War Strategy', *Diplomatic History*, 5/2 (1981): 107–20.

Fenby, Jonathan, *Generalissimo: Chiang Kai-Shek and the China He Lost* (London, 2005).

Ferris, John, 'Worthy of Some Better Enemy?: The British Estimate of the Imperial Japanese Army, 1919–41, and the Fall of Singapore', *Canadian Journal of History*, 28/2 (1993): 223–56.

Feuerwerker, Albert, 'Economic Trends, 1912–49', in John K. Fairbank (ed.), *The Cambridge History of China, volume 12: Republican China 1912–1949*, part 1 (Cambridge, 1983).

Fiebig-von Hase, Ragnhild, 'Introduction', in Ragnhild Fiebig von Hase and Ursula Lehmkuhl (eds), *Enemy Images in American History* (Providence and Oxford, 1997).

Fielding, Raymond, *The March of Time: 1935–1951* (New York, 1978).

Findlay, Ronald and Kevin O'Rourke, *Power and Plenty: Trade, War, and the World Economy in the Second Millenium* (Princeton and Oxford, 2007).

Finlay, Richard J., 'The Scottish Press and Empire, 1850–1914', in Simon J. Potter (ed.), *Newspapers and Empire in Ireland and Britain: Reporting the British Empire, c. 1857–1921* (Dublin, 2004).

Fischer, Heinz-Dietrich and Erika Fischer (eds), *Editorial Cartoon Awards 1922–1997* (München, 1999).

Fischer, Roger, *Them Damned Pictures: Explorations in American Cartoon Art* (North Haven, 1996).

Fitzgerald, John, *Awakening China: Politics, Culture, and Class in the Nationalist Revolution* (Stanford, 1996).

Fleischmann, Anja, *Das Japanbild in England vom 16. bis 20. Jahrhundert* (München, 1999).

Flory, Harriette, 'The Arcos Raid and the Rupture of Anglo-Soviet Relations, 1927', *Journal of Contemporary History*, 12/4 (1977): 707–23.

Folly, Martin, *Churchill, Whitehall and the Soviet Union, 1940–1945* (Basingstoke, 2000).

Foucault, Michel, *The Archaeology of Knowledge* (New York, 1972).

——, *The History of Sexuality, volume 1: An Introduction* (New York, 1978).

——, *Power/Knowledge: Selected Interviews and Other Writings 1972–1977*, edited by Colin Gordon (New York, 1980).

Fowler, Roger, *Language in the News: Discourse and Ideology in the Press* (London and New York, 1991).

Frank, Gustav and Klaus Sachs-Hombach, 'Bildwissenschaft und Visual Culture Studies', in Klaus Sachs-Hombach (ed.), *Bild und Medium: Kunstgeschichtliche und philosophische Grundlagen der interdisziplinären Bildwissenschaft* (Köln, 2006).

Frei, Daniel, *Assumptions and Perceptions in Disarmament* (New York, 1984).

Frei, Fritz, 'L'avvicinamento alla Cina: Il caso della Società delle Missioni Estere die Betlemme, Immensee', in Pier Francesco Fumagalli, Gerardo Rigozzi and Luca Salitni (ed.), *Occidente verso la Cina* (Lugano, 2008).

French, Paul, *Through the Looking Glass: China's Foreign Journalists from Opium Wars to Mao* (Hong Kong, 2009).

Friday, Karl F., 'Bushido or Bull? A Medieval Historian's Perspective on the Imperial Army and the Japanese Warrior Tradition', *The History Teacher*, 27/3 (1994): 339–49.

Fulton, Marianne, 'Bearing Witness: The 1930s and 1950s', in Marianne Fulton (ed.), *Eyes of Time: Photojournalism in America* (Boston, Toronto and London, 1988).

Fung, Edmund S.K., 'Post-1949 Chinese Historiography on the 1911 Revolution', *Modern China*, 4/2 (1978): 181–214.

——, 'The Sino-British Rapprochement, 1927–1931', *Modern Asian Studies*, 17/1 (1983): 79–105.

——, *The Diplomacy of Imperial Retreat: Britain's South China Policy, 1924–1931* (Hong Kong, 1991).

Fyne, Robert, *The Hollywood Propaganda of World War II* (Metuchen and London, 1994).

Gäbler, Ulrich, 'The Swiss: A Chosen People?', in William R. Hutchison and Hartmut Lehmann (eds), *Many Are Chosen: Divine Election and Western Nationalism* (Minneapolis, 1994).

Gaddis, John Lewis, *Strategies of Containment: A Critical Appraisal of American National Security Policy during the Cold War*, second edition (Oxford and New York, 2005).

——, *The Cold War: A New History* (New York, 2005).

Gallagher, John and Ronald Robinson, 'The Imperialism of Free Trade', *The Economic History Review*, 6/1 (1953): 1–15.

Gamson, William A., 'News as Framing', *American Behavioral Scientist*, 33/2 (1989): 157–61.

Gamson, William A., David Croteau, William Hoynes and Theodore Sasson, 'Media Images and the Social Construction of Reality', *Annual Review of Sociology*, 18 (1992): 373–93.

Gehrig-Straube, Christine, *Beziehungslose Zeiten: Das schweizerisch-sowjetische Verhältnis zwischen Abbruch und Wiederaufnahme der Beziehungen (1918–1946) aufgrund schweizerischen Akten* (Zürich, 1994).

Gelber, Harry G., *Opium, Soldiers and Evangelicals: England's 1840–42 War with China, and Its Aftermath* (Basingstoke and New York, 2004).

Goetschel, Laurent, 'Aussenpolitik', in Ulrich Klöti, Peter Knoepfel, Hanspeter Kriesi, Wolf Linder, Yannis Papadopoulos and Pascal Sciarini (eds), *Handbuch der Schweizer Politik*, fourth edition (Zürich, 2006).

Goffman, Erving, 'A Reply to Denzin and Keller', *Contemporary Sociology*, 10/1 (1981): 60–68.

Goldberg, Vicki, *The Power of Photography: How Photographs Changed Our Lives* (New York, London and Paris, 1991).

Goldstein, Erik, 'Britain and the Origins of the Cold War', in Michael F. Hopkins, Michael D. Kandiah and Gillian Staerck (eds), *Cold War Britain, 1945–1964: New Perspectives* (Basingstoke, 2003).

Goldstein, Jonathan, Jerry Israel and Hilary Conroy (eds), *America Views China: American Images of China Then and Now* (London, 1991).

Gollwitzer, Heinz, *Die Gelbe Gefahr: Geschichte eines Schlagworts* (Göttingen, 1962).

Goodbody, John, 'The Star: Its Role in the Rise of New Journalism', in Joel H. Wiener (ed.), *Papers for the Millions: The New Journalism in Britain, 1850s to 1914* (New York, Westport and London, 1988).

Gordon, David M., 'The China-Japan War, 1931–1945', *The Journal of Military History*, 70/1 (2006): 137–82.

Goto-Shibata, Harumi, *Japan and Britain in Shanghai, 1925–31* (Basingstoke and London, 1995).

Gould, Lewis L., *The Presidency of William McKinley* (Lawrence, 1980).

Goutor, David, 'Constructing the "Great Menace": Canadian Labour's Opposition to Asian Immigration, 1880–1914', *The Canadian Historical Review*, 88/4 (2007): 549–76.

Graebner, Norman A., 'Hoover, Roosevelt, and the Japanese', in Dorothy Borg and Shumpei Okamoto (eds), *Pearl Harbor as History: Japanese-American Relations 1931–1941* (New York and London, 1973).

Graham, Edward D., *American Ideas of a Special Relationship with China* (New York and London, 1988).

Greenberg, Michael, *British Trade and the Opening of China, 1800–1842* (New York and London, 1951).

Greenwood, Sean, *Britain and the Cold War 1945–91* (Basingstoke, 2000).

Gregory, John S., *The West and China since 1500* (Basingstoke and New York, 2003).

Griffiths, Dennis, *Fleet Street: Five Hundred Years of the Press* (London, 2006).

Grossberg, Lawrence. 'Identity and Cultural Studies: Is That All There Is?', in Stuart Hall and Paul du Gay (eds), *Questions of Cultural Identity* (London, 1996).

Gruner, Erich, *Die Parteien in der Schweiz*, second edition (Bern, 1977).

——, *Arbeiterschaft und Wirtschaft in der Schweiz 1880–1914: Soziale Lage, Organisation und Kämpfe von Arbeitern und Unternehmern, politische Organisation und Sozialpolitik*, volume 3 (Zürich, 1988).

Guillermaz, Jacques, *A History of the Chinese Communist Party, 1921–1949* (London, 1972).

Gull, E.M., *British Economic Interests in the Far East* (London, 1943).

Haddad, John, 'The Laundry Man's Got a Knife! China and Chinese America in Early United States Cinema', *Chinese America: History and Perspectives*, 15 (2001): 31–46.

Hall, Catherine, 'Remembering Edward Said (1935–2003)', *History Workshop Journal*, 57 (2004): 235–43.

——, 'Culture and Identity in Imperial Britain', in Susan Stockwell (ed.), *The British Empire: Themes and Perspectives* (Malden, Oxford and Carlton, 2008).

Hall, Stuart, 'Introduction: Who Needs "Identity"?', in Stuart Hall and Paul du Gay (eds), *Questions of Cultural Identity* (London, 1996).

Hamby, Alonzo L., 'Progressivism: A Century of Change and Rebirth', in Sidney M. Milkis and Jerome M. Mileur (eds), *Progressivism and the New Democracy* (Amherst, 1999).

Hammond, J.L., *C.P. Scott of the Manchester Guardian* (London, 1934).

Hampton, Mark, *Visions of the Press in Britain, 1850–1950* (Urbana and Chicago, 2004).

Hansen, Anders (ed.), *Mass Communication Research Methods* (3 vols, London, Thousand Oaks, New Delhi and Singapore, 2009).

Hao, Yen-P'ing, 'Chinese Teas to America: A Synopsis', in Ernest R. May and John F. Fairbank (eds), *America's China Trade in Historical Perspective* (Cambridge, 1986).

Harbutt, Fraser J., *The Cold War Era* (Malden, 2001).

Harris, Paul W., 'Cultural Imperialism and American Protestant Missionaries: Collaboration and Dependency in Mid-Nineteenth-Century China', *The Pacific Historical Review*, 60/3 (1991): 309–38.

Hart, James, 'Harper's Magazine', in Alan Nourie and Barbara Nourie (eds), *American Mass-Market Magazines* (New York, Westport and London, 1990).

Harvey, A.D., *Collision of Empires: Britain in Three World Wars, 1793–1945* (London and Rio Grande, 1992).

Hayashi, Brian Masaru, *Democratizing the Enemy: The Japanese American Internment* (Princeton and Oxford, 2004).

Haynes, John E., *Red Scare or Red Menace? American Communism and Anticommunism in the Cold War Era* (Chicago, 1996).

Haynes, John Earl and Harvey Klehr, *Early Cold War Spies: The Espionage Trials That Shaped American Politics* (Cambridge and New York, 2006).

He, Di, 'The Evolution of the Chinese Communist Party's Policy toward the United States, 1944–1949', in Harry Harding and Yuan Ming (eds), *Sino-American Relations, 1945–1955: A Joint Reassessment of a Critical Decade* (Wilmington, 1989).

Heale, M.J., *American Anticommunism: Combating the Enemy Within, 1830–1970* (Baltimore and London, 1990).

Healey, R.M., 'Punch', in Sam G. Riley (ed.), *Consumer Magazines of the British Isles* (Westport, 1993).

Henning, Joseph M., 'White Mongols? The War and American Discourses on Race and Religion', in Rotem Kowner (ed.), *The Impact of the Russo-Japanese War* (New York and Milton Part, 2007).

Herre, Franz, *Kaiser Wilhelm II.: Monarch zwischen den Zeiten* (Köln, 1993).

Herring, Robert, 'The News-Reel', in Luke McKernan (ed.), *Yesterday's News: The British Cinema Newsreel Reader* (London, 2002).

Hess, Stephen and Sandy Northrop, *American Political Cartoons: The Evolution of a National Identity, 1754–2010* (New Brunswick and London, 2011).

Hevia, James L., *English Lessons: The Pedagogy of Imperialism in Nineteenth-Century China* (Durham and London, 2003).

Higashi, Sumiko, 'Melodrama, Realism, and Race: World War II Newsreels and Propaganda Film', *Cinema Journal*, 37/3 (1998): 38–61.

Higham, John, *Strangers in the Land: Patterns of American Nativism 1860–1925*, second edition (Westport, 1963).

Hinds, Lynn Boyd and Theodore Otto Windt, Jr., *The Cold War as Rhetoric: The Beginnings, 1945–1950* (New York and London, 1991).

Hixson, Walter L., *The Myth of American Diplomacy: National Identity and U.S. Foreign Policy* (New Haven and London, 2008).

Hoare, J.E., *Embassies in the East: The Story of the British Embassies in Japan, China and Korea from 1859 to the Present* (Richmond, 1999).

Hobsbawm, Eric, 'Introduction: Inventing Traditions', in Eric Hobsbawm and Terence Ranger (eds), *The Invention of Tradition* (Cambridge, 1983).

Hodge, Robert and Gunther Kress, *Language as Ideology*, second edition (London and New York, 1993).

Hoffer, Peter C., 'American Businessmen and the Japan Trade, 1931–1941: A Case Study of Attitude Formation', *The Pacific Historical Review*, 41/2 (1972): 189–205.

Hogan, Michael J., *The Marshall Plan: America, Britain, and the Reconstruction of Western Europe, 1947–1952* (Cambridge and New York, 1987).

Holmes, Colin, 'Bushido and the Samurai: Images in British Public Opinion, 1894–1914', *Modern Asian Studies*, 14/2 (1980): 309–29.

Honda, Katsuichi, *The Nanjing Massacre: A Japanese Journalist Confronts Japan's National Shame*, edited by Frank Gibney (Armonk and London, 1999).

Hopkin, Deian, 'The Left-Wing Press and the New Journalism', in Joel H. Wiener (ed.), *Papers for the Millions: The New Journalism in Britain, 1850s to 1914* (New York, Westport and London, 1988).

Horne, Gerald, *Race War! White Supremacy and the Japanese Attack on the British Empire* (New York and London, 2004).

Horten, Gerd, *Radio Goes to War: The Cultural Politics of Propaganda during World War II* (Berkeley, Los Angeles and London, 2002).

Hou, Chi-ming, *Foreign Investment and Economic Development in China, 1840–1937* (Cambridge, 1965).

Hsiao, Liang-lin, *China's Foreign Trade Statistics, 1864–1949* (Cambridge, 1974).

Hsüeh, Chün-tu, 'New Aspects of the 1911 Revolution', in Chün-tu Hsüeh (ed.), *The Chinese Revolution of 1911: New Perspectives* (Hong Kong, 1986).

Hu, Shizhang, *Stanley K. Hornbeck and the Open Door Policy, 1919–1937* (Westport and London, 1995).

Huang, Kailai, 'Myth or Reality: American Perceptions of the China Market', in Hongshan Li and Zhaohui Hong (eds), *Image, Perception, and the Making of U.S.-China Relations* (Lanham and Cummor Hill, 1998).

Huber, Peter, *Kommunisten und Sozialdemokraten in der Schweiz 1918–1935: Der Streit um die Einheitsfront in der Zürcher und Basler Arbeiterschaft* (Zürich, 1986).

Hückel, W., *Bunte Bilder aus dem heidnischen und christlichen China* (Berlin, 1925).

Hug, Peter, 'Verhinderte oder verpasste Chancen? Die Schweiz und die Vereinten Nationen, 1943–1947', in Georg Kreis (ed.), *Die Schweiz im internationalen System der Nachkriegszeit 1943–1950* (Basel, 1996).

——, *Schweizer Rüstungsindustrie und Kriegsmaterialhandel zur Zeit des Nationalsozialismus: Unternehmensstrategien – Marktentwicklung – politische Überwachung* (Zürich, 2002).

Huggan, Graham, '(Not) Reading Orientalism', *Research in African Literatures*, 36/3 (2005): 124–36.

Hunt, Michael H., 'Pearl Buck – Popular Expert on China, 1931–1949', *Modern China*, 3/1 (1977): 33–64.

——, *The Making of a Special Relationship: The United States and China to 1914* (New York, 1983).

——, *Ideology and U.S. Foreign Policy* (New Haven and London, 1987).

——, *The American Ascendancy: How the United States Gained and Wielded Global Dominance* (Chapel Hill, 2007).

Hürlimann, Martin, 'Die Entwicklung der schweizerisch-japanischen Beziehungen', in Schweizerisch-Japanische Gesellschaft (ed.), *Schweiz–Japan* (Zürich, 1975).

Husband, William B., 'The New Economic Policy (NEP) and the Revolutionary Experiment, 1921–1929', in Gregory L. Freeze (ed.), *Russia: A History* (Oxford, 1997).

Hutchison, William R., *Errand to the World: American Protestant Thought and Foreign Missions* (Chicago and London, 1987).

Ihle, Pascal, *Die journalistische Landesverteidigung im Zweiten Weltkrieg: Eine kommunikationshistorische Studie* (Zürich, 1997).

Ikeda, Kiyoshi, 'Anglo-Japanese Relations, 1941–45', in Ian Nish and Yoichi Kibata (eds), *The History of Anglo-Japanese Relations, 1600–2000, volume 2: The Political-Diplomatic Dimension, 1931–2000* (Basingstoke, 2000).

Im Hof, Ulrich, *Mythos Schweiz: Identität – Nation – Geschichte, 1291–1991* (Zürich, 1991).

Imam, Zafar, *Colonialism in East-West Relations: A Study of Soviet Policy towards India and Anglo-Soviet Relations: 1917–1947*, second edition (New Delhi, 1987).

Imboden, William, *Religion and American Foreign Policy, 1945–1960: The Soul of Containment* (New York, 2008).

Imhof, Kurt, 'Vermessene Öffentlichkeit – vermessene Forschung? Vorstellung eines Projektes', in Kurt Imhof, Heinz Kleger and Gaetano Romano (eds), *Zwischen Konflikt und Konkordanz: Analyse von Medienereignissen in der Schweiz der Vor- und Zwischenkriegszeit* (Zürich, 1993).

——, 'Kriegskommunikation im sozialen Wandel', in Kurt Imhof and Peter Schulz (eds), *Medien und Krieg – Krieg in den Medien* (Zürich, 1995).

——, 'Das kurze Leben der geistigen Landesverteidigung: Von der "Volksgemeinschaft" vor dem Krieg zum Streit über die "Nachkriegsschweiz" im Krieg', in Kurt Imhof, Heinz Kleger and Gaetano Romano (eds), *Konkordanz und Kalter Krieg: Analyse von Medienereignissen in der Schweiz der Zwischen- und Nachkriegszeit* (Zürich, 1996).

——, 'Wiedergeburt der geistigen Landesverteidigung: Kalter Krieg in der Schweiz', in Kurt Imhof, Heinz Kleger and Gaetano Romano (eds), *Konkordanz und Kalter Krieg: Analyse von Medienereignissen in der Schweiz der Zwischen- und Nachkriegszeit* (Zürich, 1996).

——, 'Sonderfallsdiskurse und Pfadabhängigkeit: Der Fall Schweiz', in Thomas S. Eberle and Kurt Imhof (eds), *Sonderfall Schweiz* (Zürich, 2007).

Impey, Oliver, *Chinoiserie: The Impact of Oriental Styles on Western Art and Decoration* (London, 1977).

Iriye, Akira, 'Japan as a Competitor, 1895–1917', in Akira Iriye (ed.), *Mutual Images: Essays in American-Japanese Relations* (Cambridge and London, 1975).

——, *The Globalizing of America, 1913–1945* (Cambridge, 1995).

——, *Japan and the Wider World: From the Mid-Nineteenth Century to the Present* (London and New York, 1997).

——, *Pearl Harbor and the Coming of the Pacific War* (Boston and New York, 1999).

Isaacs, Harold R., *Images of Asia: American Views of China and India* (New York, 1962).

Ishii, Osamu, 'Markets and Diplomacy: The Anglo-Japanese Rivalries over Cotton Good Markets, 1930–36', in Ian Nish and Yoichi Kibata (eds), *The History of Anglo-Japanese Relations, 1600–2000, volume 2: The Political-Diplomatic Dimension, 1931–2000* (Basingstoke, 2000).

Israel, Jerry, '"Mao's Mr. America": Edgar Snow's Images of China', *Pacific Historical Review*, 47 (1978): 107–22.

——, 'Carl Crow, Edgar Snow, and Shifting American Journalistic Perceptions of China', in Jonathan Goldstein, Jerry Israel and Hilary Conroy (eds), *America Views China: American Images of China Then and Now* (London, Toronto and Cranbury, 1991).

Jacobi, Astrid, *Die Pressefotografie: Geschichte, Entwicklung und Ethik des Fotojournalismus* (Saarbrücken, 2007).

Jacobs, Dan M., *Borodin: Stalin's Man in China* (Cambridge and London, 1981).

Jacobson, Dawn, *Chinoiserie* (London, 1993).

Jäger, Siegfried, 'Diskurs und Wissen: Theoretische und methodische Aspekte einer Kritischen Diskurs- und Dispositivanalyse', in Reiner Keller, Andreas Hirseland, Werner Schneider and Willy Viehöver (eds), *Handbuch Sozialwissenschaftliche Diskursanalyse, Band I: Theorien und Methoden* (Opladen, 2001).

Jansen, Marius B., 'The 1911 Revolution and United States East Asian Policy', in Etō Shinkichi and Harold Z. Schiffrin (eds), *The 1911 Revolution in China: Interpretive Essays* (Tokyo, 1984).

Jarren, Ottfried and Patrick Donges, *Politische Kommunikation in der Mediengesellschaft: Eine Einführung, Band 2: Akteure, Prozesse und Inhalte* (Wiesbaden, 2002).

Jeans, Roger B., 'Victims or Victimizers? Museums, Textbooks, and the War Debate in Contemporary Japan', *The Journal of Military History*, 69/1 (2005): 149–95.

Jespersen, Christopher T., *American Images of China, 1931–1949* (Stanford, 1996).

Jin, Chongji, 'The 1911 Revolution and the Awakening of the Chinese Nation', in Etō Shinkichi and Harold Z. Schiffrin (eds), *The 1911 Revolution in China: Interpretive Essays* (Tokyo, 1984).

Johnson-Cartee, Karen S., *News Narratives and News Framing: Constructing Political Reality* (Lanham and Oxford, 2005).

Jones, Alfred Haworth, 'The Making of an Interventionist on the Air: Elmer Davis and CBS News, 1939–1941', *The Pacific Historical Review*, 42/1 (1973): 74–93.

Jones, Maldwyn A., *The Limits of Liberty: American History 1607–1992*, second edition (Oxford and New York, 1995).

Jost, Hans Ulrich, *Linksradikalismus in der deutschen Schweiz 1914–1918* (Bern, 1973).

——, 'Bedrohung und Enge', in Comité pour une Nouvelle Histoire de la Suisse (ed.), *Geschichte der Schweiz und der Schweizer* (Basel and Frankfurt am Main, 1983).

Jucker, Andreas, *Social Stylistics: Syntactic Variation in British Newspapers* (Berlin and New York, 1992).

Judd, Denis and Keith Surridge, *The Boer War* (London, 2002).

Kaestli, Tobias, *Selbstbezogenheit und Offenheit: Die Schweiz in der Welt des 20. Jahrhunderts. Zur politischen Geschichte eines neutralen Kleinstaats*, fourth edition (Zürich, 2005).

Kaldor, Mary, *The Imaginary War: Understanding the East-West Conflict* (Oxford and Cambridge, 1990).

Kamber, Ester, 'Medienereignishierarchien 1910–1940', in Kurt Imhof, Heinz Kleger and Gaetano Romano (eds), *Zwischen Konflikt und Konkordanz: Analyse von Medienereignissen in der Schweiz der Vor- und Zwischenkriegszeit* (Zürich, 1993).

——, 'Medienereignishierarchien 1930–1960: Neue Zürcher Zeitung, Tages-Anzeiger, Tagwacht, Vaterland', in Kurt Imhof, Heinz Kleger and Gaetano Romano (eds), *Konkordanz und Kalter Krieg: Analyse von Medienereignissen in der Schweiz der Zwischen- und Nachkriegszeit* (Zürich, 1996).

Kaul, Chandrika, *Reporting the Raj: The British Press and India c. 1880–1922* (Manchester and New York, 2003).

——, 'Monarchical Display and the Politics of Empire: Prince of Wales and India 1870–1920s', *Twentieth Century British History*, 17/4 (2006): 464–88.

Kawamura, Noriko, 'Wilsonian Idealism and Japanese Claims at the Paris Peace Conference', *The Pacific Historical Review*, 66/4 (1997): 503–26.

——, 'Emperor Hirohito and Japan's Decision to Go to War with the United States: Reexamined', *Diplomatic History*, 31/1 (2007): 51–79.

Keeble, Curtis, *Britain, the Soviet Union and Russia* (Basingstoke, 2000).

Keene, Sam, *Faces of the Enemy: Reflections of the Hostile Imagination* (San Francisco, 1986).

Keller, Reiner, Andreas Hirseland, Werner Schneider and Willy Viehöver (eds), *Handbuch Sozialwissenschaftliche Diskursanalyse, Band I: Theorien und Methoden* (Opladen, 2001).

Kennamer, J. David, 'Public Opinion, the Press, and Public Policy: An Introduction', in J. David Kennamer (ed.), *Public Opinion, the Press, and Public Policy* (Westport, 1992).

Kenney, Keith and Michael Colgan, 'Drawing Blood: Images, Stereotypes, and the Political Cartoon', in Paul Martin Lester and Susan Dente Ross (eds), *Images that Injure: Pictorial Stereotypes in the Media*, second edition (Westport and London, 2003).

Kernell, Samuel, 'The Truman Doctrine Speech: A Case Study of the Dynamics of Presidential Opinion Leadership', *Social Science History*, 1/1 (1976); 20–44.

Kersten, Uwe, 'Die Perzeption des Imperialismus im Kleinstaat Schweiz, 1882–1904', unpublished Lizentiatsarbeit, Universität Zürich, 1990.

Kessler, Lawrence D., '"Hands across the Sea": Foreign Missions and Home Support', in Patricia Neils (ed.), *United States Attitudes and Policies toward China: The Impact of American Missionaries* (Armonk and London, 1990).

Kiernan, Victor, *The Lords of Human Kind: European Attitudes to Other Cultures in the Imperial Age* (London, 1995).

Kimball, Warren F., *Forged in War: Roosevelt, Churchill, and the Second World War* (New York, 1997).

Kimble, James J., *Mobilizing the Home Front: War Bonds and Domestic Propaganda* (College Station, 2006).

Kirby, William C., 'The Internationalization of China: Foreign Relations at Home and Abroad in the Republican Era', in Frederic Wakeman Jr. and Richard Louis Edmonds (eds), *Reappraising Republican China* (Oxford, 2000).

Kitchen, Martin, 'The Empire, 1900–1939', in Chris Wrigley (ed.), *A Companion to Early Twentieth-Century Britain* (Malden and Oxford, 2003).

Kitts, Charles R., *The United States Odyssey in China, 1784–1990* (Lanham, New York and London, 1991).

Klehr, Harvey, John Earl Haynes and Kyrill M. Anderson, *The Soviet World of American Communism* (New Haven and London, 1998).

Klein, Christina, *Cold War Orientalism: Asia in the Middlebrow Imagination, 1945–1961* (Berkeley, Los Angeles and London, 2003).

Klein, Thoralf, 'Anti-Imperialism at Grassroots: Christianity and the Chinese Revolution in Northeast Guangdong, 1919–1930', in Mechthild Leutner, Roland Felber, Mikhail L. Titarenko and Alexander M. Grigoriev (eds), The *Chinese Revolution in the 1920s: Between Triumph and Disaster* (London and New York, 2002).

——, *Die Basler Mission in Guangdong (Südchina): 1859–1931* (München, 2002).

Klugmann, James, *History of the Communist Party of Great Britain, volume 2: The General Strike* (London, 1969).

Knieper, Thomas, *Die politische Karikatur: Eine journalistische Darstellungsform und deren Produzenten* (Köln, 2002).

Knuesel, Ariane, 'British Diplomacy and the Telegraph in Nineteenth-Century China', *Diplomacy and Statecraft*, 18/3 (2007): 517–37.

Knüsel, Ariane, '"Western Civilization" against "Hordes of Yellow Savages": British Perceptions of the Boxer Rebellion', *Asiatische Studien*, 62/1 (2008): 43–83.

Koginos, Manny T., *The Panay Incident: Prelude to War* (Lafayette, 1967).

Koselleck, Reinhart, 'Begriffsgeschichte und Sozialgeschichte', in Reinhart Koselleck, *Vergangene Zukunft: Zur Semantik geschichtlicher Zeiten* (Frankfurt am Main, 1989).

Koss, Stephen, *The Rise and Fall of the Political Press in Britain, volume 1: The Nineteenth Century* (London, 1981).

——, *The Rise and Fall of the Political Press in Britain, volume 2: The Twentieth Century* (Chapel Hill and London, 1984).

Koureas, Gabriel, *Memory, Masculinity and National Identity in British Visual Culture, 1914–1930: A Study of 'Unconquerable Manhood'* (Aldershot, 2007).

Kowner, Rotem, '"Lighter than Yellow, but Not Enough": Western Discourse on the Japanese "Race", 1854–1904', *The Historical Journal*, 43/1 (2000): 103–31.

——, 'Between a Colonial Clash and World War Zero: The Impact of the Russo-Japanese War in a Global Perspective', in Rotem Kowner (ed.), *The Impact of the Russo-Japanese War* (Abingdon and New York, 2007).

Kramer, Paul A., 'Empires, Exceptions, and Anglo-Saxons: Race and Rule between the British and United States Empires, 1880–1910', *The Journal of American History*, 88/4 (2002): 1315–53.

Kreis, Georg, *Der Mythos von 1291: Zur Entstehung des schweizerischen Nationalfeiertags* (Basel, 1991).

——, 'Der "homo alpinus helveticus": Zum schweizerischen Rassendiskurs der 30er Jahre', in Guy P. Marchal and Arram Mattioli (eds), *Erfundene Schweiz: Konstruktionen nationaler Identität* (Zürich, 1992).

Ku, Hung-Ting, 'Urban Mass Movement: The May Thirtieth Movement in Shanghai', *Modern Asian Studies*, 13/2 (1979): 197–216.

Kunczik, Michael, *Images of Nations and International Public Relations* (Mahwah, 1997).

Kuntz, Eva Sabine, *Konstanz und Wandel von Stereotypen: Deutschlandbilder in der italienischen Presse nach dem Zweiten Weltkrieg* (Frankfurt am Main, Berlin and Bern, 1997).

Kury, Patrick, *Über Fremde reden: Überfremdungsdiskurs und Ausgrenzung in der Schweiz 1900–1945* (Zürich, 2003).

Kynoch, Gary, 'Controlling the Coolies: Chinese Mineworkers and the Struggle for Labor in South Africa, 1904–1910', *The International Journal of African Historical Studies*, 36/2 (2003): 309–29.

LaFeber, Walter, *The Clash: A History of U.S.-Japan Relations* (New York and London, 1997).

Lake, Marilyn and Henry Reynolds, *Drawing the Global Colour Line: White Men's Countries and the International Challenge of Racial Equality* (Cambridge and New York, 2009).

Lamb, Chris, *Drawn to Extremes: The Use and Abuse of Editorial Cartoons* (New York, 2004).

Landwehr, Achim, *Geschichte des Sagbaren: Einführung in die Historische Diskursanalyse*, second edition (Tübingen, 2004).

Langendorf, Jean-Jacques and Pierre Streit, *Face à la guerre: L'armée et le peuple Suisse 1914–1918/1939–1945* (Gollion, 2007).

Langton, Loup, *Photojournalism and Today's News: Creating Visual Reality* (Chichester and Oxford, 2009).

Lasker, Bruno and Agnes Roman, *Propaganda from China and Japan: A Case Study in Propaganda Analysis* (1938).

Lasserre, André, *La Suisse des années sombres: Courants d'opinion pendant la Deuxième Guerre mondiale, 1939–1945* (Lausanne, 1989).

Latourette, Kenneth Scott, *A History of Christian Missions in China* (London, 1929).

Laybourn, Keith, *The Rise of Socialism in Britain, c. 1881–1957* (Stroud, 1997).

——, *A Century of Labour: A History of the Labour Party, 1900–2000* (Stroud, 2000).

Lazich, Michael C., *E.C. Bridgman (1801–1861): America's First Missionary to China* (Lewiston, Queenston and Lampeter, 2000).

Lee, Gregory B., *Chinas Unlimited: Making the Imaginaries of China and Chineseness* (Honolulu, 2003).

Lee, Joseph, 'Anti-Chinese Legislation in Australasia', *The Quarterly Journal of Economics*, 3/2 (1889): 218–24.

Lee, Rachel C., 'Journalistic Representations of Asian Americans and Literary Responses, 1910–1920', in King-Kok Cheung (ed.), *An Interethnic Companion to Asian American Literature* (Cambridge, New York and Melbourne, 1997).

Lee, Robert G., *Orientals: Asian Americans in Popular Culture* (Philadelphia, 1999).

Leech, Margaret, *In the Days of McKinley* (New York, 1959).

Lehmann, Jean-Pierre, *The Image of Japan: From Feudal Isolation to World Power, 1850–1905* (London, 1978).

——, 'Old and New Japonisme: The Tokugawa Legacy and Modern European Images of Japan', *Modern Asian Studies*, 18/4 (1984): 757–68.

Leong, Karen J., *The China Mystique* (London, Berkeley and Los Angeles, 2005).

Leong, Karen J. and Judy Tzu-Chun Wu, 'Filling the Rice Bowls of China: Staging Humanitarian Relief during the Sino-Japanese War', in Suchen Chang and Madeline Y. Hsu (eds), *Chinese Americans and the Politics of Race and Culture* (Philadelphia, 2008).

Levine, Lawrence W. and Cornelia R. Levine, *The People and the President: America's Conversation with FDR* (Boston, 2002).

Levine, Steven I., 'On the Brink of Disaster: China and the United States in 1945', in Harry Harding and Yuan Ming (eds), *Sino-American Relations, 1945–1955: A Joint Reassessment of a Critical Decade* (Wilmington, 1989).

Li, Danke, 'Popular Culture in the Making of Anti-Imperialist and Nationalist Sentiments in Sichuan', *Modern China*, 30/4 (2004): 470–505.

Li, Laura Tyson, *Madame Chiang Kai-Shek: China's Eternal First Lady* (New York, 2006).

Li, Shian, 'Britain's China Policy and the Communists, 1942 to 1946: The Role of Ambassador Sir Horace Seymour', *Modern Asian Studies*, 26/1 (1992): 49–63.

Lian, Xi, *The Conversion of Missionaries: Liberalism in American Protestant Missions in China, 1907–1932* (University Park, 1997).

Lieven, Dominic, 'Dilemmas of Empire, 1850–1918: Power, Territory, Identity', *Journal of Contemporary History*, 34/2 (1999): 163–200.

Lindley, William R., *20th Century American Newspapers: In Content and Production* (Manhattan, 1993).

Linhart, Sepp, *'Niedliche Japaner' oder Gelbe Gefahr? Westliche Kriegspostkarten 1900–1945* (Wien and Münster, 2005).

Linke, Manfred, 'Zwischen Bilateralismus und Multilateralismus: Die schweizerische Aussenpolitik 1944–1950', in Georg Kreis (ed.), *Die Schweiz im internationalen System der Nachkriegszeit 1943–1950* (Basel, 1996).

Little, Douglas, 'Red Scare, 1936: Anti Bolshevism and the Origins of British Non-Intervention in the Spanish Civil War', *Journal of Contemporary History*, 23/2 (1988): 291–311.

Lloyd, T.O., *Empire, Welfare State, Europe: History of the United Kingdom 1906–2001*, fifth edition (Oxford and New York, 2002).

Lockwood, William W., Jr., 'The International Settlement at Shanghai, 1924–34', *The American Political Science Review*, 28/6 (1934): 1030–46.

Longden, Martin A.L., 'From "Hot War" to "Cold War": Western Europe in British Grand Strategy, 1945–1948', in Michael F. Hopkins, Michael D. Kandiah and Gillian Staerck (eds), *Cold War Britain, 1945–1964: New Perspectives* (Basingstoke, 2003).

Lorence, James J., 'Organized Business and the Myth of the China Market: The American Asiatic Association, 1898–1937', *Transactions of the American Philosophical Society*, 71/4 (1981): 1–112.

Louis, Wm. Roger, *British Strategy in the Far East 1919–1939* (Oxford, 1971).

——, *Imperialism at Bay: The United States and the Decolonization of the British Empire, 1941-1945* (Oxford, 1972).

—— (ed.), *The Robinson and Gallagher Controversy* (New York and London, 1976).

——, 'Hong Kong: The Critical Phase, 1945–1949', *The American Historical Review*, 102/4 (1997): 1052–84.

——, 'Introduction', in Judith M. Brown and Wm. Roger Louis (eds), *The Oxford History of the British Empire: volume 4, The Twentieth Century* (Oxford and New York, 1999).

Lowe, Lisa, *Immigrant Acts: On Asian American Cultural Politics* (Durham and London, 1996).

Lowe, Peter, *Containing the Cold War in East Asia: British Policies towards Japan, China and Korea, 1948–53* (Manchester and New York, 1997).

Lu, Suping, *They Were in Nanjing: The Nanjing Massacre Witnessed by American and British Nationals* (Hong Kong, 2004).

Lucas, Scott and Kaeten Mistry, 'Illusions of Coherence: George F. Kennan, U.S. Strategy and Political Warfare in the Early Cold War, 1946–1950', *Diplomatic History*, 33/1 (2009): 39–65.

Luk, Michael Y.L., *The Origins of Chinese Bolshevism: An Ideology in the Making, 1920–1928* (Oxford, 1990).

Lüsebrink, Hans-Jürgen and Rolf Reichardt, *Die Bastille: Zur Symbolgeschichte von Herrschaft und Freiheit* (Frankfurt am Main, 1990).

Lüthi, Karl J., *Die Schweizer Press einst und jetzt* (Bern, 1933).

Lutz, Jessie Gregory, *China and the Christian Colleges, 1850–1950* (Ithaca and London, 1971).

——, 'China and Protestantism, 1807–1949', in Stephen Uhalley, Jr. and Xiaoxin Wu (eds), *China and Christianity: Burdened Past, Hopeful Future* (Armonk and London, 2001).

Lutze, Thomas D., *China's Inevitable Revolution: Rethinking America's Loss to the Communists* (New York and Basingstoke, 2007).

Lyman, Stanford M., 'The "Yellow Peril" Mystique: Origins and Vicissitudes of a Racist Discourse', *International Journal of Politics, Culture and Society*, 13/4 (2000): 683–747.

Ma, L. Eve Armentrout, *Revolutionaries, Monarchists, and Chinatowns: Chinese Politics in the Americas and the 1911 Revolution* (Honolulu, 1990).

MacKenzie, John M., *Propaganda and Empire: The Manipulation of British Public Opinion, 1880–1960* (Manchester and Dover, 1984).

——, 'The Press and the Dominant Ideology of Empire', in Simon J. Potter (ed.), *Newspapers and Empire in Ireland and Britain: Reporting the British Empire, c. 1857–1921* (Dublin, 2003).

Mackerras, Colin, *Western Images of China* (Hong Kong, 1991).

MacKinnon, Stephen R. and Oris Friesen, *China Reporting: An Oral History of American Journalism in the 1930s and 1940s* (Berkeley, Los Angeles and London, 1987).

Mainer, Hubert and Herward Sieberg, *Der Boxerkrieg in China 1900–1901* (Hildesheim, 2001).

Maissen, Thomas, 'Neue Zürcher Zeitung (NZZ)', in Stiftung Historisches Lexikon der Schweiz (ed.), *Historisches Lexikon der Schweiz*, Band 9 (Basel, 2010).

Mandler, Peter, *The English National Character: The History of an Idea from Edmund Burke to Tony Blair* (London, 2006).

Marder, Arthur J., *Old Friends, New Enemies: The Royal Navy and the Imperial Japanese Navy, Strategic Illusions, 1936–1941* (Oxford, 1981).

Martin, Brian G., 'The Green Gang and the Guomindang State: Du Yuesheng and the Politics of Shanghai, 1927–1937', *The Journal of Asian Studies*, 54/1 (1995): 64–91.

Masland, John W., 'Missionary Influence upon American Far Eastern Policy, *The Pacific Historical Review*, 10/3 (1941): 279–96.

Matsukaka, Yoshishi Tak, *The Making of Japanese Manchuria, 1904–1932* (Cambridge and London, 2001).

Matsumura, Takao, 'Anglo-Japanese Trade Union Relations Between the Wars', in Gordon Daniels and Chushichi Tsuzuki (eds), *The History of Anglo-Japanese Relations 1600–2000, volume 5: Social and Cultural Perspectives* (Basingstoke and New York, 2002).

Matthes, Jörg and Matthias Kohring, 'The Content Analysis of Media Frames: Toward Improving Reliability and Validity', *Journal of Communication*, 58/2 (2008): 258–79.

Maughan, Steven, '"Mighty England Do Good": The Major English Denominations and Organisation for the Support of Foreign Missions in the Nineteenth Century', in Robert A. Bickers and Rosemary Seton (eds), *Missionary Encounters: Sources and Issues* (Richmond, 1996).

May, Ernest R., 'U.S. Press Coverage of Japan, 1931–1941', in Dorothy Borg and Shumpei Okamoto (eds), *Pearl Harbor as History: Japanese-American Relations 1931–1941* (New York and London, 1973).

——, 'When Marshall Kept the U.S. out of War in China', *Journal of Military History*, 66/4 (2002): 1001–10.

May, J.P., 'The Chinese in Britain, 1860–1914', in Colin Holmes (ed.), *Immigrants and Minorities in British Society* (London, Boston and Sydney, 1978).

McCormick, Thomas J., *China Market: America's Quest for Informal Empire, 1893–1901* (Chicago, 1967).

McDermott, Kevin and Jeremy Agnew, *The Comintern: A History of International Communism from Lenin to Stalin* (New York, 1997).

McGerr, Michael, *A Fierce Discontent: The Rise and Fall of the Progressive Movement in America, 1870–1920* (New York, 2003).

McGiffert, Carola (ed.), *Chinese Images of the United States* (Washington, DC, 2005).

McKee, Delber L., 'The Chinese Boycott of 1905–1906 Reconsidered: The Role of Chinese Americans', *The Pacific Historical Review*, 55/2 (1986): 165–91.

Mclean, David, 'Finance and "Informal Empire" before the First World War', *The Economic History Review*, new series, 29/2 (1976): 291–305.

McWilliams, Wilson Carey, 'Standing at Armageddon: Morality and Religion in Progressive Thought', in Sidney M. Milkis and Jerome M. Mileur (eds), *Progressivism and the New Democracy* (Amherst, 1999).

Mehnert, Ute, *Deutschland, Amerika und die 'Gelbe Gefahr': Zur Karriere eines Schlagworts in der Großen Politik, 1905–1917* (Stuttgart, 1995).

Melancon, Glenn, *Britain's China Policy and the Opium Crisis: Balancing Drugs, Violence and National Honour, 1833–1840* (Aldershot and Burlington, 2003).

Melby, John F., 'The Origins of the Cold War in China', *Pacific Affairs*, 41/1 (1968): 19–33.

Meng, Hua and Sukehiro Hirakawa (eds), *Images of Westerners in Chinese and Japanese Literature* (Amsterdam, 2000).

Mersmann, Birgit, 'Bildkulturwissenschaft als Kulturbildwissenschaft?: Von der Notwendigkeit eines inter- und transkulturellen Iconic Turn', *Zeitschrift für Ästhetik und Allgemeine Kunstwissenschaft*, 49/1 (2004): 91–109.

Metallo, Michael V., 'American Missionaries, Sun Yat-sen, and the Chinese Revolution', *The Pacific Historical Review*, 47/2 (1978): 261–82.

Meyer, Michael, 'Between Theory, Method, and Politics: Positioning of the Approaches to CDA', in Ruth Wodak and Michael Meyer (eds), *Methods of Critical Discourse Analysis* (London, Thousand Oaks and New Delhi, 2007).

Miles, Robert, *Racism* (London and New York, 2002).

Miller, Edward S., *War Plan Orange: The U.S. Strategy to Defeat Japan, 1897–1945* (Annapolis, 1991).

Miller, Karen A.J., *Populist Nationalism: Republican Insurgency and American Foreign Policy Making, 1918–1925* (Westport and London, 1999).

Miller, Mark and Bonnie Parnell Riechert, 'The Spiral of Opportunity and Frame Resonance: Mapping the Issue Cycle in News and Public Discourse', in Stephen D. Reese, Oscar H. Gandy, Jr. and August E. Grant (eds), *Framing Public Life: Perspectives on Media and Our Understanding of the Social World* (Mahwah and London, 2001).

Minger, Ralph Eldin, *William Howard Taft and United States Foreign Policy: The Apprenticeship Years 1900–1908* (Urbana, Chicago and London, 1975).

Mitchell, B.R., *British Historical Statistics* (Cambridge, New York and Melbourne, 1988).

Mittler, Max, *Der Weg zum Ersten Weltkrieg: Wie neutral war die Schweiz?* (Zürich, 2003).

Möckli, Daniel, 'The Long Road to Membership: Switzerland and the United Nations', in Jürg Martin Gabriel and Thomas Fischer (eds), *Swiss Foreign Policy, 1945–2002* (Basingstoke, 2003).

Moeller, Susan D., *Shooting War: Photography and the American Experience of Combat* (New York, 1989).

Mooser, Josef, 'Die Geistige Landesverteidigung in den 1930er Jahren: Profile und Kontexte eines vielschichtigen Phänomens der schweizerischen politischen Kultur in der Zwischenkriegszeit', *Schweizerische Zeitschrift für Geschichte*, 47 (1997): 685–708.

Morgan, Kenneth, *The Oxford History of Britain* (Oxford, 2001).

Morgan, Ted, *Reds: McCarthyism in Twentieth-Century America* (New York, 2003).

Morris, Margaret, 'The General Strike in Retrospect', in Chris Wigley (ed.), *The British Labour Movement in the Decade after the First World War* (Loughborough, 1979).

Morrouchi, Mustapha, 'Counternarratives, Recoveries, Refusals', in Paul A. Bové (ed.), *Edward Said and the Work of the Critic: Speaking Truth to Power* (London, 2000).

Mott, Frank Luther, *American Journalism: A History of Newspapers in the United States through 260 Years: 1690 to 1950* (New York, 1950).

——, *A History of American Magazines, volume 4: 1885–1905* (Cambridge, 1957).

Mottini, Roger, *Die Schweiz und Japan während der Meiji-Zeit (1868–1912): Begegnung, Berichterstattung und Bilder* (Bamberg, 1998).

Mungello, D.E., *The Great Encounter of China and the West, 1500–1800*, second edition (Lanham and Oxford, 2005).

Murfett, Malcolm H., *Hostage on the Yangtze: Britain, China, and the Amethyst Crisis of 1949* (Annapolis, 1991).

Myers, Henry A. (ed.), *Western Views of China and the Far East, volume 2: The Early Modern Times to the Present (since 1800)* (Hong Kong, 1984).

Nakai, Paul Akio, 'Die Aufnahme der diplomatischen Beziehungen zwischen der Schweiz und Japan im Jahre 1864', in Comité du centenaire (ed.), *Helvetia – Nippon: 1864–1964* (Tokio, 1964).

Narizny, Kevin, 'The Political Economy of Alignment: Great Britain's Commitments to Europe, 1905–39', *International Security*, 27/4 (2003): 184–219.

Neils, Patricia, *China Images in the Life and Times of Henry Luce* (Savage, 1990).

Neilson, Keith, 'The Anglo-Japanese Alliance and British Strategic Foreign Policy, 1902–1913', in Phillips Payson O'Brien (ed.), *The Anglo-Japanese Alliance, 1902–1922* (London and New York, 2004).

Neval, Daniel A., *'Mit Atombomben bis nach Moskau': Gegenseitige Wahrnehmung der Schweiz und des Ostblocks im Kalten Krieg 1945–1968* (Zürich, 2003).

Newsinger, John, 'Recent Controversies in the History of British Communism', *Journal of Contemporary History*, 41/3 (2006): 557–72.

Ng, Wendy, *Japanese American Internment during World War II: A History and Reference Guide* (Westport, 2002).

Ngai, Mae M., 'The Architecture of Race in American Immigration Law: A Reexamination of the Immigration Act of 1924', *The Journal of American History*, 86/1 (1999): 67–92.

Nicholas, Siân, 'The Construction of National Identity: Stanley Baldwin, "Englishness" and the Mass Media in Inter-War Britain', in Martin Francis and Ina Zweiniger-Bargielowska (eds), *The Conservatives and British Society, 1880–1990* (Cardiff, 1996).

Ninkovich, Frank, *The United States and Imperialism* (Oxford and Malden, 2001).

Nish, Ian, *Japanese Foreign Policy in the Interwar Period* (Westport and London, 2002).

——, 'Britain and Japan: Long-Range Images', *Diplomacy and Statecraft*, 15/1 (2004): 149–61.

Niu, Jun, 'The Origins of the Sino-Soviet Alliance', Odd Arne Westad (ed.), *Brothers in Arms: The Rise and Fall of the Sino-Soviet Alliance, 1945–1963* (Washington, DC, 1998).

Nord, David Paul, *Communities of Journalism: A History of American Newspapers and Their Readers* (Urbana and Chicago, 2001).

Northedge, F.S. and Audrey Wells, *Britain and Soviet Communism: The Impact of a Revolution* (London and Basingstoke, 1982).

O'Neill, William L., *A Democracy at War: America's Fight at Home and Abroad in World War II* (London and Cambridge, 1997).

O'Sullivan, Donal, *Furcht und Faszination: Deutsche und britische Russlandbilder, 1921–1933* (Köln, Weimar and Wien, 1996).

Okihiro, Gary Y. and Julie Sly, 'The Press, Japanese Americans, and the Concentration Camps', *Phylon*, 44/1 (1983): 66–83.

Orr, James J., 'Victims and Perpetrators in National Memory: Lessons from Post-World War Two Japan', *Schweizerische Zeitschrift für Geschichte*, 57/1 (2007): 42–57.

Osman, Colin and Sandra S. Phillips, 'European Visions: Magazine Photography in Europe between the Wars', in Marianne Fulton (ed.), *Eyes of Time: Photojournalism in America* (Boston, Toronto and London, 1988).

Osterhammel, Jürgen, 'Semi-Colonialism and Informal Empire in Twentieth Century China: Towards a Framework of Analysis', in Wolfgang Mommsen and Jürgen Osterhammel (eds), *Imperialism and After: Continuities and Discontinuities* (London, 1986).

——, 'British Business in China, 1860s–1950s', in R.P.T. Davenport-Hines and Geoffrey Jones (eds), *British Business in Asia since 1860* (Cambridge and New York, 1989).

——, *China und die Weltgesellschaft: Vom 18. Jahrhundert bis in unsere Zeit* (München, 1989).

——, *Shanghai, 30. Mai 1925: Die chinesische Revolution* (München, 1997).

——, 'China', in Judith M. Brown and Wm. Roger Louis (eds), *The Oxford History of the British Empire, volume 4: The Twentieth Century* (Oxford and New York, 1999).

Otte, T.G., 'The Boxer Uprising and British Foreign Policy: The End of Isolation', in Robert Bickers and R.G. Tiedemann (eds), *The Boxers, China, and the World* (Plymouth and Lanham, 2007).

——, 'The Fragmenting of the Old World Order: Britain, the Great Powers, and the War', in Rotem Kowner (ed.), *The Impact of the Russo-Japanese War* (Abingdon and New York, 2007).

Ovendale, Ritchie, 'Britain, the United States, and the Cold War in South-East Asia, 1949–1950', *International Affairs*, 58/3 (1982): 447–64.

Padover, Saul K., 'Japanese Race Propaganda', *The Public Opinion Quarterly*, 7/2 (1943): 191–204.

Pan, Lynn, *Sons of the Yellow Emperor: A History of the Chinese Diaspora* (New York, Tokyo and London, 1994).

Pan, Zhongdang and Gerald M. Kosicki, 'Framing Analysis: An Approach to News Discourse', *Political Communication*, 10/1 (1993): 55–75.

Pantsov, Alexander, *The Bolsheviks and the Chinese Revolution, 1919–1927* (Richmond, 2000).

Parins, James W. and Marilyn Parins, 'Twentieth Century', in Alvin Sullivan (ed.), *British Literary Magazines: The Modern Age, 1914–1984* (Westport and London, 1986).

Paris, Michael, *Warrior Nation: Images of War in British Popular Culture, 1850–2000* (London, 2000).

Parker, Jean M., 'Time', in Alan Nourie and Barbara Nourie (eds), *American Mass-Market Magazines* (New York, Westport and London, 1990).

Paul, Gerhard, 'Von der Historischen Bildkunde zur Visual History: Eine Einführung', in Gerhard Paul (ed.), *Visual History: Ein Studienbuch* (Göttingen, 2006).

Peatling, G.K., 'Home Rule for England, English Nationalism, and Edwardian Debates about Constitutional Reform', *Albion*, 35/1 (2003): 71–90.

Peck, James, *Washington's China: The National Security World, the Cold War, and the Origins of Globalism* (Amherst and Boston, 2006).

Penney, Matthew, 'Far from Oblivion: The Nanking Massacre in Japanese Historical Writing for Children and Young Adults', *Holocaust and Genocide Studies*, 22/1 (2008): 25–48.

Pepper, Suzanne, 'The KMT-CCP Conflict 1945–1949', in John K. Fairbank and Albert Feuerwerker (eds), *The Cambridge History of China, volume 13: Republican China 1912–1949*, part 2 (Cambridge, 1986).

Perlmutter, David D., *Picturing China in the American Press: The Visual Portrayal of Sino-American Relations in Time Magazine, 1949-1973* (Lanham, 2007).

Perry, Curtis Lewis, *Apes and Angels: The Irishman in Victorian Caricature* (Newton Abbot, 1971).

Perry, Elizabeth, *Shanghai on Strike: The Politics of Chinese Labor* (Stanford, 1993).

Perry, Hamilton Darby, *The Panay Incident: Prelude to Pearl Harbor* (Toronto, 1969).

Phillips, Clifton J., 'The Student Volunteer Movement and Its Role in China Missions, 1886–1920', in John K. Fairbank (ed.), *The Missionary Enterprise in China and America* (Cambridge, 1974).

Phillips, Morgan, 'Introduction: Labour Yesterday and Today', in Herbert Tracey (ed.), *The British Labour Party: Its History, Growth Policy and Leaders*, volume 1 (London, 1948).

Pierce, Anne R., *Woodrow Wilson and Harry Truman: Mission and Power in American Foreign Policy* (Westport and London, 2003).

Porter, Andrew, '"Cultural Imperialism" and Protestant Missionary Enterprise, 1780–1914', *Journal of Imperial and Commonwealth History*, 25/3 (1997): 367–91.

——, *Religion versus Empire? British Protestant Missionaries and Overseas Expansion, 1700–1914* (Manchester and New York, 2004).

——, 'An Overview, 1700–1914', in Norman Etherington (ed.), *Missions and Empire* (Oxford, 2005).

Porter, Bernard, *The Absent-Minded Imperialists: Empire, Society, and Culture in Britain* (Oxford and New York, 2004).

Porter, Brian, *Britain and the Rise of Communist China: A Study of British Attitudes, 1945–1954* (London, New York and Toronto, 1967).

Powell, David, *The Edwardian Crisis: Britain 1901–14* (Basingstoke and London, 1996).

——, *Nationhood and Identity: The British State since 1800* (London and New York, 2002).

Powers, Richard Gid, *Not without Honor: The History of American Anticommunism* (New York, 1995).

Preston, Diana, *A Brief History of the Boxer Rebellion: China's War on Foreigners, 1900* (London, 2002).

Pugach, Noel H. 'American Friendship for China and the Shantung Question at the Washington Conference', *The Journal of American History*, 64/1 (1977): 67–86.

Pugh, Michael, 'Pacifism and Politics in Britain, 1931–1935', *The Historical Journal*, 23/3 (1980): 641–56.

——, *State and Society: A Social and Political History of Britain, 1870–1997*, second edition (London, 1999).

Qing, Simei, 'American Visions of Democracy and the Marshall Mission to China', in Hongshan Li and Zhaohui Hong (eds), *Image, Perception, and the Making of U.S.-China Relations* (Lanham and Cummor Hill, 1998).

Quested, R.K.I., *Sino-Russian Relations: A Short History* (London and New York, 2005).

Rand, Peter, *China Hands: The Adventures and Ordeals of the American Journalists Who Joined Forces with the Great Chinese Revolution* (New York, 1995).

Rapold, Hans, *Der Schweizerische Generalstab, Band 5: Zeit der Bewährung? Die Epoche um den Ersten Weltkrieg 1907–1924* (Basel and Frankfurt am Main, 1988).

Rauber, André, 'L'anticommunisme en Suisse, une quasi-doctrine d'Etat, entre phobie et manipulation de la légalité', in Michel Caillat, Mauro Cerutti, Jean-François Fayet and Stéphanie Roulin (eds), *Histoire(s) de l'anticommunisme en Suisse/Geschichte(n) des Antikommunismus in der Schweiz* (Zürich, 2009).

Reed, James, *The Missionary Mind and American East Asia Policy, 1911–1915* (Cambridge and London, 1983).

Reese, Stephen D., 'Prologue – Framing Public Life: A Bridging Model for Media Research', in Stephen D. Reese, Oscar H. Gandy, Jr. and August E. Grant (eds), *Framing Public Life: Perspectives on Media and Our Understanding of the Social World* (Mahwah and London, 2001).

——, 'The Framing Project: A Bridging Model for Media Research Revisited', *Journal of Communication*, 57/1 (2007): 148–54.

Reichardt, Rolf (ed.), *Aufklärung und Historische Semantik: Interdisziplinäre Beiträge zur westeuropäischen Kulturgeschichte* (Berlin, 1998).

Reinders, Eric, *Borrowed Gods and Foreign Bodies: Christian Missionaries Imagine Chinese Religion* (Berkeley, Los Angeles and London, 2004).

Rembold, Elfie, *Die festliche Nation: Geschichtsinszenierungen und regionaler Nationalismus in Grossbritannien vor dem Ersten Weltkrieg* (Berlin and Wien, 2000).

Remer, C.F., *Foreign Investments in China* (New York, 1933).

Remer, C.F. and William B. Palmer, *A Study of Chinese Boycotts: With Special Reference to Their Economic Effectiveness* (Taipei, 1966).

Rennstich, Karl, 'The Understanding of Mission, Civilisation and Colonialism in the Basel Mission', in Torben Christensen and William R. Hutchison (eds), *Missionary Ideologies in the Imperialist Era: 1880–1920* (Aarhus, 1982).

Renshaw, Patrick, 'Anti-Labour Politics in Britain, 1918–27', *Journal of Contemporary History*, 12/4 (1977): 693–705.

Reynolds, Bruce L., 'The East Asian "Textile Cluster" Trade, 1868–1973: A Comparative-Advantage Interpretation', in Ernest R. May and John F. Fairbank (eds), *America's China Trade in Historical Perspective* (Cambridge, 1986).

Reynolds, David, '1940: Fulcrum of the Twentieth Century?', *International Affairs*, 66/2 (1990): 325–50.

——, *From Munich to Pearl Harbor: Roosevelt's America and the Origins of the Second World War* (Chicago, 2001).

——, *From World War to Cold War: Churchill, Roosevelt, and the International History of the 1940s* (Oxford, 2006).

Richardson, Peter, 'The Recruiting of Chinese Indentured Labour for the South African Gold-Mines, 1903–1908', *Journal of African History*, 18/1 (1977): 85–108.

Riedi, Eliza, 'Women, Gender, and the Promotion of Empire: The Victoria League, 1901–1914', *The Historical Journal*, 45/3 (2002): 569–99.

Riegel, O.W., 'Channels of Communication', *The Public Opinion Quarterly* (October 1938): 651–8.

Rigby, Richard W., *The May 30 Movement: Events and Themes* (Canberra, 1980).

Riklin, Alois and Silvano Möckli, 'Werden und Wandel der schweizerischen Staatsidee', in Alois Riklin (ed.), *Handbuch Politisches System der Schweiz*, volume 1 (Bern and Stuttgart, 1983).

Ritzmann-Blickenstorfer, Heiner (ed.), *Historische Statistik der Schweiz* (Zürich, 1996).

Roberts, Chalmers M., *In the Shadow of Power: The Story of the Washington Post* (Cabin John, 1989).

Roeder, George H., Jr., *The Censored War: American Visual Experience during World War Two* (New Haven and London, 1993).

Röhl, John C.G., *Wilhelm II.: Der Aufbau der persönlichen Monarchie 1888–1900* (München, 2001).

Rosenberg, Emily S., *Financial Missionaries to the World: The Politics and Culture of Dollar Diplomacy, 1900–1930* (Durham and London, 2003).

Ross, Susan Dente, 'Unconscious, Ubiquitous Frames', in Paul Martin Lester and Susan Dente Ross (eds), *Images that Injure: Pictorial Stereotypes in the Media*, second edition (Westport and London, 2003).

Roux, Alain, *Grèves et politique à Shanghai: Les disillusions (1927–1932)* (Paris, 1995).

Rubinstein, Murray A., 'Witness to the Chinese Millenium: Southern Baptist Perceptions of the Chinese Revolution, 1911–1921', in Patricia Neils (ed.), *United States Attitudes and Policies toward China: The Impact of American Missionaries* (Armonk and London, 1990).

Rüegg, Willy, 'Die Chinesische Revolution in der Berichterstattung der Basler Mission', unpublished PhD thesis, Universität Zürich, 1988.

Rüger, Jan, *The Great Naval Game: Britain and Germany in the Age of Empire* (Cambridge, 2007).

Ruotsila, Markku, *British and American Anticommunism before the Cold War* (London, 2001).

Rust, Ambros, *Die Betlehem-Missionare Immensee* (Freiburg, 1961).

Rutenberg, Daniel, 'Nineteenth Century, The', in Alvin Sullivan (ed.), *British Literary Magazines: The Victorian and Edwardian Age, 1837–1913* (Westport and London, 1984).

Ryan, Charlotte, 'Getting Framed: The Media Shape Reality', in Anders Hansen (ed.), *Mass Communication Research Methods*, volume 3 (London, Thousand Oaks, New Delhi and Singapore, 2008).

Ryan, David, *US Foreign Policy in World History* (London, 2000).

Said, Edward, *Orientalism* (New York, 1979).

Salzmann, Stephanie, *Great Britain, Germany and the Soviet Union: Rapallo and After, 1922–1934* (Woodbridge, 2005).

Sanger, Gerald, 'We Lived in the Presence of History: The Story of British Movietone News in the War Years', in Luke McKernan (ed.), *Yesterday's News: The British Cinema Newsreel Reader* (London, 2002).

Sarasin, Philipp, 'Geschichtswissenschaft und Diskursanalyse', in Philipp Sarasin, *Geschichtswissenschaft und Diskursanalyse* (Frankfurt am Main, 2003).

Sarasin, Philipp, Andreas Ernst, Christoph Kübler and Paul Lang, 'ImagiNation. Eine Einleitung', in Barbara Welter (red.), *Die Erfindung der Schweiz 1848– 1948: Bildentwürfe einer Nation* (Zürich, 1998).

Saul, Norman E., *Friends or Foes? The United States and Russia, 1921–1941* (Lawrence, 2006).

Saussy, Haun, *Great Walls of Discourse and Other Adventures in Cultural China* (Cambridge and London, 2001).

Savoy, Jerold J., 'Punch', in Alvin Sullivan (ed.), *British Literary Magazines: The Victorian and Edwardian Age, 1837–1913* (Westport and London, 1984).

Sbrega, John J., *Anglo-American Relations and Colonialism in East Asia, 1941– 1945* (New York and London, 1983).

——, 'The Anticolonial Policies of Franklin D. Roosevelt: A Reappraisal', *Political Science Quarterly*, 101/1 (1986): 65–84.

Schaffer, Gavin, *Racial Science and British Society, 1930–62* (Basingstoke, 2008).

Schaller, Michael, *The U.S. Crusade in China, 1938–1945* (New York, 1979).

Schanne, Michael, 'Einführung in die Mediengeschichte der Schweiz', in Michael Schanne and Peter Schulz (eds), *Journalismus in der Schweiz: Fakten, Überlegungen, Möglichkeiten* (Aarau, 1993).

Schanne, Michael and Ruedi Matter, 'Auswahl und Inszenierung von Themen zur öffentlichen Kommunikation', in Michael Schanne and Peter Schulz (eds), *Journalismus in der Schweiz: Fakten, Überlegungen, Möglichkeiten* (Aarau, 1993).

Schiffrin, Harold Z., *Sun Yat-sen and the Origins of the Chinese Revolution* (Berkeley and Los Angeles, 1968).

Schindler, Dietrich, 'Dauernde Neutralität', in Alois Riklin, Hans Haug and Hans Christoph Binswanger (eds), *Handbuch der schweizerischen Aussenpolitik* (Bern and Stuttgart, 1975).

Schlesinger, Arthur Jr., 'The Missionary Enterprise and Theories of Imperialism', in John K. Fairbank (ed.), *The Missionary Enterprise in China and America* (Cambridge, 1974).

Schmid-Ammann, Paul, *Die Wahrheit über den Generalstreik von 1918* (Zürich, 1968).

Schmidt, Hans, 'Democracy for China: American Propaganda and the May Fourth Movement', *Diplomatic History*, 22/1 (1998): 1–28.

Schnyder, Matthias, 'Das schweizerische Konsularwesen von 1798 bis 1895', *Politorbis*, 36 (2004): 5–68.

Scholes, Walter V. and Marie V. Scholes, *The Foreign Policy of the Taft Administration* (Columbia, 1970).

Schrecker, Ellen, *Many Are the Crimes: McCarthyism in America* (Princeton, 1998).

Schrijvers, Peter, *The GI War against Japan: American Soldiers in Asia and the Pacific during World War II* (New York, 2002).

Schweizerisches Bundesarchiv (ed.), *Expos.ch: Ideen, Interessen, Irritationen* (Bern, 2000).

Scott, David, 'Diplomats and Poets: "Power and Perceptions" in American Encounters with Japan, 1860', *Journal of World History*, 17/3 (2006): 297–337.

See, Irwin, 'Alone against the Waking Dragon: Britain's Failure to Secure International Cooperation in China, 1925–1926', *Journal of Modern Chinese History*, 2/2 (2008): 167–84.

Seed, John, 'Limehouse Blues: Looking for Chinatown in the London Docks, 1900–40', *History Workshop Journal*, 62 (2006): 58–85.

Seshagiri, Urmila, 'Modernity's (Yellow) Perils: Dr. Fu-Manchu and English Race Paranoia', *Cultural Critique*, 62 (2006): 162–94.

Sewell, William H., 'The Concept(s) of Culture', in Victoria E. Bonnell and Lynn Hunt (eds), *Beyond the Cultural Turn: New Directions in the Study of Society and Culture* (Berkeley and Los Angeles, 1999).

Seymour-Ure, Colin and Jim Schoff, *David Low* (London, 1985).

Shaffer, Robert, 'Pearl S. Buck and the East and West Association: The Trajectory and Fate of "Critical Internationalism," 1940–1950', *Peace and Change*, 28/1 (2003): 1–36.

Shai, Aron, *Origins of the War in the East: Britain, China and Japan 1937–39* (London, 1976).

——, *Britain and China, 1941–47* (Basingstoke and London, 1984).

Shao, Wenguang, *China, Britain and Businessmen: Political and Commercial Relations, 1949–57* (Basingstoke and London, 1991).

Sheafer, Tamir, 'How to Evaluate It: The Role of Story-Evaluative Tone in Agenda Setting and Priming', *Journal of Communication*, 57/1 (2007): 21–39.

Sheng, Michael M., 'America's Lost Chance in China? A Reappraisal of Chinese Communist Policy toward the United States before 1945', *The Australian Journal of Chinese Affairs*, 29 (1993): 135–57.

——, 'The United States, the Chinese Communist Party, and the Soviet Union, 1948–1950: A Reappraisal', *Pacific Historical Review*, 63 (1994): 521–36.

Shichor, Yitzhak, 'Ironies of History: The War and the Origins of East Asian Radicalism', in Rotem Kowner (ed.), *The Impact of the Russo-Japanese War* (Abingdon and New York, 2007).

Shimazu, Naoko, *Japan, Race and Equality: The Racial Equality Propsosal of 1919* (London and New York, 1998).

Shoemaker, Pamela J., 'Media Gatekeeping', in Anders Hansen (ed.), *Mass Communication Research Methods*, volume 1 (London, Thousand Oaks, New Delhi and Singapore, 2009).

Shoemaker, Pamela J. and Stephen D. Reese, *Mediating the Message: Theories of Influences on Mass Media Content* (New York and London, 1991).

Shukla, Vivekanand, *Soviet Revolutions and the Indian National Movement: Perceptions of Indian Media* (New Delhi, 1989).

Siederer, N.D., 'The Campbell Case', *Journal of Contemporary History*, 9/2 (1974): 143–62.

Siegel, Katherine A.S., *Loans and Legitimacy: The Evolution of Soviet-American Relations, 1919–1939* (Lexington, 1996).

Simpson, Jacqueline, 'Fifty British Dragon Tales: An Analysis', *Folklore*, 89/1 (1978): 79–93.

Smith, Beverly E., 'New Statesman and Society', in Sam G. Riley (ed.), *Consumer Magazines of the British Isles* (Westport, 1993).

Smith, Simon C., *British Imperialism: 1750–1970* (Cambridge, 1989).

Smith, Steve, 'Moscow and the Second and Third Armed Uprisings in Shanghai, 1927', in Mechthild Leutner, Roland Felber, Mikhail L. Titarenko and Alexander M. Grigoriev (eds), *The Chinese Revolution in the 1920s: Between Triumph and Disaster* (London and New York, 2002).

Smith, Tony, *America's Mission: The United States and the Worldwide Struggle for Democracy in the Twentieth Century* (Princeton, 1994).

Smythe, Ted Curtis, *The Gilded Age Press, 1865–1900* (Westport and London, 2003).

Somers, Paul P., '"Right in the Führer's Face": American Editorial Cartoons of the World War II Period', *American Journalism*, 13/3 (1996): 333–53.

Sozialdemokratische Partei der Schweiz (ed.), *Historisch Notizen über ihre Entstehung, ihr Wachstum und ihre Aktion* (Bern, 1928).

Spence, Jonathan D., *The Chan's Great Continent: China in Western Minds* (New York and London, 1998).

Spillmann, Kurt R., Andreas Wenger, Christoph Breitenmoser and Marcel Gerber, *Schweizer Sicherheitspolitik seit 1945: Zwischen Autonomie und Kooperation* (Zürich, 2001).

Splichal, Slavko, *Public Opinion: Developments and Controversies in the Twentieth Century* (Lanham and Oxford, 1999).

Stämpfli, Regula, 'Die Schweiz und China, 1945–1950', *Studien und Quellen*, 13/14 (1988): 163–224.

Stangor, Charles and Mark Schaller, 'Stereotypes as Individual and Collective Representations', in Charles Stangor (ed.), *Stereotypes and Prejudice: Essential Readings* (Philadelphia, 2000).

Startt, James D., 'Good Journalism in the Era of the New Journalism: The British Press, 1902–1914', in Joel H. Wiener (ed.), *Papers for the Millions: The New Journalism in Britain, 1850s to 1914* (New York, Westport and London, 1988).

Steffen, Therese, 'Gegensätzliche Partner – Die Beziehungen Schweiz-Sowjetunion 1946–1956', *Studien und Quellen*, 21 (1995): 45–91.

Steinmann, Stephan, 'Seldwyla im Wunderland: Schweizer im alten Shanghai (1842–1941): Eine Untersuchung ausländischer Präsenz im China der Kapitularverträge', unpublished PhD thesis, Zürich, 1998.

Stepan, Nancy, *The Idea of Race in Science: Great Britain 1800–1960* (Hamden, 1984).

Stephanson, Anders, *Manifest Destiny: American Expansion and the Empire of Right* (New York, 1995).

Stettler, Peter, *Die Kommunistische Partei der Schweiz, 1921–1931* (Bern, 1980).

Stimson, Henry L., *The Far Eastern Crisis: Recollections and Observations* (New York, 1974).

Straubel, Daniel, 'North American Review', in Alan Nourie and Barbara Nourie (eds), *American Mass-Market Magazines* (New York, Westport and London, 1990).

Sun, Youli, *China and the Origins of the Pacific War, 1931–1941* (New York, 1993).

Takaki, Ronald, *Strangers from a Different Shore: A History of Asian Americans* (Boston, Toronto and London, 1989).

Tang, James T.H., 'From Empire Defence to Imperial Retreat: Britain's Postwar China Policy and the Decolonization of Hong Kong', *Modern Asian Studies*, 28/2 (1994): 317–37.

Tanner, Jakob, 'Die Schweiz und Europa im 20. Jahrhundert: Wirtschaftliche Integration ohne politische Partizipation', in Paul Bairoch and Martin Körner (eds), *Die Schweiz in der Weltwirtschaft* (Zürich, 1990).

———, '1910–1930: Konjunkturen, Kontinuitäten und Brechung zweier Jahrzehnte: Versuch einer Synopsis', in Andreas Ernst and Erich Wigger (eds), *Die neue Schweiz? Eine Gesellschaft zwischen Integration und Polarisierung (1910–1930)* (Zürich, 1996).

———, '"Réduit national" und Aussenwirtschaft: Wechselwirkungen zwischen militärischer Dissuasion und ökonomischer Kooperation mit den

Achsenmächten', in Philipp Sarasin and Regina Wecker (eds), *Raubgold, Reduit, Flüchtlinge: Zur Geschichte der Schweiz in Zweiten Weltkrieg* (Zürich, 1998).

——, 'Switzerland and the Cold War: A Neutral Country between the "American Way of Life" and "Geistige Landesverteidigung"', in Joy Charnley and Malcolm Pendler (eds), *Switzerland and War* (Bern, 1999).

Taylor, Antony, *'Down with the Crown': British Anti-monarchism and Debates about Royalty since 1790* (London, 1999).

Tchen, John Kuo Wei, *New York before Chinatown: Orientalism and the Shaping of American Culture 1776–1882* (Baltimore and London, 2001).

Teel, Leonard Ray, *The Public Press, 1900–1945: History of American Journalism* (Westport and London, 2006).

Temple, Mick, *The British Press* (Maidenhead, 2008).

Thompson, Andrew S., 'Tariff Reform: An Imperial Strategy, 1903–1913', *The Historical Journal*, 40/4 (1997): 1033–54.

——, 'The Language of Imperialism and the Meanings of Empire: Imperial Discourse in British Politics, 1895–1914', *The Journal of British Studies*, 36/2 (1997): 147–77.

——, *Imperial Britain: The Empire in British Politics, c. 1880–1932* (Harlow, 2000).

——, *The Empire Strikes Back? The Impact of Imperialism on Britain from the Mid-nineteenth Century* (Harlow, 2005).

Thompson, James, '"Pictorial Lies"?: Posters and Politics in Britain c. 1880–1914', *Past and Present*, 197 (2007): 177–210.

Thompson, John A., *Woodrow Wilson* (London, 2002).

Thompson, Richard Austin, *The Yellow Peril, 1890–1924* (New York, 1978).

Thorne, Christopher, *The Limits of Foreign Policy: The West, the League and the Far Eastern Crisis of 1931–1933* (London, 1972).

——, *Allies of a Kind: The United States, Britain and the War against Japan, 1941–1945* (London, 1978).

——, *The Issue of War: States, Societies, and the Far Eastern Conflict of 1941–1945* (London, 1985).

——, 'Racial Aspects of the Far Eastern War of 1941–1945', in Michael L. Krenn (ed.), *Race and U.S. Foreign Policy from 1900 through World War II* (New York and London, 1998).

Thornton, Richard C., *The Comintern and the Chinese Communists, 1928–1931* (Seattle and London, 1969).

Thorpe, Andrew, *The British Communist Party and Moscow, 1920–1943* (Manchester, 2000).

——, 'The Membership of the Communist Party of Great Britain, 1920–1945', *The Historical Journal*, 43/3 (2000): 777–800.

Tiedemann, R.G., 'Indigenous Agency, Religious Protectorates, and Chinese Interests: The Expansion of Christianity in Nineteenth-Century China', in

Dana L. Robert (ed.), *Converting Colonialism: Visions and Realities in Mission History, 1706–1914* (Grand Rapids and Cambridge, 2008).

Tifft, Susan E. and Alex S. Jones, *The Trust: The Private and Powerful Family behind The New York Times* (Boston and New York, 1999).

Tovy, Tal and Sharon Halevi, 'America's First Cold War: The Emergence of a New Rivalry', in Rotem Kowner (ed.), *The Impact of the Russo-Japanese War* (Abingdon and New York, 2007).

Trachsler, Daniel, *Neutral zwischen Ost und West? Infragestellung und Konsolidierung der schweizerischen Neutralitätspolitik durch den Beginn des Kalten Krieges, 1947–1952* (Zürich, 2002).

Trampedach, Tim, 'Chiang Kaishek between Revolution and Militarism, 1926/27', in Mechthild Leutner, Roland Felber, M.L. Titarenko and A.M. Grigoriev (eds), *The Chinese Revolution in the 1920s: Between Triumph and Disaster* (London and New York, 2002).

Trask, David F., 'Sino-Japanese-American Relations during the Paris Peace Conference of 1919', in Thomas H. Etzold (ed.), *Aspects of Sino-American Relations since 1784* (New York and London, 1978).

Traxel, David, *Crusader Nation: The United States in Peace and the Great War, 1898–1920* (New York, 2006).

Trotter, Ann, *Britain and East Asia 1933–1937* (London and New York, 1975).

Ts'ai, Shih-sham, 'Reaction to Exclusion: The Boycott of 1905 and Chinese National Awakening', *Historian*, 29/1 (1976): 95–110.

Tsang, Steve, *The Cold War's Odd Couple: The Unintended Partnership between the Republic of China and the UK, 1950–1958* (London and New York, 2006).

Tuchman, Barbara W., *Stilwell and the American Experience in China, 1911–1945* (New York, 1985).

Tucker, Nancy Bernkopf, 'America First', in Carola McGiffert (ed.), *China in the American Political Imagination* (Washington, DC, 2003).

Twells, Alison, *The Civilising Mission and the English Middle Class, 1792–1850* (Basingstoke and New York, 2009).

Unabhängige Expertenkommission Schweiz-Zweiter Weltkrieg (ed.), *Die Schweiz, der Nationalsozialismus und der Zweite Weltkrieg: Schlussbericht* (Zürich, 2002).

Unverfehrt, Gerd, 'Der Mensch-Tier-Vergleich: die Spinne als Zeichen', in Gerhard Langemeyer, Gerd Unverfehrt, Herwig Guratzsch and Christopf Stölzl (eds), *Bild als Waffe: Mittel und Motive der Karikatur in fünf Jahrhunderten* (München, 1984).

Van de Ven, Hans, *War and Nationalism in China, 1925–1945* (London and New York, 2003).

——, 'Robert Hart and Gustav Detring during the Boxer Rebellion', *Modern Asian Studies*, 40/3 (2006): 631–62.

Van Dyke, Paul A., *The Canton Trade: Life and Enterprise on the China Coast, 1700–1845* (Hong Kong, 2005).

Van Gorp, Baldwin, 'The Constructionist Approach to Framing: Bringing Culture Back In', *Journal of Communication*, 57/1 (2007): 60–78.

Varg, Paul A., *Missionaries, Chinese, and Diplomats: The American Protestant Missionary Movement in China, 1890–1952* (Princeton, 1958).

——, *The Making of a Myth: The United States and China, 1897–1912* (East Lansing, 1968).

——, *The Closing of the Door: Sino-American Relations 1936–1946* (East Lansing, 1973).

Varisco, Daniel Martin, *Reading Orientalism: Said and the Unsaid* (Seattle and London, 2007).

Vinacke, Harold M., 'Woodrow Wilson's Far Eastern Policy', in Edward H. Buehrig (ed.), *Wilson's Foreign Policy in Perspective* (Bloomington, 1957).

Voiret, Jean-Pierre, 'Genf und die Verbreitung der Chinoiserie in der Schweiz', in Paul Hugger (ed.), *China in der Schweiz: Zwei Kulturen in Kontakt* (Zürich, 2005).

Walker, Martin, *Powers of the Press: The World's Great Newspapers* (London, Melbourne and New York, 1982).

Wallace, Aurora, *Newspapers and the Making of Modern America: A History* (Westport and London, 2005).

Waller, P.J., 'The Chinese', *History Today*, 35/9 (1985): 8–15.

Walls, Andrew F., 'British Missions', in Torben Christensen and William R. Hutchison (eds), *Missionary Ideologies in the Imperialist Era: 1880–1920* (Aarhus, 1982).

——, 'Carrying the White Man's Burden: Some British Views of National Vocation in the Imperial Era', in William R. Hutchison and Hartmut Lehmann (eds), *Many Are Chosen: Divine Election and Western Nationalism* (Minneapolis, 1994).

Walton, John K., 'Britishness', in Chris Wrigley (ed.), *A Companion to Early Twentieth-Century Britain* (Malden and Oxford, 2003).

Wang, Chen-main, 'A Re-examination of the Instructions Used by Marshall's Mission in China (December 1945–January 1947)', in Priscilla Roberts (ed.), *Sino-American Relations since 1900* (Hong Kong, 1991).

Wang, Dong, *China's Unequal Treaties: Narrating National History* (Lanham and Oxford, 2005).

Wang, Guanhua, *In Search of Justice: The 1905–1906 Chinese Anti-American Boycott* (Cambridge and London, 2001).

Wang, Jerry L., 'The Profitability of Anglo-Chinese Trade, 1861–1913', *Business History*, 35/3 (1993): 39–65.

Wang, Jianwei, *Limited Adversaries: Post-Cold War Sino-American Mutual Images* (Oxford and New York, 2000).

Ward, Paul, *Red Flag and Union Jack: Englishness, Patriotism and the British Left, 1881–1924* (Woodbridge, 1998).

Warner, Geoffrey, 'From "Ally" to Enemy: Britain's Relations with the Soviet Union, 1941–8', in Francesca Gori and Silvio Pons (eds), *The Soviet Union and Europe in the Cold War, 1943–53* (Basingstoke and London, 1996).

Warraq, Ibn, *Defending the West: A Critique of Edward Said's Orientalism* (Amherst, 2007).

Weale, Putnam, *The Re-Shaping of the Far East* (London, 1905).

Weaver, David, 'Thoughts on Agenda Setting, Framing, and Priming', *Journal of Communication*, 57/1 (2007): 142–7.

Weber, Karl, *The Swiss Press: An Outline* (Bern, 1948).

Weigold, Auriol, *Churchill, Roosevelt and India: Propaganda during World War II* (New York and London, 2008).

Weiler, Peter, 'British Labour and the Cold War: The Foreign Policy of the Labour Governments, 1945–1951', *Journal of British Studies*, 26 (1987): 54–82.

Wells, David and Sandra Wilson, 'Introduction', in David Wells and Sandra Wilson (eds), *The Russo-Japanese War in Cultural Perspective, 1904–1905* (Basingstoke, 1999).

Wendt, Lloyd, *Chicago Tribune: The Rise of a Great American Newspaper* (Chicago, New York and San Francisco, 1979).

Westad, Odd Arne, *Cold War and Revolution: Soviet-American Rivalry and the Origins of the Chinese Civil War, 1944–1946* (New York, 1993).

——, *Decisive Encounters: The Chinese Civil War, 1946–1950* (Stanford, 2003).

Wettig, Gerhard, *Stalin and the Cold War in Europe: The Emergence and Development of East-West Conflict, 1939–1953* (Lanham and Boulder, 2008).

White, Christine A., *British and American Commercial Relations with Soviet Russia, 1918–1924* (Chapel Hill and London, 1992).

Widmer, Paul, *Die Schweiz als Sonderfall: Grundlagen, Geschichte, Gestaltung* (Zürich, 2007).

Wiedmann, Arnd, *Imperialismus – Militarismus – Sozialismus: Der deutschschweizerische Protestantismus in seinen Zeitschriften und die grossen Fragen der Zeit 1900–1930* (Bern, Berlin, Frankfurt am Main, 1995).

Wigger, Erich, 'Geschichtsbilder und Zukunftserwartungen: Zur Konstruktion von freisinniger Orientierung im Krisenkontext nach dem Ersten Weltkrieg in der Schweiz', in Andreas Ernst and Erich Wigger (eds), *Die neue Schweiz? Eine Gesellschaft zwischen Integration und Polarisierung (1910–1930)* (Zürich, 1996).

——, *Krieg und Krise in der politischen Kommunikation* (Zürich, 1997).

Wilbur, C. Martin, *The Nationalist Revolution in China, 1923–1928* (Cambridge, 1984).

Wild, Dölf, 'Auf wen schoss Wilhelm Tell? Überlegungen zu Entstehung und Gehalt der schweizerischen Staatsmythen', in Silvia Ferrari, Josef Lang, Heinz Looser, Isabelle Meier, Brigitte Ruckstuhl, Dominik Siegrist, Dölf Wild, Claudia Wirthlin and Manfred Züfle, *Auf wen schoss Wilhelm Tell? Beiträge zu einer Ideologiegeschichte der Schweiz* (Zürich, 1991).

Wilford, Hugh, 'The Communist International and the American Communist Party', in Tim Rees and Andrew Thorpe (eds), *International Communism and the Communist International 1919–43* (Manchester and New York, 1998).

Wilgus, Mary H., *Sir Claude MacDonald, the Open Door, and British Informal Empire in China, 1895–1900* (New York and London, 1987).

Wilke, Jürgen, *Grundzüge der Medien- und Kommunikationsgeschichte: Von den Anfängen bis ins 20. Jahrhundert* (Köln and Weimar, 2000).

Wilkins, Mira, 'The Impact of American Multinational Enterprise on American-Chinese Economic Relations, 1786–1949', in Ernest R. May and John F. Fairbank (eds), *America's China Trade in Historical Perspective* (Cambridge, 1986).

——, 'The Role of U.S. Business', in Dorothy Borg and Shumpei Okamoto (eds), *Pearl Harbor as History: Japanese-American Relations 1931–1941* (New York and London, 1973).

Williams, Andrew J., *Labour and Russia: The Attitude of the Labour Party to the USSR, 1924–34* (Manchester and New York, 1989).

Wilson, A.N., *After the Victorians: The World Our Parents Knew* (London, 2006).

Wilson, Sandra, 'Containing the Crisis: Japan's Diplomatic Offensive in the West, 1931–1933', *Modern Asian Studies*, 29/22 (1995): 337–72.

——, *The Manchurian Crisis and Japanese Society, 1931–1933* (London and New York, 2002).

Wodak, Ruth, 'What CDA Is About: A Summary of Its History, Important Concepts and Its Developments', in Ruth Wodak and Michael Meyer (eds), *Methods of Critical Discourse Analysis* (London, Thousand Oaks and New Delhi, 2007).

——, 'The Discourse-Historical Approach', in Ruth Wodak and Michael Meyer (eds), *Methods of Critical Discourse Analysis* (London, Thousand Oaks and New Delhi, 2007).

Wodak, Ruth and Michael Meyer (eds), *Methods of Critical Discourse Analysis* (London, Thousand Oaks and New Delhi, 2007).

Wodak, Ruth and Gilbert Weiss (eds), *Critical Discourse Analysis: Theory and Interdisciplinarity* (Basingstoke, 2007).

——, 'Introduction: Theory, Interdisciplinarity and Critical Discourse Analysis', in Ruth Wodak and Gilbert Weiss (eds), *Critical Discourse Analysis: Theory and Interdisciplinarity* (Basingstoke, 2007).

Wolf, David C. '"To Secure a Convenience": Britain Recognizes China – 1950', *Journal of Contemporary History*, 18/2 (1983): 299–326.

Wong, K. Scott, *Americans First: Chinese Americans and the Second World War* (Cambridge and London, 2005).

Wong, Sin-Kiong, 'Die for the Boycott and Nation: Martyrdom and the 1905 Anti-American Movement in China', *Modern Asian Studies*, 35/3 (2001): 565–88.

Wood, Alan, *The True History of Lord Beaverbrook* (London, 1965).

Wood, Herbert J., 'Nelson Trusler Johnson: The Diplomacy of Benevolent Pragmatism', in Richard Dean Burns and Edward M. Bennett (eds), *Diplomats in Crisis: United States – Chinese – Japanese Relations, 1919–1941* (Santa Barbara and Oxford, 1974).

Woodhouse, Eiko, *The Chinese Hsinhai Revolution: G.E. Morrison and Anglo-Japanese Relations, 1897–1920* (London and New York, 2004).

Worley, Matthew, *Class against Class: The Communist Party in Britain between the Wars* (London and New York, 2002).

Wright, Quincy, 'The Washington Conference', *The American Political Science Review*, 16/2 (1922): 285–97.

Wrigley, Chris, '1919: The Critical Year', in Chris Wrigley (ed.), *The British Labour Movement in the Decade after the First World War* (Loughborough, 1979).

Wu, William F., *The Yellow Peril: Chinese Americans in American Fiction 1850–1940* (Hamden, 1982).

Xiang, Lanxin, 'The Recognition Controversy: Anglo-American Relations in China, 1949', *Journal of Contemporary History*, 27/2 (1992): 319–43.

——, *Recasting the Imperial Far East: Britain and America in China, 1945–1950* (Armonk and London, 1995).

——, *The Origins of the Boxer War: A Multinational Study* (London, 2003).

Xu, Guangqiu, 'The Issue of US Air Support for China during the Second World War, 1942–45', *Journal of Contemporary History*, 36/3 (2001): 459–84.

Yamamoto, Masahiro, *The History and Historiography of the Rape of Nanking* (Ann Arbor, 1998).

——, *Nanking: Anatomy of an Atrocity* (Westport and London, 2000).

Yapp, M.A., 'British Perceptions of the Russian Threat to India', *Modern Asian Studies*, 21/4 (1987): 647–65.

Yoshida, Takashi, *The Making of the 'Rape of Nanking': History and Memory in Japan, China, and the United States* (Oxford and New York, 2006).

Young, Leonard K., *British Policy in China: 1895–1902* (Oxford, 1970).

Young, Louise, *Japan's Total Empire: Manchuria and the Culture of Wartime Imperialism* (Berkeley, Los Angeles and London, 1999).

Yung, Judy, Gordon Chang and Him Mark Lai (eds), *Chinese American Voices: From the Gold Rush to the Present* (Berkeley, Los Angeles and London, 2006).

Zangger, Andreas, 'Von schnellem Geld und dauerhaften Bindungen: Schweizer im kolonialen Südostasien, 1860–1930', unpublished PhD thesis, Universität Zürich, 2010.

Zarrow, Peter, *China in War and Revolution, 1895–1949* (London and New York, 2005).

Zhai, Qiang, *The Dragon, the Lion, and the Eagle: Chinese-British-American Relations, 1949–1958* (Kent and London, 1994).

Zhang, Baijia, 'Chinese Policies toward the United States, 1937–1945', in Harry Harding and Yuan Ming (eds), *Sino-American Relations, 1945–1955: A Joint Reassessment of a Critical Decade* (Wilmington, 1989).

Zhang, Han Ying, 'The Marshall Mission and United States Relations with the Nationalists and Communists in China', in Priscilla Roberts (ed.), *Sino-American Relations since 1900* (Hong Kong, 1991).

Zhang, Hong, *America Perceived: The Making of Chinese Images of the United States, 1945–1953* (London and Westport, 2002).

Zhang Kaiyuan, 'A General Review of the Study of the Revolution of 1911 in the People's Republic of China', *The Journal of Asian Studies*, 39/3 (1980): 525–31.

——, 'Introduction: Historical Background', in Zhang Kaiyuan (ed.), *Eyewitnesses to Massacre: American Missionaries Bear Witness to Japanese Atrocities in Nanjing* (Armonk and London, 2001).

—— (ed.), *Eyewitnesses to Massacre: American Missionaries Bear Witness to Japanese Atrocities in Nanjing* (Armonk and London, 2001).

Zhao, Qiguang, *A Study of Dragons, East and West* (New York, 1992).

Zhou, Yufang, *Die Exterritorialitätsrechte der Schweiz in China (1918–1946)* (Frankfurt and Bern, 2003).

Zimmer, Oliver, '"A Unique Fusion of the Natural and the Man-made": The Trajetory of Swiss Nationalism, 1933–1939', *Journal of Contemporary History*, 39/1 (2004): 5–24.

Index

Acheson, Dean 220, 228–31, 237–9
*Allgemeiner Evangelisch-Protestantischer
    Missionsverein* 66–7
Amerasia 225
American Exceptionalism 53–5, 59, 67,
    109–11, 227, 229–30, 236, 252–8
American Workers' Party 103
Amethyst Incident 208–9
Anglo-Japanese Alliance 132–8, 201, 251,
    256
*Annals of the American Academy of
    Political and Social Science* 20,
    58, 161
anticommunism 74–5, 205, 253–5
    in Britain 73, 76–84, 86–9, 91–3, 98–9
    in China 93, 97
    in Switzerland 115–117, 239–41, 245,
        248
    in the USA 99–105, 111, 225–32, 239
Arcos Raid 98
Atlanta Constitution 13, 18–19, 49–50, 59,
    61–2, 183

Bachmann, Peter 246–7
Baldwin, Stanley 81, 84, 88, 98
Basel Mission 65–7
Beijing 30–31, 54, 62, 71, 94–5, 97, 112,
    143, 210
Berner Intelligenzblatt 22, 68–9, 71
Bethlehem-Mission Immensee 119
Bevin, Ernest 207, 212, 214–215, 220–221
Boer War 33, 44
Bolshevism 73, 76–81, 84, 86–91, 94–5,
    97–8, 101, 104, 106, 112, 115–116,
    119–120, 255; *see also* Russia
Boscovits, J.F. 70–71
Boston Globe 19, 48, 57–8, 61
Boxer Uprising 25, 30–31, 256
    American reactions 53–5, 59, 234,
        255–6

British reactions 31–5, 46, 127, 134,
    252, 255–6
Swiss reactions 64–66
boycott
    during the May Thirtieth Movement
        85, 87–8, 112, 255
    of American goods in 1905 49–51
    of Japanese goods in the 1930s 143,
        179
Bridgman, Elijah Coleman 51
British Empire
    and the British press 3, 33, 35–8, 44–6,
        86–8, 97, 147, 151–2, 155, 209,
        212–213, 216–219, 252–4
    and British missionaries 28
    and Chinese immigration 136
    and monarchy 42, 44–45
    and political parties 86–7, 254
    and trade with China 35, 87–8, 93
    challenges to the Empire 44–6, 94,
        105, 132, 151–2, 205, 212, 214–6,
        254
    communist threat 76–8, 86–8, 92,
        97–9, 105, 115, 117, 215, 217–19
British monarchy 25, 38–43, 46, 252; *see
    also* George V
British Movietone News 209–10, 213
Buck, Pearl S. 170, 182, 194
Bundesblatt 64, 198
Burma 138, 151, 205, 212, 215, 217,
    221–2, 234
bushido 132–3, 171–2
Business Week 169–70, 179

Campbell Case 79
cartoonists *see* editorial cartoonists
cartoons *see* editorial cartoons
censorship
    newspaper censorship 146–7, 176–7,
        196–7

newsreel censorship 144, 175–6, 197

Chiang Kai-shek 93, 95, 97, 111, 113, 139, 174–5, 182, 203–5, 222–4, 227–32, 238, 249

Chicago Daily News 146, 177

Chicago Tribune 13, 18–19, 25, 48–9, 53–4, 58–9, 99, 104–5, 109, 111–113, 161, 163–4, 166–7, 177–9, 188, 224–5, 229–1, 236–7, 239, 254

China Lobby 228–9, 238

China trade 4, 6, 11, 27, 71, 73
   American trade with China 46–51, 54–7, 59, 105, 112–113, 162–3, 169–70, 176, 206, 252
   British trade with China 26–8, 30, 35, 53, 87–8, 93–4, 119, 140–141, 206, 220, 252, 249
   Swiss trade with China 62–5, 68–9, 119, 193, 246, 248–9

Chinese Civil War (1945–1949) 2, 23, 203, 206–8, 210, 212–213, 215, 220–222, 224, 227–33, 241–6, 253, 255

Chinese Communist Party 84–5, 88, 105, 203, 206–13, 220–224, 228, 234–7, 244

Chinese Exclusion Act (USA) 49–50, 158, 190

Chinese immigration 190, 256
   to Britain 134, 136–7
   to Switzerland 190
   to the USA 49, 51, 158–60, 234

Chinese Maritime Customs Service 28, 151

Chinese Nationalists 84–5, 90, 93–5, 97, 111, 182, 203, 205–6, 210, 220–224, 227–9, 231–2, 236–7, 242, 249

Chinese People's Republic 221–2, 245, 248–9

chinoiserie 46, 62

Christian Century 20, 104, 111, 113–114, 178, 184, 190, 232

Christian Science Monitor 19, 59, 61–2, 232

Christianity 2, 52, 61, 67, 130, 160, 182, 252,

Churchill, Winston 76, 93, 205, 214, 226

Cold War 203–5, 217, 226, 232, 241, 245–6, 249, 251, 255–6

Collier's 188–9

Comintern 76–7, 80–81, 85, 91, 93, 97, 103, 105–106, 112–113, 115,

communism *see* anticommunism; Bolshevism; Chinese Communist Party; Comintern; Communist Labor Party; Communist Party of America; Communist Party of Great Britain; Communist Party of the USA

Communist International *see* Comintern

Communist Labor Party 100

Communist Party of America 100; *see also* Communist Party of the USA

Communist Party of Great Britain 73–4, 77, 79–80, 84, 91–2, 94–6

Communist Party of the USA 103

Communist Victory in China (1949) 2, 23, 203–5, 210, 215, 218, 229–30, 232–6, 242, 244–6, 249, 252–4, 256

Conger, Edwin H. 54

Conservative Party (UK) 40, 78–81, 83–4, 86, 90, 93, 98, 104, 254

Coolidge Administration 112–113

Daily Express 13–16, 44, 79–81, 84, 87–9, 94, 141, 146, 150, 152

Daily Mail 13–16, 31, 35–6, 38–9, 42–4, 79–81, 84, 86, 88, 97, 114, 144, 146, 148, 150, 152, 155, 157, 203–4, 209, 213, 255

Daily Mirror 13–16, 35, 39, 43–4, 79, 81, 83, 88, 94, 132, 134, 146, 148, 150, 209, 213, 221

Daily Telegraph 44, 114

democracy 186, 204, 226
   American mission to spread democracy 2–3, 53, 58–61, 107–9, 111, 114, 120, 160, 170–171, 188, 222, 226–7, 236, 252–4
   democracy in Britain 39–40, 77–8, 212
   democracy in Switzerland 71, 117, 122, 124–5, 198, 253–4
   perceptions of democracy in China 25, 43, 61, 107, 111, 124–5, 160,

174–5, 182, 207, 210, 212, 222,
    236, 253
Democratic Party (USA) 19, 100
Department of Foreign Affairs
    (Switzerland) 197
Die Weltwoche 22, 193–4, 198–9, 201,
    242, 244
Dollar Diplomacy 55–7
dragon 38, 120–121, 127–30, 134–5, 162,
    218–219, 234–5, 242, 257
Durdin, Tillman 177–8

editorial cartoonists 5, 11, 12, 73, 81, 84,
    111, 127, 134, 148, 166, 193, 205,
    210, 256
editorial cartoons
    syndication 2, 4
    and media discourses 5–6, 10–12, 23,
        81, 111, 166, 215, 256–7
    on the antiforeign agitation in China in
        1927 1–2, 117–120
    on the axis powers 127, 129, 196–7
    on the Boxer Uprising 55–6, 127–8,
        134–5
    on the Chinese Boycott of American
        goods (1905) 50–51
    on the Chinese Communist Victory
        203–5, 210–211, 214–216, 234–5,
        241–4, 246–247, 249
    on Chinese immigration to the USA
        158–9
    on communist expansion in Asia
        217–219
    on the general election in Britain
        (1924) 73–4, 81–4
    on the "Hands off China" Movement
        (1926–1927) 94–96
    on Japan in the Second World War 148,
        152–7, 186–9
    on the Japanese occupation of
        Manchuria 141–2, 166–9, 193
    on the May Thirtieth Movement
        88–89108–111
    on the Sino-Japanese War (1937–1945)
        144–5, 149–150, 171–3, 194–5
    on the 21 Demands 161–3
    on the Xinhai Revolution 59–60,
        70–71; *see also* racial stereotypes

editorial policies 5–6, 11–12, 31, 33,
    59, 69, 79, 90, 99, 105, 147, 171,
    173, 181, 185, 193, 196, 209, 225,
    229, 231, 240, 254–5
editors *see* editorial policies
Elderman, Eugene 171–2
Evangelische Missionsgesellschaft *see*
    Basel Mission
Evening Standard 15–16, 79, 141–2, 152,
    154–7, 196, 210–211, 214–216
extraterritoriality in China 107
    British views 89, 91, 157
    Swiss views 117, 119–120, 122, 124,
        241
    US views 107, 112, 190,

FDR *see* Roosevelt, Franklin D.
Federal Council (Switzerland) 63, 68, 198,
    248
film 5, 137–8, 146, 170, 175, 177, 182,
    194, 251, 256; *see also* newsreels
First World War 16, 87, 100–101, 105, 109,
    115, 123, 178, 191
Foreign Affairs (publication) 20, 111
Foreign Office (UK) 31, 38, 80, 88, 90,
    94, 97–8, 113, 139, 206–7, 215,
    220–221
Foreign Policy Reports 232
Fox Movietone 183
frames 3, 9–12, 23, 25, 35, 38, 44, 65, 69,
    71, 80, 86, 98–9, 104–5, 111, 114,
    116, 122, 125, 171, 196, 217, 232,
    241, 245, 252–5, 257; *see also* Red
    Menace; Yellow Peril
France 2–3, 27, 30, 36, 48, 55–6, 69, 95,
    111, 114, 120–122, 128, 130, 214
Freisinnig-Demokratische Partei der
    Schweiz 21
Frenzeny, Paul 32–3
Fu Manchu 137–8
Fun (publication) 127–8

Gallup Poll 148, 178–180, 185–6, 225–6,
    237, 239
Gaumont British News 144, 209–10, 213
Geistige Landesverteidigung 197–201,
    239–41, 253–4
General Election of 1924 (UK) 79–84, 253

General Strike
  in Britain 91–2
  in China 85, 92
  in Switzerland 115
  in the USA 101; *see also* strikes
George V 39–40, 45
Germany 3, 14, 27, 30, 35–6, 48, 55, 64–7,
      69, 109, 119, 128, 130, 132–3, 141,
      143–4, 148, 150, 162, 179, 185,
      196–7, 201, 214, 239, 251–2, 255
Gilsi, René 117–118
Greater East Asia Co-Prosperity Sphere
      148, 180
Grey, Sir Edward 38
Guangzhou 34, 46, 51, 64, 85, 119
gunboat diplomacy 36, 51, 91, 93–4, 246
Guomidang *see* Chinese Nationalists

"Hands off China" Movement (1926–
      1927) 94–6
Hankou 2, 34, 93–5, 112, 256
Harmsworth, Alfred *see* Lord Northcliffe
Harmsworth, Harold *see* Lord Rothermere
Harper's Magazine 20, 53, 106, 111, 223,
      231
Haselden, W.K. 81, 83
Hay, John 48, 54
Hearst Metrotone News 183
Hiss, Alger 228–30, 234
Hitler, Adolf 127, 143, 180, 185, 188, 196
Hong Kong 34–5, 38, 66, 85, 87, 147,
      150–151, 205, 209, 212–213
Hornbeck, Stanley K. 178
Hull, Cordell 180
Hurley, Patrick 224

Illingworth, Leslie 203–4
Illustrated London News 17, 32–3, 36, 44
India 26, 28, 36, 45–6, 63, 76–7, 88, 105,
      117, 123, 151, 205, 215, 217–9,
      221–2
Industrial Workers of the World (USA)
      100–102
Ireland 15, 40, 42, 117, 84, 91
Irish Times 35–6, 39, 42–3, 133
Italy 30, 48, 69, 95, 143–4, 148, 179, 196,
      201
James, Weldon 147

Japan 2, 23, 27, 30, 33, 35, 48, 55–7, 69,
      127, 130–131, 203, 246, 256
  and Britain 91, 127–8, 132–3, 138–57,
      213–215, 246, 256
  and the May Thirthieth Movement
      85–6
  and the Nanjing Incident 95
  and Shandong 109
  and Switzerland 120, 123–5, 190–201,
      253
  and the USA 105, 109–111, 160–190,
      222–4, 230–231, 234, 246, 254–6
Japanese American Internment 181–2
Jiang Jieshi *see* Chiang Kai-shek
Jingoism (UK) 33, 86, 147, 208–9, 254;
      see also nationalism
Johnson, Nelson T. 111, 178
Jordan, Sir John 38, 42
Journal de Genève 13, 21–2, 65, 68–9,
      117, 119–120, 124–5, 191–4, 248
Joynson-Hicks, William 84, 93, 98

Keller, George Frederick 158–9
Kellogg Pact 141, 165–6
Kellogg, Frank B. 111, 113
Keppler, Joseph Jr. 50–1
Knatchbull-Hugessen, Hughe 143
Kommunistische Partei der Schweiz
      116–117

labour movement
  in Britain 76–8, 88, 92–3, 99, 104, 256
  in Switzerland 115–117
  in the USA 101–4
Labour Party (UK) 76–81, 91–2, 94, 104,
      116, 256
Lattimore, Owen 231, 238
League of Nations 139, 141–3, 162–4, 166,
      192–4
Lee, Joseph 152, 154
Lenin (Vladimir Ilich Ulianov) 80, 115,
      207, 234
Liberal Party (UK) 40, 76, 90, 136
Life (publication) 20, 171, 173–174, 179,
      183–184
Limehouse fiction 137–138, 191
Lippmann, Walter 180, 182, 188–189,
      231–232, 238

Literary Digest 166, 173, 176, 179
Little, Tom 234–235
Lloyd George, David 76
Lord Beaverbrook (Max Aitken) 15, 71–81, 87, 90, 147, 253–4
Lord Curzon (George Nathaniel Curzon) 76
Lord Northcliffe (Alfred Harmsworth) 15, 43, 254
Lord Rothermere (Harold Harmsworth) 15, 79, 90, 254
Los Angeles Times 1–2, 18–19, 48–9, 53–7, 108–11, 164, 166, 169, 175–8, 181–2, 184, 186–188, 190, 224, 231–4, 236, 238
Low, Sir David 73–4, 84, 141–2, 155–7, 196–7, 210–211, 214–216
Luce, Henry R. 20, 174–5, 182–3

Macauley, Charles Raymond 59–60
MacDonald, Ramsay 79–84
MacMurray, John van Antwerp 113
Madame Chiang *see* Soong Meiling
Manchester Guardian 13–16, 31, 33, 36, 39, 42–4, 46, 88–91, 97–8, 132–3, 136–41, 144, 146–8, 151–2, 155–7, 206, 208–210, 212–213, 217, 220–222, 254–5
Manchu Dynasty *see* Qing Dynasty
Manchuria 56–57, 252
    Japanese occupation 23, 139–42, 164–9, 192–3
    Manzhouguo 141, 143
Mao Zedong 203, 205, 207, 221, 223–4, 239
March of Time 175
Marshall Plan 227–8, 231
Marshall, George C. 224
May Thirtieth Movement (1925) 23, 73, 84–6, 89–90
    British reactions 86–93, 114–115, 253, 255
    Swiss reactions 115, 117, 119–125, 253
    US reactions 104, 106–109, 253
McCarran, Patt 229–230
McCormick, Anne O'Hare 185
McCormick, Robert R. 99, 105, 229–30
McCutcheon, John T. 161–3

McKinley, William 48
McLean, Ned 105, 163
Meyer, Eugene 185
missionaries 3, 11, 20, 29–30, 34, 73, 251
    British missionaries 26, 28–30, 33, 251–2
    Swiss missionaries 3, 62, 65–7, 119, 244, 248, 251–2
    US missionaries 3, 20, 46, 49, 51–3, 59–61, 106–9, 114, 119–120, 160, 170, 174, 228, 236, 251–2, 256
Morley, Felix 185
Morrell, G. F. 36–7, 40–41
Morris, William Charles 108–111
Morrison, George E. 31, 44
Morrison, Robert 29

Nanjing 95, 143, 208, 220
Nanjing Incident (1927) 23, 73, 95
    British reactions 97–8, 114–115, 253
    Swiss reactions 117–119, 253
    US reactions 112–114, 253
Nanjing Massacre (1937) 131, 146
    British reactions 146–7, 194
    US reactions 175–9, 194
    Swiss reactions 193–6
Nanking Road Massacre 85
Nation (publication) 20, 106, 177, 223, 231, 238
national identity 2, 4–6, 25, 75, 131, 253, 256
    Britain 25, 28, 39–40, 76, 253, 256
    Switzerland, 75, 122–5, 198, 245, 253–6
    USA 25, 53, 55, 75, 107, 114, 229–30, 234, 236, 252–4, 256; *see also* American Exceptionalism; Geistige Landesverteidigung; neutrality; British monarchy; British Empire
National Review 16–17, 95, 207–8, 210, 213, 217
nationalism 130
    Asian nationalism 215, 221
    British nationalism 45, 105
    Chinese nationalism 85, 89–91, 93, 95, 104, 106, 112–113, 117–120, 237
    Indian nationalism 76–77
    Swiss nationalism 67, 197–199, 239

US nationalism 51, 67, 105, 111; *see also* jingoism; American Exceptionalism; Chinese Nationalists
NATO 229, 231, 241
Nebelspalter 22, 70–72, 117–118, 120–121, 123, 192, 194–5, 241–3, 246–7, 249
Neue Zürcher Zeitung 21–2, 63–5, 68–9, 71, 114, 117, 119–120, 122, 124–5, 191–4, 197–9, 242, 244–5, 248–9
neutrality 38, 68, 120, 122–125, 176, 194, 197–8, 240–241, 245–56, 248, 251, 253–4, 257
New Statesman 17, 91, 97–8, 141, 144, 147–8, 206, 208, 210, 217, 221, 254,
New York Times 13, 18–19, 47, 49, 53–4, 57–8, 61–2, 99, 103, 107, 109, 111, 113–114, 161–163, 166, 169, 176–80, 185–6, 188, 223, 225–6, 230–236, 239, 254
New York World *see* The World
newsreels 4–5, 144, 174, 175–6, 183, 197, 203, 209–210, 212–213, 233, 239
Nineteenth Century (publication) 17, 91, 97, 132, 140, 208, 210, 217
Nomura Kichisaburō 180
North American Review 19–20, 50, 53, 55, 111, 130

Observer 15–16, 133, 143, 151, 221, 242
Ochs, Adolph 99
October Revolution 76, 101, 115
Open Door Notes 48, 50–51, 54–6, 59, 119, 139, 140, 148, 164
opium
    stereotypes 137, 158
    opium trade 26–7, 47
    Opium Wars 2, 27, 134
orientalism 6–7, 170
Orr, Carey 166–7
Otto Baumberger, 120–121

Panay Incident 147–8, 175–8
Partridge, Bernard 81–2, 88–9, 94–6, 144–5
Pathé News 209–210, 212–213

Pearl Harbor 131, 155, 181–5, 188, 201
Pearson, Charles H. 136, 160
People's Republic of China 221–2, 238–9, 248–9
photographs 5, 15, 17, 20, 34–5, 107, 132, 146, 171, 173–4, 193–194
Progressive Movement (USA) 58, 253
Pulitzer Prize 161, 166, 170
Pulitzer, Joseph 18, 59, 99
Punch 16–17, 44, 81–2, 88–9, 94–6, 127, 129, 134–5, 144–5, 148–9, 152–3, 155, 217–219
Pyle, Ernie 186

Qing Dynasty 28, 34–5, 38–9, 59, 71

Rabinovitch, Gregor 194–5
racial stereotypes 51, 127, 130, 137–8, 150–155, 158–60, 186–8, 191, 242–3 *see also* Yellow Peril
racial theories 127, 130, 136, 152, 160, 185, 190–191
radio 4, 137–8, 181, 183, 209, 239
Rape of Nanjing *see* Nanjing Massacre
Red Menace 73, 75, 204–5, 245, 255–6
    in Britain 73–4, 76–8, 81–4, 86, 92, 95–8, 218, 245, 253, 255–6
    in Switzerland 114, 116–118, 125, 242, 244–7, 253, 255–6
    in the USA 99, 101–6, 109, 111, 113–114, 244–5, 255–6; *see also* anticommunism; Bolshevism; Comintern; red wave
Red Scare (1919–1920) 101–2, 111
red wave 203–4, 210 230–233, 244–5, 256
Republic of China (1912–1949) 2, 23, 34, 38–9, 42, 43, 46, 57–8, 61–2, 69–71, 112–113
Republican Party (USA) 19, 100, 225–6, 228–31, 236, 238, 253–4
Revolution of 1911 *see* Xinhai Revolution
Rohmer, Sax (Arthur Sarsfield Ward) 137–8, 191
Roosevelt, Franklin D. 166, 175, 179, 180, 222, 224, 230–231, 237
Roosevelt, Theodore 50
Russell, Bruce 186–7
Russia

among foreign powers in China 27,
    30, 35, 46, 48, 55–6, 86, 120–121,
    124, 139
and the British labour movement 77–8,
    80–84, 86, 91–2, 94–5
British relations with Russia 46, 76–80,
    84, 86–91, 93, 95, 97–9, 105,
    115–116, 132–3, 214, 217–218,
    221, 255
and the Communist Victory in China
    207, 209, 228–30, 232–8, 241,
    244–7
and the May Thirtieth Movement
    84–91, 104–6, 111–112, 114, 117,
    119
and the Nanjing Incident 95, 97, 104,
    112–114, 117
as a rival to British interests in China
    35–6, 139–140
as a rival to US interests in China 57
and the Swiss labour movement
    116–117
Swiss relations with Russia 115–116,
    191, 240–241, 245–6
and US Communist Parties 103
and the US labour movement 101, 103
US relations with Russia 99, 101,
    104–5, 115, 203, 225–30, 232–4,
    236–9; *see also* anticommunism;
    Bolshevism; Cold War; Comintern;
    Red Menace
Russo-Japanese War 132, 138, 160

San Francisco Chronicle 13, 18–19, 53–4,
    57, 58, 62
Schweizer Illustrierte 22, 117, 120, 123–4,
    191, 193–4, 198–200, 242
Schweizer Rundschau 240, 244
Scotland 14–15, 39, 42, 86
Scott, C.P. 90
Second World War 127, 131, 151, 182–3,
    186, 188, 196, 214, 222, 239–41,
    244, 246, 251, 254, 256
Service, John S. 224–5
Shanghai 38, 63, 68–9, 85, 92, 94–5, 112,
    119, 122–3, 125, 143–4, 146–7,
    169, 171, 175, 193, 194, 197,
    208–10, 212, 246, 248

Shepard, E. H. 127, 129, 148–9, 152–3,
    155, 217–219
Sino-Japanese War (1894–1895) 130
Sino-Japanese War (1937–1945) 23,
    143–5, 170–174, 192–3, 196,
    198–200, 253–4
Snow, Edgar 223
Social Darwinism *see* racial theories
Socialism 75, 204
    in Britain 14, 17, 75–84, 86, 95, 116,
        140–141, 254
    in Switzerland 73, 75, 115–116
    in the USA 73, 75, 99–102, 104–6,
        116; *see also* Red Menace;
        anticommunism
Socialist Party (USA) 100, 102
Soong Meiling 175, 182–3
Soviet Union *see* Russia
Sozialdemokratische Partei der Schweiz
    (SPS) 115–117
Spectator 16–17, 36, 39, 43, 91, 97–8,
    140–141, 147, 208–10, 213, 217,
    220–221
spheres of influence in China 3, 27, 48, 64,
    66–7, 109, 122, 139, 192
Spira, Bill
Stalin, Joseph 214, 217–218, 234, 241
State Department (USA) 104, 111, 113,
    178, 225, 228, 230–231, 237–9
Steele, Archibald T. 146, 177
Stilwell, Joseph 222–4
strikes
    in Britain 78, 88, 134
    in China 85
    in Switzerland 115
    in the USA 100–102; *see also* General
        Strike
Strube, Sidney 84
Stuart, John Leighton 239
Sulzberger, Arthur 179
Sun Yat-sen 33–4, 43, 61–2, 85, 93, 105,
    182
Sun Zhongshan *see* Sun Yat-sen
Sykes, Charles Henry 1–2
Szyk, Arthur 184, 188–9

Taft, William Howard 55–7, 61

Tages-Anzeiger 13, 21–2, 63–6, 71, 114, 117, 120, 123–4, 191–4, 241–2, 244–5, 248–9
Talburt, Harold M. 165–6
Tenniel, Sir John 134–5
The Graphic 17, 36–7, 40–41, 44–5, 133
The Scotsman 14, 16, 35–6, 38, 42–3, 45–6, 132, 137, 147, 155, 217
The Star 14, 16, 73–4, 84
The Times 13, 15–16, 25, 31, 35, 39, 42, 43–4, 81, 88–9, 93–4, 97–8, 114, 132–3, 136, 140, 144, 146–8, 150, 152, 155–7, 206, 208–210, 213, 217, 221–2
The Wasp 158–9
The World 13, 18–19, 59–60, 62, 106, 111
Tianjin 30, 63, 112, 143
Time Magazine 20, 106, 111, 174–5, 177–8, 183–4, 188, 199, 232–3, 237, 239
Times-Picayune 168, 171, 176
Timperley, Harold 146–7
Tongmenhui 33
Trades Union Congress (UK) 78, 91–2, 117
transnational circulation of images 4–5, 73, 75, 127, 131, 136, 138, 155, 190, 199, 201, 204–5, 245, 251, 253, 255–6; *see also* Yellow Peril; Red Menace
treaties with China
 treaty ports 28, 90, 122
 treaty revisions 88–94, 98, 106–7, 111–113, 255
 Treaty of Tianjin 63
 Treaty of Wangxia 47
 unequal treaties 2, 47, 89, 94, 106, 192, 246, 255
Tripartite Pact 148, 179
Truman, Harry S. 224–32, 237–9, 253–5

Universal Pictures 175

Voitinsky (Grigory Naumovich Zarkhin) 84
Von Salis, Ferdinand 68–9, 71

Wales 15, 39–40, 42, 86
War Office (UK) 38, 93, 207
Ward, Arthur Sarsfield *see* Sax Rohmer
Warner Pathé 233, 239
Washington Daily News 165–6
Washington Post 18–19, 47–9, 53–4, 57–8, 105, 109, 111, 163–4, 166, 169, 171–2, 176, 178–81, 185–6, 188, 190, 231–2, 234, 236–9, 254
Wilkinson, Gilbert Welby 127–8
Wilson, Woodrow 100, 109, 161–2, 255
Winteler, Matthias 68
Wong, Hai-Sheng 174

Xinhai Revolution 23, 25–26, 34
 British reactions to 34–46, 252–3
 Swiss reactions 65–71
 US reactions 39, 57–62, 253

Yellow Peril 23, 127, 130–131, 141, 255–256
 British portrayals 31–3, 35, 127–9, 133–8, 144–5, 148, 150–151, 155, 201, 218–219, 251–2, 254, 256
 Swiss portrayals 120–121, 127, 190–191, 193, 196, 201, 242–4, 256–7
 transnational circulation of Yellow Peril imagery 127, 131, 134, 190–191, 199, 201, 244, 251, 255–7
 US portrayals 59, 127, 158–60, 162, 171–2, 178, 180–182, 184–9, 193, 201, 233–5, 251, 256; *see also* racial stereotypes
Yuan Shikai 34, 43–4

Zhou Enlai 239
Zinoviev (Grigory Evseevich Radomilsky) 80–81, 115

For Product Safety Concerns and Information please contact our
EU representative GPSR@taylorandfrancis.com Taylor & Francis
Verlag GmbH, Kaufingerstraße 24, 80331 München, Germany